Ageism

Ageism
Stereotyping and Prejudice against Older Persons

edited by Todd D. Nelson

A Bradford Book
The MIT Press
Cambridge, Massachusetts
London, England

First MIT Press paperback edition, 2004

© 2002 Massachusetts Institute of Technology

This book was set in New Baskerville by Graphic Composition, Inc.

Printed and Bound in the United States of America

Library of Congress Cataloging-in-Publication Data

Ageism : stereotyping and prejudice against older persons / edited by Todd D. Nelson.
     p. cm.
   "A Bradford book."
   Includes bibliographical references and index.
ISBN 978-0-262-14077-5 (hc. : alk. paper) — 978-0-262-64057-2 (pb. : alk. paper)
     1. Ageism. 2. Ageism—United States. I. Nelson, Todd D., 1966–

HQ1061 .A42442 2002
305.26'0973—dc21

                                          2001044756

10 9 8 7

Contents

Preface

In social perception, people tend rather automatically to categorize others along three major dimensions: race, sex, and age (Kunda 1999). Ever since the early days of social psychology, researchers have been interested in the causes and consequences of such categorization, with specific focus on the stereotypes and prejudice that arise from this automatic social perception. Much empirical and theoretical attention has been devoted to the study of racism and sexism, but comparatively very little research in psychology has been directed at understanding what some refer to as the "third ism," ageism (Barrow and Smith 1979). To illustrate this, consider the results of a PsycInfo database search I conducted minutes ago. I ran three searches and set up the search criteria to look for the words *racism, sexism,* and *ageism* anywhere in the abstract of each article. The results indicated 2,215 articles for racism, 1,085 articles for sexism, and a mere 215 articles with the term *ageism* in the citation (a title search yielded a similar pattern: 548, 249, and 68 articles, respectively). Clearly there has been a pattern of underinterest in ageism research in the mainstream psychological literature.

But why the lack of interest? There are a myriad of possible reasons, but perhaps the most obvious is that age prejudice is one of the most socially condoned, institutionalized forms of prejudice in the world—especially in the United States—today. For example, there is a whole industry in the greeting card business built around the "over the hill" theme. Such cards are often portrayed as humorous, but the essential message is that it is undesirable to get older. As you will see in reading the chapters of this book, most Americans tend to have little tolerance for older persons and very few reservations about harboring negative attitudes toward older people. Whatever the reasons for the comparative dearth of theoretical and empirical research on ageism among psychologists, it is clear that much more research is sorely needed.

According to the U. S. Bureau of the Census (1990), the number of people over age 65 is expected to double by 2030. This "graying of America" represents a great challenge to the social, political, medical, and economic structure of society, and it also represents a challenge for prejudice researchers. In about ten years, many baby boomers (those born roughly between 1946 and 1965) will begin to retire, and the population of the elderly will begin to mushroom. In preparation, the National Institute of Aging is issuing a massive push for grant proposals for researchers to begin, in earnest, programs of research to understand the psychological effects of aging. Prejudice researchers should seek to be at the forefront of this research.

This book is organized into three major sections, dealing with the origens of ageism, the effects of ageism, and reducing ageism and future directions.

Origins of Ageism

One of the unique features of ageism is that age, unlike race and sex, represents a category in which most people from the in-group (the young) will eventually (if they are fortunate) become a member of the out-group (older persons). Thus, it seems strange that young people would be prejudiced toward a group to which they will eventually belong. Where does this negative affect originate? To begin, Cuddy and Fiske examine the basic cognitive and affective processes underlying stereotyping and prejudice. They then present evidence from their research that supports earlier research (Brewer, Dull, and Lui 1981; Hummert 1990; Kite and Johnson 1988; Schmidt and Boland 1986) concluding that people have multiple, often contradictory views of older persons. Cuddy and Fiske suggest that today's elders are seen as incompetant (low status) but warm (passive), and discuss the functional basis for the creation of prejudice agaist older people. Chapter 2, by Greenberg, Schimel, and Mertens, suggests that age prejudice arises out of a fear of our own mortality. These authors present evidence to support the contention that one likely reason that people develop prejudice agaist older persons is due to thoughts and feelings about their own mortality that are evoked at thinking about the older person. That is, merely thinking about (or seeing) an older person tends to arouse anxiety about the fact that one has a short time on earth, and the fear associated with such cognitions tends to provoke the perceiver to dislike the individual (or group) who elicits such fear. Greenberg's terror management theory well for ageism by attributing it to our desire to dissociate ourselves with any reminder of our own impending mortality.

In chapter 3, Levy and Banaji discuss their research on how age stereotypes can implicitly (without conscious awareness) affect our thoughts, feelings, and behaviors. Levy and Banaji make a compelling case for the notion that because there is a lack of strong hatred toward older persons coupled with a widespread, institutionalized acceptance of negative beliefs about older people, it is even more important to understand the effects of implicit cognitions about age. The authors show that avoiding thinking about automatically activated age stereotypes may be more dificult than we think. In chapter 4, Montepare and Zebrowitz present a detailed analysis of the developmental literature that indicated children learn age prejudice at a very early age. Additionally, structural changes in society have changed the extended family unit to a nuclear family, with grandparents often out of contact their grandchildren. The influence of media, peers, and parental attitudes toward older people also converges to foster in the child a negative impression of older people. Montepare and Zebrowitz conclude by suggesting directions for future research on the development of ageist attitudes in children.

Effects of Ageism

This section examines how ageist attitudes affect the targets of such prejudice (older persons), as well as the influence of ageism on the perceiver. Kite and Wagner start us off in chapter 5 with a social-cognition perspective on ageist attitudes. They discuss ways researchers have tried to measure ageism and the difference between positive and negative ageism. They then turn their attention to address reasons that we view older men and older women differently and conclude with suggestions about how various social psychological theories can advance the study of ageism. In chapter 6, McCann and Giles examine the devastating consequences of ageism for older persons in the workplace. They argue that a better understanding of workplace discrimination of older people will be attained through an examination of the ways older and younger persons communicate their attitudes, values, and expectations to each other. They then conclude by highlighting the need for further theory development and empirical inquiry in the area of intergenerational communication of ageism. Continuing the examination of age discrimination, Pasupathi and Löckenhoff take an in-depth look at a wide range of discriminatory behaviors, from policy to interpersonal actions. They introduce an important distinction between age-differentiated behavior and ageist behavior. They then highlight unanswered questions in ageism discrimination research. In the last chapter of this section, Whitbourne and Sneed discuss the effects of ageism on the older person's sense of self and identity. As other chapters have aptly shown, our society favors the young and devalues older people. So Whitbourne and Sneed ask, What is it that allows some older individuals to maintan high self-esteem and sense of self-woth while other elders internalize society's negative views of older people and feel demoralized and a burdon to others?

Reducing Ageism and Future Directions

In chapter 9, Golub, Filipowicz, and Langer discuss ageism from the perspective of Langer's theory of mindfulness. They suggest that mindfulness can account for how ageist attitudes are formed and how they are maintained, and also illuminate ways to reduce ageism. For example, they touch on a rather unique angle with regard to how ageism is perpetuated, suggesting that younger adults often create stereotype-perpetuating environments for older persons which foster dependence. We tend to categorize people rather automatically according to their age. Of course, a problem with this is that our stereotypes and prejudice associated with a certain age group could then also become automatically activated upon perception of that person.

While many of the chapters in the previous two sections have touched on the reduction of ageism and future directions of ageism research, the chapters in this section specifically focus on these issues. In chapter 10, Ng discusses the need to understand cross-cultural variations in attitudes toward older persons. Most ageism research has not considered this important perspective, and if we are to have a more accurate understanding of the factors that increase or decrease age prejudice, then it is crucial that we consider the ways that culture influences age-related attitudes. Braithwaite, in chapter 11, discusses ways that society can reduce stereotypes, prejudice, and the stigma associated with aging. She presents research suggesting that through policies and intervention programs, society can move toward ageism reduction. However, Braithwaite argues, it is only when society is willing and able to confront its fears about aging and loss (physical, status, social, economic) that it will be able to make significant inroads in the reduction of prejudice against older persons. Finally, Wilkinson and Ferraro nicely conclude the book with a detailed review of the history of ageism research, spanning over thirty years, to present. They highlight the major findings in four areas of inquiry—language, physical appearance, media, and values—and discuss directions for future research on ageism.

Conclusion

It is my hope that this book will represent a loud and clear call to all prejudice researchers to examine the problem of ageism and find out ways to use their theoretical and empirical talents to address the issues that confront society as we just begin to scratch the surface of this long neglected area of prejudice research. This book addresses ageism from several different perspectives (e.g., gerontology, communication, psychology), and the distinguished chapter authors present the latest theoretical and empirical advances in our understanding of the causes and effects of ageism. Ideally, researchers will use the theory and findings set out here as a point of inspiration for their own future research on ageism and bring us ever closer to an understanding of how age prejudice begins, how it is maintained, and how it can be reduced.

Acknowledgments

Many people helped get this project off the ground. First, I am grateful to Amy Brand, former editor at MIT Press, who had the vision to give this project the green light. I also thank Thomas Stone, senior editor at MIT Press, for being so understanding with extending the deadline and being so great to work with throughout all the stages of the book preparation. Of course, none of this would be possible without the contributions of the chapter authors. I cannot thank them enough for their time and the effort they have invested in their chapters, resulting in an in-depth examination of ageism. I thank my wife, Barb, and my 18-month old son, Brandon, for being so patient and understanding while much of my time was devoted to this volume. I love you both.

Todd D. Nelson, January, 2001.

References

Barrow, G. M., and Smith, P. A. (1979). *Aging, ageism, and society.* New York: Westt Publishing.

Brewer, M. B., Dull, V., and Lui, L. (1981). Perceptions of the elderly: Stereotypess as prototypes. *Journal of Personality and Social Psychology, 41* (4), 656–670.

Hummert, M. L. (1990). Multiple stereotypes of elderly and young adults: A comparison of structure and evaluations. *Psychology and Aging,* 5 (2), 182–193.

Kite, M. E., and Johnson, B. T. (1988). Attitudes toward older and younger adults: A meta-analysis. *Psycology and Aging,* 3 (3), 233–244.

Kunda, Z. (1999). *Social cognition.* Cambridge, MA: MIT Press.

Schmidt, D., and Boland, S. (1986). Structure of perceptions of older adults: Evidence for multiple stereotypes. *Psychology and Aging,* 1 (3), 255–260.

U.S. Bureau of the Census (1990). 1990 Census of population: General population characteristics. Washington, D.C.: U.S. Department of Commerce.

Contributors

Mahzarin Banaji
Yale University

Valerie Braithwaite
Australian National University

Amy J. C. Cuddy
Princeton University

Kenneth F. Ferraro
Purdue University

Allan Filipowicz
Harvard University

Susan T. Fiske
Princeton University

Howard Giles
University of California, Santa Barbara

Sarit A. Golub
Harvard University

Jeff Greenberg
University of Arizona

Mary E. Kite
Ball State University

Ellen J. Langer
Harvard University

Becca R. Levy
Yale University

Corinna E. Löckenhoff
Stanford University

Andy Martens
University of Arizona

Robert McCann
University of California, Santa Barbara

Joann M. Montepare
Emerson College

Sik Hung Ng
City University of Hong Kong

Monisha Pasupathi
University of Utah

Jeff Schimel
University of Arizona

Joel R. Sneed
University of Massachusetts

Lisa Smith Wagner
University of San Francisco

Susan Krause Whitbourne
University of Massachusetts

Jody A. Wilkinson
University of Arizona

Leslie A. Zebrowitz
Brandeis University

I

Origins of Ageism

1

Doddering but Dear: Process, Content, and Function in Stereotyping of Older Persons

Amy J. C. Cuddy and Susan T. Fiske

In first encounters, age is one of the earliest characteristics we notice about other people (Fiske 1998; Kite, Deaux, and Miele 1991). Conscious or not, noticing age drives our interactions with others. Age seems to answer: How should I address them? What are their political views? What do they know about popular culture? Will they be competent? Socially aware? How slowly should I talk? How loudly? From an individual's perceived age, we infer social and cognitive competencies, political and religious beliefs, and physical abilities. These inferences guide how we behave and what information we seek, heed, and remember.

Age is far from the only social marker that shapes our attitudes toward other people. We form opinions based on sex, race, and religion, among other social categories. But unlike these other categories, old age is one that most of us eventually join. For the most part, people do not move from one gender, racial, ethnic, or religious category to another. Moreover, stereotyping people based on their age, unlike these other groupings, goes largely unchallenged and even unnoticed in the United States. We disparage elderly people without fear of censure. Indeed, noticing a person's age early in a social encounter is not surprising or inherently offensive. It is what we do with that information that can be destructive. As Butler (1980) notes in an edition of the *Journal of Social Issues* devoted to the topic, ageism, like racism and sexism, becomes institutionalized, affecting hiring decisions, medical care, and social policy.

Many people approach old age with dread. What was once viewed as a natural process is now seen as a social problem. Television portrays only 1.5 percent of its characters as elderly, and most of them in minor roles (Zebrowitz and Montepare 2000). Older adults are also more likely than any other age group to appear in television and film as conduits for comic relief, exploiting stereotypes of physical, cognitive, and sexual ineffectiveness (Zebrowitz and Montepare 2000). Today in America, we no longer see our elders as sources of wisdom but as feeble yet lovable, doddering but dear.

Our goal in writing this chapter is to shed light on the social-psychological underpinnings of stereotyping processes, contents, and functions and to use this as a scaffold to discuss stereotyping of elderly people. We begin by elucidating the systematic nature of the processes of stereotyping, including those of older people. After process, we discuss the less examined area of stereotype content. We suggest that content, including the content of stereotypes about elderly people, is systematic. Finally, the chapter examines the functions served by stereotyping and discusses the conditions most likely to elicit the use of stereotypic information in impression formation. Overall, the processes, contents, and functions of elderly stereotypes fit well with the general principles of stereotyping.

Social-Psychological Processes of Stereotyping

Processes of stereotyping primarily address cognition. One context for this comes from the traditional tripartite view that three mechanisms constitute attitudes: affect, behavior, and cognition (Breckler 1984; Eagly and Chaiken 1998). In category-based attitudes, these are represented as prejudice (affective), discrimination (behavioral), and stereotyping (cognitive). Ageism contains the same three mechanisms. This chapter focuses primarily on stereotypes, which are cognitive structures that store our beliefs and expectations about the characteristics of members of social groups, and stereotyping, the process of applying stereotypic information.

Stereotypes develop over time as people perceive their changing environments, interpret the perceived information, and encode it in memory. Biased by various cognitive processes, these collections of beliefs are later retrieved for use in interpreting social cues, and consequently directing how we behave in social interactions (Stangor and Schaller 1996). Accurate or not, stereotypes guide our social behavior and often govern what information we seek, heed, and remember (for a review, see Fiske 1998). At the root of stereotyping is our impulse to assign objects, events, and people to meaningful classes, about which we have established beliefs and expectations.

Categorization and Stereotype Formation
Human functioning requires cognitive categorization. To make sense of the world, we group objects and events based on their similar features.

Identifying these shared characteristics serves to reduce the amount of re-dundant data to be processed and provides additional useful information (for a review, see Fiske 1998). If we walked into a retirement home with-out the ability to categorize people into residents, staff, and visitors, we would quickly be confused and overloaded by the complexities.

Just as we cluster objects and events based on perceived similarities, we cluster people based on perceived similarities. In his classic volume, *The Nature of Prejudice,* Gordon Allport suggests, "The human mind must think with the aid of categories. Once formed, categories are the basis for normal prejudgment. We cannot possibly avoid this process. Orderly liv-ing depends on it" (1954, p. 20).

Perceived category membership does not necessarily result from an in-dividual's actual possession of necessary category traits. Instead, it is based on our perceptions of how well a person fits a certain social group, based on characteristics we believe to represent a category. Two estab-lished models have explained how we determine the degree of fit: the prototype model and the exemplar model. The former was the first to suggest that categories do not have rigid boundaries and compulsory cri-teria, but that we subjectively categorize people based on how well we per-ceive them to resemble the average category member, or *prototype* (Cantor and Mischel 1979). A prototype need not be an actual person, but instead an imagined individual who embodies the central tendencies of the group's key attributes. Common experience suggests that the prototype *elderly person* may be portrayed on television as slow, confused, bent, and dowdy, characteristics that quickly categorize the character.

Whereas prototypes are usually abstractions derived from an individ-ual's collected experiences with the category, *exemplars* are memories of actual people or events. Ronald Reagan, one's grandmother, and Nor-man Thayer (Henry Fonda's *On Golden Pond* character) all might be eld-erly exemplars. The exemplar model suggests that we have multiple exemplars for each social category and that we assign membership to in-dividuals who resemble many of the category's exemplars (see Fiske and Taylor 1991 for a review). The field acknowledges that neither of the models can account for all social cognitive representations; different sit-uations call for different processes. But the shared contribution of the prototype and exemplar models to our understanding of stereotyping is that mental representations of social categories have nebulous bound-aries and are the baselines people use to organize and construct their social taxonomies. Thus, the category *elderly people* is not defined by necessary and sufficient rules; a 70 year old who plays bridge and runs marathons might or might not qualify, depending on resemblance to one's abstract prototype or specific exemplars.

Several consequences follow from mental representations of social categories (Mackie et al. 1996). First, we perceive people as more similar to each other when they are presented as members of the same group (within-group assimilation) and less similar when presented as members of different groups (between-group contrast) (Allen and Wilder 1979). Thus, two people over age 80 would be viewed as more similar compared to 20 year olds, but as quite different if one were a Japanese person in a group of Japanese businessmen and the other a German person in a group of German tourists.

Second, we perceive out-groups as less variable than in-groups, a phenomenon termed the *out-group homogeneity effect* (Park and Rothbart 1982). Young people perceive all old people to be alike, varying very little on stereotypic traits such as political affiliation and open-mindedness. Similarly, older people may see teenagers as indistinguishable on dimensions such as discipline and thoughtfulness.

Third, the perceived contrast between groups is evaluative, favoring the in-group (Tajfel et al. 1971). Young people make favorable in-group comparisons to older counterparts, evaluating the in-group more positively on relevant trait dimensions, such as attractiveness and wit.

Levels of Categorization

People perceive groups at various levels of specificity. Usually when we refer to social groups, such as "elderly people," we are speaking of the superordinate, or global, level of categorization. But sometimes superordinate categories splinter into meaningful subcategories, which we will refer to as subtypes (Taylor 1981).[1] The next section describes some elderly subtypes, but first note that relative to individual instances and superordinate-level representations of a category, subtypes occur at an intermediate level of generality (Ryan, Park, and Judd 1996). Because our cognitive representations of out-groups are less differentiated than our representations of in-groups, we are less likely to use a subordinate level for out-groups (Park, Ryan, and Judd 1992). However, when superordinate categories impart too little data even for out-groups, people sometimes develop subtypes (Stangor et al. 1992), which provide richer information about how to behave in specific situations, thereby amplifying predictive potential.

Subtypes develop in response to stereotype-incongruent information (Fiske and Taylor 1991). They allow for characteristics that are inconsistent with beliefs about the global category, guarding the perceiver from having to integrate new, disconfirming information into an existing stereotype (Hewstone, Johnston, and Aird 1992). Several subtypes describe variations on the theme of the broad, elderly category.

Subtypes of Elderly People

Multiple subtypes of older adults have emerged in research on ageism (Brewer, Dull, and Lui 1981; Hummert 1990, 1997; Hummert et al. 1998; Schmidt and Boland 1986). In early work on elderly subtypes, participants sorted pictures and traits into categories as they thought appropriate and later assigned descriptive statements to photos of older people (Brewer et al. 1981). Three elderly subtypes emerged: the *grandmotherly* type, described as helpful, kindly, serene, and trustworthy; the *elder statesman,* described as intelligent, competitive, aggressive, and intolerant; and the *senior citizen,* described as lonely, old-fashioned, weak, and worried. Later research (Schmidt and Boland 1986) generated a dozen elderly subtypes, eight of which (*perfect grandparent, liberal matriarch/patriarch, John Wayne conservative, recluse, severely impaired, vulnerable, shrew/curmudgeon,* and *despondent*) were replicated by Hummert (1990). Even market researchers have identified multiple elderly subtypes: the *adventurer,* the *contented,* the *cautious,* the *getby,* the *restrained,* and the *survivor* (Slater 1995).

Stereotype Content

The majority of research on stereotyping devotes itself to stereotyping processes, with ample reason (for a review, see Fiske 1998). Stereotyping processes respond to systematic principles and are stable over time, place, and out-group. Stereotype content, on the other hand, has been presumed to be volatile and random, morphing over time and unique to each social group. Thus, researchers have neglected content for its own sake. Recent research counters these assumptions, demonstrating that content may also prove systematic, in two fundamental respects: Across groups, stereotype contents share common dimensions, and where groups fall along these dimensions of stereotype content can be predicted from social structural variables (Fiske et al. 1999, 2001).

Two Dimensions of Stereotype Content

To many people, the term *stereotype* implies uniform antipathy toward a social group, a postulate that has been supported by many prominent social psychologists (Allport 1954; Crosby, Bromley, and Saxe 1980; Sigall and Page 1971). Moreover, stereotypes have been considered unidimensional; groups are stereotyped along a single dimension reflecting general goodness (or badness). In recent work, we suggest that stereotypes are neither univalent nor one-dimensional. Instead, they contain both negative and positive beliefs, along multiple dimensions (Fiske et al. 1999, 2001). Stereotypes of out-groups frequently reflect ambivalence with groups often tagged as proficient in one sphere and inferior in the other. Some additional background on this theory will frame our subsequent placement of elderly people in this scheme.

The two core dimensions of general stereotype content that we propose, competence (e.g., independent, skillful, confident, able) and warmth (e.g., good-natured, trustworthy, sincere, friendly), have received copious support from several areas of psychology. These dimensions are rooted in classic person perception studies (Asch 1946; Rosenberg, Nelson, and Vivekanathan 1968) and have emerged in numerous in-depth analyses of specific social groups.

Similar factors have also appeared in more general stereotype content research. Peeters (1983, 1995) has argued for the dimensions of *self-profitability* (e.g., confident, ambitious, industrious, intelligent)—resembling our notion of competence—and *other-profitability* (e.g., conciliatory, tolerant, trustworthy, sensitive)—not unlike our concept of warmth. In the context of national stereotypes, Phalet and Poppe (1997) use a comparable distinction of competence and "morality"—honest, helpful, and tolerant—to interpret Eastern Europeans' national stereotypes.

Akin to our concept of warmth and Peeters's other-profitability, *communal* traits (helpful, aware of other's feelings, able to devote self to others) concern interpersonal sensitivity, whereas *agentic* (or self-profitable) traits (independent, self-confident, and dominant) concern abilities in traditionally valued domains and are similar to our competence notion (Bakan, 1966). Likewise, Spence and Helmreich (1979) named two factors as accounting for most gender stereotypes, with instrumental (agentic) traits as stereotypically male and expressive (communal) traits as stereotypically female. In a related vein, the Ambivalent Sexism Inventory (e.g., Glick and Fiske 1996) delineates two types of prejudice against two types of women. Hostile sexism is directed at nontraditional women, perceived to possess agentic traits, and benevolent sexism is directed at traditional women, believed to possess communal traits.

Research on another specific social group, Asian Americans, has uncovered stereotypes comprising excessive competence (too ambitious, too hardworking) and deficient sociability (Hurh and Kim 1989; Lin and Fiske 1999; Kitano and Sue 1973). Alternatively, some stereotypes of disabled people fit the opposite cluster; blind people are perceived as socially sensitive (intuitive and friendly) but otherwise incompetent (helpless, dependent, incapable) (McGroarty and Fiske 1997).

Along these two dimensions, three clusters of stereotyped out-groups emerge: (1) warm and incompetent, (2) competent and cold, and (3) incompetent and cold. What is missing is the merger of warm *and* competent—because people reserve that description for in-groups. Each one of these constellations of stereotypes reflects a unique prejudice. Groups perceived as warm and incompetent, such as traditional women, will be the targets of paternalistic prejudice (liked but disrespected), while competent and cold groups such as Asians, are the targets of envious prejudice (disliked but respected). Groups stereotyped as cold and incompetent receive contemptuous prejudice (disliked and disrespected). Only groups perceived as warm and competent will evoke pride (liked and respected).

In short, the stereotype content model makes three proposals that have been relevant in this section (Fiske et al. 1999, 2001). (1) the two pivotal dimensions of stereotype content are warmth and competence, (2) people perceive most out-groups as significantly higher on one dimension (with in-groups high on both), and (3) distinct prejudices accompany each category of stereotype content (Fiske, Cuddy, and Glick, forthcoming).

Survey data collected by Fiske and colleagues illustrates how stereotypes of social groups array along these two dimensions (figure 1.1) and provide support for the hypotheses. Across multiple survey studies (Fiske et al. 1999, 2001) participants rated systematically derived rosters of American social groups on warmth and competence, and status and competition. A small minority of groups (homeless people, poor people, and welfare recipients) were stereotyped as both incompetent *and* cold, presumably because people blame them for their lot in life. Only in-groups (in white, female, middle-class samples) were perceived to be both warm and competent (whites, Christians, women, and the middle class).

Consistently, however, participants rated the majority of groups as significantly higher on one dimension than on the other.[2] That is, most out-groups were viewed as either competent and cold (Asians, Jews, and rich people), or incompetent and warm (disabled and retarded). Elderly people fell into the incompetent-warm category. Moreover, a distinct type of prejudice accompanied each quadrant of stereotype content: envy

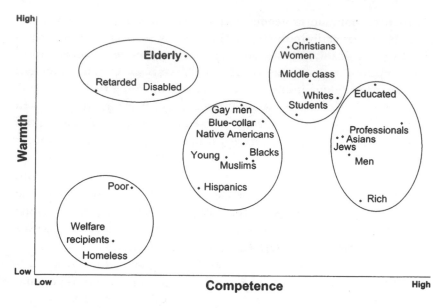

Figure 1.1
American social groups arrayed along perceived competence and perceived warmth and sorted by cluster analysis.

(highest for the competent-cold cluster), admiration (highest for the competent-warm cluster), pity (highest for the incompetent-warm cluster), and contempt (highest for the incompetent-cold cluster).

Content of Elderly Stereotypes
Strong evidence independently suggests that the global category *elderly people* falls squarely into the warm and incompetent cluster of stereotyped groups (Fiske et al. 1999, 2001; Heckhausen, Dixon, and Baltes 1989; Kite et al. 1991). In the Fiske et al. (1999, 2001) survey studies, elderly people reliably fell into the warm-incompetent cluster, alongside disabled and retarded people (figure 1.1). Elderly people were rated as less competent than eighteen of twenty-four groups and warmer than twenty-two of twenty-four groups (see figure 1.1). Competence ratings averaged only 2.63 out of 5.00 (below the scale midpoint), and warmth ratings averaged 3.78 (well above the scale midpoint). The two scores differed significantly from each other in all samples. These clusters were accompanied by distinct prejudices. When asked about the warm-incompetent cluster that included elderly people, participants most endorsed items reflecting paternalistic prejudice (pity and sympathy) and least endorsed emotions reflecting envy (envy and jealousy).

In an examination of gender and age stereotypes, Kite, Deaux, and Miele (1991) similarly found that older people were believed less likely to possess agentic characteristics, whereas ratings of communal characteristics were unaffected by aging. Erber (1989; Erber, Etheart, and Szuchman 1992; Erber, Szuchman, and Etheart, 1993) revealed an age-based double standard concerning attributions of memory failure, such that when young people forget, it is attributed to lack of effort or attention, but when older people do the same, it is attributed to incompetence. In other studies, older people were rated as intellectually incompetent (Rubin and Brown 1975) and less ambitious and responsible than younger people but also as friendlier and warmer than younger people (Andreoletti, Maurice and Whalen 2001). Furthermore, research on automatic stereotyping shows that people are quicker at associating elderly names with incompetence traits than with competence traits (Zemore and Cuddy, 2000).

A similar pattern of stereotype content appears in research on people's beliefs about development throughout adulthood (Heckhausen, Dixon, and Baltes 1989). Participants rated hundreds of traits on desirability and estimated their average ages of onset (when people first develop these traits) and closing (when people lose these traits). Desirability ratings were negatively correlated with both onset and closing ages, indicating that traits believed common to younger populations are more desirable. Consistent with our hypothesis, additional analyses reveal that traits most similar to those on our warmth scale (affectionate, friendly, good-natured, kind, and trustworthy) were not predicted to close until as late as age 81.3. This average estimate is nine years later (a significant difference) than the mean predicted closing date (72.3) of competence traits (independent, industrious, intelligent, productive, self-confident, and smart). Older adults become incompetent first, according to stereotypes of life span development.

Researchers in industrial-organizational psychology and in business and management programs have produced abundant research on stereotyping and aging (Britton and Thomas 1973; Haefner 1977; Kirchner and Dunnette 1954; Locke-Connor and Walsh 1980; Rosen and Jerdee 1976a, 1976b; Singer 1986; Waldman and Avolio 1986). While there is a main effect of age, such that younger employees and applicants are generally rated more positively than older employees and applicants, a closer look reveals findings consistent with our view of a global elderly stereotype reflecting warmth and incompetence. In the workplace, older people are perceived as less competent in job performance–related tasks than in interpersonal ones (Avolio and Barrett 1987; Rosen and Jerdee 1976a, 1976b; Singer 1986). Incidentally, researchers have failed to demonstrate any actual relationship between age and job performance (for a review, see Salthouse and Maurer 1996). Older people's alleged incompetence lies solely in the eye of the beholder.

Social Structure Predicts Stereotype Content in General

The stereotype content model makes another prediction, concerning the origins of competence and warmth stereotypes. Why do people choose these two dimensions as benchmarks for stereotyping? Structural relationships among different social groups foretell the content of the stereotypes of those groups. Specifically, the stereotype content model predicts that perceived relative status predicts which groups will be stereotyped as competent, whereas perceived lack of competition predicts who is seen as warm. Glick and Fiske (1999) contend that these social structural variables inform us about whether members of another group will be helpers or competitors.

In the Fiske et al. (1999, 2001) survey data, correlations between status and competence ratings (positive) and competition and warmth ratings (negative) were significant, in line with the hypothesis that social structural variables predict stereotype content. High-status groups, as rated by participants, were viewed as highly competent, and highly competitive groups were perceived as cold.

Social Structure Predicts Stereotype Content of Elderly People

As expected, in the Fiske et al. (1999, 2001) survey data, elderly people were perceived as low status and relatively noncompetitive. Their status scores across samples averaged 2.64 (on a 5-point scale), lower than eighteen of twenty-four groups. Similarly, competition scores averaged 2.59, lower than fifteen of twenty-four groups. Both ratings fall below the respective scale midpoints.

Because the competence and status scales in our survey research are general, to accommodate beliefs about a wide range of social groups, we can only speculate about what elderly-specific beliefs are being activated. We suggest that perceived group status is a strong predictor of perceived competence. Changes in social status accompany the life cycle, such that young and old people rank lowest and middle-aged people highest (Stokes 1992).

Modernization theory explains the reduced status of older people as a function of the transformation from traditional, agrarian societies to modern, industrial societies (for a review, see Branco and Williamson 1982). Four shifts in social structure are indicted. First, improved health care has inevitably extended the span of life, thereby increasing the size of the older population. As a result, retirement has become institutionalized, and elderly people no longer hold prestigious jobs or possess as much financial muscle as they once did. Second, technological advances created new jobs, for which older people were not trained. Job experience was eclipsed by cutting-edge skills, which also contributed to putting older people out of work. Third, urbanization pulled young people away from their homes, triggering the collapse of close ties among extended family members. As a result, we no longer seek out our grandparents and great-grandparents for wisdom and guidance. Fourth, the implementation of public education has created a literate majority, effectively eliminating the elders' long-held position as transmitter of cultural knowledge and wisdom. In short, older people have suffered the loss of status as a result of displacement from the workforce, loss of income, transience of extended family members, and the obsolescence of the spoken word.

Linked to changes in the relative social status of older people is their absence from competitive social roles, which leads to their stereotype as harmless and socially sensitive. In 1990, less than 3 percent of the workforce was over age 65 (Smolak 1993). Based on our concept of competition, which measures the degree to which a group is a perceived threat to resources, it is understandable that older adults are perceived as non-competitive.

Subtypes of Elderly People, Revisited

In line with our view that stereotypes fall along the dimensions of warmth and competence, we believe that each of the primary elderly subtypes (Brewer, Dull, and Lui 1981) clearly falls into one of the quadrants. The grandmother most closely mirrors the global elderly stereotype as nurturing but ineffectual, reflected in feelings of pity. She is high on communal qualities, but absent from her description are competence-related traits, such as independence, intelligence, and confidence.

The senior citizen lacks both competence and warmth. Presumably, people view this subtype as complaining and lazy, responsible for their predicament. Anger and resentment target people whose negative outcomes are believed to be individually controllable (Weiner 1985).

The elder statesman is agentic but socially insensitive (e.g., aggressive and intolerant), reflecting feelings of respect and mirroring the competent but not warm category. This subtype raises an issue worthy of note. The American Association of Retired Persons (AARP) is among the most powerful lobbying forces in Washington. What is remarkable is that this fact, which is clearly stereotype incongruent, has not penetrated the global stereotype of older people. Instead, it has apparently contributed to the development of the elder statesman subtype, reflecting characteristics not normally associated with older Americans.

Functions of Stereotyping

Interpersonal Level: The Social Cognitive Perspective

People have limited cognitive resources but must function in a complex social environment. To be successful, we employ cognitive short-cuts and commit countless approximations. Sometimes we are cognitive misers, using our mental resources frugally (Fiske and Taylor 1984), yet we are also motivated tacticians who think harder when it is useful to do so (Fiske and Taylor 1991). Distinguishing each person as unique (individuating) requires ample time and effort, draining us of our mental assets. When we do individuate, we must attend to and process complex information. Categorization, on the other hand, is simple and relatively effortless. Based on certain salient features, such as race, sex, or age, we assign individuals to categories. Those category assignments provide stereotypic information, which we use to infer further information about the individual in question.

Stereotyping serves two primary functions in interindividual situations. First, it allows us to make judgments (for better or for worse) when effortful processing is difficult (Bodenhausen 1990; Bodenhausen and Lichtenstein 1987; Kruglanski and Freund 1983; Macrae, Milne, and Bodenhausen 1994). When participants are asked to form impressions about people while completing a complex cognitive task, they recall more information about the individual when stereotypic labels are provided (Macrae, Milne, and Bodenhausen 1994). Our mental representations of out-groups are also simpler and more extreme than representations of in-groups, thereby facilitating the processing of information about unfamiliar groups. When college students were asked to describe a group of older adults, they assigned to them simpler and more extreme descriptions than their in-group descriptions of young people (Linville 1982).

Second, stereotyping provides us with information that guides our interactions with others. These category inferences often lead us to behave in ways that confirm the stereotypes, a process known as *behavioral confirmation* or *self-fulfilling prophecy* (for a review, see Darley and Fazio 1980).

Countless elderly people will attest to their treatment as incompetent, undermining their ability to function effectively.

Nonconscious activation of the elderly stereotype has specifically been shown to affect people's social behavior. Subjects who were subliminally primed with elderly faces during computer tasks later walked significantly more slowly upon departing the lab than did those who did not receive the prime (Bargh, Chen, and Burrows 1996). This suggests that people use stereotypic information to direct their own behaviors in social interactions. People's social behaviors may reflect their stereotypic expectations of the behaviors of their interaction partners. They adapt their behavior to facilitate smoother social exchanges.

People are not always tight-fisted with their cognitive capital. Short-cuts may be the default, but people are not fools. Fiske and Taylor (1991) suggest that people are motivated tacticians, strategically choosing situations that warrant additional mental resources when they are motivated and able to do so. For example, the continuum model (Fiske and Neuberg 1990; Fiske, Lin, and Neuberg 1999) proposes two poles of impression formation: category-based processing and attribute-based, or individuating, processing. Category-based processing relies on a top-down route; perceivers place a person in a category, from which they infer stereotypic information about the individual. Attribute-based processing is a bottom-up approach, wherein people actually attend to details about the individual, forming an impression based on fine points. What determines when perceivers will use attribute-based versus category-based processing is the accessibility of stereotype-incongruent information, along with the ability and motivation to deal with it. When stereotype-inconsistent information is offered, when cognitive resources are not taxed, and when people are motivated to be accurate, they are more likely to modify their stereotypes by integrating the new information into the overall impression (Fiske et al. 1987; Macrae, Hewstone, and Griffiths 1993).

Researchers in the past decade have begun to shift from an exclusive focus on cognition to a joint focus on cognition and motivation. Five core social motives—belonging, understanding, controlling, enhancing, and trusting—can help explain stereotyping-relevant goals (Fiske 2000). Belonging, the primary social goal, concerns people's need for affiliation with others. To foster in-group relationships, people attend to individuating information about in-group members, echo the beliefs of in-group members, comply with in-group norms, and mimic in-group behavior. These all affect the degree to which people will or will not stereotype elderly people, who may be treated as in-group members (family) or out-group members (elderly people).

People are also motivated to maintain a shared social understanding and control of socially effective interactions, both of which are relatively cognitive motives. The goal to understand others starts with automatic categorization and leads people to search for and remember stereotypic information. Social representations of elderly people constitute a shared cultural understanding. The motivation to control can cause people to treat stereotyped groups, including older people, in particularly preemptory ways, to maintain power hierarchies with older people toward the bottom.

Finally, people strive to enhance the self and trust in-group members, both of which are more affective goals. The former, self-enhancement, fits the suggestion by Snyder and Meine (1994) that stereotyping, specifically of elderly people, may also serve an ego-protective function. That is, inasmuch as older people threaten younger people by reminding them of the transience of youth, young people will be motivated to protect themselves against this threat. By attributing the perceived mental and physical deficiencies of older adults to some personal weakness, rather than blaming the aging process for these perceived losses, young people protect themselves from the truth of the inevitability of aging, enhancing self in the process.

Trust relates to maintaining in-group boundaries. Given that interdependence is essential to in-group functioning, it is adaptive for people to trust in-group members; thus, older people can be excluded. When people are interdependent with out-group members, however, they will be motivated to trust them. Successful intergroup cooperation builds trust, undercutting stereotyping toward out-group members. Interdependence across age groups can therefore undercut mutual stereotypes (for a review of the five core social goals, see Fiske 2000).

Intergroup Level: Social Identity and Self-Categorization Theories

A complementary approach to interpersonal cognitive analyses of stereotyping comes from social identity and self-categorization theories, which focus on intergroup explanations. Social identity theory (SIT) views the divisions of groups into "us" (in-groups) and "them" (out-groups) as having both cognitive (categorization) and motivational (positive social identity) benefits (Tajfel and Turner 1979, 1986; Turner and Oakes 1989). Motivated to obtain positive social identities from the groups to which we belong, we distinguish in-groups from out-groups, which leads to a self-beneficial contrast. If an in-group advantage is not obvious, we create positive distinctiveness by favoring the in-group over the out-group on pertinent dimensions. By relying on stereotypes that exaggerate intergroup differences, we assign positive evaluations to our own group, relative to our evaluations of the out-group (for a review, see Brewer and Brown 1998). Elderly people demonstrate an in-group evaluative bias, rating characteristics associated with older people more favorably than characteristics associated with younger adults (Brubaker and Powers 1976; Fitzgerald 1978; Porter and O'Connor 1978; Rothbaum 1983; and Traxler 1971).

Self-categorization theory (SCT) extends SIT by dropping the motivational aspects of SIT and by explaining that the self can be conceived on many levels of categorization, which is contextually determined by how one relates to others, including in-group members (Turner and Oakes 1989; Oakes, Haslam, and Turner 1994). Viewed through the lens of SIT and SCT, young in-groups will favor themselves, to the exclusion of older out-groups. Although the reverse also occurs, the nonelderly are more likely to control significant resources, so their in-group favoritism has more severe consequences.

Conclusion

Amid the clamor of the 2000 presidential election vote-counting debacle, we were struck by media portrayals of older Palm Beach County voters who inadvertently voted for the wrong candidate as incompetent and harebrained. "If there's a county in the world that would have a population that would struggle with the ballot, it would be that one," said one political science professor, citing demographics (i.e., age) as the culprit (Gordon 2000, para 3). Another interviewee added that elderly voters are "not as sharp as they used to be" (Gordon 2000, para 11). The nightly news even showed one Florida demonstrator carrying a sign that read, "Stupid people shouldn't vote."

We propose that today in the United States, elderly people are stereotyped as incompetent but also as warm. People view them ambivalently as physically and cognitively inept but socially sensitive. Preliminary data suggest that elderly people are subject to a paternalistic breed of prejudice; they are pitied but not respected. Because of historical and cultural changes, today's elders are seen as low status, which elicits perceptions of incompetence, and passivity, leading to perceptions of warmth. Transformations in the content of elderly stereotypes stem from social structural changes, resulting from historical and cultural transformations. In particular, they result from the diminished social status of older adults and the absence of older adults from competitive social roles.

From workplaces to medical settings, stereotyping of elderly people manifests itself through discriminatory communication and treatment (Zebrowitz and Montepare 2000). Believing older people are incompetent leads others to treat them as if they are incompetent. Young people use baby talk—higher voices and simpler words—and sound more unpleasant when communicating with older people (Hummert et al. 1998; Montepare, Steinberg, and Rosenberg 1992; Thimm, Rademacher, and Kruse 1998). People are less willing to engage in challenging conversations with elderly people by asking them difficult questions (Rodin and Langer 1980).

Our stereotypes of elderly ineptitude also come to life in the workplace. When evaluating supposed job interviews, people rated younger interviewees more positively overall, even when they had the same qualifications as the older interviewees (Avolio and Barrett 1987). Older job applicants are less likely to be hired, are viewed as more difficult to train, harder to place into jobs, more resistant to change, less suitable for promotion, and expected to have lower job performances (for a review, see Avolio and Barrett 1987).

Older people are victims of discrimination in medical settings as well. Sometimes we deny older people services afforded to younger people. For instance, when reporting the same symptoms as young people, older people are less likely to be referred for psychiatric assessments (Grant 1996; Hillerbrand and Shaw 1990). When reporting psychiatric symptoms commonly associated with aging, older patients are treated less thoroughly than young people reporting the same symptoms (Butler 1975). Medical doctors condescend to and patronize older patients by providing oversimplified information and presenting it in less engaging ways (Greene et al. 1989; Caporael and Culbertson 1986).

By keeping older people at a social distance, we deny ourselves exposure to stereotype-incongruent information, which could force us to see older people as a more variable group. Under certain conditions, interage contact (Caspi 1984; Schwartz and Simmons in press) and the presentation of stereotype-inconsistent information (Jackson and Sullivan 1988) curtail discrimination against elderly people. When presented with individuating information, young adults are less likely to make age-stereotype-consistent attributions (Erber, Etheart, and Szuchman 1992) and, in some cases, even likely to assign more positive ratings to older people than to younger counterparts (Erber, Szuchman, and Etheart 1993).

Attributing the errors of older Palm Beach voters to intellectual incompetence perpetuates the worst of our cultural stereotypes. Stereotyping of elderly people goes largely unchallenged and even unnoticed in the United States. Nevertheless, intergroup contact among age groups and interdependence among young, middle-aged, and old people may restore a sense of respect, as well as liking for, all age groups in their glorious human variety.

Notes

1. It is important to distinguish subtypes from subgroups. The former results from the clustering of group members who disconfirm the stereotype, and the latter is the product of the linking together of group members based on their similarities (Jones 1997). The crucial difference is that subtypes leave the stereotype unchanged, whereas subgroups lead perceivers to appreciate within-group variability. When we discuss subordinate categories in this chapter, we are referring to subtypes, not subgroups.

2. It may be unclear from figure 1.1 that 21 of 24 of these groups differed significantly on competence and warmth, including 4 of 7 groups in the middle cluster.

References

We thank Kathleen and William Dexter, for sharing their experiences and insights on this topic and Matt Cuddy and Kenworthey Bilz for valuable feedback on drafts of this chapter.

Allen, V. L., and Wilder, D. A. (1979). Group categorization and attribution of belief similarity. *Small Group Behavior, 10,* 73–80.

Allport, G. W. (1954). *The nature of prejudice.* Reading, MA: Addison-Wesley.

Andreoletti, C., Maurice, J. K., and Whalen, H. (2001). *Gender, race, and age: Compound stereotypes across the lifespan.* Poster presented at the Second Annual Meeting of the Society for Personality and Social Psychology, February 2001, San Antonio, TX.

Asch, S. E. (1946). Forming impressions of personality. *Journal of Abnormal and Social Psychology, 41,* 1230–1240.

Avolio, B. J., and Barrett, G. J. (1987). Effects of age stereotyping in a simulated interview. *Psychology and Aging, 2,* 56–63.

Bakan, D. (1966). *The duality of human existence: An essay on psychology and religion.* Chicago: Rand McNally.

Bargh, J. A., Chen, M., and Burrows, L. (1996). Automaticity of social behavior: Direct effects of trait construct and stereotype activation on action. *Journal of Personality and Social Psychology, 71,* 230–244.

Bodenhausen, G. V. (1990). Stereotypes as judgmental heuristics: Evidence of circadian variations in discrimination. *Psychological Science, 1,* 319–322.

Bodenhausen, G. V., and Lichtenstein, M. (1987). Social stereotypes and information-processing strategies: The impact of task complexity. *Journal of Personality and Social Psychology, 52,* 871–880.

Branco, K. J., and Williamson, J. B. (1982). In A. G. Miller (Ed.) *In the eye of the beholder: Contemporary issues in stereotyping* (pp. 364–410). New York: Praeger.

Breckler, S. J. (1984). Empirical validation of affect, behavior, and cognition as distinct components of attitude. *Journal of Personality and Social Psychology, 47,* 1191–1205.

Brewer, M. B., and Brown, R. J. (1998). Intergroup relations. In D. T. Gilbert, S. T. Fiske, and G. Lindzey (Eds.), *The handbook of social psychology* (4th ed.). New York: McGraw-Hill.

Brewer, M. B., Dull, V., and Lui, L. (1981). Perceptions of the elderly: Stereotypes as prototypes. *Journal of Personality and Social Psychology, 41,* 656–670.

Britton, J. O., and Thomas, J. R. (1973). Age and sex as employment variables: Views of employment service interviewers. *Journal of Employment Counseling, 10,* 180–186.

Brubaker, T. H., and Powers, E. A. (1976). The stereotype of "old": A review and alternative approach. *Journal of Gerontology, 31,* 441–447.

Butler, R. N. (1975). Psychiatry and the elderly: An overview. *American Journal of Psychiatry, 132,* 893–900.

Butler, R. N. (1980). Ageism: A foreword. *Journal of Social Issues, 36,* 8–11.

Cantor, N., and Mischel, W. (1979). Prototypes in person perception. In L. Berkowitz (Ed.), *Advances in experimental social psychology* (Vol. 12, pp. 3–52). New York: Academic Press.

Caporael, L. R., and Culbertson, G. H. (1986). Verbal response modes of baby talk and other speech at institutions for the aged. Language and Communication, 6, 99–112.

Caspi, A. (1984). Contact hypothesis and inter-age attitudes: A field study of cross-age contact. *Social Psychology Quarterly, 47,* 74–80.

Crosby, F. J., Bromley, F., and Saxe, L. (1980). Recent unobtrusive studies of black and white discrimination and prejudice: A literature review. *Psychological Bulletin, 87,* 546–563.

Darley, J. M., and Fazio, R. H. (1980). Expectancy-confirmation processes arising in the social interaction sequence. *American Psychologist, 35,* 867–881.

Eagly, A. H., and Chaiken, S. (1998). Attitude structure and function. In D. T. Gilbert, S. T. Fiske, and G. Lindzey (Eds.), *The handbook of social psychology* (4th ed.). New York: McGraw-Hill.

Erber, J. T. (1989). Young and older adults' appraisal of memory failures in young and older adult target person. *Journal of Gerontology: Psychological Sciences, 44,* 170–175.

Erber, J. T., Etheart, M. E., and Szuchman, L. T. (1992). Age and forgetfulness: Perceivers' impressions of targets' capability. *Psychology and Aging, 7,* 479–483.

Erber, J. T., Szuchman, L. T., and Etheart, M. E. (1993). Age and forgetfulness: Young perceivers' impressions of young and old neighbors. *International Journal of Aging and Human Development, 37,* 91–103.

Fiske, S. T. (1998). Stereotyping, prejudice, and discrimination. In D. T. Gilbert, S. T. Fiske, and G. Lindzey (Eds.), *The handbook of social psychology* (4th ed.). New York: McGraw-Hill.

Fiske, S. T. (2000). Stereotyping, prejudice, and discrimination at the seam between the centuries: Evolution, culture, mind, and brain. *European Journal of Social Psychology, 30,* 299–322.

Fiske, S. T., Cuddy, A. J. C., Glick, P., and Xu, J. (2001). *A model of stereotype content as often mixed: Separate dimensions of competence and warmth respectively follow from status and competition.* Unpublished manuscript, Princeton University.

Fiske, S. T., Cuddy, A. J. C., and Glick, P. (Forthcoming). Emotions up and down: Intergroup emotions result from perceived status and competition. In D. M. Mackie and E. R. Smith (Eds.), *From prejudice to intergroup emotions: Differentiated reactions to social groups.* Psychology Press: Philadelphia.

Fiske, S. T., Lin, M., and Neuberg, S. L. (1999). The continuum model ten years later. In S. Chaiken and Y. Troppe (Eds.), *Dual-process theories in social psychology* (pp. 231–254). New York: Guilford Press.

Fiske, S. T., and Neuberg, S. L. (1990). A continuum model of impression formation from category-based to individuating processes: Influences of information and motivation on attention and interpretation. In M. P. Zanna (Ed.), *Advances in experimental social psychology* (Vol. 3, pp. 1–74). San Diego, CA: Academic Press.

Fiske, S. T., Neuberg, S. L., Beattie, A., and Milberg, S. (1987). Category-based and attribute-based reactions to others: Some informational conditions of stereotyping and individuating processes. *Journal of Experimental Social Psychology, 23,* 399–427.

Fiske, S. T., and Taylor, S. (1984). *Social Cognition* (1st ed.). New York: McGraw-Hill.

Fiske, S. T., and Taylor, S. (1991). *Social Cognition* (2nd ed.). New York: McGraw-Hill.

Fiske, S. T., Xu, J., Cuddy, A. C., and Glick, P. (1999). (Dis)respecting versus (dis)liking: Status and interdependence predict ambivalent stereotypes of competence and warmth. *Journal of Social Issues, 55,* 473–489.

Fitzgerald, J. M. (1978). Actual and perceived sex and generational differences in interpersonal style, structure, and quantitative issues. *Journal of Gerontology, 33,* 388–393.

Glick, P., and Fiske, S. T. (1996). The Ambivalent Sexism Inventory: Differentiating hostile from benevolent sexism. *Journal of Personality and Social Psychology, 70,* 491–512.

Glick, P., and Fiske, S. T. (1999). Sexism and other "isms": Interdependence, status, and the ambivalent content of stereotypes. In W. B. Swann, Jr., L. A. Gilbert, and J. Langlois (Eds.), *Sexism and stereotypes in modern society: The gender science of Janet Taylor Spence* (pp. 193–221). Washington, D.C.: American Psychological Association.

Gordon, M. (2000, November 11). Palm Beach County had ballot problems in past elections. *The Associated Press.* [Online]. Available: *http://www.lexis-nexis.com/universe.*

Grant, L. (1996). Effects of ageism on individual and health care providers' responses to healthy aging. *Health and Social Work, 21,* 9–15.

Greene, M. G., Adelman, R. D., Charon, R., and Friedmann, R. (1989). Concordance between physicians and their older and younger patients in the primary care medical encounter. *Gerontologist, 29,* 808–813.

Haefner, J. R. (1977). Race, age, sex, and competence as factors in employer selection of the disadvantaged. *Journal of Applied Social Psychology, 62,* 199–202.

Heckhausen, J., Dixon, R. A., and Baltes, P. B. (1989). Gains and losses in development throughout adulthood as perceived by different adult age groups. *Developmental Psychology, 25,* 109–121.

Hewstone, M., Johnston, L., and Aird, P. (1992). Cognitive models of stereotype change: II. Perceptions of homogeneous and heterogeneous groups. *European Journal of Social Psychology, 22,* 235–249.

Hillerbrand, E., and Shaw, D. (1990). Age bias in a general hospital: Is there ageism in psychiatric consultation? *Clinical Gerontologist, 2,* 3–13.

Hummert, M. L. (1990). Multiple stereotypes of elderly and young adults: A comparison of structure and evaluations. *Psychology and Aging, 5,* 182–193.

Hummert, M. L. (1997). Age stereotyping: Are we oversimplifying the phenomenon? *International Journal of Aging and Human Development, 22,* 315–325.

Hummert, M. L., Shaner, J. L., Garstka, T. A., and Henry, C. (1998). Communication with older adults: The influence of age stereotypes, context, and communicator age. *Human Communication Research, 25*(1), 124–151.

Hurh, W. M., and Kim, K. C. (1989). The "success" image of Asian Americans: Its validity and its practical and theoretical implications. *Ethnic and Racial Studies, 12,* 512–538.

Jackson, L. A., and Sullivan, L. A. (1988). Age stereotype disconfirming information and evaluations of old people. *Journal of Social Psychology, 128,* 721–729.

Jones, J. M. (1997). *Prejudice and racism.* New York: McGraw-Hill.

Kirchner, W. K., and Dunnette, M. D. (1954). Attitudes toward older workers. *Personnel Psychology, 7,* 257–265.

Kitano, H. H. L., and Sue, S. (1973). The model minorities. *Journal of Social Issues, 29,* 1–9.

Kite, M., Deaux, K., and Miele, M. (1991). Stereotypes of young and old: Does age outweigh gender? *Psychology and Aging, 6,* 19–27.

Kruglanski, A. W., and Freund, T. (1983). The freezing and unfreezing of lay inferences: Effects on impression primacy, ethnic stereotyping, and numerical anchoring. *Journal of Experimental Social Psychology, 19,* 448–468.

Lin, M., and Fiske, S. T. (1999). *Attitudes toward Asian Americans: Developing a prejudice scale.* Unpublished paper, University of Massachusetts at Amherst.

Linville, P. (1982). The complexity-extremity effect and age-based stereotyping. *Journal of Personality and Social Psychology, 42,* 193–211.

Locke-Connor, C., and Walsh, P. R. (1980). Attitudes toward the older job applicant: Just as competent, but more likely to fail. *Journal of Gerontology, 35,* 920–927.

Mackie, D. M., Hamilton, D. L., Susskind, J., and Rosselli, F. (1996). Social psychological foundations of stereotype formation. In C. N. Macrae, C. Stangor, and M. Hewstone (Eds.), *Stereotypes and stereotyping* (pp. 41–78). New York: Guilford.

Macrae, C. N., Hewstone, M., and Griffiths, R. (1993). Processing load and memory for stereotype-based information. *European Journal of Social Psychology, 23,* 77–87.

Macrae, C. N., Milne, A. B., and Bodenhausen, G. V. (1994). Stereotypes as energy-saving devices: A peek inside the cognitive toolbox. *Journal of Personality and Social Psychology, 66,* 37–47.

McGroarty, C., and Fiske, S. T. (1997). *Attitudes toward blind people.* Unpublished scale, University of Massachusetts at Amherst.

Montepare, J. M., Steinberg, J., and Rosenberg, B. (1992). Characteristics of vocal communication between young adults and their parents and grandparents. *Communication Research, 19,* 479–492.

Oakes, P. J., Haslam, S. J., and Turner, J. C. (Eds.). (1994). *Stereotyping and social reality.* Oxford: Blackwell.

Park, B., and Rothbart, M. (1982). Perception of out-group homogeneity and levels of social categorization: Memory for the subordinate attributes of in-group and out-group members. *Journal of Personality and Social Psychology, 42,* 1051–1068.

Park, B., Ryan, C. S., and Judd, C. M. (1992). Role of meaningful subgroups in explaining differences in perceived variability for ingroups and outgroups. *Journal of Personality and Social Psychology, 42,* 1051–1068.

Peeters, G. (1995). What's negative about hatred and positive about love? On negation in cognition, affect, and behavior. In H. C. M. de Swart, L. J. M. Bergman (Eds.), *Perspectives on negation: Essays in honour of Johan J. de Iongh on his 80th birthday* (pp. 123–133). Tilburg, Netherlands: Tilburg University Press.

Peeters, G. (1983). Relational and informational patterns in social cognition. In W. Doise and S. Moscovici (Eds.), *Current issues in European social psychology,* 201–237. UK: Maison des Sciences de l'Homme and Cambridge University Press.

Phalet, K., and Poppe, E. (1997). Competence and morality dimensions of national and ethnic stereotypes: A study in six eastern-European countries. *European Journal of Social Psychology, 27,* 703–723.

Porter, K., and O'Connor, N. (1978). Changing attitudes of university students to old people. *Educational Gerontology, 3,* 139–145.

Rodin, J., and Langer, E. J. (1980). Aging labels: The decline of control and the fall of self-esteem. *Journal of Social Issues, 36,* 12–29.

Rosen, B., and Jerdee, T. H. (1976a). The nature of job-related age stereotypes on managerial decisions. *Journal of Applied Social Psychology, 62,* 180–183.

Rosen, B., and Jerdee, T. H. (1976b). Influence of age stereotypes on managerial decisions. *Journal of Applied Psychology, 61,* 428–432.

Rosenberg, S., Nelson, C., and Vivekanathan, P. S. (1968). A multidimensional approach to the structure of personality impressions. *Journal of Personality and Social Psychology, 9,* 283–294.

Rothbaum, F. (1983). Aging and age stereotypes. *Social Cognition, 2(2),* 171–184.

Ryan, C. S., Park, B., and Judd, C. M. (1996). Assessing stereotype accuracy: Implications for the understanding of stereotyping process. In C. N. Macrae, C. Stangor, and M. Hewstone (Eds.), *Stereotypes and stereotyping* (pp. 3–37). New York: Guilford.

Salthouse, T. A., and Maurer, T. J. (1996). Aging, job performance, and career development. In J. E. Birren and K. W. Schaie (Eds.), *Handbook of psychology of aging* (pp. 353–364). San Diego: Academic Press.

Schmidt, D. F., and Boland, S. M. (1986). Structure of perceptions of older adults: Evidence for multiple stereotypes. *Psychology and Aging, 1,* 255–260.

Schwartz, L. K., and Simmons, J. P. (2001). Contact quality and attitudes toward the elderly. *Educational Gerontology, 27,* 127–137.

Sigall, H., and Page, R. (1971). Current stereotypes: A little fading, a little faking. *Journal of Personality and Social Psychology, 18,* 247–255.

Slater, R. (1995). *The psychology of growing old.* Buckingham, England: Open University Press.

Singer, M. S. (1986). Age stereotypes as a function of profession. *Journal of Social Psychology, 126,* 691–692.

Smolak, L. (1993). *Adult Development.* Englewood Cliffs, NJ: Prentice-Hall.

Snyder, M., and Meine, P. K. (1994). Stereotyping of the elderly: A functional approach. *British Journal of Social Psychology, 33,* 63–82.

Spence, J. T., and Helmreich, R. L. (1979). The many faces of androgyny: A reply to Locksley and Colten. *Journal of Personality and Social Psychology, 37,* 1032–1046.

Stangor, C., Lynch, L., Duan, C., and Glass, B. (1992). Categorization of individuals on the basis of multiple social features. *Journal of Personality and Social Psychology, 62,* 207–218.

Stangor, C., and Schaller, M. (1996). Stereotypes as individual and collective representations. In C. N. Macrae, C. Stangor, and M. Hewstone (Eds.), *Stereotypes and stereotyping* (pp. 3–37). New York: Guilford.

Stokes, G. (1992). *On being old: The psychology of later life.* London: Falmer Press.

Tajfel, H., Billig, M., Bundy, R. P., and Flament, C. (1971). Social categorization and intergroup behavior. *European Journal of Social Psychology, 1,* 149–177.

Tajfel, H., and Turner, J. C. (1979). An integrative theory of intergroup conflict. In W. G. Austin and S. Worchel (Eds.), *The social psychology of intergroup relations* (pp. 33–47). Monterey, CA: Brooks/Cole.

Tajfel, H., and Turner, J. C. (1986). The social identity theory of intergroup behavior. In S. Worchel and W. G. Austin (Eds.), *Psychology of intergroup relations* (pp. 7–24). Chicago: Nelson-Hall.

Taylor, S. E. (1981). A categorization approach to stereotyping. In D. L. Hamilton (Ed.), *Cognitive processes in stereotyping and intergroup behavior* (pp. 88–114). Hillsdale, NJ: Elbaum.

Thimm, C., Rademacher, U., and Kruse, L. (1998). Age stereotypes and patronizing messages: Features of age-adapted speech in technical instructions to the elderly. *Journal of Applied Communication Research, 26,* 66–82.

Traxler, A. J. (1971). Intergenerational differences in attitudes toward old people. *Gerontologist, 11,* 34.

Turner, J. C., and Oakes, P. J. (1989). Self-categorization theory and social influence. In P. B. Paulus (Eds.), *The psychology of group influence* (pp. 233–275). Hillsdale, NJ: Erlbaum.

Waldman, D. A., and Avolio, B. J. (1986). A meta-analysis of age differences in job performance. *Journal of Applied Psychology, 71*, 33–38.

Weiner, B. (1985). An attributional theory of achievement motivation and emotion. *Psychological Review, 92*, 548–573.

Zebrowitz, L. A., and Montepare, J. M. (2000). Too young, too old: Stigmatizing adolescents and elders. In T. F. Heatherton, R. E. Kleck, M. R. Hebl, and J. G. Hull (Eds.), *The social psychology of stigma* (pp. 334–373). New York: Guilford Press.

Zemore, S., and Cuddy, A. J. C. (2000). [Elderly stereotype contents at the automatic level]. Unpublished raw data.

2

Ageism: Denying the Face of the Future
Jeff Greenberg, Jeff Schimel, and Andy Martens

Ageism, like all other forms of prejudice, undoubtedly has a variety of causes and serves a variety of functions. Ageism can most simply be defined as negative attitudes or behaviors toward an individual solely based on that person's age. Defined this way, negative attitudes toward people because they are young would qualify as ageism. However, throughout this chapter and consistent with the spirit of this book, we will use the term ageism to refer specifically to negative attitudes and behavior toward the elderly, focusing exclusively on this most troubling and consequential form of ageism.

In the United States, once a person is categorized as elderly, the non-elderly are likely to apply a host of negative stereotypes to the aged (e.g., Kite and Johnson 1988), assume attitude and value differences, and expect that the elderly have very different economic and social interests than they do (e.g., Bytheway 1995; Palmore 1999). In Tucson, Arizona, there are vivid examples of ageism, in part because the elderly population is particularly substantial. Because of the warm weather, beyond native residents who grow old, there are lots of permanent resident retirees who have escaped colder climates, in addition to their temporary winter counterparts, known as "snowbirds." The most salient stereotype is that the elderly create consternation and congestion on the highways with their slow driving, more often than not in the left lane. And in the political spectrum, the elderly are despised for being narrowly focused on reducing taxes at the expense of education. Of course, other, probably more harmful manifestations of ageism undoubtedly abound in Tucson as well as elsewhere—phenomena like age discrimination in hiring and forced retirement (Esposito 1987) and negative depictions of the elderly in the mass media (Palmore 1999).

These examples surely suggest that the many causes of ethnic prejudice discussed by Allport (1954) and researched over the past half-century most likely apply to age prejudice as well. However, certain special aspects of ageism suggest some unique causes for this type of prejudice. Although the young may view the elderly as an out-group, the truth is that the elderly used to be young and that the young, barring premature death, will one day be elderly. Thus, the relationship of the nonold to the old is unique. If the elderly are viewed as an out-group, they consist of an out-group that used to be part of the nonelderly's in-group, and one that the nonelderly will someday join if they are lucky enough to survive that long! These complexities do not apply to relations between blacks and whites or the French and Germans. They also do not apply to religious differences, except in the rare case of conversion, or relations between the sexes except for the rare case of sex change operations.

Another complexity concerns the nature of the threat posed by the elderly. National and ethnic out-groups often pose economic threats, such as competition for jobs and material resources, but this does not seem to be a major concern people have regarding the elderly within their own culture. Out-groups can also be threatening because they may claim superiority to one's own group. For example, some of the animosity among Germany, France, and Great Britain over the years may stem from each culture's perceiving that the other one claims to be superior. In this way, out-groups may threaten an individual's self-esteem. Indeed, as we have suggested elsewhere (Greenberg et al. 1990), this may help explain the widespread prejudice against Jews, who have long claimed to be the chosen people. It seems unlikely, however, that the elderly pose a threat to the self-esteem of the nonelderly in this manner.

The Elderly and the Threat of Death

Terror management theory (Greenberg, Pyszczynski, and Solomon 1986), based on the writings of Ernest Becker (1962, 1973, 1975), proposes an even more fundamental way that out-groups can be psychologically threatening. The theory proposes that individuals' faith in their cultural worldviews provides them with psychological equanimity in a threatening universe where death is the only certainty. By subscribing to different worldviews, members of out-groups either explicitly or implicitly imply that one's own worldview may not be valid. This psychological threat is posited to be a major contributor to prejudice and discrimination.

This threat may play a role in ageism, but probably a minor one. In most cultures, the elderly are staunch supporters—in fact, key representatives—of the mainstream worldview. To the extent they are, they should provide psychological comfort rather than distress. The one exception is when the elderly are viewed as holding on to an antiquated worldview that is no longer compatible with the views held by the young of the particular culture. In many cultures, there may be some element of this generation gap, but at the same time, the elderly generally are likely to be quite supportive of the traditions and fortunes of the culture and there appears to be "general agreement between generations about our basic value system" (Palmore 1999, p. 15). Thus, this type of threat to one's worldview may contribute to some ageism, but only under a limited set of circumstances.

Terror management theory suggests yet another threat that may commonly contribute to ageism, one that is fundamentally tied to the elderly. The elderly represent the threat to the young of their own fate: the prospects of diminishing beauty, health, sensation, and, ultimately, death. These threats are recognized in aspects of most, if not all, cultures, albeit perhaps most clearly in Western cultures. In the Shakespearean comedy *As You Like It*, in one of the most well-known passages in English literature ("all the world's a stage"), the melancholy philosopher Jacques refers to the seventh and final stage of life as "second childishness and mere oblivion / sans teeth, sans taste, sans everything," John Keats (1820/1991), in two of the most revered poems in the English language, echoes this negative view of aging. In "Ode to a Nightingale" (pp. 34-35), he laments the human knowledge of our fate:

Where palsy shakes a few last gray hairs,
Where youth grows pale, and spectre-thin and dies;
Where but to think is to be full of sorrow
And leaden-eyed despairs,
Where Beauty cannot keep her lustrous eyes,
Or new Love pine at them beyond to-morrow.

Similarly, in "Ode on a Grecian Urn" (p. 37), Keats exalts the scene portrayed on the urn because those portrayed will never grow old or perish:

Fair youth, beneath the trees, thou canst not leave
Thy song, nor ever can those trees be bare;
Bold Lover, never, never canst thou kiss,...
She cannot fade, though thou hast not thy bliss,
For ever wilt thou love, and she be fair...
When old age shall this generation waste,
thou shalt remain, in midst of other woe
Than ours, a friend to man.

Ironically, Keats never had to cope with these problems of aging because he died at the ripe old age of 26, having met that one inevitable fate with which aging is linked all too soon.

Evidence of the linking of aging with death is also apparent in distinctly non-Western cultures. Indeed, the evolutionary anthropological philosopher Susanne Langer (1982) has argued that it is precisely the dawning awareness by our ancestors that aging leads to death that magnifies the problem of death. Her argument is that death by lion, boulder, or even evil spirit can be avoided, but death as a natural consequence of the aging process to which we are all subject makes death a permanent, unavoidable constant, which burdens us psychologically like nothing else. People may face a variety of reminders of death over the course of their daily lives, such as news stories and television shows about murders and natural disasters, car and plane accidents. But people can feel that they have qualities or can engage in actions that allow them to avoid these problems. However, when the young see a very elderly person, they see a fate that is their inevitable destiny if they are lucky enough to avoid the many hazards that can cause an earlier death. Thus, from this perspective, the elderly may be the most threatening reminder to people of their inevitable mortality.

In these and many other examples from anthropology, literature, painting, and film, aging is associated with a variety of negative consequences, the most psychologically important of these being death. Because of these widespread associations, the elderly are likely to bring to mind these very threatening prospects for ourselves. Terror management theory (Greenberg et al. 1986; Solomon, Greenberg, and Pyszczynski 1991) was developed to explain how we humans cope with the knowledge of our own vulnerability and mortality, and so it may be useful to review the theory and associated research and then draw implications from this work to understand how people defend against the threatening aspects of knowledge of and experiences with the elderly and the consequences of such defenses for attitudes and behavior toward the elderly.

Terror Management Theory

Terror management theory was based on the writings of cultural anthropologist Ernest Becker (1962, 1973, 1975), and neither the theory nor this chapter should be taken as an adequate substitute for the rich analyses Becker put forth. Terror management theory was formulated to pull together Becker's essential points, supplement them as needed, and pro-

vide a basis for investigating empirically how the problem of the awareness of death affects a wide range of human behaviors.

Becker sought to synthesize knowledge from all the academic disciplines concerned with people to understand why human beings behave
the way they do. Particularly prominent among the influences on his the-
orizing were Søren Kierkegaard, Charles Darwin, Sigmund Freud, Otto
Rank, Alfred Adler, Erving Goffman, Gregory Zillborg, and Norman
Brown. The analysis of human behavior that he formulated can be viewed
as an existential psychodynamic one, quite similar to those of contempo-
raries Robert Jay Lifton and Irvin Yalom.

Becker noted the common heritage shared by humans and other animals and focused especially on the notion that all animals are driven to
survive, or have an instinct for self-preservation. We most likely evolved
out of our ape ancestors into a unique species. According to Becker, what
makes us the unique and thriving species we are is our highly developed
cerebral cortex, most different from our ape relatives in the elaborate nature of our prefontal lobes. While our closest cousins, the great apes,
number around 100,000 worldwide, the human population is continuing
to grow beyond 6 billion, and it is our intellectual prowess, made possible
by our highly evolved cortex, that is probably most responsible for our
advantage.

So for Becker, to understand human behavior, including ageism, we
have to understand that humans are animals with basic organismic needs
but with unique intellectual tools for satisfying those needs. Among the
intellectual capacities that Becker proposed as critical to our nature are
the capacity for language and symbolic thought, the capacity for concep-
tualizing subjective experience in terms of past, present, and future—facilitating our ability to learn from experience and plan ahead—and the
capacity for self-awareness. These capabilities in combination allow humans an unprecedented capacity for self-regulation and regulation of external circumstances—to delay and modify reactions to impending
stimuli, to communicate with others as well as the self about mentally
stored information and hypothetical possibilities, to plan out potential
courses of action and monitor our progress toward goals, and to imagine
and make modifications to the external environment. These regulatory
advantages have enhanced our inclusive fitness far beyond that of the
other species most similar to us and have played a major role in our re-
productive success—our ability to survive and thrive in virtually every environmental niche on earth.

Thus, as a species, we owe much to the intellectual capacities made possible by the evolution of our cerebral cortex. Unfortunately, this inheritance we all share does not come without its burdens. To be aware that one exists as a material creature in the world with a future full of possible threats and with death as one's only certainty is, as the existential philosophers have made clear, a very heavy burden indeed. Stephen Jay Gould (1997) has referred to this knowledge as perhaps the most important spandrel (i.e., accidental by-product) of the evolution of our intellectual capacities. Becker argued that this knowledge makes us unique as a species in our potential for anxiety and constitutes a threat we cannot simply face squarely and unadorned. If we are in fact driven to survive and programmed to react with fear and defense to threats to our survival, how do we deal with the knowledge that mortality is our only certainty?

In *The Denial of Death* (1973), Becker concluded that this existential paradox—being driven to live but knowing the only certainty is death—creates the potential for paralyzing terror, a potential we carry with us at all times. The way we control or manage this potential for terror is by using culturally based mechanisms to deny death. The core of death denial, or what we refer to as terror management, is a cultural worldview that allows individuals who are socialized within a given culture to view reality as stable, meaningful, and permanent. At the most fundamental level, these worldviews allow us to mature cognitively over the course of development without having to view ourselves merely as animals purposelessly clinging to a clump of dirt hurtling through space destined only to decay and death. And so we live embedded in a world of symbols and meaning, full of clocks and calendars, cultural myths and histories, nations and deities, soccer games and art exhibits. And the fact that the content of these worlds of symbols and meanings varies so much from culture to culture suggests that they are all ultimately social constructions, or as Becker preferred to call them, fictions.

Along with imparting meaning and value, each of these fictions provides possibilities of death transcendence through literal and symbolic forms of immortality. Literal immortality is provided by concepts such as an eternal soul, heaven, nirvana, and reincarnation. Symbolic immortality is provided by enduring cultural achievements and other enduring indicators of our existence, such as that great novel we are all going to write or the scientific discovery we are going to make, offspring, estates, memorials, and tributes. It is also provided by identification with entities that will endure indefinitely, such as family lines, cultural institutions, nations, and great causes. In this way, all cultural worldviews provide ways by which we can feel that our existence will continue beyond our death.

Becker argued that this cultural worldview lays the groundwork for psychological equanimity but is not sufficient. These worldviews are constructed such that qualification for protection and ultimately death transcendence requires meeting standards of value that confer significance as contributors to this meaningful reality. This structure is an extension of the original way in which we as children attain and sustain our security: by living up to the standards of value of our parents, which qualifies us for their continued love and protection. The transition from the parents as the security base to the culture, which Becker refers to as the primary transference process, begins as the child comes to the realization that the parents are fallible and are unable to protect him or her from all the evils and dangers in the world, including death. As a result of this realization, the child extends his or her security base by investing in the standards, values, and prescriptions of the broader culture. This transition is typically quite smooth because the parents, who were once the child's sole source of protection, also serve as agents of the culture and its standards.

The culture then extends the linkage, "valued boy or girl equals safe and secure," throughout life by prescribing good qualities and valued social roles by which one can attain and sustain a sense of personal significance, which we refer to in everyday parlance as self-esteem. This significance means we are more than animals; we are cultural beings—people with names, positions, and permanence. Depending on one's cultural worldview, an individual could, for example, feel secure by being a good Christian, a good basketball player, a good warrior, or, in 1936 in Germany, a good Nazi. Each culture provides a variety of such roles by which self-esteem and a sense of security and death transcendence could be attained and sustained. And as the examples illustrate, the same attributes and behaviors that could make an individual in one culture feel good and secure could have the very opposite effect on an individual within a different culture. This observation highlights a key implication of this analysis: that self-esteem is predicated on faith in a particular cultural worldview, and each one in its own unique way imbues reality with meaning and the possibility of perceiving oneself to be of enduring value.

In formulating terror management theory, we have summarized Becker's analysis in the following way. The juxtaposition of an innate desire for survival and the awareness of our vulnerability and inevitable mortality creates a potential for paralyzing terror. Humans manage this potential terror by sustaining faith in a cultural anxiety buffer consisting of (1) an individualized but culturally derived view of reality that imbues life with order, meaning and permanence, and standards of value that qualify the individual for death transcendence (cultural worldview), and (2) one's value within the context of that worldview (self-esteem).

Our next step was to assess basic hypotheses derived from the theory. The first hypothesis we tested was that self-esteem serves as an anxiety buffer. Indeed, what first attracted us to Becker's work was the fact that his analysis explains why people want self-esteem and defend it so vigorously when it is threatened. The extant literature on self-esteem is highly consistent with the anxiety-buffer notion. First, a large body of evidence has shown that self-esteem is negatively correlated with anxiety and anxiety-related psychological and behavioral problems. Second, experimental research has shown that threats to self-esteem arouse anxiety and that this anxiety motivates a variety of defenses to minimize, counteract, or compensate for the threat. Third, defense of self-esteem in turn reduces anxiety.

To assess the anxiety-buffer hypothesis more directly, we designed a series of studies in which we manipulated level of self-esteem in the lab, exposed participants to threat, and measured anxiety. Across three studies we found that using both physiological and self-report measures, participants whose self-esteem had been raised experienced less anxiety in response to threat than did participants whose self-esteem had not been raised (Greenberg et al. 1992). Subsequent studies also showed that both individuals whose self-esteem was raised experimentally and individuals with naturally high self-esteem are less likely to engage in defensive responses to reminders of death (Harmon-Jones et al. 1997). Thus, the evidence provided clear support for the idea that self-esteem serves the psychological function of protecting people from anxiety.

The second basic hypothesis we tested concerned the fear of death and people's investment in their cultural worldview. Another attribute of Becker's analysis that we found appealing was that it provides an organizing framework for understanding many aspects of human social behavior that are typically studied as independent phenomena. From the terror management perspective, altruism and aggression, tolerance and prejudice, conformity and asserting uniqueness all can be viewed as resulting from attitudes and behaviors designed to sustain faith in one's worldview and sense of self-worth in the context of that worldview.

The key notion, of course, is that we attempt to preserve these psychological structures because they protect us from our potential terror of death. The difficult empirical issue was how to assess this notion. The problem is twofold. First, because this potential for terror is posited to drive behavior from outside consciousness, we could not rely on self-reports to assess its existence. Second, following Zillborg (1943), Becker argued that we all have this potential; it is an organismic annihilation anxiety, the emotional manifestation of the instinct for self-preservation. Consequently, for Becker, this terror potential is not a variable but a constant. Thus, it cannot be measured or altered.

The solution we arrived at was to posit that if the theory was valid, then perhaps conscious reminders of death would motivate actions to bolster faith in the cultural worldview. In other words, making the constant potential for annihilation anxiety more accessible to consciousness should drive us to push the troubling thoughts back into the unconscious by means of strengthening our cultural armor. Over eighty studies, conducted in seven countries, have since assessed and found support for variants of this hypothesis (for a review, see Greenberg, Solomon, and Pyszczynski 1997). In the first such experiment (Rosenblatt et al. 1989), we had municipal court judges fill out a series of questionnaires and then make a judgment on a hypothetical case in which they needed to set bond for an alleged prostitute. For a randomly chosen half of the judges, we embedded in the questionnaires two questions about their own death. In this way, we manipulated mortality salience. Our reasoning was that if we made mortality salience high for judges, they should be extra motivated to bolster their worldview by treating an apparent violator of that worldview, an alleged prostitute, especially harshly. And that is precisely what we found. The judges reminded of their own death set an average bond of $455, whereas the judges not reminded of their own death recommended an average bond of $50.

Since that study, researchers have manipulated mortality salience in a variety of ways (ranging from proximity to a funeral home to subliminal death primes) and assessed judgments and behavior toward a wide variety of targets (e.g., pro and anti-U.S. essayists, Germans and Turks, Christians and Jews, Republicans and Democrats, American and Japanese auto manufacturers, thieves and heroes). The consistent finding has been that mortality salience increases positive reactions to those who uphold or validate the individual's worldview and negative reactions to those who violate or challenge the individual's worldview (which we refer to as worldview defense). Research has also found that these effects are not mediated by negative affect or arousal and are not replicated by thoughts of a host of other potentially aversive future events (e.g., one's next important exam, dental pain, social exclusion).

Recent research has found other theory-consistent effects of mortality salience. Mortality salience-induced worldview defense is reduced when individuals have particularly strong cultural anxiety buffers or subscribe to worldviews that emphasize tolerance and is increased in those with weak anxiety buffers or who have particularly rigid worldviews (see Greenberg et al. 1997 for a review). In addition, mortality salience makes it difficult for people to violate cultural norms and increases people's perceptions that they are similar to others, unless their uniqueness has recently been called into question (Greenberg et al. 1995; Pyszczynski et al. 1996; Simon et al. 1997). Mortality salience has also been found to increase self-esteem striving in the following ways: engaging in risky driving in those who base their self-worth in part on their driving (Ben-Ari, Florian, and Mikulincer 1999); focusing on bodily appearance in those who think well of their bodies (Goldenberg, McCoy, et al. 2000); and shifting identifications toward successful groups and away from unsuccessful groups (Dechesne et al. 2000). Thus, mortality salience motivates bolstering of the self-esteem component of the cultural anxiety buffer as well as the worldview component.

Another set of studies has tested a mortality salience hypothesis based on Becker's argument that the recognition that we are animals reminds us that we are material beings subject to decay and death. This research has shown that mortality salience increases people's aversions to stimuli and activities that remind them that humans are animals. For example, mortality salience reduces people's interests in the physical aspects of sex and increases disgust reactions to body products (Goldenberg, Pyszczynski, et al., 2000). Mortality salience also increases people's preferences for an essay extolling human uniqueness over one extolling our similarities to other animals (Goldenberg, Pyszczynski, et al. 2000).

Recent research has also shed light on the sequences of psychological processes activated by thoughts of mortality (for a review see Pyszczynski, Greenberg, and Solomon 1999). The initial response to mortality salience is to get such thoughts out of consciousness by rationally convincing oneself that death is far into the future, distracting oneself from the threat, denying one's vulnerability to death, or physically removing oneself from salient reminders of death. We refer to this type of defense as proximal because it is an immediate way to address the presenting problem of scary thoughts in consciousness. Once such thoughts have receded from consciousness, bolstering of the worldview and self-esteem is increased, presumably to quell the deeper unconscious problem of our knowledge of our ultimate mortality. We refer to these defenses as distal

defenses because they are not rationally related to the presenting problem, but rather symbolic means of quelling an unconscious concern.
What the research essentially shows is that following mortality salience,
further death-related thoughts are immediately suppressed, but such
thoughts gradually increase in accessibility, motivating the distal defenses, which then bring the accessibility of death-related thought down
to its baseline level.

Terror Management and Ageism

The body of research on mortality salience suggests that some manifestations of ageism may result from the tendency for the elderly to arouse
thoughts of death in others. If the elderly do indeed arouse the threat of
mortality, then a variety of defenses may be engaged to address it. Both
proximal and distal defenses in response to the elderly may contribute to
ageism. As noted earlier, proximal defenses protect against the immediate, conscious awareness of death, and distal defenses serve to keep unwanted thoughts of death far away at the level of the unconscious.

Proximal Defenses in Response to the Elderly
First we consider proximal defenses. Perhaps the most direct way to assuage this threatening aspect of the elderly is through physical distancing—that is, by avoiding them. If they are not around, they cannot arouse
death-related thoughts. The elderly can be avoided by staying away from
places where they are likely to be found—for example, senior citizen centers, bingo parlors, nursing homes, golf courses, Florida, and Rolling
Stones concerts. Another way to avoid the elderly is to keep them out of
the workplace. Age discrimination is one of the most clearly documented
and economically and socially harmful consequences of ageism (e.g., Esposito 1987). Although there may be a number of factors contributing to
age discrimination in hiring, including negative stereotypes about the
competence of old people, one such factor is likely to be simply not wanting old people around to remind other employees of their own fate. At a
more personal level, people may seek to place elderly relatives in retirement homes or nursing communities, in part to reduce the extent to
which the elderly will become a salient aspect of their lives, and thus a
salient reminder of their own potential to grow old and closer to death.
Indeed, elderly relatives may be an especially strong reminder of old age
and death to the extent that we perceive ourselves as sharing many
personality and genetic characteristics with them. This similarity may

contribute to the perception that we ourselves are vulnerable to the same fate (e.g., Schimel et al. 2000).

In addition to physical distancing, people may also use psychological distancing to minimize the threat of the elderly. This strategy could take two forms. The first is to view the elderly as very different from oneself. One way to do this is to view elderly individuals not as individuals but as "old people" or, even worse, refer to them with derogatory terms like *old fart, geezer, old-timer, blue-hair, codger, old hag, fossil,* or *dinosaur.* Indeed, Kite and Johnson (1988) found that in studies where the elderly were evaluated in a general way without individuating information, they were viewed in a particularly negative light.

The second way people psychologically distance themselves from the elderly is to view an elderly person, or all old people, as very different from them, with different attitudes, interests, and personality traits. Research has shown that people are prone to exaggerate the differences between themselves and others who have characteristics or conditions that they fear having themselves. One example is people with cancer. Pyszczynski et al. (1995) found that student participants rated their own personality as very different from another student if that student was reported to have cancer. Similarly, Schimel et al. (2000) found that people see their personalities as very different from someone who engages in actions that they fear they themselves may be capable of committing. In the same way, people may tend to exaggerate their differences from elderly individuals to deny their own susceptibility to the aging process and increasing proximity to death. In fact, we have found support for this phenomenon in a recent study in which, after a mortality salience manipulation, we asked college students to indicate their own attitudes on a variety of topics along with their beliefs regarding the attitudes of teenagers and elderly people. Those participants who were reminded of their own mortality viewed the attitudes of elderly people as especially different from their own. As noted by Simone de Beauvoir (1972) among others, one disconcerting result of this may be the treatment of the elderly not "as real people" but as "different, as *another being*" (pp. 2–3).

According to terror management theory, these distancing strategies should be most pronounced in those most actively troubled by their own mortality. Terror management research has shown that people with a shaky faith in their worldview such as the mildly depressed, the neurotic, and people lacking high self-esteem show the strongest defensive reactions following mortality salience (Goldenberg et al. 1999; Harmon-Jones et al. 1997; Simon et al. 1996). Thus, people whose faith in the worldview is most tenuous and people with low or unstable, fragile self-esteem should be most likely to distance from and derogate the elderly. Consistent with this hypothesis, Schweibert (1978) found a positive relationship between an individual's level of death anxiety (as measured by Templer's Death Anxiety Scale) and ageist attitudes (as measured by Kogan's Attitudes Toward Old People Scale). A similar relationship between a tenuous worldview and increased death anxiety can be seen in the Kafir children of South Africa (Langer 1982). These children possess a form of gerontophobia (fear of growing old) whereby they ward off old age by physically plucking hairs from their chin and praying to ancestral spirits to keep them from growing old. Interestingly, this tendency appears only in those children who have not yet absorbed the religious doctrines instilled by ritual. Thus, until the Kafir children have been securely embedded in the meaningful value system of their culture through ritual, they feel vulnerable to the curse of old age and engage in their own compulsive rituals to alleviate their fears.

Distal Terror Management Defenses in Response to the Elderly

By reminding people of their own death, old people may also activate in others distal terror management mechanisms. Such distal defenses include increased self-esteem striving, increased negative reactions to those who challenge one's worldview, and increased positive reactions to those who support one's worldview. Thus, after exposure to the elderly, people may try to enhance their self-esteem by derogating the elderly and engaging in downward social comparison with them. To the extent that an individual perceives the elderly as holding different attitudes and values from themselves, following exposure to old people, derogation of the elderly may also serve to bolster the individual's faith in his or her worldview.

Similarly, elderly people, particularly given the negative stereotypes of them, may threaten the durability of the ways in which people feel good about themselves. Old people may serve as a reminder that many of people's bases of self-esteem will not endure. For example, the young person whose self-esteem is based largely on good looks, athleticism, driving ability, sexual prowess, or verbal alacrity may consider, when exposed to an elderly person, the transitory nature of these qualities. This of course would threaten such an individual's basis of terror management. Such a threat may be especially strong when individuals see photos of elderly people taken when they were young, exuding health and youthful good looks.

As death may be more salient in general for the elderly, we would also expect that distal terror management defense mechanisms be activated within the elderly themselves. In particular, if the dominant worldview is one pervasive with negative stereotypes about aging and the elderly, then the older generation's increased exposure to death-related thoughts may make them even more susceptible to buying into those negative stereotypes, thus compounding the harmfulness of ageism. Levy (1996) demonstrated that activating negative stereotypes about the elderly tended to decrease memory performance and views of the aging in elderly persons. Additionally, Levy (unpublished manuscript) recently demonstrated the destructive effects of ageism where negative stereotypes primed in elderly participants lead to worsened memory task performance and also a decrease in the will to live. This last assessment was measured by asking participants whether they hypothetically, would choose to prolong their life with a certain treatment, even if it meant great financial costs and a heavy time commitment from family members. As Levy has noted, this dependent measure may have also served as a mortality salience manipulation, further compounding the effects of negative ageism.

Characteristics of the Elderly That May Moderate Defensive Responses to Terror

More complex reactions to the elderly can also be predicted from terror management theory. Although the elderly may generally remind people of death, old people who are particularly healthy or convey that they have lived a full life with meaning and value continuing beyond death may not do so, and even under conditions of mortality salience, could be viewed quite positively. Healthy old people offer the hope that through exercise and diet, one's life expectancy can be greatly extended and enjoyed well into the elder years. Additionally, elderly individuals who appear healthy and fit may reduce people's tendency to use proximal defenses against death to the extent that health and fitness also reduces the salience of death and decay.

Similarly, the elderly person coping well psychologically gives hope that the younger individual too can face proximity to death with equanimity. For example, an elderly person who feels good about his or her life, enduring accomplishments, children, and grandchildren may reinforce paths toward death transcendence rather than threaten them. As Menaker (1982) summarized Rank's view, what we are all looking for is identification with the continuity of life, and so people who are approaching death while conveying such identification may reinforce our faith in our own ability to do so.

Conversely, the elderly person lacking health or meaning may be particularly threatening. Such people may remind the rest of us of the possibility of nameless animal death and absolute annihilation. If some die in this way, we may too, and perhaps it is no different for anyone. In a related manner, the physical problems associated with aging (such as incontinence, loss of teeth, and diminishing senses) may serve as vivid reminders of our animal and therefore mortal nature, something we spend much of our lives trying to deny. Perhaps this is why "old" is often viewed as "ugly" or "disgusting." As Kite and Johnson (1988) reported in a meta-analysis, one of the clearest and most consistent findings across studies is that the elderly are rated as less physically attractive than nonelderly people.

Additionally, people are often repulsed by the thought of the elderly engaging in sex. Perhaps because the elderly remind us of our animality, the thought of their having sex, an activity also likely to remind us of our animality, provides a potent threat. Goldenberg and others (1999), for instance, have shown that the thought of sex when people have been reminded of their animality is particularly threatening. As Goldenberg, Pyszczynski et al. (in press) have also proposed and shown, one way to minimize such a threat is to react to it with disgust and contempt, effectively asserting one's distance from such activities and facilitating denial of one's animality. Consequently, this reaction may manifest itself in the disparaging and ageist labeling of older people who are interested in sex as "dirty old men and women" (Palmore 1999, p. 4). This negative image of elderly desires is echoed by de Beauvoir (1972), who writes that "if old people show the same desires, the same feelings and the same requirements as the young, the world looks upon them with disgust: in them love and jealousy seem revolting or absurd, sexuality repulsive and violence ludicrous. They are required to be a standing example of all the virtues. Above all they are called upon to display serenity: the world asserts that they possess it, and this assertion allows the world to ignore their unhappiness" (pp. 3–4)—and, we would add, allows us to ignore our own impending decay, unhappiness, and mortality.

Implications of Terror Management Theory for Reducing Ageism

This chapter seems to paint a bleak picture of the situation in which the elderly reside. As reminders of death, they are likely to arouse a host of proximal and distal terror management defenses, largely directed at derogating, avoiding, and psychologically distancing from the elderly. These defenses and resulting negative attitudes and behaviors can then obviously have a profound effect on the older population and their quality of life. Although we hope that this analysis is useful in helping to account for the pervasive nature of ageism and many of its particular manifestations, we are also hopeful that the analysis suggests at least some broad approaches to combating ageism.

Cultural Valuing of the Elderly

Based on the terror management literature, three avenues for ameliorating negative reactions to the aged may be fruitful. The first is to foster social norms and values supportive of respect for and cherishing the elderly (Palmore 1999). Of course, this is no great insight and no easy thing to accomplish. However, if individuals internalized worldviews in which personal value was based in part on treating the elderly well, then reminders of death would encourage intensified positive treatment of the elderly rather than negative treatment of them. Indeed, some collectivist cultures possess such norms of valuing and respecting the elderly. For example, in China there is a value known as filial piety, whereby younger children and adults are expected to respect the elderly for their wisdom and include them in important family decisions (Hwang 1999; chapter 10, this volume; Sung 1998; Yue and Ng 1999). The young are also expected to give financial blessings back to their parents as they prosper in their careers (chapter 10, this volume; Yue and Ng 1999). To the extent that people in collectivist cultures believe that the elderly should be valued, respected, and cared for, we would hypothesize that reminders of mortality would promote positive reactions to the elderly in these cultures.

The way collectivist cultures include the elderly in the social network might also reduce the extent to which contact with the elderly increases death anxiety. In collectivist cultures, the elderly are included in social activities and given important roles within the family network, such as counselors and advice givers. Thus, the process of growing old is not associated with becoming obsolete but as gradually taking on new and important roles. To the extent that elderly persons are viewed as an ongoing part of the social network, they are not as potent a reminder that death is around the corner. In these cultures, the elderly may even instill a sense of longing in adults approaching old age for the day when they will fill these roles and receive filial piety from other family members.

Conversely, in Western culture, there is a subtle form of segregation of the elderly from mainstream society. Once the elderly reach retirement age, it is common for them to enter retirement homes or move to regions of the country where they can live out the remaining portion of their lives in comfort. Although this segregation is often in the service of allowing the elderly to enjoy their remaining years, the separation of the elderly in this way may also be a form of proximal defense against thoughts about old age and death. Separating the elderly and preventing them from being a functioning part of society may propagate the belief that the elderly have entered a stage of life where they are now useless and obsolete (Esposito 1987). To the extent that the elderly are viewed as obsolete, they may also be seen as being closer to death. Thus, there may exist a cycle of psychological defense and increased fear of the elderly in Western cultures: the more the elderly remind us of our own mortality, the more they are separated from society, and the more they are separated from society, the more they become potent reminders of death. From this perspective, enhancing social norms about caring for the elderly and providing important social roles for them within the social network could reduce many forms of ageism that result from our fear of aging and death.

This shift in social norms would also serve to reduce costs of ageism on the nonelderly that may not be immediately apparent, such as the loss of emotional support from the older generation, the loss of their wisdom and guidance gained from life experience, and the guilt suffered as a result of ignoring the elderly and responsibility to them. It has even been suggested that problems such as "lack of adequate child care, juvenile delinquency, and high crime rates" are in part due "to the neglect of...elder resources" and the failure to include and incorporate them fully into the lives of the nonelderly (Palmore 1999, p. 7).

Bolstering Terror Management
A second direction is to buttress people's worldviews and senses of value. If people are effectively managing their own terror, they should be far less threatened by exposure to the elderly and should be better able to acknowledge their similarities to and obligations toward the elderly. This requires social changes toward more compelling worldviews that offer more secure and accessible bases of self-worth.

Death Awareness
The third direction is to have people become more aware of their own fears of death and aging. If people could face up to their own fears, acknowledge them, and perhaps reinforce productive ways to incorporate their mortality into their worldviews and strivings for self-worth, they should be far less threatened in general, and in particular should be less threatened by and more empathetic to the elderly.

Implications for Education

All three of these directions for improvement are difficult to achieve, particularly when we think of them at a society-wide or global level of change. However, we could use the school system to attempt to shift worldviews to be more favorable to the elderly and could similarly encourage students to face up to their own fears of aging and mortality and develop ways to cope with them. Family life and health education classes that potentially could deal with such issues often avoid the topic of old age and death altogether, because it is deemed by some as inappropriate and even harmful (Weeks and Johnson 1992). Consequently, much as with parenting, we could do much more within the educational system to prepare people for their lives and for nondefensively relating to other people and their own futures as well.

Some schools, however, have developed elective courses designed to teach about the dying process and death. When taught with sensitivity and compassion, these courses seem to be extremely meaningful for the students who take them. Weeks and Johnson (1992), documenting one class, mentioned that although the course is often initially met with reluctance, there have been "no negative reactions" received by the school since the course's inception in 1973. Instead, there has been only positive feedback as students have had "an opportunity to clarify their values and come to terms with their feelings regarding death and quality-of-life issues. They learn specific facts about legal matters pertaining to dying and burial, begin to understand the complex psychological dynamics of grief, and learn to deal with many different types of losses more effectively" (p. 271).

In addition, students in community service programs (and sometimes paying jobs) aid elderly men and women with chores and shopping and in the process form relationships with the aged "clients." Not only have these programs proved immensely beneficial to the elderly in need of basic services and human contact, but they are rewarding for the youthful participants as well. Indeed, they often come to treasure the relationships developed, as do the elderly. Furthermore, these programs appear to demystify old age for many young men and women, revealing the elderly as human and as individuals (Shanks 1976).

Conclusion

Providing these types of experiences is a step in the right direction in terms of aiding the younger generation in confronting and coping with fears about the elderly and their own aging processes, altering our social norms, and viewing the elderly as individuals instead of in a general or generic and hurtful way. But what the terror management analysis suggests is that whatever we do to try to promote more accurate and positive attitudes and behaviors toward the elderly, we have to do so in a way that is cognizant of the role of the fear of death in attitudes and treatment of the elderly. With a more sober and realistic understanding of our own fears and reactions to the elderly, we may be better able to understand ageism as something we are all prone to but nevertheless can combat.

Movement in a positive direction can occur with attempts to buttress both young and old people's sense of value in this potentially lonely and horrifying universe, and with the realization that the young can learn a great deal from the old about coping with aging and life's limitations and also about how courage, meaning, and passion might be preserved and remain "strong enough to prevent us turning in upon ourselves" (de Beauvoir 1972). With the recognition of the fact that one day the young will be old and will want to be treated with dignity, de Beauvoir writes, "Let us recognize ourselves in this old man or in that old woman. It must be done if we are to take upon ourselves the entirety of our human state. And when it is done we will no longer acquiesce in the misery of the last age; we will no longer be indifferent, because we shall feel concerned, as indeed we are" (p. 5).

We are concerned about our future and our fate, and so it would be a mistake not to try to understand better the elderly for whom death is most likely closest (as is often painfully apparent) and to understand better ourselves and our own fearful yet natural responses to aging and death. Imagine the benefits if we could all value, cherish, and emulate the wisdom and strength of the elderly in dealing with something that, to our detriment as well as theirs, we try so hard to deny.

References

This work was supported in part by National Science Foundation Grants SBR-9212798, SBR-9312546, and SBR-9601474.

Allport, G. (1954). *The nature of prejudice.* Reading, MA: Addison-Wesley.

Anderson, I. (1971). Aqualung. On *Aqualung.* Compact Disk: Hollywood: Chrysalis Records, 1996.

Becker, E. (1962). *The birth and death of meaning.* New York: Free Press.

Becker, E. (1973). *The denial of death.* New York: Free Press.

Becker, E. (1975). *Escape from evil*. New York: Free Press.

Ben-Ari, O. T., Florian, V., and Mikulincer, M. (1999). The impact of mortality salience on reckless driving: A test of terror management mechanisms. *Journal of Personality and Social Psychology, 71*, 35-45.

Bytheway, B. (1995). *Ageism*. Bristol, PA: Open University Press.

de Beauvoir, S. (1972). *The coming of age*. New York: Putnam.

Deschesne, M., Greenberg, J., Arndt, J., and Schimel, J. (2000). Terror management and sports fan affiliation: The effects of mortality salience on fan identification and optimism. *European Journal of Social Psychology, 30*, 813-835.

Esposito, J. L. (1987). *The obsolete self: Philosophical dimensions of aging*. Los Angeles: University of California Press.

Goldenberg, J., McCoy, S., Pyszczynski, T., Greenberg, J., and Solomon, S. (2000). The body as a source of self-esteem: The effects of mortality salience on identification with one's body, interest in sex, and appearance monitoring. *Journal of Personality and Social Psychology, 79*, 118-130.

Goldenberg, J., Pyszczynski, T., Greenberg, J., and Solomon, S. (2000). Fleeing the body: A terror management perspective on the problem of human corporeality. *Personality and Social Psychology Review, 4*, 200-218.

Goldenberg, J., Pyszczynski, T., McCoy, S. K., Greenberg, J., and Solomon, S. (1999). Death, sex, love, and neuroticism: Why is sex such a problem? *Journal of Personality and Social Psychology, 77*, 1173-1187.

Gould, S. J. (1997, October 9). Evolutionary psychology: An exchange. *New York Review of Books, 44*, 55-57.

Greenberg, J., Portteus, J., Simon, L., Pyszczynski, T., and Solomon, S. (1995). Evidence of a terror management function of cultural icons: The effects of mortality salience on the inappropriate use of cherished cultural symbols. *Personality and Social Psychology Bulletin, 21*, 1221-1228.

Greenberg, J., Pyszczynski, T., and Solomon, S. (1986). The causes and consequences of the need for self-esteem: A terror management theory. In R. F. Baumeister (Ed.), *Public and private self* (pp. 189-212). New York: Springer-Verlag.

Greenberg, J., Pyszczynski, T., Solomon, S., Rosenblatt, A., Veeder, M., Kirkland, S., and Lyon, D. (1990). Evidence for terror management theory II: The effects of mortality salience reactions to those who threaten or bolster the cultural worldview. *Journal of Personality and Social Psychology, 58*, 308-318.

Greenberg, J., Solomon, S., and Pyszczynski, T. (1997). Terror management theory of self-esteem and cultural worldviews: Empirical assessments and conceptual refinements. In M. Zanna (Ed.), *Advances in experimental social psychology* (Vol. 29, pp. 61-139). San Diego, CA: Academic Press.

Greenberg, J., Solomon, S., Pyszczynski, T., Rosenblatt, A., Burling, J., Lyon, D., Pinel, E., and Simon, L. (1992). Why do people need self-esteem? Convergent evidence of an anxiety-buffering function. *Journal of Personality and Social Psychology*, *63*, 913-922.

Harmon-Jones, E., Simon, L., Greenberg, J., Pyszczynski, T., Solomon, S., and McGregor, H. (1997). Terror management theory and self-esteem: Evidence that increased self-esteem reduced mortality salience effects. *Journal of Personality and Social Psychology*, *72*, 24-36.

Hwang, K. (1999). Filial piety and loyalty. Two types of social identification in Confucianism. *Asian Journal of Social Psychology*, *2*, 163-183.

Keats, J. (1821/1991). *Lyric poems*. New York: Dover.

Kite, M. E., and Johnson, B. T. (1988). Attitudes toward older and younger adults: A meta-analysis. *Psychology and Aging*, *3*, 233-244.

Langer, S. K. (1982). *Mind: An essay on human feeling*. Baltimore: Johns Hopkins University Press.

Levy, R. (1996). Improving memory in old age through implicit self-stereotyping. *Journal of Personality and Social Psychology*, *71*, 1092-1107.

Levy, R., Ashman, O., and Dror, I. (2000). To be or not to be: The effects of aging stereotypes on the will to live. *Journal of Death and Dying*, *40*, 409-420.

Menaker, E. (1982). *Otto Rank: A rediscovered legacy*. New York: Columbia University Press.

Palmore, E. (1999). *Ageism: Negative and positive*. New York: Springer.

Pyszczynski, T., Greenberg, J., and Solomon, S. (1999). A dual process model of defense against conscious and unconscious death-related thoughts: An extension of terror management theory. *Psychological Review*, *106*, 835-845.

Pyszczynski, T., Greenberg, J., Solomon, S., Cather, C., Gat, I., and Sideris, J. (1995). Defensive distancing from victims of serious illness: The role of delay. *Personality and Social Psychology Bulletin*, *21*, 13-20.

Pyszczynski, T., Wicklund, R. A., Floresku, S., Gauch, G., Koch, H., Solomon, S., and Greenberg, J. (1996). Whistling in the dark: Exaggerated estimates of social consensus in response to incidental reminders of mortality. *Psychological Science*, *7*, 332-336.

Rosenblatt, A., Greenberg, J., Solomon, S., Pyszczynski, T., and Lyon, D. (1989). Evidence for terror management theory I: The effects of mortality salience on reactions to those who violate or uphold cultural values. *Journal of Personality and Social Psychology*, *57*, 681-690.

Schimel, J., Pyszczynski, T., Greenberg, J., O'Mahan, H., and Arndt, J. (2000). Running from the shadow: Psychological distancing from others to deny characteristics people fear in themselves. *Journal of Personality and Social Psychology, 78,* 446-462.

Schwiebert, D. C. (1978). Unfavorable stereotyping of the aged as a function of death anxiety, sex, perception of elderly relatives, and a death anxiety-repression interaction. *Dissertation Abstracts International, 39* (6-B), 3007.

Shanks, A. Z. (1976). *Old is what you get: Dialogues on aging by the old and young.* New York: Viking Press.

Simon, L., Greenberg, J., Arndt, J., Pyszczynski, T., Clement, R., and Solomon, J. (1997). Perceived consensus, uniqueness, and terror management: Compensatory responses to threats to inclusion and distinctiveness. *Personality and Social Psychology Bulletin, 23,* 1055-1065.

Simon, L., Greenberg, J., Harmon-Jones, E., Solomon, S., and Pyszczynski, T. (1996). Mild depression, mortality salience, and defense of the worldview: Evidence of intensified terror management in the mildly depressed. *Personality and Social Psychology Bulletin, 22,* 81-90.

Sung, K., (1998). Filial piety in modern times: Timely adaptation and practice patterns. *Australasian Journal of Ageing, 17,* 88-92.

Weeks, D., and Johnson, C. (1992). A second decade of high school death education. *Death Studies, 16,* 269-279.

Yue, X., and Ng, S. H. (1999). Filial obligations and expectations in China: Current views from young and old people in Beijing. *Asian Journal of Social Psychology, 2,* 215-226.

Zillboorg, G. (1943). Fear of death. *Psychoanalytic Quarterly, 12,* 465-475.

3

Implicit Ageism
Becca R. Levy and Mahzarin R. Banaji

In a chapter entitled "Age and Human Society" in the 1935 *Handbook of Social Psychology*, Walter Miles chronicled everything a social scientist would want to know about the topic. Yet this all-encompassing treatise, beginning with the insight that "Men are not all equal partly for the reason that they cannot all be born at the same time" (p. 596), had nothing to say about the inequality that old age elicits through the two central psychological processes of attitude and belief: negative feelings and thoughts toward those who are so marked. Even at the time of Miles's writing, equivalent treatments of other social groups, such as women, African Americans, and Jews, included a discussion of the content of the prejudices and stereotypes of the day, the processes by which they operate, and their consequences (Dollard 1937; Lasker 1930; Plewa 1936). Fifty years later, Roger Brown's textbook *Social Psychology* included an extended discussion of stereotypes and prejudice as they related to race, gender, nationality, and sexual orientation. Again, age prejudice was absent from the presentation. It appears that the recognition, even among social scientists, that age can serve as a potent attribute from which psychological and social benefit or harm can radiate has been slow in coming. However, as this book and others over the past decade attest, the notion that age is a social category worthy of attention for the study of stereotypes and prejudice is recently but firmly in place now (for reviews see Hummert 1999; Palmore 1998).

Beliefs about the elderly as unable to contribute to society, and hence as dispensable members of a community, and attitudes toward them of dislike and distancing are prevalent (Kite and Johnson 1988). Social scientists have focused on the effects of negative beliefs and attitudes to examine discrimination toward the aged in a variety of spheres, including everyday conversations (Hummert and Ryan 1996; Williams and Giles 1998), politics (Sigelman and Sigelman 1982) and the workplace (Butler

1980; Finkelstein, Burke, and Raju 1995). To take just one example of discriminatory treatment, many older Americans do not receive necessary care for common and treatable medical conditions, including heart disease (Asch et al. 2000; Bowling 1999; Guigliano et al. 1998; Hillerbrand and Shaw 1990). Although poverty, insofar as its effects are magnified in old age, is obviously involved, the reason for discrimination does not appear to be solely financial, because the vast majority of treatments are covered by Medicare (Asch et al. 2000). Instead, some believe that "ageism in clinical medicine and health policy reflects the ageism evident in wider society" (Bowling 1999, p. 1353). As health maintenance organizations and medical centers place pressure on physicians to spend increasingly less time with each patient, discrimination against the elderly is likely to increase. In time-pressured situations in which attention is called to a number of tasks at once, individuals may be more likely to engage in stereotyping (Gilbert and Hixon 1991; Blair and Banaji 1996; Jamieson and Zanna 1989; Pratto and Bargh 1991).

In this chapter, we make two claims regarding ageism, which we define as an alteration in feeling, belief, or behavior in response to an individual's or group's perceived chronological age. First, one of the most insidious aspects of ageism is that it can operate without conscious awareness, control, or intention to harm. Although the idea of the implicit nature of stereotyping and prejudice is not new to social science research (Katz and Braly 1935; Crosby, Bromley, and Saxe 1980; Devine 1989), the idea of implicit ageism is unique in at least one way. There are no hate groups that target the elderly as there are hate groups that target members of religious and racial and ethnic groups. Even gender prejudice has produced the recognition that there are those who have explicit antipathy toward one or the other group (e.g., misogynists, male chauvinists, man haters). In contrast, social sanctions against expressions of negative attitudes and beliefs about the elderly are almost completely absent. In fact, the widespread occurrence of socially acceptable expressions of negativity toward the elderly has been well documented (Williams and Giles 1998). This state of affairs stands in contrast to other social groups, where, at least in public discourse, there has been a notable change in recognition of social disadvantage and the need for action to ameliorate its consequences.

In this context of a lack of strong, explicit hatred toward the elderly, on the one hand, and a wide acceptance of negative feelings and beliefs about them, on the other, the role of implicit attitudes and knowledge about age becomes especially important. Such an analysis can reveal the extent to which the roots of prejudice can be found at levels that are unnoticed or uncontrollable.

In the early decades of research on ageism (the 1970s and 1980s), when self-report measures were almost exclusively used to measure prejudice and stereotypes, it was assumed that such prejudice was to be found in some but not in others (Kogan 2000). The second claim of this chapter is that all humans, to varying degrees, are implicated in the practice of implicit ageism. The mental processes and behaviors that show sensitivity to age as an attribute are automatically produced in the everyday thoughts and feelings, judgments and decisions, of ordinary folk, such as the writers of this chapter. Yet there are also large individual differences in such attitudes, and the emerging research findings on implicit age stereotypes and prejudice usher in new implications for policies intended to guard and protect equal treatment that otherwise erodes with age.

We define implicit age stereotypes (also called automatic or unconscious stereotypes) as thoughts about the attributes and behaviors of the elderly that exist and operate without conscious awareness, intention, or control. We define implicit age attitudes (also called automatic or unconscious prejudice) as feelings toward the elderly that exist and operate without conscious awareness, intention, or control. In this chapter we use the term *implicit ageism* to cover both implicit age stereotypes and prejudice. We realize that ageism can also apply to stereotypes and prejudice directed at the young, but our focus here remains on the negative attitudes and beliefs that have come to be associated with old age.

In contrast to implicit age stereotypes and prejudice, the conscious or controllable thoughts and feelings of explicit stereotypes and prejudice might be elicited by such questions as, "Do you prefer those who are young to those who are old?" The challenge for those interested in implicit social cognition has been to find ways to measure unconscious thoughts and feelings, for they cannot be easily assessed through verbal self-report. Alongside the many studies of implicit biases involving race and gender, a small but sufficient number of studies of implicit ageism is now available, making it possible to evaluate the trends and implications of the emerging findings. As we do so, we are aware of the disparity in the attention given in research settings to age as a social category compared with other groups. The far-less research attention accorded to age is yet another indicator of the ease with which this form of discrimination appears to be acceptable compared with others. Ageism, unlike racism, does not provoke shame. It may be a matter of some interest to track changes in the recognition of ageism as a form of discrimination worthy of study even in the community of social scientists working on the topic of prejudice.

In this chapter, we review the two methodologies that have been most extensively used to study implicit ageism: the Implicit Association Test

(IAT; Greenwald, McGhee, and Schwarz 1998) and priming. The age IAT studies have tended to explore individual and group differences in unconscious attitudes, stereotypes, and identity as they relate to age. The stereotype priming studies, on the other hand, have tended to examine the impact of implicit age stereotypes and attitudes on cognitive, behavioral, and affective outcomes. In this chapter, we review both the IAT and stereotype priming measures and their assumptions, then outline the major findings related to implicit ageism. We discuss research findings based on both young participants, who do not yet share group membership in the category, and older participants, for whom old age has relevance to self and identity. Finally, we speculate about how implicit ageism may develop and the cause of one of the more striking implicit ageism findings: implicit out-group favoritism expressed by older individuals. Throughout the chapter, we seek to show the commonalities between implicit ageism and biases involving other social categories as well as its seemingly unique properties.

Implicit Ageism: Background

Implicit social cognition is an umbrella term used to capture the idea that thoughts and feelings may operate outside the purview of conscious awareness, control, and intention; in contrast, explicit social cognition involves thought and deliberation (Greenwald and Banaji 1995). Numerous studies have demonstrated a disassociation between specific types of implicit and explicit processes of social cognition, such as stereotypes, attitudes, and identity. Race has been prominently studied, with research showing strong and clear negativity toward African Americans compared with European Americans on implicit or automatic measures of social cognition, even when it fails to be observed on more explicit measures (Dasgupta et al. Banaji, 2000; Devine 1989; Dovidio et al., Greenwald et al. 1998; Fazio et al. 1995; Nosek, Banaji, and Greenwald in press). Similar findings have been obtained regarding the automatic use of gender stereotypes (Banaji and Hardin 1996; Blair and Banaji 1996) and implicit age stereotypes (Levy 1996, Nosek, et al., in press).

During the past decade, methods have been developed to facilitate experimental demonstrations and explorations of unconscious processes whose existence was first identified more than a hundred years ago by Sigmund Freud and William James. Several recently developed techniques have specifically focused on assessing implicit attitudes and stereotypes. Their development has drawn on the availability of computers that can capture the speed of mental processes, as well as the numerous studies on attitudes and stereotypes published over the past century. In addition, the research conducted on other mental processes (e.g., memory), where transitions from purely conscious to both conscious and unconscious measures were achieved earlier, have served as models for developing methods to examine implicit attitudes and stereotypes. To take the construct of implicit attitude as an example, one can work through definitions to show a clear developmental path (see Banaji, 2001). If attitude is "a psychological tendency that is expressed by evaluating a particular entity with some degree of favor or disfavor" (Eagly and Chaiken 1998) and if implicit memory is "revealed when previous experiences facilitate performance on a task that does not require conscious or intentional recollection of these experiences" (Schacter 1987), then implicit attitudes can be "introspectively unidentified (or inaccurately identified) traces of past experience that mediate favorable or unfavorable feeling, thought, or action toward social objects" (Greenwald and Banaji 1995).

Implicit Association Test

A popular measure of implicit social cognition, the IAT (Greenwald, McGhee, and Schwartz 1998; see Banaji 2001 for a review of criticisms), has been largely used to measure automatic attitudes, stereotypes, and identity in a variety of domains including age (see Greenwald and Nosek in press). The IAT relies on a response latency indicator obtained in the process of pairing the attitude object (say, a social group such as *old-young*) with an evaluative dimension (*good-bad*) or knowledge attributes (such as *self-other, home-career, science-arts*). In the computerized version, the pairing is achieved by using the keyboard (say, a left key) to be pressed in response to items from the two paired categories, *old+bad*, while another key (say, a right key) is used for the other pair, *young+good*. The speed at which this pairing is completed compared to the opposite one is interpreted as a measure of the strength of an implicit evaluation (attitude). Similarly, the strength of association between concept and attribute (that is, *old-young* with *home-career*) is interpreted as a measure of the strength of implicit knowledge (stereotype). The IAT effect is based on a difference score reflecting both the valence of implicit attitude (positive versus negative) and the magnitude of the attitude (larger numbers reflecting larger differences between pairings in milliseconds). (To sample the IAT, visit www.yale.edu/implicit.)

The use of the IAT involves several assumptions that are best listed explicitly: (1) the strength of evaluative (e.g., favorable-unfavorable) and other attributes (e.g., strong-weak) elicited by a social object can be measured; (2) associations between object and attribute are revealed in the ease with which they are mentally paired; (3) one measure of the strength of such associations is the mental speed involved in making object+attribute pairs; and (4) the mental strength of object+attribute pairs is a rough index of automatic knowledge, attitude, or identity. For instance, the strength of the *elderly+good* pairing is taken as an indicator of automatic attitude, the strength of *elderly+frail* pairing is taken as a measure of that automatic stereotype, and the strength of the *elderly+me* pairing is taken as a measure of that automatic identity between self and elderly.

Of the basic findings regarding implicit ageism we have to date, the following summary may be offered. Nosek, Banaji, and Greenwald (in press) measured the speed of *old+good/young+bad* pairings and compared them to the opposite pairings of *old+bad/young+good* at a demonstration web site (for a description of e-research, see Nosek, Banaji and Greenwald, in press). Based on 68,144 tests that included those along a wide spectrum of ages, we present three findings of general interest. Among the first and most striking aspects of the results plotted in figure 3.1 is the magnitude of the effect. It remains, in our experience with the effects obtained using this task, among the largest negative implicit attitudes we have observed

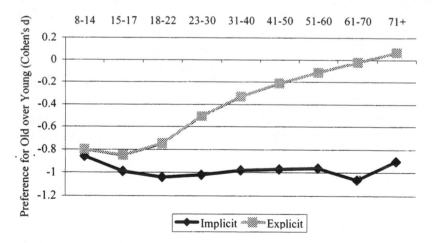

Figure 3.1
Implicit and explicit age attitudes by age group. This figure is adapted from one appearing in Nosek, B. A., Banaji, M. R., and Greenwald, A. G. (in press). Harvesting intergroup attitudes and stereotype data from the Implicit Association Test website. *Group Dynamics*. (c) 2001 by the American Psychological Association. Adapted with permission.

(effect sizes invariably larger than 1)—consistently larger than the antiblack attitude among white Americans.

Second, as can be seen in figure 3.1, the implicit age attitudes stand in contrast to explicit attitudes, with the explicit attitude showing less negativity toward the elderly than the implicit association measure reveals. The explicit age attitudes for all age groups, except those over the age of 70, are negative. The implicit age attitudes are far more negative overall. Although this dissociation between implicit and explicit attitudes is consistent with that observed in other domains, it is not as large as has been found with race, for example, where the positivity of explicit attitudes outperforms the implicit effects by a wider margin. For now, we simply note the dissociation in mean values between implicit and explicit attitudes, which has come to be a signature finding of experiments that compare conscious versus unconscious social group cognition.

Third, we point to a peculiar feature of implicit age effects that distinguishes it from other group attitudes: implicit age bias does not appear to vary as a function of the respondent's age. As can be observed in figure 3.1, older participants, like younger participants, tend to have negative implicit attitudes toward the elderly and positive implicit attitudes toward the young (Greenwald et al. 2000; Nosek, Banaji, and Greenwald in press). This lack of an effect of group membership stands in contrast to the explicit attitude that becomes more positive toward the elderly as the age of the respondent increases. The lack of an effect of group membership also stands in contrast to other implicit attitudes—religion (Jews, Christians), race (black, white Americans), gender (female, male)— where group membership plays a role, and sometimes a strong role, in the implicit attitudes that are revealed. For example, groups often show preference for the in-group over the out-group (e.g., Korean and Japanese participants each showed preference for their own group over the other group, Greenwald, McGhee, and Schwartz 1998). Even when they do not, as when African Americans show on average no preference one way or the other, members of all groups tested to date—other than the aged—invariably show more positive implicit attitudes toward their own group compared to nongroup members.

This finding may be understood in the context of the psychologically permeable nature of the boundary between age groups, which perhaps allows oneself to be dissociated from the group, thereby allowing none of the typical benefit of group membership (i.e., positive implicit attitudes toward the in-group) observed in many other cases. Yet the rise in positivity of explicit attitudes as chronological age rises is in contrast to the unbending nature of the implicit attitude and suggests that conscious attitudes are more sensitive to group membership than are unconscious attitudes. In this regard, the implicit-explicit divergence in attitude bears similarity to that of African Americans, who show exceptionally strong, positive explicit attitudes toward the group—far stronger than seen in samples of white Americans—and in contrast to their own neutral implicit attitude toward their group (African Americans). We speculate on this implicit out-group favoritism finding in the last part of the chapter.

To our knowledge, no similar large-scale analyses of age stereotypes (as opposed to attitude) using the IAT are available. Based on other work, we would not be surprised to find similar effects across the life span, indicating the presence of stereotypes linking weak, frail, and passive with the elderly, and perhaps even that they are relatively constant with age. Such assessments nevertheless need to await further evidence.

Most recently the IAT has been used to measure age identity and age attitudes. (Greenwald, Banaji, Rudman, Farnham, Nosek, and Mellot, in press) Greenwald and his colleagues (in press) found that unlike most other groups, older individuals tend to identify implicitly with the category young as strongly as did young individuals. The researchers compared elderly and young participants on an in-group-identity IAT (association of self with old) and a self-esteem IAT (association of self with good). Before conducting their research, the authors expected that higher self-esteem elders would have a positive attitude toward old age and would have a stronger age identity "presumably reflecting psychological comfort with their identity as old" (Greenwald, et al. in press, p. 41). Instead, they found the opposite: "the higher the self-esteem of elders the more they both implicitly preferred youth to old age and implicitly identified as young rather than old" (Greenwald et al. in press, p. 42). We provide a possible interpretation for this set of findings at the end of the chapter in the section entitled, "Implicit Outgroup Favoritism."

Stereotype Priming

Another recently developed method of measuring implicit age stereotypes is through implicit priming of age stereotypes, or activating a preexisting schema. This method allows researchers to examine the impact that age stereotypes and attitudes may have on thinking, behavior, and decisions without awareness.

In the first research that implicitly primed the construct of age, Perdue and Gurtman (1990) conducted a two-part study to examine whether ageism, which they defined as "differential association of negative traits with the aged" (p. 199), occurred automatically in young adults. In the first part, they randomly presented twenty positive (e.g., "cheerful") and twenty negative (e.g., "rude") traits on a computer screen. After each trait appeared, participants were randomly asked one of several questions that included, "Is this a term that would describe an old person?" and "Is this a term that would describe a young person?" Participants responded by pressing keys labeled "yes" or "no." Then, in an unexpected free-recall task, participants were asked to list all the traits they had read on the computer. Perdue and Gurtman found that significantly more negative than positive traits were recalled when they were paired with the question about an elderly person. In contrast, significantly more positive traits than negative traits were recalled when they were paired with the question about a young person. From these results Perdue and Gurtman concluded that an unintentional age bias probably exists. To test more directly if the bias operates outside conscious control, they conducted a second study.

In the second experiment, thirty college students sat in front of a computer and the word *old* or *young* randomly appeared on the screen for 55 ms, a speed selected to avoid conscious recognition. Following the subliminal age primes, one of eighteen positive or eighteen negative traits randomly appeared on the screen. Afterward, participants were asked to decide if the trait is a good or bad quality for a person to possess. They found that the negative traits were judged more quickly after exposure to the "old" prime as opposed to the "young" prime. In contrast, the positive traits were judged more quickly when they followed the "young" prime as opposed to the "old" prime. From these results, the authors concluded that "cognitively categorizing a person as 'old' may create a subset of predominantly negative constructs which are more accessible and more likely to be employed in evaluating that person—and this will tend to perpetuate ageism from the beginning of the social perception process" (p. 213).

The Impact of Implicit Age Stereotypes on the Elderly

In 1994, Levy and Langer conducted a study in China and the United States that found stereotypes of aging correlated with memory performance among older individuals. Levy (1996) undertook a follow-up study in order to examine whether more positive stereotypes of aging lead to better memory performance (rather than the other way around) and whether activating negative stereotypes of aging might worsen memory performance.

To create the implicit age stereotype intervention, Levy (1996) created two priming tasks: one that subliminally activated positive and one that subliminally activated negative stereotypes of aging. To ensure that the positive and negative age stereotype primes reflected the meaning of stereotypes used in everyday life, Levy surveyed a number of people of different ages and asked them to generate behaviors and traits that reflected senility or wisdom. Then she asked another intergenerational panel to rate these words on how characteristic of old age and how positive or negative they seemed. The words selected for the negative age stereotype intervention included *incompetent, decrepit,* and *diseased.* The words selected for the positive age stereotype intervention included *guidance, sage,* and *accomplished.* These sets of words, with a predominance of positive or negative stereotypes in each, were flashed on a computer screen at a speed designed to prevent conscious recognition. Individuals, who sat in front of the computer, were told to try to identify whether a flash appeared above or below a bull's-eye by pressing one of two arrow keys. (For a complete description of the stereotype intervention, see Levy 1996).

Previous explicit interventions carried out by other researchers that tried to alter individuals' views of aging or their assumptions about memory performance in old age had not been successful (e.g., Lachman et al. 1992). Levy's premise was that to shift individuals' stereotypes of aging from the predominantly negative ones to the less common positive ones in the United States, the most likely approach would be an intervention that draws on the unconscious so that it can bypass the negative stereotypes that are repetitively internalized throughout older individuals' lifetimes.

Before and after participants were randomly assigned to the age stereotype intervention, they took five memory tests and were asked questions about how well they thought they would perform. Levy (1996) found that older participants exposed to the positive age stereotype primes performed significantly better on the memory test than those older participants exposed to the negative age stereotype primes. Although all four visual memory tasks showed this pattern, the auditory memory task did not. This may indicate that self-stereotypes of aging evoke visual imagery and processes rather than verbal descriptions and processes. In addition, those older individuals exposed to the positive age stereotypes reported higher memory self-efficacy than those exposed to the negative age stereotype, suggesting that older individuals' expectations may mediate the performance effect.

A secondary finding of the Levy (1996) study was that older individuals' perceptions can be affected by implicit self-stereotypes. This was illustrated by the interpretations of a story about a 73-year-old woman named Margaret that included details designed to prompt contrasting interpretations (Levy 1996). For example, Margaret spends the night at her daughter's house. Older individuals in the positive age-stereotype condition tended to interpret her as a key member of the family who could provide valuable services, whereas those in the negative age-stereotype condition tended to see her as dependent and drawing on the daughter's resources. This result further suggests that implicit age self-stereotypes can influence older individuals' views of other older individuals as well as of themselves.

An assumption of this study is that self-perceptions and performance are activated by stereotypes. To increase the likelihood that the older individuals' old age identities were activated, the researcher recruited participants through signs that asked for individuals age 60 and older and they were told that the study was assessing "aging memory." In addition, the twenty-four stereotype prime words that were used for the priming intervention were all judged as characteristic of old age by members of an intergenerational panel. Further, in the stereotype priming intervention for both the positive and the negative condition, the word *old* and the word *senior* were presented five times each. As a result, since altogether 100 stereotype words were presented in either the positive or negative intervention, 10 percent of the words were age-category words. Finally, the influence of age stereotypes on memory performance was found in the old, but not in the young, participants.

Although previous priming studies had found that activating stereotypes of a social group could influence participants' perceptions of members of another group (Devine 1989; Banaji, Hardin and Rothman 1993), Levy (1996) examined whether implicitly activating stereotypes of individuals' own social group influenced their performance. It was also the first study to activate both positive and negative stereotypes of the same social group. Research on the content of age stereotypes had suggested that most individuals are aware of both positive (e.g., *wise*) and negative (e.g., *senile*) stereotypes of older individuals (Brewer, Dull, and Lui 1981; Hummert, 1990; Schmidt and Boland 1986). However, stereotype priming research previously had focused on one stereotype per group (Devine 1989). Also, while previous implicit stereotype studies had been limited to college students as participants (Perdue and Gurtman 1990), Levy's respondents included older individuals.

The implicit self-stereotyping effect has been replicated among individuals in diverse groups. For example, Shih, Pittinsky, and Ambady

(1999) took advantage of the cultural stereotypes that Asians have superior quantitative skills compared to other ethnic groups and that women have inferior quantitative skills compared to men. When the researchers implicitly primed Asian American women's gender identity, they performed worse on a mathematics test, and when they implicitly primed the women's Asian identity, the women performed better on the mathematical test than a control group who had neither identity activated. By conducting a cross-cultural analysis, the researchers concluded that it was the participants' stereotypes, and not their identity, that was influencing their performance. Steele and Aronson (1998) demonstrated that merely asking African American students to record their race was sufficient to impair test performance. From such research, we gather firm support for the idea of automatic self-stereotyping. With friends like oneself, who needs enemies?

In addition, the depth and breadth of the impact of implicit self-stereotypes on aging have been demonstrated in a series of studies using subliminal priming procedures. In research following the memory performance finding, Levy, Ashman, and Dror (2000) found that self-stereotype activation influenced older individuals' reported will to live. Again, old and young participants were randomly assigned to either negative or positive stereotypes of old age. As predicted, the priming selectively influenced the responses of the older participants to hypothetical medical situations. Aged participants primed with negative age stereotypes tended to refuse life-prolonging interventions, whereas the old participants primed with positive age stereotypes tended to accept the same interventions. As expected, this priming did not emerge among younger participants, for whom the stereotypes were less personally relevant. The results go further than the ones showing lowered performance on a test to suggest that societally transmitted negative stereotypes of aging can weaken elderly people's will to live.

In order to determine whether self-stereotypes of aging affect behavior that is assumed to operate without the control of conscious processes (Allport and Vernon 1933), Levy (2000) examined whether stereotypes can influence a behavior associated with age change: handwriting. She found that those exposed to negative stereotypes of aging demonstrated shakier handwriting than those exposed to positive stereotypes, as determined by judges blind to the participants' stereotype condition. This study suggests that handwriting may prove to be a useful tool for monitoring the influence of negative stereotypes in future experiments, as well as in clinical settings.

Because implicit self-stereotypes of aging operate without awareness, the process may be particularly harmful. Just as younger individuals who are not aware of the impact of implicit age stereotypes are unlikely to correct for resulting discriminatory behavior, older individuals are unlikely to recognize outcomes they experience as being due to implicit age self-stereotypes. An adverse health outcome, for instance, might be attributed to an inevitable consequence of aging rather than to a response triggered by a negative implicit self-stereotype.

The potential for this misinterpretation is suggested by the results of a study that examined whether aging self-stereotypes can influence cardiovascular function (Levy et al. 2000). After elderly persons were subliminally exposed to either positive or negative aging stereotypes, they faced mathematical and verbal challenges. Those exposed to the negative aging stereotypes demonstrated a heightened cardiovascular response to stress, measured by heart rate, blood pressure, and skin conductance, as compared to those exposed to positive aging stereotypes (see figure 3.2). It appears that the negative aging stereotypes acted as direct stressors, whereas the positive aging stereotypes helped protect participants from

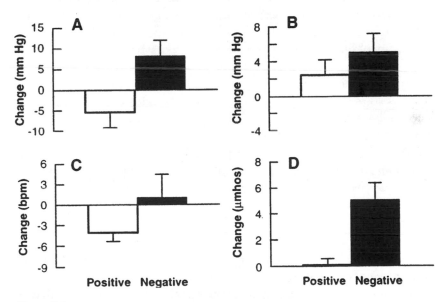

Figure 3.2
The influence of implicit aging self-stereotypes on cardiovascular response to stress. Change from baseline for (A) systolic blood pressure, (B) diastolic blood pressure, (C) heart rate, and (D) skin conductance.

experiencing elevated cardiovascular reactivity or response to stress (associated with the onset and progression of cardiovascular disease; Barnett et al. 1997).

Overall, these studies suggest that ageism may have an impact on older individuals' cognition, behavior, and health without their awareness. Although most studies tend to select a particular dependent variable for ease and tractability, there is no reason to believe that only one system is affected at a time. Instead, it seems likely that these different effects of implicit age stereotypes could be interrelated and perhaps mutually reinforcing.

The process of implicit aging self-stereotypes could be activated by many of the manifestations of stereotypes that permeate society. In turn, the manifestations of age self-stereotypes are perceived by others. There is, then, a reciprocal nature to this automatic exchange between stereotypes and self-stereotypes. For example, elderly individuals often encounter an expectation that they are subject to memory loss. This expectation takes forms that range from enforced early retirement to casual references by middle-aged individuals to their own "senior moments" when they have forgotten something. It is also possible that when young people are around older people, they adjust their behaviors in ways that reflect age stereotypes and thus activate the age stereotypes in older individuals.

In an experiment aimed at determining the effect of stereotype priming on younger individuals' behavior, Bargh and his colleagues used scrambled sentences containing words intended to activate age stereotypes (Bargh, Chen, and Burrows 1996). Although the priming did not occur subliminally, the participants were unaware of the purpose of the experiment (they were told it was to test language proficiency), and they were unaware of what constituted the outcome of the experiment (the rate at which they walked down the hall after the test was seemingly over). The researchers found that participants in the stereotype group walked slower afterward than did the participants who had been in the neutral group.

The assumption that the influence of stereotypes is tied to their relevance, so that the old would be more affected than the young by primed stereotypes of aging, is not necessarily at odds with the finding by Bargh, Chen, and Burrows (1996) that the aging primes induced young subjects to walk more slowly. Using the subliminal stereotype of aging priming technique, the effect of aging self-stereotypes on the gait of older participants was examined. When positive stereotypes of aging were activated in the study, walking speed increased from baseline by 9 percent, and the percentage of swing time—the time spent with a foot off the ground, which reflects balance capabilities—increased significantly (Hausdorff, Levy, and Wei 1999). The improved gait speed is similar to gains that have been seen in older participants after weeks of participation in exercise programs. Participants exposed to the negative stereotypes of aging primes showed no significant changes in walking, perhaps because the association between slow walking and negative stereotypes of aging had already been saturated after a lifetime of exposure.

Since neither study included the complementary age group and the study conducted by Bargh and his colleagues did not include a positive stereotypes age group, a precise comparison of performance in the two studies is not easily possible. Nonetheless, the striking improvement among the positively primed older participants in the Hausdorff, Levy, and Wei study may be a guide to how it can be reconciled with the Bargh, Chen, and Burrows study. Insofar as the elderly self-stereotypes may have been more relevant to the old than they were to the young, the old may have been affected to a greater degree than the young would have been if they were included.

There is another explanation for the results in the study conducted by Bargh and his colleagues. The college students may not have been responding to the primes that were unambiguously related to aging, such as *old, retired,* and *wrinkle.* Instead, other words that were intended as additional aging primes might have been relevant to the participants in a nonaging way. Among these words were several that might have acted as primes to walk slowly, such as *careful, helpless,* and *cautious.* Either way, the effectiveness of priming was demonstrated.

The Development of Implicit Ageism

Although there are no analyses yet of the precise processes by which implicit ageism develops, we can speculate using the related research with children and accounts of the development of automatic biases more generally. Some research suggests that implicit social cognition begins in explicit form and that through chronic activation, what initially requires conscious thought and feeling eventually becomes automatic (Bargh 1997). Children as young as 6 years old can report the age stereotypes of their culture (Isaacs and Bearison 1986). Yet it is possible that age attitudes and stereotypes need not be explicitly stated to be acquired early in life. Comments such as, "Poor Grandma can't walk fast," may be part of what causes negative attitudes to be learned, but simple observation of the disabilities of age, as well as a neglect of the elderly, may be learned without explicit reference on the part of adults.

Unlike negative attitudes and stereotypes of race and gender, negative feelings and thoughts about age are still prevalent in public spheres. Through fairy tales, children are likely to be exposed to older characters who are portrayed as evil and sinister (Hansel and Gretel) or weak and gullible (Little Red Riding Hood; Cohen, 2000). Television may also promote images of aging that contribute to the formation of implicit age stereotypes. The old are often absent or else appear in comical roles that highlight stereotypes of their decline and incompetence (Kubey 1980; Zebrowitz and Montepare 2000). For example, an advertisement for the search engine hotbot.com showed its rival search engine as a group of dangerously incompetent old men promoting such products as asbestos children's pajamas. The advertisement ends with the statement: "Don't waste time with old links."

The elderly seem distant to the young in the sense that acquisition of old age is seen for what it is: a slow and lengthy process. This may in fact encourage the development of implicit age stereotypes in children because old age has little relevance to their emerging selves, and children may have little reason to question these stereotypes since they are not referring to their in-group (Langer 1989). Children's uncritical acceptance of age stereotypes may contribute to the process by which chronic exposure to negative images of aging in the environment are the data that constitute the associations that continue to operate in both conscious and unconscious form throughout life.

Once age stereotypes have been acquired, they are likely to be automatically triggered by the presence of an elderly person. The broader process has been described by Ichheiser (1970) as one in which "the situation evokes automatically the appropriate attitude and thus controls the selection of classificatory types applied in concrete human relations" (p. 63).

A number of studies have demonstrated that the automatic categorization of individuals into social groups occurs easily and effortlessly in the domains of age, race, and gender (Banaji and Hardin 1996; Devine 1989; Hamilton and Sherman 1994; Perdue and Gurtman 1990). There may well be a functional advantage to automatic stereotypes, for without them, the encounter with any new individual would require continuous new learning. Implicit stereotypes reflect generalizations that are in the interest of simplifying the demands on thinking and feeling and promoting adaptation. By automatic categorization into social groups, such as age, the perceiver, it is assumed, is able to reorient cognitive resources and attention to nonroutine tasks (Bodenhausen, Kramer, and Susser 1994; MacCrae, Milne, and Bodenhausen 1994).

Maintenance of Implicit Age Bias

Implicit age stereotypes are probably maintained, and may even be strengthened, over time by several processes. Research shows that repetitive exposure to primes can increase the strength of an implicit stereotype (Dijksterhuis and van Knippenberg 1998; Levy et al. 2000; Murphy, Monahan, and Zajonc 1995).

In addition, once an implicit stereotype is formed, the stereotype is usually not diminished when a person encounters contradictory evidence (Hill et al. 1990). If anything, the contradiction, such as the successfully aging 78-year-old astronaut John Glenn, may be classified as an exception. Hilton and von Hippel (1996), in their review of stereotypes, discuss the process of self-perpetuation of bias in the context of implicit race and gender stereotypes; it seems reasonable to assume that age stereotypes operate similarly. They show that individuals may strengthen stereotypes in spite of encountering contradictory evidence. For example, children often report that all doctors are male, even when their own pediatricians are female (Adler 2000). Such automatic associations between doctor and male (among many other gender-profession associations) are also observed in studies of college students, regardless of their explicit beliefs (Banaji and Hardin 1996).

The maintenance of negative implicit age stereotypes may also benefit from the process of implicit negative evaluations that lead to avoidance of information (Bargh 1997). When encountering a new object or person, individuals tend to assign a global evaluation of good or bad within a quarter of a second (Zajonc 1980). This implicit evaluation has been linked to approach-avoidance motivation (Lewin 1935). For example, study participants pushed a lever away faster following unpleasant words than the pleasant words and pulled the lever toward themselves faster in response to pleasant than the unpleasant words (Chen and Bargh 1997; Solarz 1960). If the old are automatically assigned a negative evaluation, as suggested by Perdue and Gurtman (1990), younger adults may find ways to avoid interacting with the elderly. This avoidance in turn could reduce the opportunity for younger adults to have meaningful interaction and contact with the elderly, a context in which positive explicit age stereotypes may develop (Palmore 1998).

Recent research by Cunningham, Nezlek, and Banaji (2002) suggests a connection between implicit and explicit attitudes that challenges previous assumptions that they may be fully dissociated. These investigators demonstrate that when multiple measures are used and the data are subjected to covariance structural modeling, previous assumptions of a complete lack of relationships between conscious and unconscious measures are invalid. Instead, they showed that implicit and explicit attitudes toward five social groups (black-white, gay-straight, American-foreign, Jewish-Christian, and rich-poor) are significantly correlated (while confirmatory factor analysis also reveals the two families of measures are unique in that a single-factor solution does not fit). Although the process by which explicit and implicit attitudes come to be associated is not adequately understood and likely to be complex, it is now possible to speculate that the two may influence each other. If younger adults have no opportunities to develop positive explicit age stereotypes, it may be difficult to change the basis of implicit age stereotypes.

Implicit Out-Group Favoritism

Although a vast body of research demonstrates strong preference for in-groups over out-groups (e.g., Tajfel 1981), the findings reviewed here suggest that age attitudes and stereotypes do not necessarily fit this pattern. Older individuals show evidence of negative attitudes and beliefs toward the elderly, at least on implicit measures. An explanation for this phenomenon may be that by the time younger individuals become elderly, they have spent over a half-century expressing and internalizing negative stereotypes of aging. When the stereotype becomes relevant to their own acquired identity, aged individuals may remain vulnerable because they have not had the opportunity to develop the mechanisms for defending against disparaging views of their group. Thus, the most effective approach may be to avoid identifying with the in-group until that becomes less and less possible, and by then it may be too late to have developed any protection against the negative attitudes and beliefs about the elderly. In support of this, research on implicit processes shows that unlike most other groups studied, such as women and African Americans, who tend to identify with their own social group, older individuals implicitly tend to identify with the young as strongly as the young themselves do (Greenwald et al. in press).

Compounding this problem, the negative implicit stereotypes directed at the elderly (and, later, at oneself) are particularly salient, as suggested by the strength of the negative response to them in the IAT Internet survey. A component of this salience probably arises from the fact that most negative stereotypes about aging relate to some form of debilitation, either physical or mental, which is a precursor to the ultimate outcome of old age, death. Since thoughts about death frequently lead to anxiety and tend to operate on an implicit level (McCoy et al. 2000), they may exacerbate the negativity of implicit age stereotypes.

Although theorists have argued that stereotypes exist to protect or enhance oneself or one's group (Adorno et al. 1950; Allport 1954; Lippman 1922; Tajfel 1981), in the case of most aging self-stereotypes, which tend to be negative, it is not the elderly as individuals or a group that is protected and enhanced. Instead, stereotypes of aging reflect the needs of younger members of society. To the extent that the elderly are perceived in negative terms, the converse becomes positive: not being old represents health, acuity, and other desirable states of being. Those who are not old are, by contrast, the beneficiaries of negative stereotypes about aging and remain so until they reach old age.

The elderly provide an example of a culturally peripheral group; therefore, according to Lewin, its members' "opinions about themselves are greatly influenced by the low esteem the majority has for them" (Lewin 1948, p. 194). Although Crocker and Major (1994) have shown that membership in disadvantaged groups need not destroy self-esteem, this fortuitous state of affairs may require conscious acknowledgment of prejudice toward the group and a mentally active buffering that protects against stigma associated with the group. Black Americans, we know from the Web data, show among the highest implicit self-esteem (Nosek et al. in press) and women show implicit self-esteem effects that are comparable to men's (Farnham, Greenwald, and Banaji 1999).

Additionally, women, who represent a group that is socially and politically marginalized like the elderly, do not show the same lack of positive attitudes toward the in-group, even though they may hold implicit negative stereotypes of the group. Women show strong, positive implicit attitudes toward their own group (Carpenter and Banaji 2000), and this effect appears whether or not the group *male* is directly present in the evaluation context (Mitchell, Nosek, and Banaji 2002). In this regard, women's group attitudes differ in a crucial way from those of the elderly. To our knowledge, the elderly is the only group that shows as strong negative implicit attitudes toward their own group as does the out-group (the young). This state of affairs raises the question of the importance of positive explicit attitudes; insofar as the elderly are not the beneficiaries of positive implicit attitudes and stereotypes, it is especially important to achieve the benefits of positive attitudes and beliefs through conscious, explicit modes.

Reducing Negative Implicit Age Stereotypes

Once implicit negative age stereotypes are formed, even though they operate below awareness, several studies suggest that they may be susceptible to appropriate interventions by either reinforcing implicit positive age stereotypes through subliminal priming (Levy 1996; Levy et al. 2000) or through exposure to pictures and descriptions of admired older individuals and disliked younger individuals (Dasgupta and Greenwald (in press), see also Blair and Ma 2002 and Carpenter and Banaji 2000 for similar results with gender). Blair and Ma (2002) found that by encouraging women to think about a "strong woman," they increased automatic stereotypes of women as strong. Similarly, Haines (1999) was able to increase women participants' association of self with strength by using a simulation game in which they were assigned to play a powerful woman.

An equivalent process has been applied to racial and age stereotypes. Dasgupta and Greenwald (in press) demonstrated that pro-white automatic stereotypes could be reduced through exposure to pictures and descriptions of admired black individuals (e.g., Martin Luther King) and disliked white individuals (e.g., Timothy McVeigh), as opposed to a group that was exposed to admired white individuals (e.g., John F. Kennedy) and disliked black individuals (e.g., O. J. Simpson). These authors also found that they could bring about a similar change in implicit negative age stereotypes with exposure to exemplars of admired elderly. In another study, they exposed participants to pictures and descriptions of admired older individuals (e.g., Mother Teresa) and disliked younger individuals (e.g., Tonya Harding), as opposed to admired younger individuals (e.g., Ben Affleck) and disliked older individuals (e.g., Bob Packwood). In both studies, such exposure seemingly focused attention on evaluatively distinct exemplars of the same social group (elderly or young) and produced notable differences in implicit attitude.

These studies demonstrate that an intervention can make a negatively viewed group, such as the elderly, appear more positive on a temporary basis. These experiments are also noteworthy because they show changes in attitude and stereotype that are themselves outside conscious control. In addition, these studies have demonstrated that individuals generalize the intervention exposure to primes of well-known individuals into stronger associations of positivity (or negativity) toward the category as a whole, that is, toward unknown older individuals.

To bring about long-term reduction in negative implicit age stereotypes, other interventions will be necessary. From reviewing how implicit age stereotypes are initially formed and then reinforced, one approach to change would be a stronger prescription to limit exposure to negative age stereotypes and increase exposure to positive stereotypes of the elderly across the life span. An additional measure may be necessary that requires the efforts of older individuals themselves. History suggests that reduction in discrimination is achieved with social recognition and political action. Both the civil rights and feminist movements were led in large part by members of the disadvantaged groups themselves: African Americans and women, respectively. Nothing less may be required to reduce age bias that supports the existing power structure of younger and middle-aged adults. The task may be harder to accomplish, because unlike other groups, the elderly are not their own best advocates, at least gauging by their implicit attitudes and stereotypes. Our research suggests that as all humans age, they should be aware of their own implicit negative views of their group and consciously develop an identity with old age and its positive attributes, using these to compensate for the ill effects of automatic ageism.

Note

This chapter was written with support from the Brookdale Foundation, the National Institute on Aging (AG05727), the National Institute of Mental Health (MH-57672), and the National Science Foundation (SBR-9422241, SBR-9709924).

References

Adler, R. (2000). Implicit stereotypes? *New Scientist*, 39–41.

Adorno, T., Frankel-Brunswik, E., Levinson, D. J., and Sanford, R. N. (1950). *The authoritarian personality*. New York: Harper.

Allport, G. W. (1954). *The nature of prejudice*. Reading, MA: Addison-Wesley.

Allport, G. W., and Vernon, P. (1933). *Studies in expressive movement*. New York: Macmillan.

Asch, S. M., Sloss, E. M., Hogan, C. Brook, R. H., and Kravitz, R. L. (2000). Measuring underuse of necessary care among elderly Medicare beneficiaries using inpatient and outpatient claims. *Journal of the American Medical Association, 284*, 2325–2333.ß

Banaji, M. R., Hardin, C. D., and Rothman, A. J. (1993). Implicit stereotyping in person judgment. *Journal of Personality and Social Psychology, 65*, 272–281.

Banaji, M. R. (2001). Implicit attitudes can be measured. In H. L. Roediger et al. (Eds.) *The nature of remembering: Essays in honor of Robert G. Crowder*. Washington, D.C.: American Psychological Association.

Banaji, M. R., and Hardin, C. D. (1996). Automatic stereotyping. *Psychological Science, 7,* 136–141.

Bargh, J. (1997). The automaticity of everyday life. In R. S. Wyer (Ed.), *The automaticity of everyday life: Advances in social cognition.* Mahwah, NJ: Erlbaum.

Bargh, J. A., Chen, M., and Burrows, L. (1996). Automaticity of social behavior: Direct effects of trait construct and stereotype activation on action. *Journal of Personality and Social Psychology, 71,* 230–244.

Bargh, J., and Pietromonaco, P. (1992). Automatic information processing and social perception: The influence of trait information presented outside of awareness on impression formation. *Journal of Personality and Social Psychology, 43,* 437–449.

Barnett, P. A., Spence, J. D., Manuck, S. B., and Jennings, J. R. (1997). Psychological stress and the progression of carotid artery disease. *Journal of Hypertension, 15,* 49–55.

Blair, I. V., and Banaji, M. R. (1996). Automatic and controlled processes in stereotype priming. *Journal of Personality and Social Psychology, 70,* 1142–1163.

Blair, I. V., and Ma, J. (2002). *Imagining stereotypes away: The moderation of automatic stereotypes through mental imagery.* Manuscript submitted for publication.

Bodenhausen, G. V., Kramer, G. P., and Susser, K. (1994). Happiness and stereotypic thinking in social judgments. *Journal of Personality and Social Psychology, 66,* 621–632.

Bowling, A. (1999). Ageism in cardiology. *British Medical Journal, 319,* 1353–1355.

Brewer, M. B., Dull, V., and Lui, L. (1981). Perceptions of the elderly: Stereotypes as prototypes. *Journal of Personality and Social Psychology, 41,* 656–670.

Brown, R. W. (1986). *Social psychology,* second edition. New York: Free Press.

Butler, R. N. (1980). Ageism: A foreword. *Journal of Social Issues, 36,* 8–11.

Carpenter, S., and Banaji, M. R. (2000). *Implicit gender attitudes: Group membership, cultural construal, and malleability.* Unpublished manuscript, Yale University, New Haven, CT.

Chen, M., and Bargh, J. (1997). Nonconscious behavioral confirmation processes: The self-fulfilling consequences of automatic stereotype activation. *Journal of Experimental Social Psychology, 33,* 541–560.

Cohen, G. (2000). If you were an old woman who lived in a shoe, what would you do? *American Journal of Geriatric Psychiatry, 8,* 93–95.

Crocker, J., and Major, B. M. (1994). Reactions to stigma: The moderating role of justifications. In M. P. Zanna and J. M. Olson (Eds.), *The psychology of prejudice: The Ontario symposium* (Vol. 7, pp. 289–314). Hillsdale, NJ: Erlbaum.

Crosby, F., Bromley, S., and Saxe, L. (1980). Recent unobtrusive studies of black and white discrimination and prejudice: A literature review. *Psychological Bulletin, 87,* 546–563.

Cunningham, W. A., Nezlek, J. B., and Banaji, M. R. (2002). *Conscious and unconscious ethnocentrism: Revisiting the ideologies of prejudice.* Manuscript in preparation, Yale University, New Haven, CT.

Dasgupta, N., and Greenwald, A. G. (in press). On the malleability of automatic attitudes. Combating automatic prejudice with images of admired and disliked individuals. *Journal of Personality and Social Psychology.*

Dasgupta, N., McGhee, D. E., Greenwald, A. G., and Banaji, M. R. (2000). Automatic preference for white Americans: Eliminating the familiarity explanation. *Journal of Experimental Social Psychology, 36,* 316–328.

Devine, P. (1989). Stereotypes and prejudice: Their automatic and controlled components. *Journal of Personality and Social Psychology, 56,* 5–18.

Dijksterhuis, A., and van Knippenberg, A. (1998). The relation between perception and behavior, or how to win a game of Trivial Pursuit. *Journal of Personality and Social Psychology, 74,* 865–877.

Dollard, J. (1937). *Caste and class in a southern town.* New Haven, CT: Yale University Press.

Dovidio, J. F., Kawakami, K., Johnson, B., and Howard, A. (1997). On the nature of prejudice: Automatic and controlled processes. *Journal of Experimental Social Psychology, 33,* 510–540.

Farnham, S. D., Greenwald, A. G., and Banaji, M. R. (1999). Implicit self-esteem. In D. Abrams and M. A. Hogg (Eds.), *Social identity and social cognition* (pp. 230–248). Malden, MA: Blackwell.

Fazio, R. H., Jackson, J. R., Dunton, B. C., and Williams, C. J. (1995). Variability in automatic activation as an unobtrusive measure of racial attitudes: A bona fide pipeline? *Journal of Personality and Social Psychology, 69,* 1013–1027.

Finkelstein, L. M., Burke, M. J., and Raju, N. S. (1995). Age discrimination in simulated employment contexts: An integrative analysis. *Journal of Applied Psychology, 60,* 652–663.

Gilbert, D. T., and Hixon, J. G. (1991). The trouble of thinking: Activation and application of stereotypic beliefs. *Journal of Personality and Social Psychology, 60,* 509–517.

Greenwald, A. G., and Banaji, M. R. (1995). Implicit social cognition: Attitudes, self-esteem, and stereotypes. *Psychological Review, 102,* 4–27.

Greenwald, A. G., Banaji, M. R., Rudman, L. A., Farnham, S. D., Nosek, B. A., and Mellot, D. S. (in press). A unified theory of implicit attitudes, stereotypes, self-esteem and self-concept. *Psychological Review.*

Greenwald, A. G., McGhee, D. E., and Schwartz, J. L. K. (1998). Measuring individual differences in implicit cognition: The Implicit Association Test. *Journal of Personality and Social Psychology, 74,* 1464–1480.

Greenwald, A. G., and Nosek, B. A. ([in press]). Health of the Implicit Association Test at age 3. *Zeitschrift für Experimentelle Psychologie, 48.*

Guigliano, R. P., Camargo, C. A., Lloyd-Jones, D. M., Zagrodsky, J. D., Alexis, J. D., Eagle, K. A., Fuster, V., and O'Donnell, C. J. (1998). Elderly patients receive less aggressive medical and invasive management of unstable angina: Potential impact of practical guidelines. *Archives of Internal Medicine, 158,* 1113–1120.

Haines, E. L. (1999). *Elements of a social power schema: Gender standpoint, self-concept and experience.* Unpublished doctoral dissertation, City University of New York.

Hamilton, D. L., and Sherman, J. W. (1994). Stereotypes. In R. S. Wyer and T. K. Srull (Eds.), *Handbook of social cognition* (pp. 1–68). Hillsdale, NJ: Erlbaum.

Hausdorff, J. M., Levy, B. R., and Wei, J. Y. (1999). The power of ageism on physical function of older persons: Reversibility of age-related gait changes. *Journal of the American Geriatrics Society, 47,* 1346–1349.

Hill, T., Lewicki, P., Czyzewska, M., and Schuller, G. (1990). The role of learned inferential encoding rules in the perception of faces: Effects of nonconscious self-perpetuation of a bias. *Journal of Experimental Social Psychology, 57,* 373–387.

Hillerbrand, E., and Shaw, D. (1990). Age bias in a general hospital: Is there ageism in psychiatric consultation? *Clinical Gerontologist, 2,* 3–13.

Hilton, J., and von Hippel, W. (1996). Stereotypes. *Annual Review of Psychology, 47,* 237–271.

Hummert, M. L. (1990). Multiple stereotypes of elderly and young adults: A comparison of structure and evaluations. *Psychology and Aging, 5,* 182–193.

Hummert, M. L. (1999). A social cognitive perspective on age stereotypes. In T. Hess and F. Blanchard-Fields (Eds.), *Social cognition and aging.* New York: Academic Press.

Hummert, M. L., and Ryan, E. B. (1996). Toward understanding variations in patronizing talk addressed to older adults: Psycholinguistic features of care and control. *International Journal of Psycholinguistics, 12,* 149–169.

Ichheiser, G. (1970). *Appearances and realities: Misunderstandings in human relations.* San Francisco: Jossey-Bass.

Isaacs, L., and Bearison, D. (1986). The development of children's prejudice against the aged. *International Journal of Aging and Human Development, 23,* 175–194.

Jamieson, D. A., and Zanna, M. P. (1989). Need for structure in attitude formation and expression. In A. R. Pratkanis, S. J. Breckler, and A. G. Greenwald (Eds.), *Attitude structure and function* (pp. 383–406). Hillsdale, NJ: Erlbaum.

Katz, D., and Braly, K. W. (1935). *Racial prejudice and racial stereotypes. Journal of Abnormal and Social Psychology, 30,* 175–193.

Kite, M., and Johnson, B. (1988). Attitudes toward older and younger adults: A meta-analysis. *Psychology and Aging, 3,* 233–244.

Kogan, N. (2000). *Implicit ageism symposium.* Paper presented at the annual meeting of the Gerontological Association of America, Washington, D.C.

Kubey, R. (1980). Television and aging: Past, present and future. *Gerontologist, 20,* 16–35.

Lachman, M. E., Weaver, S. L., Bandura, M., Elliott, E., and Lewkowicz, C. (1992). Improving memory and control beliefs through cognitive restructuring and self-generated strategies. *Journals of Gerontology, 47,* P293–P299.

Langer, E. (1989). *Mindfulness.* Reading, MA: Addison-Wesley.

Lasker, B. (1930). *Jewish experience in America.* New York: The Inquiry.

Levy, B. R. (1996). Improving memory in old age by implicit self-stereotyping. *Journal of Personality and Social Psychology, 71,* 1092–1107.

Levy, B. R. (2000). Handwriting as a reflection of aging self-stereotypes. *Journal of Geriatric Psychiatry, 33,* 81–94.

Levy, B. R., Ashman, O., and Dror, I. (2000). To be or not to be: The effect of stereotypes of aging on the will to live. *Omega: Journal of Death and Dying, 40,* 409–420.

Levy, B. R., Hausdorff, J., Hencke, R., and Wei, J. Y. (2000). Reducing cardiovascular stress with positive self-stereotypes of aging. *Journal of Gerontology: Psychological Sciences, 55,* 205–213.

Levy, B. R., and Langer, E. J. (1994). Aging free from negative stereotypes: Successful memory among the American deaf and in China. *Journal of Personality and Social Psychology, 66,* 935–943.

Lewin, K. (1935). *A dynamic theory of personality.* New York: McGraw-Hill.

Lewin, K. (1948). *Resolving social conflicts: Selected papers on group dynamics.* New York: Harper and Row.

Lippman, W. (1922). *Public opinion.* New York: Macmillan.

MacCrae, C. N., Milne, A. B., and Bodenhausen, G. V. (1994). Stereotypes as energy saving devices: A peek inside the cognitive toolbox. *Journal of Personality and Social Psychology, 66,* 37–47.

McCoy, S., Pyszczynski, T., Solomon, S., and Greenberg, J. (2000). Transcending the self: A terror management perspective on successful aging. In A. Tomer (Ed.), *Death attitudes and the older adult.* Philadelphia: Brunner-Routledge.

Miles, W. R. (1935). Age and human society. In C. Murchison (Ed.), *A handbook of social psychology.* New York: Russell and Russell.

Mitchell, J. A., Nosek, B. A., and Banaji, M. R. (2002). *Multitudes of attitudes: Automatic evaluation of multiply-categorizable targets.* Manuscript submitted for publication.

Murphy, S. T., Monahan, J. L., and Zajonc, R. B. (1995). Additivity of nonconscious affect: Combined effects of priming and exposure. *Journal of Personality and Social Psychology, 69,* 589–602.

Nosek, B. A., Banaji, M. R., and Greenwald, A. G. (in press). Harvesting implicit group attitudes and beliefs from a demonstration website. *Group Dynamics.*

Nosek, B. A., Banaji, M. R., and Greenwald, A. G. (in press). eResearch: Ethics, security, design, and control in psychological research on the Internet. *Journal of Social Issues.*

Palmore, E. (1998). *The Facts on Aging quiz.* New York: Springer.

Perdue, C. W., and Gurtman, M. B. (1990). Evidence for the automaticity of ageism. *Journal of Experimental Social Psychology, 26,* 199–216.

Plewa, F. (1936). The position of women in society. *Internationale Zeitschrift Fuer Individual-Psychologie, 14,* 104–118.

Pratto, F., and Bargh, J. A. (1991). Stereotyping based on apparently individuating information: Trait and global components of sex stereotypes under attention overload. *Journal of Experimental Social Psychology, 27,* 26–47.

Schacter, D. L. (1987). Implicit memory: History and current status. *Journal of Experimental Psychology: Learning, Memory, & Cognition, 13,* 501–518.

Schmidt, D., and Boland, S. (1986). Structure of perceptions of older adults: Evidence for multiple stereotypes. *Psychology and Aging, 1,* 255–260.

Shih, M., Pittinsky, T. L., and Ambady, N. (1999). Stereotype susceptibility: Identity salience and shifts in quantitative performance. *Psychological Science, 10,* 80–83.

Sigelman, L., and Sigelman, C. K. (1982). Sexism, racism, and ageism in voting behavior: An experimental analysis. *Social Psychology Quarterly, 45,* 263–269.

Solarz, A. (1960). Latency of instrumental responses as a function of compatibility with the meaning of eliciting verbal signs. *Journal of Experimental Psychology, 59,* 239–245.

Steele, C., and Aronson, J. (1998). Stereotype threat and the test performance of academically successful African Americans. In C. Jencks and P. Meredith (Eds.), *The black-white test score gap.* Washington, D.C.: Brookings Institution.

Stone, M., and Stone, L. (1997). Ageism: The quiet epidemic. *Canadian Journal of Public Health, 88,* 293–294.

Tajfel, H. (1981). *Human groups and social categories.* Cambridge: Cambridge University Press.

von Hippel, W., Sekaquaptewa, D., and Vargas, P. (1997). The linguistic intergroup bias as an implicit indicator of prejudice. *Journal of Experimental Social Psychology, 33,* 490–509.

Williams, A., and Giles, H. (1998). Communication of ageism. In M. L., Hecht and L. Michael (Eds.), *Communicating prejudice* (pp. 136–160). Thousand Oaks, CA: Sage.

Zajonc, R. B. (1980). Feeling and thinking: Preferences need no inferences. *American Psychologist, 35,* 151–175.

Zebrowitz, L. A., and Montepare, J. M. (2000). Too young, too old, stigmatizing adolescents and elderly. In T. F. Heatherton, R. E. Kleck, M. R. Hebl, and J. E. Hull (Eds.), *The social psychology of stigma.* New York: Guilford.

4

A Social-Developmental View of Ageism
Joann M. Montepare and Leslie A. Zebrowitz

The biased and unfavorable attitudes people hold of aging adults is called *ageism*. We address how these attitudes develop by examining ageism from a social-developmental perspective that views ageist attitudes as embedded in broader social perceptions that unfold with development. One advantage of this approach is that it encourages a more comprehensive analysis of the factors that contribute to ageism. Another advantage is that it increases the likelihood of discovering effective ways to combat ageism by identifying the multiple paths by which it emerges and takes shape. To begin, we discuss what children know about age by reviewing research on children's ability to differentiate age groups and their understanding of the aging process. Next, we examine children's feelings and beliefs about older adults, as well as their behavior toward them. We then examine individual variations in children's attitudes and the potential developmental impact of mechanisms that social psychologists consider to be the foundations on which stereotypes are formed. Specifically, we explore perceptual, cognitive, affective, and sociocultural mechanisms. We also discuss several methodological issues and conclude by suggesting research that is needed to further our understanding of how ageism develops and how it may be averted.

What Do Children Know about Age?

Several developmental theorists have argued that age is a fundamental dimension along which children organize their perceptions of people in their social world. In particular, Lewis and Brooks-Gunn (1979) suggest that because aging is a basic process of human experience universally associated with a wide variety of social activities, it is one of the first and most important social attributes to which children develop a sensitivity. In addition to pointing to the primacy of age as a social concept, they suggest that children's earliest social perceptions involve the categorization of people on the basis of their age-related physical characteristics. Research has identified a variety of physical characteristics that systematically covary with age, and strong empirical evidence indicates that from an early age, children readily use this information to differentiate and classify people.

Differentiating Age

Height Cues   Obviously, people grow taller as they mature and the shape of their bodies changes (Medawar 1944; Tanner 1970). Research has found that even infants make use of variations in height to differentiate among people. In their study of the reactions of 7-month-old infants to adult and child strangers, Brooks and Lewis (1976) found that infants used height information to discriminate among strangers, averting their gaze more when approached by a normal-sized adult stranger than a midget or a child stranger. Bigelow and colleagues (1990) showed that infants' stronger aversion to taller people was not because they tower more over them. Twelve-month-old infants smiled more at faces of adult strangers when they appeared on a screen at child height than when they appeared at adult height. They also averted their gaze more from faces in the adult height window, whether the faces were adults or children.

   Research with older children has shown that they are especially attuned to age-related variations in height. In fact, in some cases they disregard other sources of age information, such as facial information, in favor of that provided by height cues when judging people's age (Britton and Britton 1969; Kuczaj and Lederberg 1976; Looft 1971). For example, Britton and Britton (1969) asked children between 3 and 6 years to identify the age level of full-figure schematic drawings of individuals from five age groups. Children most easily differentiated among the youngest age groups who varied the most in height. On the other hand, individuals in the adult age groups, who were more similar in height, were less easily differentiated. With age, children's ability to make more accurate and fine-grained discriminations increased, likely owing to their greater ability to disentangle the strong natural correlation between age and height and take into account other sources of age information.

Face Cues   Considerable research has shown that people's faces change in systematic ways as they age and that children are adept at using facial cues to make age discriminations when they are not distracted by differences in height (Montepare and Zebrowitz 1998). For instance, infants as young as 4 months differentially look at pictorial representations of faces that differ in age (Fagan 1972; Lasky, Klein, and Martinez 1974; McCall and Kennedy 1980). Twelve-month-old infants show more smiles than gaze aversions to a child stranger but equal smiles and gaze aversions to an adult stranger when height cues are equated (Bigelow et al. 1990). By 15 months, children can point to pictures of faces of different-aged people in response to verbal directions and spontaneously identify them with appropriate age labels (Lewis and Brooks-Gunn 1979). By 3 years, children are proficient at systematically using age labels, such as *baby, boy,* and *man,* to identify people pictured in facial photographs (Edwards 1984; Montepare and McArthur 1986).

Research has also found that children base their age judgments on the same cues that adults use to identify age. For example, Melson, Fogel, and Toda (1986) found that 3 year olds can easily discriminate infants' faces from an array of faces of different ages and justify their choices by describing cues such as baldness. Similarly, Kogan, Stephens, and Shelton (1961) found that young children recognize that facial wrinkles are characteristic of elderly faces, and Jones and Smith (1984) found that children can use information provided by people's eyes to make age judgments. Montepare and Zebrowitz (1986) also demonstrated that facial wrinkling is a potent cue to age for preschoolers, as are age-related variations in craniofacial profile shape and the vertical placement of features on a face.

Voice Cues Although little research has explored the extent to which children can discern age from vocal cues, the available evidence suggests that they can. For example, using a face-voice matching paradigm, Lasky, Klein, and Martinez (1974) found that 5-month-old infants could discriminate between a woman's and a child's voice. Subsequent research found that infants also differentiate men's and women's voices, and they show stronger reactions to women's voices, which are higher in pitch, like children's voices (Brown 1979; Miller, Younger, and Morse 1982; Poulin-Dubois et al. 1994; Smith 1979). Poulin-Dubois and colleagues (1994) suggest that infants' greater responsiveness to women's voices may reflect vocal qualities that overlap with the baby-talk vocal register parents use when talking to young children. Indeed, research has shown that within the first few months of life, children are highly attentive to this age-dependent speech style (Cooper and Aslin 1990).

Understanding Age

The early emergence of children's sensitivity to age differences suggests that age-based categorization may be a rudimentary and universal faculty. However, other research suggests that certain aspects of children's age perceptions derive from maturational shifts in logical thinking and reasoning skills that occur as children develop (Piaget 1969; Galper et al. 1980–1981). More specifically, while children can make reliable age differentiations from early infancy, their ability to evaluate age differences improves with age, especially when it is assessed on cognitively demanding tasks that require children to rank-order stimuli and make relative age judgments using the linguistic labels *older* or *younger* (Downs and Walz 1981; Page, Olivas, Driver, and Driver 1981; Kogan, Stephens, and Shelton 1961; Seefeldt, et al. 1977; Sheehan 1978). For example, Kogan, Stepens, and Shelton (1961) asked children between 4 and 6 years to rank-order a series of photographs of men and women between 9 and 76 years and found that children's ability to identify age correctly improved with their age. These researchers maintain that certain aspects of children's appreciation of age requires higher levels of cognitive maturity, as evidenced by age-related differences in their age-identification skills. Consistent with their claim, other researchers have found that children's performance on age-identification tasks correlates with their performance on more general tests of seriation ability and their understanding of linguistic terms that reflect relative concepts (Kuczaj and Lederberg 1976; Miller, Blalock, and Ginsburg 1984; Rosenwasser et al. 1986).

Developmental changes are also found when children are asked to explain the nature of age differences, also suggesting that children's appreciation of the aging processes is tied to maturational changes in their reasoning abilities. Indeed, some researchers have suggested that children's understanding of the aging process follows a cognitive-developmental sequence paralleling the development of logical thought described by Piaget, who treated age as a temporal concept. In their research, Galper, Jantz, Seefeldt, and Serock (1980–1981) interviewed 3 to 11 year olds with a test that distinguished their level of reasoning about aging using a Piagetian framework that focused on an understanding of concepts such as duration and succession. For example, lower levels reflected children's failure to understand aging as a continuous process in time and think that people age at different rates and grow old suddenly. Thus, children at this level would believe that their parent would stay the same age while they grew older. Results showed that the level of understanding children achieved was strongly linked to their age. Moreover, their test performance was correlated with their performance on traditional Piagetian conservation tasks. Page and associates (1981) found similar age-related differences in children's understanding of age, as well as their ability to identify people's ages accurately.

Other researchers have found evidence for cognitive-developmental sequencing in children's personal explanations of the aging process. Goldman and Goldman (1981) questioned 838 international students between 5 and 15 years about the causes of aging by asking them, "Why is it that old people get wrinkled skin / get ill more easily / have to stop work?" Children's responses were categorized with respect to how logical and realistic they were. Systematic age differences were found, with younger children responding with more simplistic explanations such as having birthdays, nature or God's will, not eating enough food, and one's body wearing out. Older children more often cited physical and psychological factors as the cause of aging and described the aging process as an inevitable and irreversible one.

Summary

The research suggests that from infancy, children are sensitive to differences in people's ages and readily classify them on the basis of age-related physical cues, indicating a biological preparedness to make age-based classifications. As children grow older, their understanding of age differences and the aging process improves, suggesting that maturation or socialization, or both, plays a role in the development of their understanding of age. Having established that an appreciation of age as a social category is set in motion early in development, we now turn to our discussion of children's attitudes toward older adults.

What Are Children's Attitudes toward Older Adults?

Social psychologists typically describe attitudes as involving evaluations of a stimulus along three dimensions: affective, cognitive, and behavioral (Taylor, Peplau, and Sears, 2000). Consistent with this framework, we differentiate among these components as we explore children's ageist attitudes. More specifically, we consider children's feelings toward older adults (analogous to prejudice), children's beliefs and knowledge about older adults (analogous to stereotypes), and children's intended or actual behaviors toward older adults (analogous to discrimination).

Prejudicial Feelings

In their meta-analysis of research comparing adults' attitudes toward older and younger adults, Kite and Johnson (1988) showed that although older adults were sometimes perceived positively, they were more typically viewed negatively in comparison to younger adults. The affective valence of children's attitudes also appears to be negatively biased. In their seminal study on children's affective reactions to older versus young adults, Kogan, Stephens, and Shelton (1961) found that when asked to evaluate the extent to which they liked or disliked different-aged adults depicted in photographs, children as young as 4 years indicated a strong preference for younger adults. Using measurement techniques such as semantic differential scales and word associations, research by Seefeldt and colleagues (Seefeldt 1984; Seefeldt and Ahn 1990; Seefeldt et al. 1977) has also repeatedly found that children view older adults with generally negative feelings.

Stereotypic Beliefs

An examination of children's stereotypic beliefs about the traits, behaviors, and abilities of older adults suggests that children's age attitudes are more complex that they at first might appear. Such complexity echoes the sentiments of developmental researchers (Seefeldt et al. 1977; Marks, Newman, and Onawola 1985), as well as admonitions of social scientists, who assert that

> it is not a simple question of whether attitudes toward the elderly are indeed more negative than those expressed for younger people; attitudes toward the elderly appear to be composed of conceptually different domains and are multivariately determined. People appear to hold a variety of beliefs about older people, suggesting a need to map the terrain of these various components and, equally important, to determine how these factors influence behavior toward the elderly—a serious neglected area of research. (Kite and Johnson 1988, p. 240)

Considerable research has shown that adults do in fact hold a variety of stereotypic beliefs about older adults, including beliefs about their physical, cognitive, and interpersonal qualities (Brubaker and Powers 1976; Crockett and Hummert 1987; Green 1981; Hummert 1990; Hummert et al. 1994; Lutsky 1980; McTavish 1971; Pasupathi, Carstensen, and Tsai 1995; Schmidt and Boland 1986). Moreover, beliefs about older adults' physical and cognitive qualities are more negative than beliefs about their interpersonal ones, such as kindness or friendliness (Kite and Johnson 1988). Our evaluation of research examining children's stereotypes of older adults reveals that they are similar to those expressed by young adults, incorporating beliefs about older adults' physical, cognitive, and social characteristics (see table 4.1). Moreover, the extent to which children perceive older adults negatively appears to depend on the dimension along which they are evaluated, with more negative evaluations on physical dimensions than social ones.

Several studies have shown that by 3 years, children associate aging with decreases in physical attractiveness (Downs and Walz 1981; Kogan, Stephens, and Shelton 1961; Korthase and Trenholme 1983; Weinberger 1979). Also, negative evaluations are common when children evaluate older adults on semantic differential scales that capture physical qualities—namely, overall activity or potency (Thomas and Yamamoto 1975; Marks, Newman, and Onawola 1985). A common fear that children have about growing old is becoming sick and dying (Burke 1981–1982; Doka 1985–1986; Seefeldt et al. 1977). In addition, age-related physical changes and deficits are very salient to children, and their negative attitudes about older adults are strongly tied to their perceptions of older adults' physical appearance and health. When asked to draw pictures of older adults (Marcoen 1979), complete sentences about aging adults (Hickey, Hickey, and Kalish 1968), or describe what they expect to be like when they are old (Seefeldt et al. 1977), elementary school-aged children are quick to point to physical conditions such as baldness, wrinkling, poor vision, diminished hearing, impaired walking, general feebleness, and unhealthiness.

More positive stereotypes of older adults emerge when children are asked to evaluate certain social qualities. Although children often perceive older adults as sadder, lonelier, and duller than younger individuals (Burke 1981–1982; Doka 1985–1986; Hickey and Kalish 1968; Thomas and Yamamota 1975), they also often characterize them as unaggressive, polite, kind, good, friendly, and wise (Burke 1981–1982; Fillmer 1982; Hickey, Hickey, and Kalish 1968; Ivester and King 1977; Marks, Newman, and Onawola 1985; Mitchell et al. 1985). The positive personality traits attributed to older adults by children parallel those observed in research with adults (Kite and Johnson 1988).

Discriminatory Behavior

Although few researchers have explored the behavioral components of children's age attitudes, several studies suggest that young children maintain systematic expectations about behavior with older adults. Some research, for example, indicates that by 3 years, children voice a preference for interacting with younger as opposed to older adults (Page et al. 1981, Seefeldt et al. 1977). Miller, Blalock, and Ginsburg (1984–1985) also

Table 4.1
Studies Examining Children's Age Attitudes

Study	Subjects	Stimuli	Attitude Measures	Attitudes toward Older Adults
Kogan, Stephens, and Shelton (1961)	Boys and girls: 4–6 years	Photos of males and females, 9–76 years	Rank targets by age, attractiveness, liking	Older adults perceived as older, less attractive, and less preferred
Kasternbaum and Durkee (1964)	Adolescents	Verbal sketches	Age-appropriate Attitudes Technique and Important Years Technique	Older adults seen negatively
Hickey, Hickey, and Kalish (1968)	Boys and girls: 8 years	Verbal label of old person	Sentence writing	Older adults perceived to have negative physical characteristics and some negative and positive social characteristics
Hickey and Kalish (1968)	Boys and girls: 8, 12, 15, 19 years	Verbal labels of 25-, 45-, 65-, and 85-year-old adults	Rating scales comparing age groups	Older adults perceived more negatively
Thomas and Yamamoto (1975)	Boys and girls: 10, 12, 14, 16 years	Photos of 30-, 50-, and 70-year-old males and verbal labels of young, middle-aged, and old person	Story writing Semantic differential	Older adults perceived positively on evaluation factor and negatively on affect and activity-potency factors
Seefeldt et al. (1977)	Boys and girls: 3–11 years	Drawings of males 20–35, 35–50, 50–65, 65–80 years old	Structured interviews	Children felt negatively about being old, described old men negatively, and preferred young men
Ivester and King (1977)	Adolescents	Verbal label of an old person	Attitude toward Old People scale	Overall scores were more positive than negative

Marcoen (1979)	Boys and girls: 7–11 years	Verbal labels of older adults and grandparents	Picture drawing	Older adults drawn with negative characteristics
Weinberger (1979)	Boys and girls: 5–8 years	Photos of children and young, middle-aged, and older adults, males and females	Rank targets by traits, appearance, and potential for social interaction	Older adults least preferred and perceived as having mostly negative traits
Downs and Walz (1981)	Boys and girls: 3–4 years	Photos of 20-, 40-, and 60-year-old males and females	Children's Attitudes toward the Elderly questionnaire	Older adults perceived as less attractive and unhealthy, but having some positive social qualities
Page et al. (1981)	Boys and girls: 4–11 years	Photos of different-aged males and females	Interviews	Older adults less preferred
Burke (1981–1982)	Boys and girls: 4–7 years	Photos of males and females 25–35 and 65 years	Sociometric questions, interviews	Older adults perceived to have many negative but some positive characteristics
Fillmer (1982)	Boys and girls: 9–11 years	Pictures of males and females 20 and 60 years old	Trait and behavior scales	Older adults perceived positively on traits and negatively on behaviors
Korthase and Trenholme (1983)	Boys and girls: 7–9 years	Photos of young, middle-aged, and older adult males and females	Rank targets by attractiveness	Perceived attractiveness decreased with perceived age
Nishi-Strattner and Myers (1983)	Boys and girls: 10–11 years	Verbal labels	Attitude Perception questionnaire	Overall relatively positive attitudes

Table 4.1 (continued)

Study	Subjects	Stimuli	Attitude Measures	Attitudes toward Older Adults
Miller, Blalock, and Ginsburg (1984)	Boys and girls: 3–6 years	Drawings of a younger and older male and female	Sociometric questions	Older adults selected less often
Mitchell et al. (1985)	Boys and girls: 5–13 years	Drawings of young, middle-aged, and older males and females	Forced-choice questions	Older adults perceived to have negative physical abilities, positive personality traits, and neutral affective relations
Marks, Newman, and Onawola (1985)	Boys and girls: 8–10 years	Verbal labels of older adults	Children's Views on Aging questionnaire	Older adults perceived negatively on potency factor and positively on evaluative factor
Doka (1985–1986)	Adolescents	Verbal labels of 55, 65, 75, and 85 year olds	Sentence completions	Negative phrases and traits associated with older adults and aging
Isaacs and Bearison (1986)	Boys and girls: 4–8 years	Photos of middle-aged and older adults	Social Attitude Scale of Ageist Prejudice, behavioral measures	Older adults perceived negatively on verbal and behavioral measures
Dobrosky and Bishop (1986)	Boys and girls: 9–10 years	Verbal label of "an old person"	Nondirective questions	Physical descriptions and behaviors most salient
Rosenwasser et al. (1986)	Boys and girls: 3–5 years	Pictures of an old and young male and female	Sociometric questions	Older adults selected less often overall
Davidson, Cameron, and Jergovic (1995)	Boys and girls: 7–11 years	Drawings of older adult, male and female	Children's Attitudes toward the Elderly questionnaire	Children felt negatively about getting old and perceived older adults negatively

Note: For comparison purposes, subjects' chronological ages were estimated for studies that reported grade levels. Intervention studies are not included in this table.

found that children as young as 3 years preferred younger adults over older adults in hypothetical situations (e.g., with whom they would most like to play, whom they would like to take care of them when they are sick). Indicative of the ailments and infirmities they associate with being elderly, Seefeldt and colleagues (1977) found that when young children were asked what kinds of activities they would engage in with an elderly man, the majority said they would do things like "carry things for him," "get his glasses," "push him in a wheelchair," or "bury him." Similarly, other researchers have found that young children express a willingness to provide help to older adults, but they also express a willingness to elicit help from them in certain situations (Marks, Newman, and Onawola 1985; Weinberger 1979). More positive behavioral expectancies emerge when older adults are specified as grandparents. Burke (1981–1982) found that "older people had considerable appeal as companions" (p. 218) for 4 to 7 year olds, who described engaging in enjoyable activities with their grandparents such as playing games, working together, talking, and hugging.

Only one study, to our knowledge, has investigated children's actual behavior toward older and younger adults. In this enterprising study, Isaacs and Bearison (1986) randomly assigned 4, 6, and 8 year olds to work on a puzzle with either a 75- or 35-year-old adult. The adults interacted in similar ways with the children and were congenial, healthy, and dressed fashionably. Children's attitudes were assessed verbally with a scale measure, and their proxemic distance, eye-contact initiation, verbal interaction (number of words, number of verbal initiations, and number of appeals), and productivity (number of puzzles placed) were coded while they interacted with the adults. Children exhibited significant differences in behavior when interacting with the older versus the young adult on most behavioral measures: they sat farther away from older adults, initiated less eye contact and verbal interaction with them, and asked them less often for assistance. Moreover, children's proxemic and eye-contact behavior were correlated with their responses to the attitude scale that asked children to select which of two adults (one older and one younger) was likely to act in ways that reflecting different personality traits or abilities.

Attitudes of Different Children

The research indicates that young children possess systematic feelings, beliefs, and behavioral expectations about older adults. Moreover, although children's attitudes tend to be negatively biased, the extent of their negativity appears to depend on what characteristic of older adults they are evaluating. We now turn to research that provides information about variations in different children's attitudes and children's attitudes toward different older adults.

Age Effects   Ascertaining age-related variations in children's attitudes toward older adults is a challenging task for several reasons. Most notably, many of the studies that have chanced to compare the attitudes of younger and older children have not been guided by strong developmental theory. More typically, age differences are examined in an exploratory manner. As a result, age groups are targeted more by convenience than by theoretical motivation, and specific predictions are seldom made about particular age groups or age differences. Moreover, studies from which age comparisons may be made have employed different attitude instruments, making it difficult to sort out true age effects from measurement effects. Thus, we have chosen to restrict our discussion to a few select studies to highlight certain observations.

In one of the more extensive studies of age effects, Seefeldt and colleagues (1977) examined the attitudes of children from preschool to sixth grade using measures that assessed different components of children's attitudes. They found that children from all age levels expressed stereotypic expectations about the behaviors of older adults. Children of all ages also preferred to interact more with younger than older adults, although this preference was strongest for younger children (3 to 7 years). Younger children also reported more negative feelings about growing old. These findings suggest that negative feelings toward older adults are more characteristic of children in the preschool and early elementary school years than in later childhood.

In their study of 4, 6, and 8 year olds, Isaacs and Bearison (1986) used both verbal and behavioral measures to examine attitudes. In contrast to the findings of Seefeldt et al. (1977), the 4 year olds did not show biased responses on the verbal measure. The discrepancy in findings may simply reflect differences in the measures used and their sensitivity to different components of children's attitudes. Indeed, Isaacs and Bearison (1986) did find that 4 year olds manifested more prejudicial attitudes toward actual older than younger adults by averting their gaze and interacting with them at greater distances. By 6 years, children were consistently expressing biased attitudes verbally and also displaying differential behaviors.

Whereas negative feelings toward older adults appear to be stronger in early than middle childhood, there is evidence that negativity increases from middle childhood to adolescence. Whereas children from 8 to 19 years all viewed older adults more negatively than younger adults, the strength of this bias increased with age (Hickey and Kalish 1968). Similarly, a study of the attitudes of children 10 to 17 years revealed that the attitudes of younger children were more positive than those of adolescents (Thomas and Yamamoto 1975).

Isaacs and Bearison (1986) suggest that children's attitudes become more differentiated and elaborated with age, and research suggests that this is an apt characterization. For instance, Newman and colleagues (Newman, Faux, and Larimer 1997; Marks, Newman, and Onawola 1985) assessed 8 to 10 year olds' beliefs about aging and whether they considered these things "a good [or bad] thing to happen" or "neither good nor bad." Children's responses revealed that they viewed some aspects of aging as negative consequences and others as neutral or positive events. Their research indicates that by the middle childhood years, children attitudes reflect an appreciation of the complexity of aging and a more realistic perception than may have been true for younger age groups studied in other research. Other research has also revealed that with increasing age, children view older adults in more differentiated terms. Studying children 8 to 19 years, Hickey and Kalish (1968) found that older children differentiated older and younger adults more on some dimensions than others, showing greater differentiation when evaluating how lonely or inactive adults were. In addition, stories written by 10 to 17 year olds in research by Thomas and Yamamoto (1975) encompassed more details about older adults' daily activities and feelings than those written by 8 year olds in research by Hickey, Hickey, and Kalish (1968).

Our interpretation of these age effects suggests several developmental trends that are similar to those observed in the developmental literature on sex-role stereotypes (Serbin and Sprafkin 1986). For one thing, they echo the notion that children's attitudes entail different components, and each may have different developmental paths. Affective reactions appear to surface early and are characterized by generalized negative reactions toward older adults. Early in development, children also appear to hold systematic behavioral stereotypes that become more complex and differentiated with age. During the middle childhood years, attitudes appear to take a positive turn, perhaps as a result of greater flexibility in thinking with which greater differentiation may be associated.

It is also of interest to note that throughout the adolescent years and into young adulthood, attitudes continue to become more articulated. Indeed, ample research has shown that young adults maintain distinct stereotypes about different types of older adults (Hummert 1990; Schmidt and

Boland 1986). Nevertheless, like children, they also hold generally more negative prejudicial feelings (Kite and Johnson 1988). Interestingly, older adults also maintain biased attitudes about their own age group. In general, older adults view members of their own age group as lower in status, less likeable, unhappier, more dependent, and less goal oriented than younger adults (Zebrowitz and Montepare 2000). Piecing together the implications of age effects across the life span is a task yet to be undertaken.

Clearly, developmental research is needed to test the accuracy of our analysis. In particular, research is needed that systematically and consistently distinguishes among the various components of children's attitudes. Research also needs to focus on age groups with a developmental framework in mind that questions what groups are likely to manifest particular attitudes and why this may be so. For example, if maturational shifts in cognitive skills are thought to contribute to differences in children's attitudes, then research should compare the attitudes of age groups that developmental theory asserts should differ in these skills. Moreover, developmental measures of reasoning and thinking skills should be used in conjunction with attitude measures when age comparisons are made. In our discussion of contributing factors to ageist attitudes, we raise additional questions from a social-developmental perspective that warrant consideration in future research.

Socioeconomic Effects   Several researchers have explored relationships between children's age attitudes and their family and economic backgrounds. Not surprisingly, some research suggests that children from family backgrounds that stress the importance of intergenerational support and resources are more likely to have positive attitudes toward older adults (Slaughter-Defoe, Kuehne, and Straker 1992). However, the results of studies investigating the effects of economic background have been mixed. Some have found that children from higher-income backgrounds had more positive attitudes toward older adults (Hickey, Hickey, and Kalish 1968; Ivester and King 1977), and others have found that those from lower-income backgrounds had more positive attitudes (Dobrosky and Bishop 1986; Slaughter-Defoe, Kuehne, and Straker 1992). It has also been found that children living in urban centers had more positive attitudes than those living in rural areas, but it is unclear which group had the higher economic status (Seefeldt et al. 1977). Although it seems that social class differences may contribute to individual differences in children's attitudes, research is needed to elucidate the factors that produce these differences. Research investigating the social and psychological mechanisms underlying effects of economic differences may clarify the discrepant results that have been found.

Cultural Effects   Several researchers have considered the impact of children's racial and ethnic backgrounds on their attitudes toward older adults. Although most expected to observe differences in attitudes of children from distant regions of the world (owing to differences in modernization, traditions, kinship networks, and so on), their findings suggested that negative attitudes are universal. For example, the majority of characteristics that children aged 5 to 15 years from the United States, Canada, Australia, England, and Sweden associated with old people were negative (Goldman and Goldman 1981). Comparable negative attitudes were shown by children from the United States, Australia, Paraguay, and Thailand (Seefeldt 1984; Seefeldt and Keawkungwal 1986). In addition, Mitchell and associates (1985) failed to find significant differences in African-American and Anglo-American children's age attitudes. Although Slaughter-Defoe, Kuehne, and Straker (1992) found that African-American children had slightly more positive attitudes than Anglo-American and Anglo-Canadian children, children's attitudes from all three groups were similar and negative overall.

The few studies that have found cultural differences have done so along particular dimensions and with unanticipated patterns. Seefeldt and Ahn (1990) unexpectedly found that Korean-American children held more positive attitudes toward older adults than did Korean or Anglo American children. Moreover, Korean-American and Anglo American children perceived older adults as healthier and cleaner than did Korean children, although all children of Korean heritage viewed older adults as right, good, and friendly. Zandi, Mirle, and Jarvis (1990) also found that Anglo-American and Indian-American children's attitudes differed along particular dimensions. Anglo-American children's attitudes were more often focused on older adults' dispositions and personalities, whereas Indian-American children's attitudes more often stressed older adults' behaviors. However, these differences may reflect cultural differences in children's styles of characterizing people rather than differences in their attitudes toward older adults per se (cf. Zebrowitz 1990).

Before concluding that children's negative attitudes are culturally universal, several issues must be considered. An obvious issue concerns how attitudes have been measured. Although many studies have employed multidimensional measures, such as the one designed by Seefeldt and associates (1977), to assess children's attitudes, it is possible that they have not been sufficiently sensitive to cultural differences. It would be interesting to see if cultural differences are obtained with measures that differentiate along trait dimensions such as affect, activity, potency, and social goodness that have revealed individual variations in American children (Mitchell et al. 1985; Thomas and Yamamoto 1975). It would also be interesting to explore age attitudes with behavioral measures in addition to verbal measures.

It would also be worthwhile to explore how universality in the social roles of younger and older adults may contribute to age stereotypes, as Eagly and her colleagues (1984; 1987) suggest that universality in gender stereotypes derive from cultural similarities in the social roles of men and women. According to a social-role interpretation, older adults may be seen as less active by children from different cultures because their social roles in fact are less active, and they may be seen as more nurturing because their social roles are in fact more nurturing across cultures.

Attitudes toward Different Older Adults

Only one study has examined the impact of adults' racial background on children's age attitudes. Mitchell and associates (1985) compared African-American and Anglo-American children's attitudes toward African-American and Anglo-American older and younger adults and found significant age effects but no race effects. Children from both racial groups shared similar attitudes toward African-American and Anglo-American younger versus older adults.

Research investigating the effects of adults' gender on children's attitudes has yielded inconsistent results. Some studies report stronger negative reactions toward older women than older men. For example, Kogan, Stephens, and Shelton (1961) found that correlations between children's judgments of perceived age and the negativity of their affective judgments were stronger for female than male targets. Similarly, Isaacs and Bearison (1986) found that children selected older women more often than older men as likely to possess negative traits and act in undesirable ways. On the other hand, Mitchell and colleagues (1985) found that children viewed older women as more able to make children feel good compared to older men. Still other studies have found interaction effects in which children's ratings are more strongly tied to opposite- than same-sex older adults. Such effects have been found with respect to the accuracy of children's age judgments (Weinberger 1979), the positivity of children's trait ratings (Fillmer 1982), and the strength of relationships between children's perceptions of adults' age and attractiveness (Kortase and Trenholme 1983).

How might we account for these diverse gender-related effects? One possibility is that they reflect the use of measures that tap different aspects of children's gender-related age perceptions. It is also possible that they reflect differences in sample characteristics. For example, the children in the Mitchell et al. (1985) study were older than those in the Kogan et al. (1961) study. In addition, research may have been prone to yielding disparate effects because it was not theoretically grounded with respect to when and why gender differences might arise in children's age attitudes. Certainly, more research is needed to assess the nature and reliability of children's attitudes toward older adult men and women and the potential factors that account for them.

Summary

From an early age, children are well on the way to developing diverse and complex social perceptions of age. As our review indicates, children's age attitudes entail differentiated feelings, beliefs, and behavioral expectations about older adults, and their stereotypes differ along several dimensions. Children typically perceive older adults negatively along dimensions that reflect their activity and potency, and sometimes their affect, whereas they more often perceive older adults positively along evaluative dimensions that reflect their social goodness. Contrary to the common expectation that ageist attitudes differ cross-culturally, research suggests that children's negative attitudes toward older adults are universal. However, children's attitudes do vary with their age and social class and with older adults' gender. The question remains as to what mechanisms account for children's attitudes. In the next section, we explore various psychological processes known to contribute to social stereotypes. Although little research bears on developmental changes in these processes, it seems reasonable to suppose that changes in one or more of them contribute to the formation of children's attitudes toward older adults.

How Can We Explain Children's Attitudes toward Older Adults?

In their review of social-psychological foundations of stereotypes, Mackie and associates (1996) assert that like most other social-psychological phenomena, stereotypes are overdetermined. Specifically, they argue that

Their content and organization are influenced by the separate and combined influences of cognitive, affective, sociomotivational, and cultural factors operating in social settings. They arise from and are maintained by the way we think and the way we feel, as well as by the ways we interact and relate. A thorough analysis of the formation of stereotypes thus demands that we consider a variety of mechanisms that can instigate or contribute to their development. (p. 42)

Like these authors, we view the development of ageist attitudes as over-determined and propose that diverse factors at play in perceptual, cognitive, affective, and sociocultural processes contribute to the development of children's attitudes. Although we distinguish among the processes in terms of their primary mode of operation (perceptual, cognitive and affective, sociocultural), we have done so for the ease of presentation and do not consider these processes to be independent or mutually exclusive.

Perceptual Processes

A recurring theme in the research on children's age perceptions is that age-related physical characteristics are highly salient to children. Physical characteristics are important in enabling children to make accurate age differentiations, and they are a central component of children's attitudes toward older adults. Young children have little difficulty drawing richly detailed pictures of older adults that illustrate their aged appearance (Marcoen 1979). Even when nondirective, nonvisual methods are used to assess attitudes, physical characteristics are more frequently highlighted than other features in children's characterizations of older adults (Dobrosky and Bishop 1986). Montepare and Zebrowitz (1998) have argued that adults' age stereotypes are strongly linked to age-related variations in faces, voices, and bodies. We now consider how the distinctive physical characteristics of older adults and related perceptual processes may contribute to children's perceptions of them.

Negative Halo Effects

The lower perceived attractiveness of older adults may contribute to attitudes toward them by way of a negative halo effect, whereby those who are perceived as unattractive are also expected to possess negative traits and abilities (for reviews, see Langlois et al. 2000; Zebrowitz 1997). As noted earlier, children associate aging with decreased physical attractiveness (Downs and Walz 1981; Kogan, Stephens, and Shelton 1961; Korthase and Trenholme 1983; Weinberger 1979). Moreover, children respond more positively to attractive faces from an early age. Even young infants prefer attractive faces (Kramer et al. 1995; Langlois et al. 1987, 1991); children as young as 1 year of age show negative affective responses to unattractive adults (Langlois, Roggman, and Rieser-Dannmer 1990); and young children attribute socially undesirable personal qualities to unattractive people (Dion 1973; Langlois and Sty-czynski 1979; Langlois et al. 2000). Given that children perceive older adults to be unattractive, their negative evaluations of them may reflect a negative halo effect. However, as we have argued, stereotypes of older adults are not simply negative; they are multidimensional. Thus, an additional principle is needed to explain why older adults are often perceived negatively along some dimensions but not others.

Detection of Social Affordances   The social affordances conveyed by the physical characteristics of older adults provide another mechanism by which perceptual information may contribute to children's stereotypes. According to ecological theory (cf. McArthur and Baron 1983; Montepare and Zebrowitz 1998; Zebrowitz and Collins 1997), social perceptions serve adaptive social functions and are often accurate. Moreover, people's faces, voices, and bodies are proposed to reveal their affordances, which are the opportunities for acting, interacting, or being acted on that they provide. The concept of affordances implies that some age stereotypes may derive from the accurate perception of affordances revealed by elderly physical characteristics (e.g., wrinkled skin, balding heads, slowed movements, stooped posture, soft voices).

The hypothesis that the physical qualities that distinguish older adults accurately convey certain traits is consistent with evolutionary perspectives that suggest that age-related changes that yield an aged appearance have been selected for in the course of evolution because of their adaptive value (Forbus 1982; Jensen and Oakley 1980; Mergler and Goldstein 1983). More specifically, it has been hypothesized that appearance qualities that connote weakness and vulnerability have been selected for in older adults because they inhibit attack by other group members and thus preserve the valuable knowledge accrued by aging adults over their extended lifetime of experience (Forbus 1982; Jensen and Oakley 1980). One way a selection mechanism that favors an aged appearance might operate is by reducing the possibility of attack, increasing the likelihood of living longer, and providing greater opportunity for older- than younger-looking elders to help kin thrive, reproduce, and pass on genes that encode an aged appearance.

Similarly, Mergler and Goldstein (1983) argue that although older adults lack the capacity to reproduce, they nevertheless play an important role in species survival, and the physical qualities that differentiate them from younger adults are adaptively suited to their distinctive social roles. Specifically, they argue that older adults are a valuable resource for information about practices and customs necessary for group survival. Given the adaptive significance of the oral transmission of this knowledge, they further argue that certain qualities of older adults' vocal behavior have been favored evolutionarily because they allow for more effective communication of social knowledge. In particular, they suggest that elderly vocal qualities, especially those that are manifest when relating narrative (e.g., storytelling) as opposed to descriptive messages, are tied to stereotypic perceptions of wisdom and benevolence in older adults. Consistent with this evolutionary framework, older adults are traditionally viewed as skilled storytellers in many societies. Interestingly, children often point out that grandparents are "nice" people who talk with grandchildren and that they spend time with their grandparents "chatting together" and "laughing and laughing" (Burke 1981–1982). Thus, it may be hypothesized that age-related characteristics such as slower speech and softer, higher-pitched voices contribute to children's positive perceptions of older adults as kind, good, and friendly. The viability of this speculation is suggested by research on vocal correlates of speech stereotypes (Montepare and Zebrowitz-McArthur 1987).

Consistent with the ecological and evolutionary perspectives, Muscarella and Cunningham (1996) suggest that baldness in older adult men may signal their social maturity and give rise to perceptions of a nonthreatening form of dominance associated with wisdom and nurturance. Consistent with this hypothesis, their empirical studies have shown that decreases in the amount of men's cranial hair are associated with increases in perceptions of their age, intelligence, social status, and tenderness and decreases in perceptions of their aggressiveness. When asked to draw aging men, research has found that children use baldness as a salient feature to characterize them (Marcoen 1979), and it is possible that affordances revealed by this age cue underlie children's stereotypes of older men as less aggressive and kinder than younger men (e.g., Thomas and Yamamoto 1975). The gait of older adults also conveys information that may contribute to children's age stereotypes. Using a point-light procedure that conceals the actual age of walkers, Montepare and Zebrowitz-McArthur (1988) found that the gaits of older walkers looked less powerful than those of younger walkers, a perception that may be culturally universal (Montepare and Zebrowitz 1993). Thus, age differences in movement qualities may contribute to children's beliefs that older adults are less potent and aggressive than younger adults.

Overgeneralization Effects Although ecological theory presumes that social perceptions are typically accurate, it recognizes the possibility of error. One source of error is the overgeneralization of accurately perceived social affordances, whereby people with particular physical characteristics are perceived to have particular traits because their appearance resembles that of others who do possess those traits. Our research has examined two such overgeneralization effects: an emotion-overgeneralization effect and a babyishness-overgeneralization effect.

An emotion-overgeneralization effect occurs when people are perceived to have emotion-related traits because their physical characteristics resemble emotion cues (Montepare and Dobish 2000; Zebrowitz 1996, 1997). Consistent with this hypothesis, research has found that adults perceive older adults' faces to be sadder than those of younger adults, even when they were not displaying sad expressions, presumably because certain facial characteristics (such as wrinkled skin and drooping eyes) resemble cues associated with sad expressions (Malatesta, Fiore, and Messina 1987; Malatesta et al. 1987). Children may respond to the faces of older adults in a similar way. That is, because older faces resemble sad faces, children may perceive older adults who are not experiencing any negative emotion to be sad, lonesome, and depressed. Consistent with this notion, Goldman and Goldman (1981) quote a child in their research as remarking, "My grandparents are only a little old, but they look angry on their faces all the time" (p. 408). Interestingly, researchers who have used facial stimuli in their research with children have been very careful to construct faces with neutral expressions (Seefeldt et al. 1977). However, because some elderly facial characteristics may resemble sad expression cues, children's perceptions of the older adults depicted in these stimuli may be the result of an emotion-overgeneralization effect. One way researchers can explore and, if necessary, correct for this possibility is to use faces of both older and younger adults with smiling expressions.

The impact of an emotion-overgeneralization effect may reach beyond facial appearance to bodily appearance and movement. For example, Hummert (1994) has suggested that characteristics such as a stooped posture may contribute to perceptions of older adults as sad and sullen. Similarly, in their study examining the relationship between age-related movement cues and stereotypic expectations of aging adults, Montepare and Zebrowitz-McArthur (1988) found that the gaits of older adults made them appear to adult perceivers as unhappier than those with more youthful gaits. Moreover, several of the movement qualities that characterize an elderly gait are similar to those associated with the walking patterns of people experiencing sadness and dejection (Montepare, Goldstein, and Clausen 1987). Several researchers have noted that children's images of older adults include their bodily appearance and movement (Hickey, Kalish, and Kalish 1968; Marcoen 1979). For example, Hickey, Kalish, and Kalish (1968) found that one of the most frequently mentioned physical dimensions children used to differentiate older and younger adults was ambulatory differences. The extent to which children's perceptions of older adults' traits reflect their reactions to elderly bodily characteristics is an interesting topic for future research.

A babyish-overgeneralization effect occurs when accurate perceptions of babies are overgeneralized to adults whose appearance in some way resembles that of babies. Considerable research has found that adults with babyish faces are perceived to be weaker, gentler, more vulnerable, and less threatening than mature-faced peers. This effect has been well documented in children and adults (Zebrowitz 1997; Montepare and Zebrowitz 1998). It has also been suggested that some changes that occur in faces as they age may cause the elderly face to appear more infantile (Enlow 1982; Muscarella and Cunningham 1996). In particular, age-related losses of bone and connective tissue yield a less angular jaw, a double chin, and jowls in the elderly face, all of which are also found in the faces of babies. Thus, the resemblance of an elderly appearance to a babyish appearance may contribute to children's stereotypic perceptions of older adults as less powerful, less aggressive, and more approachable than younger adults. Our own research suggests that this speculation is partially correct. We found that older adults with babyish faces were perceived as less powerful and warmer than those with mature faces, and these effects were independent of the perceived age and attractiveness of the faces (Zebrowitz and Montepare 1992). However, the faces of older adults were judged to be less, rather than more, babyish than those of younger adults, children, and infants, likely reflecting an older perceived age derived from other age-related facial information. Thus, within-age-group variations in babyfaceness may account for stereotypes of particular older adults rather than older adults in general. Nevertheless, it would be interesting for future research to manipulate the babyishness and maturity of older adults' faces to see if children's typical age stereotypes are more pronounced when judging babyfaced older adults.

Cognitive and Affective Mechanisms

It is certain that stereotyped people like older adults can be differentiated by their appearance and that aspects of stereotyped people's appearance contribute not only to social perceivers' affective reactions toward them but also to the traits and abilities they expect people to possess (cf. Zebrowitz 1996). Moreover, the impact of appearance cues may be particularly evident in the early stages of development, because children's social judgments are highly dependent on overt stimulus information like appearances (Hoffner and Cantor 1985). Although perceptual processes may seed the early development of children's age perceptions, other processes are surely at work in shaping and perpetuating them. In the following sections, we consider how several affective and cognitive mechanisms known to influence social judgments in adults may contribute to the development of children's stereotypes of older adults. In particular, we explore the impact of categorization effects, illusory correlations, implicit theories, and personal motives.

Categorization Effects   Considerable social-psychological research has demonstrated that we are predisposed to categorizing people into groups. Moreover, despite its cognitive processing advantages, categorization produces effects that foster the acquisition of stereotypes (Mackie et al. 1996; Taylor, Peplau, and Sears, 2000). One effect of categorization is that people who are placed in the same group are perceived as more similar to each other (within-group assimilation) and as more different from those in another group than they would be had categorization not occurred (between-group contrast). From an early age, children readily categorize people into age groups. Moreover, given limitations in their information-processing capacities and their dependence on perceptual cues, very young children may be especially prone to the outcomes of categorization (Berger, 2000; Hoffner and Cantor 1985). Specifically, assimilation and contrast effects may play a key role in the biased and undifferentiated views of older adults that have been found in young children. Although such categorization effects can account for children's tendency to perceive older adults in a stereotypic manner, other mechanisms (such as the perceptual ones described above or the sociocultural ones discussed below) are needed to account for the particular traits children associate with older adults. Research is needed to examine in more detail the extent to which assimilation and contrast effects contribute to children's stereotypes of older adults. Research is also needed to examine the developmental trajectories of these effects since, with increasing age, children differentiate more strongly between younger and older adults (Burke 1981–1982; Hickey and Kalish 1968).

A second consequence of categorization is that it may affect the processing of new information about people and contribute to the perpetuation of stereotypes. For instance, adults tend to process information selectively about stereotyped groups, such that information consistent with the stereotype is given greater attention and remembered better than inconsistent information (Howard and Rothbart 1980). In this way, stereotypes are strengthened as a result of underlying cognitive processes. Research with children finds evidence for similar effects. Davidson, Cameron, and Jergovic (1995) asked elementary school children to recall positive and negative information about adults labeled as elderly or not labeled at all. Consistent with research with adults, children who expressed generally negative age attitudes recalled more negative statements about the older adults when they were labeled as elderly than when they were not labeled. Moreover, the elderly label led to negative distortions in children's recall of positive information. These results suggest that underlying cognitive processes can reinforce children's stereotypes of older adults by influencing the organization and recall of age-related information. It is of interest to note that sometimes information inconsistent with a stereotype is better recalled and processed than consistent information, and this may be especially true when individuals have either very poorly developed stereotypes or very well-developed ones (Taylor, Peplau, and Sears 2000). Thus, the results found by Davidson, Cameron, and Jergovic (1995) may not hold true for younger or older children whose stereotypes of older adults may differ in strength. Developmental research is needed to examine this issue.

A third consequence of categorization is that individuals are more likely to evaluate people based on stereotypic information about the category to which they belong than on information about their unique individual attributes. Moreover, models of impression formation view such category-based processing as more commonplace than attribute-based processing (Brewer 1988; Fiske and Neuberg 1989). Although to our knowledge no research has examined the use of these processing modes in children, several hypotheses may be offered regarding how they may influence children's evaluations of older adults. Maturational limitations in children's logical reasoning skills may cause them to attend to salient social category cues and to reason in concrete and rigid terms about people rather than in more flexible and individuated terms (Perry and Bussey 1984). As a result, younger children may be more inclined toward category-based processing, which in turn might yield more polarized attitudes about stereotyped people such as older adults. Consistent with this argument, Hoffner and Cantor (1985) found that although children between the ages of 3 and 9 years maintained systematic appearance stereotypes, older children's evaluations of a videotaped female protagonist relied less on her appearance and more on her actual behavior than did evaluations of younger children. In addition, and consistent with developmental research on person perception in childhood (Perry and Bussey 1984; Livesley and Bromley 1973), young children's descriptions of older adults often focus more on stereotypic appearance markers and overt behaviors than on older adults' underlying personalities and motivations (Dobrosky and Bishop 1986; Seefeldt et al. 1977). Moreover, our analysis of age effects indicates that younger children's attitudes are more negative than those of older children. Research examining age effects with attribution tasks that assess children's reliance on stereotypic information versus individuating characteristics when evaluating older adults would provide useful information about developmental changes in category-based processing.

Research on category- versus attribute-based processing has shown that adults' impressions are more likely to reflect people's individuating characteristics when they are motivated to attend to such information, as when their future behavior is dependent on others (Fiske and Neuberg 1989). Extending these findings to children, one may speculate that younger children may show more category-based processing and stereotyped judgments due to a poorer understanding of how their behavior depends on others and consequently lesser motivation to attend to individuating attributes. Research with adults also has shown that regardless of motivation, impressions are less likely to reflect individuating characteristics when the people are unable to inhibit salient category information. For example, von Hippel, Silver, and Lynch (2000) found that older adults who manifested age-related deficits in the ability to inhibit information relied more on stereotypes in arriving at social judgments than did younger adults with greater cognitive control. Extending these findings to children, one may speculate that younger children may show more category-based processing than older children due to greater limitations in their ability to screen information effectively. The viability of our speculations gains some support from the findings of Feldman and Ruble (1981), who examined the impact of social goals on impression formation in younger and older children. When children expected to interact with unfamiliar peers to play games, they were more likely to evaluate their potential partners in more complex and differentiated ways. However, younger children's impressions of their peers were less individuated and based more on external attributes like appearance than were those of older children. The extent to which our speculations hold true in the context of age-related impressions awaits more direct empirical testing.

However, the age-related changes that we predict are consistent with the age effects we discussed, suggesting that younger children have more biased and less elaborated attitudes than older children.

Illusory Correlation Effects   Ample research has demonstrated that perceptions of the correlation between particular people and particular behaviors are most influenced by those actor-behavior pairs that draw the most attention (Hamilton and Gifford 1976). One factor that can determine which pairs are most salient is novelty. People who are infrequent and behaviors that are infrequent draw the most attention and are seen as more strongly linked that they actually are. Because older adults are typically less frequent in the social worlds of children, they may form an illusory correlation between old age and whatever behaviors are infrequent. Because negative behaviors are typically less frequent than positive ones, illusory correlation can lead to negative attitudes toward older adults. However, it should be noted that an illusory correlation effect depends on factors that influence the salience of the behaviors apart from their relative frequency of occurrence. The illusory correlation between infrequent people and behaviors does not occur when it is the frequent behaviors that are more salient to perceivers because they are already associated with the target group, be it age, race, or sex (Zebrowitz-McArthur and Friedman 1980). Thus, illusory correlation effects due to the novelty of older adults and particular behaviors can contribute to the formation of age stereotypes, while illusory correlation effects due to pre-existing associative links between older adults and behaviors can contribute to the maintenance of those stereotypes.

Implicit Theories   The notion that people maintain naive theories about social thought and behavior is no stranger to social psychologists. Indeed, early theories of impression formation rested on assumptions about people's lay or implicit theories (Heider 1958). More recently, Dweck and her colleagues (Dweck, Chiu, and Hong 1995; Chiu, Hong, and Dweck 1997; Levy, Stroessner, and Dweck 1998; Levy and Dweck 1999) have examined the extent to which people's implicit theories about the nature of personal attributes influence the formation and endorsement of stereotypes. In general, this research has revealed that although people may share knowledge about social stereotypes, those who believe that human traits are fixed, as opposed to malleable, are more likely to endorse stereotypes and use them when evaluating others.

Consistent with research with adults, Levy and Dweck (1999) found that children who view personal attributes as fixed entities that cannot be changed were more likely to make more stereotypic and extreme attributions about people compared to those with more malleable and open-ended views. These findings have several implications for our understanding of children's age perceptions. More specifically, children's stereotypic views of older adults may derive from their view of aging as a fixed process over which people have no control (Goldman and Goldman 1981). To the extent that children's developing knowledge about the aging process incorporates information about the plasticity of aging (through maturational or experiential means), their perceptions of older adults may become more flexible with age. On the other hand, if children develop greater concerns about their own aging and mortality with age, then it is possible that these personal views will induce stronger age stereotypes, a possibility explored in the next section.

Personal Motives Although current social-psychological models of stereotypes generally cast them in cognitive terms, many acknowledge their strong affective ties to personal motives and self-relevant mechanisms. Thus, our discussion of ageism would not be complete without some attention to the role of self-related factors.

One contributing factor to ageist attitudes that has emerged in prior discussions is gerontophobia, or the fear of and devaluation of older adults because they remind people of their vulnerability and mortality (Nelson 2002; Ward 1984). This view is not unlike the rationale for age stereotyping provided by terror management theory, which suggests that people such as older adults are stereotyped and stigmatized because they exacerbate the existential anxiety caused by the fear of death and a meaningless existence (Solomon, Greenberg, and Pyszczynski 1991; Zebrowitz and Montepare 2000). Consistent with these propositions, Collette-Pratt (1976) found that negative attitudes toward death were a significant predictor of the devaluation of old age and older adults among young and middle-aged adults. Relatedly, Snyder and Miene's (1994) functional approach to stereotyping suggests that ageist attitudes serve an ego-protective function for some individuals by providing a way in which they can disassociate themselves from aging adults and the self-threatening prospects of aging.

The foregoing forces also may operate in children. Kastenbaum and Durkee (1964) found that apprehensions about personal aging are salient to adolescents, who are disinclined to think about themselves at later life stages that they expect promise little reward and satisfaction. Even younger children hold systematic beliefs about the aging of others and visions of their own aging. For example, Burke (1981–1982) found that children differentiate between "growing just old enough to acquire the privileges of skills of an older child" (p. 214) and becoming elderly. Marks, Newman, and Onawola (1985) found that when asked, "What do you think happens when you get to be an old person" (p. 93), children's positive responses reflected the advantages of becoming mature, like a young adult such as "able to do more things" or "able to drive." Negative responses reflected the disadvantages of becoming elderly, like an older adult such as, "You are sad and want to be a teenager again and have friends," "Your life goes to waste," "Nobody cares," and "You don't have much fun." Similar negative concerns about unattractiveness, physical afflictions, and unhealthiness, coupled with an aversion for personally growing old, have been noted by other researchers when children are asked to describe what they expect to be like when they are old (Seefeldt et al. 1977). A common fear that children have about growing old is dying (Burke 1981–1982; Doka 1985–1986; Seefeldt et al. 1977). Indeed, when one of us casually asked her 7-year-old son what things he feared, rather than reporting fantastic things like "monsters under the bed" as she expected him to do, he thoughtfully remarked, "Death and sex."[1]

Taken together, the findings indicate that by 4 years of age, children have begun to develop distinct perceptions of their own aging, which includes a desire to mature into an adult and a disinclination toward becoming elderly because of the fears and stigma attached to growing old. Thus, negative attitudes toward older adults seen in children may be motivated by self-serving motives. As we have discussed elsewhere, social and developmental psychologists have much to learn about the role of self-serving motives in age stereotyping and stigmatization (see Zebrowitz and Montepare 2000 for more detailed comments). Moreover, understanding how these motives contribute to the devaluation of older adults poses a particularly challenging task given that we must account for the paradox that many individuals who live long enough will become members of a group that they have stigmatized from an early age (also see Snyder and Miene 1994 for related comments).

Sociocultural Mechanisms

Social learning is often considered one of the strongest determinants of stereotyping and prejudice against stigmatized groups such as the elderly

(Taylor, Peplau, and Sears 2000). Indeed, when Newman, Faux, and Larimer (1997) asked children the source of their knowledge about old people, 62 percent of children reported that they learned about them from grandparents, 22 percent said parents, and 8 percent said television, movies, books, and friends. Empirical research has focused on these sources of knowledge by examining effects of intergenerational contacts, educational instruction, and exposure to media images on children's attitudes toward elderly adults.

Intergenerational Contact   Many theorists have argued that children's negative age attitudes reflect their limited contact and unfamiliarity with older adults. Indeed, a wealth of research has shown that simply increasing exposure to a stimulus, like a person, can have a positive impact on liking (cf. Bornstein 1989; Zajonc 1968). Moreover, research has shown that children have limited involvement with older adults and that their perceptions of familiar older adults, like grandparents, are more positive and less stereotyped than their perceptions of unfamiliar older adults, although processes other than mere exposure are likely operating (Burke 1981–1982; Marcoen 1979; Newman, Faux, and Larimer 1997).[2]

Expanding children's experience with older adults has been hypothesized as one way to improve their negative attitudes. A number of studies have tested the contact hypothesis with mixed results. Several studies using parental reports have shown little relationship between children's contact with older adults and either their ability to identify age accurately (Burke 1981–1982; Page et al. 1981) or their attitudes toward older adults (Harris and Fiedler 1988; Ivester and King 1977; Nishi-Strattner and Myers 1983). On the other hand, Sheehan (1978) found a positive relationship between reported contact and age identification ability, and Rosenwasser and associates (1986) found a negative relationship between reported contact and positive attitudes toward older adults. One likely reason for the significant effects observed in the latter studies is that they used more detailed measures of contact that involved the quality and quantity of contact.

Studies that have manipulated actual contact with older adults show stronger effects than those that have simply ascertained self-reported contact (Caspi 1984; Chapman and Neal 1990; Newman, Faux, and Larimer 1997). Not surprisingly, however, the effects of contact on children's attitudes are greatly influenced by the nature of that contact. Young children's attitudes toward older adults became more negative after weekly visits to infirm older adults in a nursing home (Seefeldt 1987), whereas their attitudes became more positive after interacting with older adults in a classroom setting (Caspi, 1984; Newman, Faux, and Larimer 1997) or working for them in their homes (Chapman and Neal, 1990).

Some theorists have argued that children's negative attitudes are the result of limited knowledge and misperceptions of aging adults and the aging process (Palmore 1990). If negative attitudes derive from inadequate knowledge, then one would expect educational instruction to have an ameliorating effect. The available research indicates that instruction does promote more positive attitudes toward older adults in children (Blunk and Williams 1977; Labouvie-Vief and Baltes 1976), particularly if it is combined with intergenerational contact (Dellman-Jenkins et al. 1986; Glass and Trent 1980; Rich, Myrick, and Campell 1983; Seefeldt et al. 1980–81). Moreover, such interventions appear to produce short- and long-term change. Labouvie-Veif and Baltes (1976) found that changed attitudes persisted after a two-week period, and Glass and Trent (1980) found changed attitudes evident over four to six months.

Not all researchers have found interventions that make use of instruction and contact to have a positive impact on children's attitudes. In particular, Doka (1985–1986) failed to find significant changes in adolescents' attitudes toward older adults after participating in an oral history program. Doka argued that his findings may have reflected participants' attributions about the uniqueness of the older adults with whom they interacted, suggesting the need for researchers to examine the psychological mechanisms by which intervention affects attitude change (whether or not it occurs).

The Influence of Television   Even if contact with older adults and education about aging can provide a positive influence on children's age attitudes, many theorists point out that children are nevertheless exposed to negative images from cultural sources that may offset or counteract the beneficial consequences of contact and instruction. Children may be especially vulnerable to the negative consequences of the media, particularly television images, since the average American child watches between 1.5 and 3.5 hours of television daily (Luecke-Aleska et al. 1995).

Research on depictions of older adults on television suggests that both the quantity and quality of images are important to consider in evaluating the potential contribution of this social influence. In general, television has idealized vigor, attractiveness, and competence, and it has portrayed being "too old" as undesirable (Northcott 1975). In line with the television ideal, considerable research attests to its underrepresentation of the elderly (Kubey 1980; Robinson 1989). For example, Northcott (1975) found that older adults appeared in 1.5 percent of all television portrayals, and mostly in minor roles. Moreover, the underrepresentation of older adults was particularly true in programs most available to children. For instance, Kovaric (1993) reports that older adults are underrepresented in most television programs by a substantial amount in relation to their frequency in the population with the exception of daytime soap operas, which children have little opportunity or inclination to watch.

Not only are older adults relatively invisible to viewers, but also they are often portrayed in a negative light when they are encountered (Harris and Feinberg 1977; Kubey 1980; Palmore 1990). Kubey (1980), for instance, notes that older adults are more likely than other adults to be portrayed in comical roles that highlight stereotypes of their physical, cognitive, and sexual impotence. Depictions of older adults on Saturday morning cartoons aimed at children show similar trends. Bishop and Krause (1984) found that aging was not a dominant theme in cartoon programming, and when it did arise, it frequently encompassed negative, incidental images of older adults who were unattractive and unhealthy.

Before drawing conclusions about the impact of television on children's age attitudes, several points should be kept in mind. First, the bulk of studies examining the representation and images of older adults on television was conducted in the 1970s and 1980s and may not reflect current trends. Second is the issue of what image of older adults and aging should be portrayed on television. Kovaric (1993) advises that even positive images can bias children's attitudes. That is, it may be equally damaging to the development of realistic age attitudes to suggest to children that the elderly are thriving, healthy, and wise as to suggest that they are passive, feeble, and slow-minded. Third, while many claim that television's limited and negative representation of older adults clearly conveys a message of their marginalization to the viewing audience, no research we know of has empirically tested the link between children's television viewing habits and either their attitudes toward older adults or their knowledge about aging.[3] However, research showing links between television viewing and children's sex-role stereotyping makes it reasonable to suggest that television also affects their age attitudes. For example, McArthur and Eisen (1976a) found that sex-stereotypical versus counterstereotypical behavior by TV models influenced children's recall, attitudes, and behavior. Children exposed to stereotypical behaviors by a male and female model recalled, displayed, and preferred relatively more stereotypical than counterstereotypical behaviors, while the reverse was true for those exposed to male and female models showing counterstereotypical behaviors.

The Influence of Children's Literature   Another source of social learning is images presented in children's books. Literature written for young children may be a particularly potent source of influence because it is typically presented by adult role models, such as parents, during close, interpersonal encounters, such as bedtime. In contrast to the negative images typically seen on television, research indicates that depictions of older adults in children's literature are more varied and likely reflect the type or status of particular books. For example, an analysis of children's books between 1870 and 1960 from the well-known E. W. King Collection of Miami University found little evidence that images of older adults were markedly negative in comparison to images of younger adults (Seltzer and Atchley 1971). It also revealed little evidence for changes in these images over time. Similarly, a more recent analysis of award-winning children's picture books published between 1972 and 1995 found that although only 12 percent of the books depicted old characters, they were described in generally positive terms (Dellmann-Jenkins and Yang 1997).

On the other hand, using a sample of books that included non–award-winning books, Hurst (1981) found a distorted and negative image of older adults in his analysis of children's books between 1958 and 1978. More specifically, although he found that older adults were slightly over-represented as characters in comparison to other adults, they more typically were depicted as sad, lonely, and in limited roles. Similarly, Ansello's (1978) analysis of juvenile and early-reader books also found that older individuals were most often depicted in relatively routine and mundane roles.

Like research on television images, research on children's literature has not directly tested the link between exposure to particular books and children's age attitudes. Thus, important questions remain unanswered. In particular, research needs to establish whether a relationship exists between children's reading habits and their attitudes toward older adults and knowledge of aging. Research showing links between children's literature and sex-role stereotyping suggests that books might also affect children's age attitudes. For example, McArthur and Eisen (1976b) found that children who heard a story in which a boy and a girl exhibited sex-stereotypical behavior subsequently showed sex-stereotyped behavior themselves, whereas they showed counterstereotypical behavior after hearing a story in which a boy and a girl had done so. If books are sufficiently potent to influence the behavioral component of children's sex stereotypes, it seems likely that they can also influence the affective and cognitive components of children's age stereotypes.

Methodological Issues

The assessment of attitudes toward older adults has been a focal concern in the gerontology literature since Tuckman and Lorge (1953) conducted their pioneering research on ageism a half-century ago. Because periodic reviews of this research had failed to draw consistent conclusions about the negativity of these attitudes (Brubaker and Powers 1976; Crockett and Hummert 1987; Green 1981; Lutsky 1980; McTavish 1971; Pasupathi, Carstensen, and Tsai 1995), Kite and Johnson (1988) subjected published research on age attitudes to meta-analytic scrutiny. They sought not only to determine quantitatively whether attitudes toward older adults were more negative than attitudes toward younger adults, but also to identify methodological factors that moderate observed differences in attitudes. They found evidence of more negative attitudes toward older adults and an impact of several methodological factors. We conducted our own exploratory analysis of the research summarized in table 4.1 and found evidence for similar methodological influences on children's attitudes. To this end, we coded the studies according to whether they used a between- or within-subjects design, a uni- or multidimensional dependent measure, visual or verbal descriptions of older adults, the year of publication, and the overall valence of their outcome (1 = more negative attitudes toward older adults, 2 = mixed attitudes, and 3 = more positive attitudes toward older adults). We then correlated outcome valence with design, dependent measure, stimuli, and publication year. The results of our analysis appear in table 4.2.

Kogan (1979) argued that measurement techniques that require individuals to make comparative judgments of older adults relative to younger adults evoke stronger age stereotypes than those in which individuals make isolated judgements of only older adults. Wingard, Heath, and Himelstein (1992) substantiated this claim experimentally, and Kite and Johnson (1988) found the effect to be robust across studies. Our analysis revealed the same effect in research with children. Studies in which children were asked to compare older adults to younger adults (Kogan, Stephens, and Shelton 1961; Miller et al. 1984; Seefeldt et al. 1977) yielded more negative attitudes than those in which only older adults were evaluated (Ivester and King 1977; Nishi-Strattner and Meyers 1983); $r(21) = .51, p < .01$.

Table 4.2

Relationship between Children's Age Stereotypes and Characteristics of Research Studies

	Outcome Valence
Study design (between versus within subjects)	.51**
Dependent measure (uni- versus multi-dimensional)	.29+
Stimuli (visual versus verbal)	.40*
Year of publication	.04

Note: Outcome valence was coded as 1 = negative, 2 = mixed, and 3 = positive. $+ p < .12$, $* p < .05$; $** p < .01$, one-tailed tests.

Echoing a concern voiced by Kogan (1979), Dobrosky and Bishop (1986) called attention to the possibility that the measures often used in research with children may favor the expression of more negative than positive attitudes. Indeed, the two studies that made clear attempts to balance the number of negative and positive items in their measures found children's attitudes to be relatively more positive than those reported elsewhere (Burke 1981–1982; Nishi-Strattner and Meyers 1983). Using more items may also produce more balance. Indeed, Kite and Johnson (1988) found that negative age stereotypes were less pronounced in studies that included a larger number of items in their attitude measures. Similarly, our analysis indicated a tendency for studies employing multidimensional measures to show more positive attitudes than those using unidimensional measures, $r(21) = .29$, $p < .12$.

Advocating the use of more nondirective methods, Dobrosky and Bishop (1986) also pointed out that many measures use potentially leading procedures that force children into thinking and responding in stereotypic and prejudicial ways. For example, while some researchers use visual stimuli that emphasize physical qualities to elicit children's attitudes (Kogan, Stephens, and Shelton 1961), others prompt children's responses by providing them with verbal labels such as "an old person like a grandparent" (Hickey, Hickey, and Kalish 1968). Different measures draw attention to different characteristics of older adults and yield responses that differ in their tone and valence. Consistent with this argument, our analysis showed that studies that used visual stimuli were more likely to find negative attitudes than those that used verbal labels, $r(21) = .40$, $p < .05$.

Weinberger and Millham (1975) experimentally demonstrated that adults' attitudes toward a personalized 70-year-old adult were more favorable than attitudes toward a general 70-year-old adult. Kite and Johnson (1988) demonstrated the robustness of this effect across studies with adults. Although we were unable to explore this effect statistically given the small number of studies that used personalized older targets, an inspection of those that did so suggests that a relationship exists between the positivity of children's attitudes and the description of the aging target. More positive attitudes emerged in the few studies in which children were asked to evaluate a specific older adult like a grandparent as opposed to a nonspecific older person like an 80-year-old man (Hickey, Hickey, and Kalish 1968; Marcoen 1979).

Kite and Johnson (1988) hypothesized that because of the rising numbers of older adults in the population, people are more informed about aging and the issues aging adults face, with a consequent change in people's overall age attitudes. Supporting this hypothesis, they found that differences between evaluations of older and younger adults grew significantly smaller the more recently a study was published. Our analysis, however, showed no relationship between children's attitudes and the year of publication, $r(21) = .04, p > .05$.

Where Do We Go from Here?

Our review reveals that the tendency to differentiate people based on their age begins in early infancy and that both negative feelings toward older adults and varied stereotypes emerge by the early preschool years. There is also evidence for developmental changes in children's attitudes toward older adults. Although more research is needed to clarify the nature and direction of these changes, it appears that with age, children's attitudes become less negative, more differentiated, and more elaborate. A number of factors may explain children's attitudes toward older adults, including perceptual, cognitive, affective, and sociocultural mechanisms. Developmental changes in attitudes may derive from developmental changes in one or more of these factors. However, little research bears on this possibility. Here we suggest research that is needed to further our understanding of the role of each of these contributing factors in the development of ageism.

The sensitivity of infants to age-related perceptual cues suggests that a biological preparedness may serve as a foundation for attitudes toward older adults. However, although infants discriminate among people on the basis of age-related size, face, and voice cues, additional research is needed to establish whether these cues also enable them to discriminate older from younger adults. Another question is whether infants show a preference for younger or older adults. This question can be addressed using visual preference paradigms and experimental paradigms like those used to document early preferences for more attractive faces (e.g., Langlois et al. 1991). An early aversion to older adults would suggest that the negative feelings documented in older children and adults might have a biological basis.

Still another question is whether infants attach different meanings to younger and older adults. This question can be addressed using classical conditioning paradigms (e.g., Balaban 1995) and cross-modal matching paradigms (e.g., Gibson and Walker 1984; Spelke 1981). Both can reveal what kinds of events are more readily associated with older faces or voices than younger ones. The latter can reveal not only the valence of events that are associated with younger versus older stimuli but also the nature of those events—the particular affordances perceived in people of different ages. For example, the finding that infants look longer at facial expressions when they are accompanied by a matching affective vocal expression (e.g., Walker 1982) could be extrapolated to an experiment designed to determine whether infants look longer at older or younger faces when they are accompanied by happy or angry or sad vocal expressions. Such research may reveal that the specific stereotypes held by older children and adults also may have a biological basis.

The contribution of perceptual mechanisms to ageism can be elucidated not only by investigating infants' responses to the perceptual qualities of older adults, but also by examining children's attitudes when such qualities are manipulated. For example, are negative feelings more pronounced the greater the number of wrinkles on an older person's face or the more aged the person's vocal qualities? Do stereotypes of weakness and kindness covary with particular facial or vocal qualities? According to ecological theory, not only do perceptual stimuli convey particular affordances, but also the detection of those affordances depends on the perceivers' perceptual experiences (McArthur and Baron 1983). Variations in perceptual experiences could account for differences that have been observed in children's reactions to familiar versus unfamiliar older adults or in the reactions of children of different ages. For example, negative reactions to the faces of particular older adults may diminish if children learn that age-related wrinkles do not predict anger and drooping eyes do not predict sadness and loneliness.

Even if perceptual qualities exert a strong effect on children's attitudes toward older adults, other mechanisms also have a significant influence.

Moreover, developmental changes in these mechanisms may explain developmental changes in attitudes. The role of cognitive processes can be seen in the maturational effects documented in research investigating the development of children's understanding of age (Galper et al. 1980–1981). However, many questions remain about the potential impact of cognitive maturation on children's attitudes toward older adults. For example, can children's attitudes be predicted from their performance on developmental tests of seriation ability? Can they be predicted from performance on developmental tests that measure the ability to decenter and focus on multiple sources of information, since such decentering would work against the category-based processing that leads to stereotyped judgments? Can they be predicted from performance on developmental tests that measure decreases in egocentrism and increases in the ability to take another's perspective, since such perspective taking may increase the likelihood of attribute-based processing? Can they be predicted from the extent to which personal attributes are viewed as fixed versus malleable? Research designed to investigate links between attitudes toward older adults and the development of specific cognitive abilities and styles may help to explain age effects in children's attitudes.

Affective mechanisms also influence attitudes toward older adults, and we have suggested that children's negative attitudes toward older adults may derive in part from their anxieties about sickness and death. However, this hypothesis needs to be tested. Given that children's anxieties about death show developmental changes (Feldman, 2000), this mechanism may contribute to age-related changes in attitudes toward older adults. It would also be instructive to assess the extent to which relationships between fears of death and ageist attitudes are mediated by children's conceptual understanding of the aging process.

Sociocultural influences are suggested by research on intergenerational contact, educational instruction, and media exposure. As found in other domains, contact with older adults may promote more positive or more negative attitudes, depending on the quality of that contact (Caspi 1984; Seefeldt 1987). Additional research is needed to establish the type of contact that is most successful in promoting positive attitudes. Such research may shed light on age differences in children's attitudes toward older adults insofar as it reveals age-related changes in the type of contact children are likely to have (see Higgins and Parsons 1983 for a more detailed discussion of relationships between changes in children's social lives and their social perceptions). Because instruction about aging has been found to promote more positive attitudes, it may play a role in age-related decreases in the negativity of children's attitudes toward older adults, insofar as older children are more likely to have received some explicit instruction and be more able to comprehend educational materials. Although research on television and children's books has documented how older adults are portrayed, additional research is needed to determine what, if any, effect exposure to these media has on children's attitudes. It would also be instructive to determine whether there is a differential impact of exposure to particular media sources on children's attitudes. For example, the fact that books portray older adults more positively than television does may contribute to more positive attitudes among older children who are likely to have more exposure to literature.

Conclusion

Social psychologists interested in understanding attitudes toward older adults (or other stigmatized groups) have typically studied them as they appear full-blown in young adults. We maintain that focusing attention on the development of ageist attitudes will help us not only to understand better the factors that contribute to children's attitudes but also those that contribute to adults' attitudes. As we have noted, adults' attitudes are overdetermined by perceptual, cognitive, affective, and sociocultural mechanisms (Mackie et al. 1996). Discovering which mechanisms are most significant in determining ageist attitudes is important not only for its theoretical value, but also for its applied value, because the most effective ways of changing attitudes depend strongly on the basis of those attitudes (Snyder and Miene 1994). Examining developmental changes in attitudes provides us an opportunity to disentangle these mechanisms and identify their independent impact. If very young infants show negative reactions to older adults, this can only be due to perceptual mechanisms, a contributing factor that is difficult to isolate in research with adults. If developmental studies show that changes in cognitive maturation yield changes in attitudes that are unlikely to involve historical changes in sociocultural influences, this would provide evidence for the independent contribution of cognitive mechanisms. Similarly, if developmental studies show that variations in death anxiety reliably predict differences in attitudes when cognitive abilities are held constant, this would provide evidence for the independent contribution of affective mechanisms. Finally, whereas studies of the effects of media exposure among adults run up against a ceiling effect, there is likely to be more variation in children's exposure, permitting better experimental and naturalistic investigations of its effects on attitudes toward older adults. Having determined what mechanisms contribute to attitudes toward older adults and when they do so developmentally, those who wish to ameliorate ageism will be in a better position to design effective interventions.

Notes

1. In their study of the effectiveness of an educational curriculum on elementary school children's age attitudes, Seefeldt and associates, (1981) found that their intervention successfully altered children's attitudes toward older adults but had little impact on their negative attitudes toward their own aging. The resistance of these personal attitudes to change suggests that subjective age perceptions may be a core dimension along which the self is organized. It is also possible that coming to terms with one's aging requires a level of reasoning and reflection not attained until an older age. Research examining the nature of these personal attitudes in more detail would be worthwhile.

2. Although familiarity has been strongly implicated in children's attitudes toward older adults, its impact has not been directly tested. To assert that familiarity yields positive attitudes, research needs to compare children's attitudes toward familiar and unfamiliar older adults with their attitudes toward familiar and unfamiliar younger adults. If familiarity mediates positive attitudes, then attitudes toward familiar older adults should be equally as positive as attitudes toward familiar younger adults. If age difference persists when familiarity is equated, then other factors must be at work.

3. Passuth and Cook (1985) examined the relationship of the amount of television viewing, attitudes toward older adults, and knowledge about aging using data from a 1974 survey of a nationally representative sample of adults between the ages of 18 and 99. Consistent with the often-cited observations of Gerbner and associates (1980), heavy viewing was correlated with stronger stereotypes and lesser knowledge. However, this was true only for young adults under the age of 30. The determinants of these effects, as well as whether they hold true using experimental paradigms and extend to children, are issues that await further empirical scrutiny.

References

Ansello, E. F. (1978). Ageism—The subtle stereotype. *Childhood Education, 54,* 118–123.

Balaban, M. T. (1995). Affective influences on startle in five-month-old infants. Reactions to facial expressions of emotion. *Child Development, 58,* 889–909.

Berger, K. S. (2000). *The developing person through the life span.* New York: Worth Publishers.

Bigelow, A., MacLean, J., Wood, C., and Smith, J. (1990). Infants' responses to child and adult strangers: An investigation of height and facial configuration variables. *Infant Behavior and Development, 13,* 21–32.

Bishop, J. M., and Krause, D. R. (1984). Depictions of aging and old age on Saturday morning television. *Gerontologist, 24,* 91–94.

Blunk, E. M., and Williams, S. E. (1997). The effects of curriculum on preschool children's perceptions of the elderly. *Educational Gerontology, 29,* 233–241.

Bornstein, R. F. (1989). Exposure and affect: Overview and meta-analysis of research, 1968–1987. *Psychological Bulletin, 106,* 265–289.

Brewer, M. (1988). A dual processing model of impression formation. In T. K. Srull and R. S. Wyer (Eds.), *Advances in social cognition* (pp. 1–36). Hillsdale, NJ: Erlbaum.

Britton, J. O., and Britton, J. H. (1969). Discrimination of age by preschool children. *Journal of Gerontology, 24,* 457–460.

Brooks, J., and Lewis, M. (1976). Infants' responses to strangers: Midget, adult, and child. *Child Development, 45,* 323–332.

Brown, C. (1979). Reactions of infants to their parents' voices. *Infant Behavior and Development, 2,* 295–300.

Brubaker, T. H., and Powers, E. A. (1976). The stereotype of "old": A review and alternative approach. *Journal of Gerontology, 31,* 441–447.

Burke, J. L. (1981–1982). Young children's attitudes and perceptions of older adults. *International Journal of Aging and Human Development, 14,* 205–222.

Caspi, A. (1984). Contact hypothesis and inter-age attitudes: A field study of cross-age contact. *Social Psychology Quarterly, 47,* 74–80.

Chapman, N. J., and Neal, M. B. (1990). The effects of intergenerational experiences on adolescents and older adults. *Gerontologist, 30,* 825–832.

Chiu, C., Hong, Y., and Dweck, C. (1997). Lay dispositionism and implicit theories of personality. *Journal of Personality and Social Psychology, 73,* 19–30.

Collette-Pratt, C. (1976). Attitudinal predictors of devaluation of old age in a multigenerational sample. *Journal of Gerontology, 31,* 193–197.

Cooper, R. P., and Aslin, R. N. (1990). Preference for infant-directed speech in the first month after birth. *Child Development, 61,* 1584–1595.

Crockett, W. H., and Hummert, M. L. (1987). Perceptions of aging and the elderly. In C. Eisdorfer (Ed.), *Annual review of gerontology and geriatrics* (Vol. 7, pp. 217–241). New York: Springer.

Davidson, D., Cameron, P., and Jergovic, J. (1995). The effects of children's stereotypes on their memory for elderly individuals. *Merrill-Palmer Quarterly, 41,* 70–90.

Dellman-Jenkins, M., Lambert, D., Fruit, D., and Dinero, T. (1986). Old and young together: Effect of an educational program on preschoolers' attitudes toward older people. *Children Education*, 206–213.

Dellmann-Jenkins, M., and Yang, L. (1997). The portrayal of older people in award-winning literature for children. *Journal of Research in Childhood Education*, *12*, 96–100.

Dion, K. (1973). Young children's stereotyping of facial attractiveness. *Developmental Psychology*, *9*, 183–188.

Dobrosky, B. J., and Bishop, J. M. (1986). Children's perceptions of old people. *Educational Gerontology*, *12*, 429–439.

Doka, K. J. (1985–1986). Adolescent attitudes and beliefs toward aging and the elderly. *International Journal of Aging and Human Development*, *22*, 173–187.

Downs, A. C., and Walz, P. J. (1981). Sex differences in preschoolers' perceptions of young, middle-aged, and elderly adults. *Journal of Psychology*, *109*, 119–122.

Dweck, C. S., Chiu, C., and Hong, Y. (1995). Implicit theories and their role in judgments and reactions: A world from two perspectives. *Psychological Inquiry*, *6*, 267–285.

Eagly, A. H. (1987). *Sex differences in social behavior: A social-role interpretation*. Hillsdale, NJ: Erlbaum.

Eagly, A. H., and Steffen, V. J. (1984). Gender stereotypes stem from the distribution of women and men into social roles. *Journal of Personality and Social Psychology*, *46*, 735–753.

Edwards, C. P. (1984). The age group labels and categories of preschool children. *Child Development*, *55*, 440–452.

Enlow, D. H. (1982). *Handbook of facial growth* (2nd ed.). Philadelphia: Saunders.

Fagan, J. F. (1972). Infants' recognition memory for faces. *Journal of Experimental Child Psychology*, *14*, 453–476.

Feldman, R. S. (2000). *Development across the life span*. Upper Saddle River, NJ: Prentice Hall.

Feldman, N. S., and Ruble, D. N. (1981). The development of person perception: Cognitive and social factors. In S. S. Brehm, S. M. Kassin, and F. X. Gibbons (Eds.), *Developmental social psychology: Theory and research* (pp. 191–206). New York: Oxford University Press.

Fillmer, H. T. (1982). Children's descriptions of and attitudes toward the elderly. *Educational Gerontology*, *10*, 99–107.

Fiske, S. T., and Neuberg, S. L. (1989). Category-based and individuating processes as a function of information and motivation: Evidence from our laboratory.

In D. Bar-Tal, C. F. Graumann, A. Kruglanski, and W. Stroebe (Eds.), *Stereotyping and prejudice: Changing conceptions* (pp. 83–105). New York: Springer.

Forbus, P. R. (1982). Age appearance and behavior: A further comment. *Gerontologist, 22,* 5–7.

Galper, A., Jantz, R. K., Seefeldt, C., and Serock, K. (1980–1981). The child's concept of age and aging. *International Journal of Aging and Human Development, 12,* 149–156.

Gerbner, G., Gross, L., Signorielli, N., and Morgan, M. (1980). Aging with television: Images in television drama and conceptions of social reality. *Journal of Communication, 30,* 37–47.

Gibson, E. J., and Walker, A. S. (1984). Development of knowledge of visual-tactual affordances of substance. *Child Development, 55*(2), 453–460.

Glass, J. C., and Trent, C. (1980). Changing ninth-graders' attitudes toward older persons. *Research on Aging, 2,* 499–512.

Goldman, R. J., and Goldman, J. (1981). How children view old people and aging: A developmental study of children in four countries. *Australian Journal of Psychology, 33,* 405–418.

Green, S. K. (1981). Attitudes and perceptions about the elderly: Current and future perspectives. *International Journal of Aging and Human Development, 13,* 99–119.

Hamilton, D. L., and Gifford, R. K. (1976). Illusory correlation in interpersonal perception: A cognitive basis of stereotypic judgments. *Journal of Experimental Social Psychology, 12,* 392–407.

Harris, A. J., and Feinberg, J. F. (1977). Television and aging: Is what you see what you get? *Gerontologist, 17,* 464–468.

Harris, J., and Fiedler, C. M. (1988). Preadolescent attitudes toward the elderly: An analysis of race, gender, and contact variables. *Adolescence, 23,* 335–340.

Heider, F. (1958). *The psychology of interpersonal relations.* New York: Wiley.

Hickey, T., Hickey, L. A., and Kalish, R. A. (1968). Children's perceptions of the elderly. *Journal of Genetic Psychology, 112,* 227–235.

Hickey, T., and Kalish, R. A. (1968). Young people's perceptions of adults. *Journal of Gerontology, 112,* 227–235.

Higgins, E. T., and Parsons, J. E. (1983). Social cognition and the social life of the child: Stages as subcultures. In E. T. Higgins, D. N. Ruble, and W. W. Hartup (Eds.), *Social cognition and social development* (pp. 15–61). Cambridge: Cambridge University Press.

Hoffner, C., and Cantor, J. (1985). Developmental differences in responses to a television character's appearance and behavior. *Developmental Psychology, 21,* 1065–1074.

Howard, J. W., and Rothbart, M. (1980). Social categorization and memory for in-group and outgroup behavior. *Journal of Personality and Social Psychology, 38,* 301–310.

Hummert, M. L. (1990). Multiple stereotypes of elderly and young adults: A comparison of structure and evaluations. *Psychology and Aging, 5,* 182–193.

Hummert, M. L. (1994). Physiognomic cues and activation of stereotypes of the elderly in interaction. *International Journal of Aging and Human Development, 39,* 5–20.

Hummert, M. L., Gartska, T. A., Shaner, J. L., and Strahm, S. (1994). Stereotypes of the elderly held by young, middle-aged, and elderly adults. *Journals of Gerontology: Psychological Sciences, 49,* P240–P249.

Hurst, J. B. (1981, February). Images in children's picture books. *Social Education,* 138–143.

Isaacs, L. W., and Bearison, D. J. (1986). The development of children's prejudice against the aged. *International Journal of Aging and Human Development, 23,* 175–195.

Ivester, C., and King, K. (1977). Attitudes of adolescents toward the aged. *Gerontologist, 17,* 85–89.

Jensen, G. D., and Oakely, F. B. (1980). Age appearance and behavior: An evolutionary and ethological perspective. *Gerontologist, 20,* 595–597.

Jones, G., and Smith, P. K. (1984). The eyes have it: Young children's discrimination of age in masked and unmasked facial photographs. *Journal of Experimental Child Psychology, 38,* 328–337.

Kasternbaum, R., and Durkee, N. (1964). Young people view old age. In R. Kasternbaum (Ed.), *New thoughts on old age* (pp. 236–249). New York: Springer.

Kite, M. E., and Johnson, B. T. (1998). Attitudes toward older and younger adults: A meta-analysis. *Psychology and Aging, 3,* 233–244.

Kogan, N. (1979). Beliefs, attitudes and stereotypes about old people: A new look at some old issues. *Research on Aging, 1,* 11–36.

Kogan, N., Stephens, J. W., and Shelton, F. C. (1961). Age differences: A developmental study of discriminability and affective response. *Journal of Abnormal and Social Psychology, 62,* 221–230.

Korthase, K. M., and Trenholme, I. (1983). Children's perceptions of age and physical attractiveness. *Perceptual and Motor Skills, 56,* 895–900.

Kovaric, P. M. (1993). Television, the portrayal of the elderly, and children's attitudes. In G. L. Berry and J. K. Asamen (Eds.), *Children and television: Images in a changing sociocultural world* (pp. 243–254). Newbury Park, CA: Sage.

Kramer, S., Zebrowitz, L. A., San Giovanni, J. P., and Sherak, B. (1995). Infant preferences for attractiveness and babyfaceness. In B. G. Bardy, R. J. Bootsma, and Y. Girard (Eds.), *Studies in perception and action III* (pp. 389–392). Hillsdale, NJ: Erlbaum.

Kratochwill, T. R., and Goldman, J. A. (1973). Developmental changes in children's judgments of age. *Developmental Psychology, 9,* 358–362.

Kubey, R. (1980). Television and aging: Past, present, and future. *Gerontologist, 20,* 16–35.

Kuczaj, S. A., and Lederberg, A. R. (1976). Height, age, and function: Difference influences in children's comprehension of "younger" and "older." *Journal of Child Language, 4,* 395–416.

Labouvie-Vief, G., and Baltes, P. B. (1976). Reduction of adolescent misperception of the aged. *Journal of Gerontology, 31,* 68–71.

Langlois, J. H., Kalakanis, L. E., Rubenstein, A. J., Larson, A. D., Hallam, M. J., and Smoot, M. T. (2000). Maxims and myths of beauty: A meta-analytic and theoretical review. *Psychological Bulletin, 126,* 390–423.

Langlois, J. H., Ritter, J. M., Roggman, L. A., and Vaughn, L. S. (1991). Facial diversity and infant preferences for attractive faces. *Developmental Psychology, 27,* 79–84.

Langlois, J. H., Roggman, L. A., Casey, R. J., Ritter, J. M., Reiser-Danner, L. A., and Jenkins, V. Y. (1987). Infant preferences for attractive faces: Rudiments of a stereotype? *Developmental Psychology, 23,* 363–369.

Langlois, J. H., Roggman, L. A., and Rieser-Danner, L. A. (1990). Infants' differential social responses to attractive and unattractive faces. *Developmental Psychology, 26,* 153–159.

Langlois, J. H., and Stephan, C. W. (1977). The effects of physical attractiveness and ethnicity on children's behavioral attributions and peer preferences. *Child Development, 48,* 1694–1698.

Langlois, J. H., and Styczynski, L. (1979). The effects of physical attractiveness on the behavioral attributions and peer preferences in acquainted children. *International Journal of Behavioral Development, 2,* 325–341.

Lasky, R. E., Klein, R. E., and Martinez, S. (1974). Age and sex-discriminations in five- and six-month-old infants. *Journal of Psychology, 88,* 317–324.

Levy, S. R., and Dweck, C. S. (1999). The impact of children's static versus dynamic conceptions of people on stereotype formation. *Child Development, 70,* 1163–1180.

Levy, S. R., Stroessner, S. J., and Dweck, C. S. (1998). Stereotype formation and endorsement: The role of implicit theories. *Journal of Personal and Social Psychology, 74,* 1421–1436.

Lewis, M., and Brooks-Gunn, J. (1979). *Social cognition and the acquisition of self.* New York: Plenum Press.

Livesley, W. J., and Bromley, D. B. (1973). *Person perception in childhood and adolescence.* New York: Wiley.

Looft, W. R. (1971). Children's judgments of age. *Child Development, 42,* 1282–1284.

Luecke-Aleska, D., Anderson, D. R., Collins, P., A., and Schmitt, K. L. (1995). Gender constancy and television viewing. *Developmental Psychology, 31,* 773–780.

Lutsky, N. S. (1980). Attitudes toward old age and elderly persons. In C. Eisdorfer (Ed.), *Annual review of gerontology and geriatrics* (Vol. 1, pp. 287–336). New York: Springer.

Mackie, D. M., Hamilton, D. L., Susskind, J., and Rosselli, F. (1996). Social psychological foundations of stereotype formation. In N. McRae, M. Hewstone, and C. Stangor (Eds.), *Foundation of stereotypes and stereotyping* (pp. 41–78). New York: Guilford Press.

Malatesta, C., Fiore, M., and Messina, J. (1987). Affect, personality and expressive characteristics of older people. *Psychology and Aging, 2,* 64–69.

Malatesta, C., Izard, C., Culver, C., and Nicholich, M. (1987). Emotion communication skills in young, middle-aged, and older women, *Psychology and Aging, 2,* 193–203.

Marcoen, A. (1979). Children's perceptions of age persons and grandparents. *International Journal of Behavioral Development, 2,* 87–105.

Marks, R., Newman, S., and Onawola, R. (1985). Latency-aged children's views of aging. *Educational Gerontology, 11,* 89–99.

McArthur, L. Z., and Baron, R. M. (1983). Toward an ecological theory of social perception. *Psychological Review, 90,* 215–238.

McArthur, L. Z., and Eisen, S. V. (1976a). Television and sex-role stereotyping. *Journal of Applied Social Psychology, 6,* 329–351.

McArthur, L. Z., and Eisen, S. V. (1976b). Achievements of male and female storybook characters as determinants of achievement behavior by boys and girls. *Journal of Personality and Social Psychology, 33,* 467–473.

McCall, R. B., and Kennedy, C. B. (1980). Attention of 4-month infants to discrepancy and babyishness. *Journal of Experimental Child Psychology, 29,* 189–201.

McTavish, D. G. (1971). Perceptions of old people: A review of research methodologies and findings. *Gerontologist, 11,* 90–101.

Medawar, P. B. (1944). The shape of human beings as a function of time. *Proceedings of the Royal Society of London, 91,* 1–12.

Melson, G. F., Fogel, A., and Toda, S. (1986). Children's ideas about infants and their care. *Child Development, 57,* 1519–1527.

Mergler, N. L., and Goldstein, M. D. (1983). Why are there old people? Senescence as biological and cultural preparedness for the transmission of information. *Human Development, 26,* 72–90.

Miller, C. L., Younger, B. A., and Morse, P. A. (1982). The categorization of male and female voices in infancy. *Infant Behavior and Development, 5,* 143–159.

Miller, S. M., Blalock, J., and Ginsburg, H. J. (1984–1985). Children and the aged: Attitudes, contact, and discriminative ability. *International Journal of Aging and Human Development, 19,* 47–53.

Mitchell, J., Wilson, K., Revicki, D., and Parker, L. (1985). Children's perceptions of aging: A multidimensional approach to differences by age, sex, and race. *Gerontologist, 25,* 182–187.

Montepare, J. M., and Dobish, H. (2000). *The contribution of social affordances of emotional expressions to trait impressions.* Unpublished manuscript, Emerson College, Boston.

Montepare, J. M., Goldstein, S., and Clausen, A. (1987). Identification of emotions from gait information. *Journal of Nonverbal Behavior, 11,* 33–42.

Montepare, J. M., and McArthur, L. Z. (1986). The influence of facial characteristics on children's age perceptions. *Journal of Experimental Child Psychology, 42,* 303–314.

Montepare, J. M., and McArthur, L. Z. (1987). Perceptions of adults with childlike voices in two cultures. *Journal of Experimental Social Psychology, 23,* 331–349.

Montepare, J. M., and Zebrowitz, L. (1993). A cross-cultural comparison of impressions created by age-related variations in gait. *Journal of Nonverbal Behavior, 17,* 55–67.

Montepare, J. M., and Zebrowitz, L. A. (1998). Person perception comes of age: The salience and significance of age in social judgment. In M. P. Zanna (Ed.), *Advances in experimental social psychology* (Vol. 30, pp. 93–161). New York: Academic Press.

Montepare, J. M., and Zebrowitz-McArthur, L. (1987). Perceptions of adults with childlike voices in two cultures. *Journal of Experimental Social Psychology, 23,* 331–349.

Montepare, J. M., and Zebrowitz-McArthur, L. (1988). Impressions of people created by age related qualities of their gait. *Journal of Personality and Social Psychology, 55,* 547–556.

Muscarella, F., and Cunningham, M. R. (1996). The evolutionary significance and social perception of male pattern baldness and facial hair. *Ethology and Sociobiology, 17,* 99–117.

Nelson, T. D. (2002). Ageism: A critical review of current research and theory. In T. Nelson (Ed.), *The psychology of prejudice.* Needham Heights, MA: Allyn and Bacon.

Newman, S., Faux, R., and Larimer, B. (1997). Children's views on aging: Their attitudes and values. *Gerontologist, 37*, 412–417.

Nishi-Strattner, M., and Myers, J. E. (1983). Attitudes toward the elderly: An intergenerational examination. *Educational Gerontology, 9*, 389–397.

Northcott, H. (1975). "Too young, too old"—Age in the world of television. *Gerontologist, 15*, 184–186.

Palmore, E. B. (1990). *Ageism: Negative and positive.* New York: Springer.

Page, S., Olivas, R., Driver, J., and Driver, R. (1981). Children's attitudes toward the elderly and aging. *Educational Gerontology, 7*, 43–47.

Passuth, P. M., and Cook, F. L. (1985). Effects of television viewing on knowledge and attitudes about older adults: A critical reexamination. *Gerontologist, 25*, 69–77.

Pasupathi, M., Carstensen, L. L., and Tsai, J. L. (1995). Ageism in interpersonal settings. In B. Lott and D. Maluso (Eds.), *The social psychology of interpersonal discrimination* (pp. 16–182). New York: Guilford.

Perry, D. G., and Busscy, K. (1984). *Social development.* Englewood Cliffs, NJ: Prentice-Hall.

Piaget, J. (1969). *The children's conception of time.* New York: Basic Books.

Poulin-Dubois, D., Serbin, L. A., Kenyon, B., and Derbyshire, A. (1994). Infants' intermodal knowledge about gender. *Developmental Psychology, 30*, 436–442.

Rich, P. E., Myrick, R. D., and Campbell, C. (1983). Changing children's perceptions of the elderly. *Educational Gerontology, 9*, 483–491.

Robinson, J. D. (1989). Mass media and the elderly: A uses and dependency interpretation. In J. F. Nussbaum (Ed.), *Life-span communication: Normative processes* (pp. 319–338). Hillsdale, NJ: Erlbaum.

Rosenwasser, S. M., McBride, P., Brantley, T., and Ginsburg, H. J. (1986). Children and aging: Attitudes differentiation ability, and quantity and quality of contact. *Journal of Genetic Psychology, 147*, 407–415.

Schmidt, D. F., and Boland, S. M. (1986). The structure of impressions of older adults: Evidence for multiple stereotypes. *Psychology and Aging, 1*, 255–260.

Seefeldt, C. (1984). Children's attitudes toward the elderly: A cross-cultural comparison. *International Journal of Aging and Human Development, 19*, 319–328.

Seefeldt, C. (1987). The effects of preschoolers' visits to a nursing home. *Gerontologist, 27*, 228–232.

Seefeldt, C., and Ahn, U. R. (1990). Children's attitudes toward the elderly in Korea and the United States. *International Journal of Comparative Sociology, 31*, 248–256.

Seefeldt, C., Jantz, R. K., Galper, A., and Serock, K. (1977). Using pictures to explore children's attitudes toward the elderly. *Gerontologist, 17,* 506–512.

Seefeldt, C., Jantz, R. K., Galper, A., and Serock, K. (1981). Healthy, happy, and old: Children learn about the elderly. *Educational Gerontology, 7,* 79–87.

Seefeldt, C., and Keawkungwal, S. (1986). Children's attitudes toward the elderly in Thailand. *Educational Gerontology, 12,* 151–158.

Seltzer, M. M., and Atchley, R. C. (1971). The concept of old: Changing attitudes and stereotypes. *The Gerontologist, 11,* 226–230.

Serbin, L. A., and Sprafkin, C. (1986). The salience of gender and the process of sex typing in three to seven-year-old children. *Child Development, 57,* 1188–1199.

Sheehan, R. (1978). Young children's contact with elderly. *Journal of Gerontology, 33,* 567–574.

Slaughter-Defoe, D. T., Kuehne, V. S., and Straker, J. K. (1992). African-American, Anglo-American, and Anglo-Canadian grade 4 children's concepts of old people and of extended family. *International Journal of Aging and Human Development, 35,* 161–179.

Smith, P. M. (1979). Sex markers in speech. In K. R. Scherer and H. Giles (Eds.), *Social markers in speech* (pp. 109–146). Cambridge: Cambridge University Press.

Snyder, M., and Miene, P. K. (1994). Stereotyping of the elderly: A functional approach. *British Journal of Social Psychology, 33,* 63–82.

Solomon, S., Greenberg, J., and Pyszczynski, T. (1991). Terror management theory of self-esteem. In C. R. Snyde and D. Forsyth (Eds.), *Handbook of social and clinical psychology: The health perspective* (pp. 21–40). New York: Pergamon.

Spelke, E. S. (1981). The infant's acquisition of knowledge of bimodally specified events. *Journal of Experimental Child Psychology, 31,* 279–299.

Tanner, J. M. (1970). Physical growth. In P. H. Mussen (Ed.), *Carmichael's manual of child psychology.* New York: Wiley.

Taylor, S. E., Peplau, L. A., and Sears, D. O. (2000). *Social psychology.* Upper Saddle River, NJ: Prentice Hall.

Thomas, E. C., and Yamamoto, K. (1975). Attitudes toward age: An exploration in school-age children. *International Journal of Aging and Human Development, 6,* 117–129.

Tuckman, J., and Lorge, I. (1953). Attitudes toward old people. *Journal of Social Psychology, 37,* 249–260.

von Hippel, W., Silver, L. A., and Lynch, M. E. (2000). Stereotyping against your will: The role of inhibitory ability in stereotyping and prejudice among the elderly. *Personality and Social Psychology Bulletin, 26,* 523–532.

Ward, R. A. (1984). *The aging experience.* New York: Harper and Row.

Weinberger, A., (1979). Stereotyping of the elderly: Elementary school children's responses. *Research on Aging, 1,* 113–136.

Weinberger, L. E., and Millham, J. (1975). A multi-dimensional, multiple method analysis of attitudes toward the elderly. *Journal of Gerontology, 30,* 343–348.

Wingard, J. A., Heath, R., and Himelstein, S. A. (1992). The effects of contextual variations on attitudes toward the elderly. *Journal of Gerontology, 37,* 475–482.

Zajonc, R. B. (1968). Attitudinal effects of mere exposure. *Journal of Personality and Social Psychology, 9,* Monograph Supplement, No. 2, part 2.

Zandi, T., Mirle, J., and Jarvis, P. (1990). Children's attitudes toward elderly individuals: A comparison of two ethnic groups. *International Journal of Aging and Human Development, 30,* 161–174.

Zebrowitz, L. A. (1990). *Social perception.* Pacific Grove, CA: Brooks-Cole.

Zebrowitz, L. A. (1996). Physical appearance as a basis for stereotyping. In N. McRae, M. Hewstone, and C. Stangor (Eds.), *Foundation of stereotypes and stereotyping* (pp. 79–120). New York: Guilford Press.

Zebrowitz, L. A. (1997). *Reading faces.* Boulder, CO: Westview Press.

Zebrowitz, L. A., and Collins, M. A. (1997). Accurate social perception at zero acquaintance: The affordances of a Gibsonian approach. *Personality and Social Psychology Review, 1,* 203–222.

Zebrowitz, L. A., and Montepare, J. M. (1992). Impressions of babyfaced individuals across the life span. *Developmental Psychology, 28,* 1143–1152.

Zebrowitz, L. A., and Montepare, J. M. (2000). "Too young, too old": Stigmatizing adolescents and elders. In T. Heatherton, R. Kleck, M. Hebl, and J. G. Hull (Eds.), *Stigma* (pp. 334–373). New York: Guilford Publications.

Zebrowitz-McArthur, L., and Friedman, S. A. (1980). Illusory correlation in impression formation: Variations in the shared distinctiveness effect as a function of the distinctive person's age, race, and sex. *Journal of Personality and Social Psychology, 39,* 615–624.

Walker, A. S. (1982). Intermodal perception of expressive behaviors by human infants. *Journal of Experimental Child Psychology, 33,* 514–535.

II

Effects of Ageism

5

Attitudes toward Older Adults
Mary E. Kite and Lisa Smith Wagner

Old age is a social category we join or anticipate joining with feelings of ambivalence. As has often been noted, most of us aspire to reach old age; after all, the alternative is to die young. Yet most North Americans are reluctant to accept aging gracefully and often hold ageist attitudes and beliefs. In our society, youth is the standard held in highest esteem. From commercials promoting products to stop the aging process to party decorations labeling age 50 "over the hill," the message that youth is valued is impossible to ignore. At the same time, the population is aging at an unprecedented rate. The proportion of U.S. residents over the age of 65 rose from 9.2 percent in 1960 to 12.6 percent in 1990 and is predicted to reach 17.7 percent in 2020 (U.S. Bureau of the Census, 1989). The baby boomers are rapidly moving into retirement, bringing with them a model for prosperity and fulfillment in one's later years. The freedom and opportunities open to these individuals offer a positive perspective on the aging process.

For over a half a century, gerontologists have puzzled over our fascination with youth and our reluctance to accept aging gracefully. Early work stemmed from the assumption that negative attitudes about and prejudice toward older adults was widespread. Yet as McTavish (1971) noted in his seminal review of the literature, the answer to the seemingly simple question, "Does ageism exist?" is not an unequivocal yes. Instead, our views about aging are multidimensional, with both positive and negative elements. Our ideas about aging also reflect an appreciation for individual differences and context. These are the layers of complexity that must be wrestled with by those attempting to understand attitudes toward the aging process and toward those who have reached "old age."

Throughout this chapter, we implicitly or explicitly assume that ageist attitudes stem from cultural beliefs about older adults and the aging process. Without a doubt, messages conveying North American's cultural unease with aging are everywhere—messages that are so well learned that people respond to them below the conscious level. Recent research demonstrates the automaticity of this unconscious processing. Studies using implicit attitude measures (Implicit Association Test and Response Window Priming), for example, found that both older and younger adults showed evidence of automatic ageism. Respondents in these studies have been found to associate old and unpleasant stimuli (and young and pleasant stimuli) more easily than old and pleasant (and young and unpleasant) stimuli (Mellott and Greenwald 2000). Similarly, people remember more negative traits when those characteristics previously have been associated with an older person and more positive traits when those characteristics previously have been associated with a younger person (Perdue and Gurtman 1990). A detailed discussion of this research is the focus of Chapter 3 in this book, yet it is important to acknowledge the implications of these findings for the research we describe.

In this chapter, we examine the literature on attitudes toward and beliefs about older adults. We begin with a discussion of what constitutes an ageist attitude and provide a historical perspective of the quest to measure these attitudes. Next, we describe how modern researchers have built on and expanded the contributions of this groundbreaking work. In particular, we explain why attitudes toward older adults cannot be considered unequivocally negative and highlight the factors that moderate age-related perceptions. We also examine how gender stereotypes intersect with age-based attitudes and discuss when and why older women and men are viewed differently. Throughout the chapter, we address how current social-psychological theory can advance the study of ageism. Theory-driven perspectives, long absent from the literature on age-related attitudes, are essential because they guide research, suggest hypotheses, and aid in the interpretation of results (see Crockett and Hummert 1987; Lutsky 1980). Adding to the insights of many recent theorists (Erber and Prager 1999; Hummert 1999), we consider the theoretical perspectives of social role theory (Eagly 1987; Eagly, Wood, and Diekman, 2000), and social identity theory (SIT; Harwood, Giles, and Ryan 1995; Tajfel and Turner 1979).

What Is Ageism?

Attitudes have been defined traditionally as psychological tendencies that are expressed by evaluating a particular entity with some degree of favor or disfavor (Eagly and Chaiken 1993). Butler (1969) coined the term *ageist* to refer to evaluative judgments toward a person or persons simply due to their advanced age. Yet researchers have not always agreed on what constitutes an ageist attitude (see Lutsky 1980 for an excellent discussion). Indeed, the number and type of dependent variables that authors have used to represent attitude cover such a wide range that it defies easy categorization or explanation. For our purposes, we adopt the traditional tripartite model (see Eagly and Chaiken 1993). This model, applied to older adults, proposes that attitudes comprise three components: an affective component, represented by feelings that one has toward older individuals; a cognitive component, represented by beliefs or stereotypes about older people; and a behavioral component, represented by behavior or behavioral intentions toward older adults. Ageist attitudes are best thought of as a constellation of these three factors, each of which can have a positive or negative component: feelings due to a person's age, stereotypes about what someone is like just because the person is "of a certain age," and differential treatment due to a person's advanced age.

Historical Perspectives

Early work on attitudes toward old age primarily centered on the development of attitude measures. One of the first measures emerged from the classic studies of Tuckman and Lorge (1952, 1953), who developed a comprehensive instrument to assess misconceptions and stereotypes about older people. Their measure consisted of 137 statements, classified into 13 evaluative categories, including personality traits, physical characteristics, mental deterioration, and best time of life. They found that agreement with stereotypic beliefs varied by category; people were most likely to agree that older adults are conservative and set in their ways and least likely to agree that older adults are inattentive to cleanliness. This instrument is rarely used today, at least in its full form, but Tuckman and Lorge's work set the standard for the field and remains highly influential. Their classic studies on attitudes toward older workers, for example, continue to be widely cited (Tuckman and Lorge 1952, 1958).

Another standard-setter was Nathan Kogan, whose contributions to the literature have spanned four decades. His early work included the construction of a sentence-completion measure of attitudes toward "old people" (Golde and Kogan 1959; Kogan and Shelton 1962), designed to address methodological problems with the Tuckman and Lorge instrument. On this measure, people complete sentences for "old people," and these are compared to completions of the same sentences for "people in general." In all, participants respond to twenty items, ranging from perceptions of older people's friendships to their fears about aging. The resulting qualitative data are then categorized by independent coders. Comparisons between the categories can be made within subjects (the same participants rate both categories) or between subjects (different participants rate each category). A review of this instrument and a discussion of beliefs, attitudes, and stereotypes of the elderly is provided by Kogan (1979). Kogan's work raised important questions that still receive considerable attention. Kogan (1979), for example, was the first to point out that a within-subjects comparison would result in more ageist attitudes than would a between-subjects comparison, a result that has held up in a variety of subsequent studies (see Finkelstein, Burke, and Raju 1995; Gordon et al. 2000; Kite and Johnson 1988). Moreover, Kogan and his colleague Florence Shelton were early advocates for distinguishing between attitudes toward older men and older women and for considering the influence of contextual information on age-related attitudes (Kogan and Shelton 1960, 1962).

Although the influence of these early scholars has not waned, their measures have been replaced by shorter instruments that are easier to complete and score. One commonly used measure is Palmore's (1977) Facts on Aging quiz, a twenty-five-item true-false test aimed toward identifying an anti-age bias. This measure is particularly useful for addressing whether education or intervention programs effectively reduce ageism (see also Palmore 1988). Another commonly used instrument is the Aging Semantic Differential (Rosencranz and McNevin 1969), designed to measure attitude valence. This thirty-two-item semantic differential scale has three factors: instrumental/effective, autonomous/dependent, and personal acceptability/unacceptability (but see Intrieri, von Eye, and Kelly 1995 for a recent discussion of the factor structure). As in other attitude areas, the semantic differential has proven an easy-to-administer and reliable measure of global attitudes toward older adults.

A more comprehensive review of the available measures is beyond the scope of this chapter. Yet even this brief historical review of the literature shows the considerable variability in the dependent variables chosen to represent ageist attitudes and beliefs. The variety of measures used to examine views about older adults has added texture and complexity to the understanding of ageism. Even so, the use of such varied dependent measures makes summarizing the literature difficult. Moreover, whether these varied measures all represent the construct "attitude" is a matter of some debate (see Lutsky 1980 for a discussion). Instruments such as the Aging Semantic Differential (Rosencranz and McNevin 1969) are undoubtedly consistent with the traditional definition of an attitude as an evaluative judgment. Many measures of stereotypic beliefs about the elderly also often have a clearly evaluative component (e.g., grouchy, have health problems; Chumbler 1994). And consistent with the tripartite definition of attitude (see Eagly and Chaiken 1993 for a review), behavior/behavioral intention measures, such as recommending evaluation by professionals following memory failure (Erber, Szuchman, and Rothberg 1990b), giving instructions to game participants (Rubin and Brown 1975), or the use of "elderspeak" (Caporael 1981; chapter 6, this volume; Ryan and See 1993) arguably represent evaluation. For a variety of other measures, however, agreement with an item may not represent a negative or positive evaluation. Examples of such dependent variables are gender stereotype measures (Canetto, Kaminski, and Felicio 1995; Kite, Deaux, and Miele 1991), measures of personal concern about the consequences of being old (Klemmack, Durand, and Roff 1980), judgments about the age at which various life markers are reached (middle age, old age; Hori 1994), and attractiveness ratings (Deutsch, Zalenski, and Clark 1986). Evidence suggests, for example, that younger people are viewed as more agentic (have attributes reflecting self-assertion, self-expansion, and the urge to master; Bakan 1966) than older people (Deutsch, Zalenski, and Clark 1986; Gekoski and Knox 1990), but this does not necessarily indicate that older people are devalued. Similarly, measures such as Palmore's (1977, 1988) Facts on Aging quiz may reflect accurate perceptions of the aging process rather than an age-linked bias. That certain cognitive abilities decline with age, for example, has been well documented (Park et al. 1996; Salthouse 1996). Older and younger adults agree that the ability to recall fades over time (Foos and Dickerson 1996); it is probably unfair, then, to conclude that those who agree that this decline exists are prejudiced. At the same time, these dimensions represent significant components of our age-related beliefs and have implications for how older adults are treated (see chapter 7, this volume, for an excellent discussion of both the positive and negative sides of age-differentiated behavior). Researchers and reviewers must therefore be careful to differentiate between those constructs that clearly convey prejudice and those that reflect other dimensions of age-linked beliefs.

When Does Old Age Begin?

Operationalizing attitudes is one piece of the puzzle, but there are a variety of other methodological issues that also deserve attention. One important concern is determining when old age begins. The actual starting point for old age is not clearly demarcated, but many researchers find the traditional retirement age of 65 a convenient indicator. Often respondents are asked to compare older adults and younger adults; for the latter category, age 25 is a commonly used marker. Of course, there is variability in this decision; some researchers use targets as young as 55 or 60 in the category "older adults" or targets in their 30s and 40s to represent the young. Still others do not specify an exact age, but instead use the general categories "young" and "old." It is also becoming increasingly common to study a range of ages, including the middle years, in studies of ageism (Hummert, Garstka, and Shaner 1997; Kogan 1979; Krueger, Heckhausen, and Hundertmark 1995). In such studies, middle age is typically defined as between 40 and 60.

Research shows that these generally accepted guidelines are not far off base. When respondents have the opportunity to define age categories themselves, their perceptions are largely in agreement with researchers' judgments. Zepelin, Sills, and Heath (1986), for example, found that those between ages 18 and 35 were considered young, those between 35 and 60 were considered middle aged, and those between 65 and 80 were considered old. These authors also found that women were perceived as reaching middle and old age about five years earlier than men were, a point we return to (see also Seccombe and Ishii Kuntz 1991). A sample of New Zealanders (Byrd and Breuss 1992) and a Japanese sample (Hori 1994) produced similar age ratings, although the New Zealanders did not report a striking difference for women's and men's entry into a particular age category.

Before accepting these categories completely, one caveat is in order. That is, to meet methodological goals, researchers often treat the beginning of old age as a fixed point. Arguably, people's experience of aging is more fluid. Middle-aged and older adult cohorts, for example, give slightly differing responses when asked at what age the average person becomes old: the start of old age appears to increase as the respondent's age increases (Seccombe and Ishii Kuntz 1991). For many people as they age, the advent of "old age" seems to advance as well, always staying just over the horizon. While at age 30, 65 may have seemed old, perhaps it does not at 60. This has research implications when, for example, older adult participants themselves fit the researcher's category of old age (e.g., over age 65), but do not see themselves as old (e.g., they feel old age starts at 75).

From a methodological perspective, the specific age used to delineate an age-based category may matter less than other factors, such as the context in which ratings are made or the specific dependent variables of interest. Hori (1994), for example, found that old age was marked by factors such as loss of physical power, changes in appearance, and memory loss more than by age itself. It is also possible that obtained personality differences between younger and older targets are not due to age itself but instead reflect the belief that members of different generations have different characteristics (Slotterback 1996). Another important point is that many theorists make the implicit assumption that the relationship between age and negative attitudes is linear. This assumption may not be warranted. Some work suggests that attitudes toward middle-aged individuals turn out to be at least as positive as, and sometimes more so than, attitudes toward younger people (Gekoski et al. 1984; Levin and Levin 1981; Rosencranz and McNevin 1969), suggesting a nonlinear relationship between evaluations and age.

Neugarten (1974) noted an important distinction between the "young-old" and the "old-old." Research highlights the wisdom of this distinction. The number of positive stereotypes associated with older people has been found to decrease significantly from photographs of the young-old to middle-old to old-old (Hummert, Garstka, and Shanon 1997; Kogan 1979). Many studies find that the most negative attitudes emerge for the oldest adults, the so-called old-old (Kidwell and Booth 1977; Sanders et al. 1984), with exceptions for some characteristics of the very oldest adults. Graham and Baker (1989) found that 90 and 100 year olds were seen as having higher status than their "younger" counterparts of 70 and 80, for example, and Hummert (1990) found that the old-old are seen as less self-centered than the middle-old or young-old. What is certain is that age-based ratings cannot be easily categorized or captured. It matters whom you ask and what you ask about. As the studies we describe next clearly demonstrate, even within a set age category of say, 65, a homogeneous target group simply does not exist.

Age-Based Stereotypes

The discussion thus far has highlighted some of the challenging issues that occur when trying to assess attitudes toward aging and older adults. The complexity of age-linked attitudes and stereotypes can also be seen through explorations of the subtypes we have of older adults. Brewer, Dull, and Lui (1981) were the first to argue that the category *elderly* represents a superordinate category under which several subcategories likely exist. Stimulated by Rosch's theory of natural categories, Brewer, Dull, and Lui (1981) argued that "elderly persons" functions as a broad social category like sex or race and that as such "elderly persons" may be too large a category to capture our attitudes toward older adults accurately. Although we may be able to measure attitudes toward this superordinate category, these measurements may yield contradictory findings if people are thinking of different subgroups while making their ratings. If we were to assess attitudes toward motor vehicles, for example, it is likely that perceptions would vary; in the absence of a more specific label, some of us would base our ratings on sedans and others on sport utility vehicles. A positive or negative rating, then, may reflect the category we are thinking of rather than our global attitude toward motor vehicles. And these ratings would likely differ in important ways from those individuals who are thinking of other types of motor vehicles. In contrast, if a subgroup is specified, our attitudes would likely be more consistent and therefore more meaningful. Parallel to this argument, Brewer, Dull, and Lui (1981) suggested it is more appropriate to examine subgroupings of older adults rather than the superordinate category of the elderly.

To test this idea, Brewer, Dull, and Lui (1981) defined three a priori subcategories of older adults: grandmother, representing a family-oriented older woman; senior citizen, representing the stereotype of an isolated, inactive elderly person of either sex; and elder statesman, representing the image of a distinguished and respected conservative gentleman. College students then sorted the photos representing each subgroup into categories of people that "went together." Participants sorted the photos into the three expected categories. They also consistently attributed traits to the photos that were appropriate to each category (e.g., the trait "kindly" was attributed to grandmother, "dignified" to elder statesman, and "lonely" to senior citizen).

Brewer and Lui (1984) replicated this finding in a sample of older women. An important aspect of this replication, however, was consideration of the category with which the older women identified. For most participants (thirty-two out of thirty-four), this was the "grandmother" subcategory. These older women showed a clear preference for this category in their evaluations, attributing almost all positive traits to this category. No such favorability bias emerged for the category not identified with: senior citizen. Brewer and Lui (1984) argued that this represented an in-group bias effect. If the older women had identified with the senior citizen category, they should have attributed positive traits to that category. Instead, older women's ratings of senior citizens corresponded almost perfectly to those made by the younger college students. As these results illustrate, an important aspect of a subtype analysis is our own perceived membership in the subgroup. In this case, older women do not identify with a general social category that includes all older adults, but rather identify with a particular subcategory. These women's ratings therefore are influenced by this process (Brewer and Lui 1984). Others report findings consistent with this claim (Heckhausen, Dixon, and Baltes 1989; Hummert et al. 1994).

Brewer's work examined subtypes determined in advance by the researchers. Expanding this work, Schmidt and Boland (1986) set out to determine people's subtypes of older adults when no a priori categories were given. To begin, they asked respondents simply to describe the typical old person, including the things they "typically think about, hear about, or read about the elderly, regardless of whether it is favorable or unfavorable or whether [they] personally believe it to be true." Results provided evidence for the complexity of older adult stereotypes; many opposite trait terms were given (e.g., sedentary-active, poor-wealthy), which clearly could not occur in the same person. In a second study, college students sorted the ninety-nine obtained traits into groups that would seem to go together in one older adult. Results showed many different stereotypes of older adults, some with positive and some with negative valences.

As Schmidt and Boland (1986) argued, these results suggest that we derogate only older adults who fit our negative stereotype and that the ageist attitudes found in earlier research would emerge only when examining specific subgroups of the elderly. Hummert has found strong support for this hypothesis. Starting from Schmidt and Boland's (1986) work, Hummert and her colleagues documented a set of stereotypes of older adults—some positive and some negative—that correspond to consistent and identifiable subtypes of older people. Based on traits generated by young, old, and middle-aged adults, Hummert and associates (1994) identified seven shared stereotypes of older adults. These included the negative subtypes Severely Impaired, Shrew/Curmudgeon, Despondent, and Recluse and the positive subtypes John Wayne Conservative, Golden Ager, and Perfect Grandparent. In addition to these shared stereotypes, middle-aged and older adults generated several additional stereotypes of older adults (e.g., Small Town Neighbor). When these unique categories were compared with the younger adults' categories, it was found that the unique categories were actually subtypes of the broader stereotypes generated by the younger adults. This suggests that there is a greater differentiation of the older adult categories as one ages. Subsequent work has shown a relationship between age of the subtype category member and valence; subtypes that are seen as older have fewer positive traits associated with them (Hummert et al. 1997). More-over, memory problems are seen as more serious for some subtypes (e.g., Despondent) than for others (e.g., Golden Ager; Hummert, Garstka, and Shaner 1995). Echoing the point raised by Schmidt and Boland (1986), Hummert, Garstka, and Shaner (1995) argued that attitudes toward older individuals vary according to the subtype that the target person likely represents rather than her or his actual age.

Social Role Perspective

Hummert's work suggests that beliefs about older adults are linked to the roles they are perceived to occupy (see Hummert 1999 for a review), a po-sition consistent with a social role analysis of attitudes toward older adults. This perspective proposes that our beliefs about social groups are de-rived, at least in part, from viewing people in various social roles (Eagly 1987; Eagly, Wood, and Diekmann, 2000). According to this perspective, our beliefs about stereotyped groups are influenced by our observation of behaviors that stem from the social roles that group members occupy. Through this observation, people come to associate the characteristics of the role with the individuals who occupy that role. Rather than emerging from biased, inaccurate beliefs, then, our ideas about group members are based on their recognized behaviors.

Although its applicability is not limited to a specific group, most tests of social role theory have emerged in the domain of gender stereotypes. Eagly and Steffen (1984), for example, demonstrated that gender stereo-types can be explained by a consideration of women's and men's occupa-tional roles. Women are traditionally in the homemaker role (or in an employee role of lower status), and men are traditionally in the bread-winner (or higher-status employee) role. As such, women are dispropor-tionately represented in roles requiring communal traits, such as kindness and concern for others, and men are disproportionately repre-sented in roles requiring agentic traits, such as self-confidence and as-sertiveness. A tenet of social role theory is that viewing women and men in these occupational roles leads people to associate the characteristics of these roles with the individuals who occupy them; hence, people con-clude that women are typically communal and men are typically agentic. A number of studies have supported this perspective. When more specific information is not provided, women are viewed as higher in communion than men, whereas men are viewed as higher in agency than women. Yet when occupational information is provided, people's judgments appear to be based on that information: regardless of the sex of the person being rated, employed individuals are seen as agentic and homemakers are seen as communal. Raters, then, take contextual information into account when making judgments about others.

A parallel argument can be offered to explain attitudes toward and beliefs about older adults. Older individuals, for example, occupy particular social roles, which should lead to a specific set of beliefs about them as a social group. Kite (1996) argued that because the employee role is occupied predominantly by people younger than 65, there is an association between agency and youth that accounts for the perception that older people are less agentic than younger people (Gekoski and Knox 1990; Kite, Deaux, and Miele 1991). Results of four experiments showed a link between occupational roles and stereotypic beliefs (Kite 1996; Kite and Cano 1998). In the absence of role information, 35-year-old targets were viewed as more agentic than 65-year-old targets. Consistent with social role theory, however, younger and older targets described as employed were viewed as equally agentic.

Contextual information has long been shown to be more influential than age information in judgments of older adults. Factors such as health status, for example, are better predictors of attitudes toward older adults than is target age (Gekoski and Knox 1990). And when older people are described at the subtype level, observers use knowledge of that subtype in their judgments. Indeed, this information outweighs age as a predictor of evaluation (Hummert, Garstka, and Shaner 1995). Contextual information drives evaluation more generally as well. That is, when an older adult is described as performing poorly, negative attitudes follow; similarly, an older adult described as competent is viewed positively (Bell and Stanfield 1973; Reno 1979; Walsh and Connor 1979).

Deciding whether ageist attitudes are operating is even more complex because gerontologists tend to examine the perceptions of older adults in relation to evaluations of other age groups. In this light, even positive absolute judgments can take on a negative cast if older adults are rated positively, but younger adults are rated even more positively. We summarize the literature comparing older and younger adults next.

Is Youth an Advantage?

As our discussion illustrates, ageist attitudes have a "now you see it, now you don't" quality that defies easy explanation. Sometimes our perceptions of older adults appear to be quite negative; other times, our views are quite favorable. Consistent with the experimental tradition so central to psychology, researchers have explored this paradox by comparing attitudes toward younger and older adults. In doing so, they have considered whether a negative bias exists against older adults, relative to their younger counterparts. Although the answer to this query is far from settled (see Crockett and Hummert 1987; Hummert 1990, 1993), considerable progress toward understanding ageist attitudes is evident.

Kite and Johnson (1988) used meta-analysis to examine this literature. They derived forty-three independent effect sizes, based on comparisons of attitudes toward younger and older adults. Thirty of those effect sizes indicated that people are more negative toward older than toward younger people, eleven indicated more negative attitudes toward younger than toward older people, and two indicated exactly no difference in attitudes toward the two groups. The overall effect size, as indexed by the d statistic, was 0.39, indicating that attitudes toward older persons are more negative than attitudes toward younger persons by approximately one-third of a standard deviation.

Although this effect indicates a bias against older adults, these effect sizes were not homogeneous. That is, the difference in attitudes expressed about older and younger adults varied widely across studies, suggesting that the studies did not share a common effect size. A number of factors accounted for additional effect-size variation. Some of these factors were methodological; as Kogan (1979) suggested, smaller differences between the evaluations of older and younger adults emerged when a between-subjects design (compared with a within-subjects design) was used. Moreover, consistent with the social role framework, the context provided for the ratings also moderated the results. When specific information was provided about the target person (compared with when a general target such as "old person" was used), age-based attitude differences were reduced significantly. Results also depended on the types of questions asked. When the study assessed personality traits (compared with competence), the effect size for the comparison of older and younger adults was reduced. As Lutsky (1980) had predicted earlier, age, in and of itself, was less important in determining attitudes toward older people than were other types of information.

In the more than a decade since Kite and Johnson's (1988) review was published, the literature on attitudes toward older adults has advanced considerably. More sophisticated questions have been posed, and the methodological techniques to answer them have also evolved. It is doubtful that these advances have dramatically changed the answer to the question of whether an age-based bias exists—North Americans likely still value youth over age—but we now have a better understanding of the basis for this bias. We describe next some of the richness brought by these important advances and explain what they tell us about North Americans' views about aging. We begin with a look at ageist attitudes in the employment setting.

Attitudes toward Older Workers

The topic itself is not new. Since the classic studies of Tuckman and Lorge (1952) and continuing through the seminal work of Rosen and Jerdee (1976a, 1976b), researchers have considered how older adults fare in employment settings. Yet the importance of this issue has arguably increased because the workforce itself is aging and because employers want to avoid age-bias lawsuits (Hassell and Perrewe 1995). Gerontologists have examined evaluations of job applicants (Connor et al. 1978), supervisors' and coworkers' attitudes toward older individuals (Davis-Berman and Robinson 1989; Taylor, Crino, and Rubenfeld 1989), and beliefs about older workers' competence (Hassell and Perrewe 1995; Rosen and Jerdee 1976a, 1976b), among other things. The pattern of findings is complex. Workplace discrimination is discussed in Chapters 6 and 7 in this book. We therefore examine this topic only briefly, describing two recent meta-analytic reviews of this literature.

There is no simple answer to the question of whether age discrimination exists in the workforce. Fortunately, the use of meta-analysis to synthesize bodies of research has recently been applied to this topic. One recent meta-analysis of age discrimination research (Gordon et al. 2000) found a small overall bias against older workers ($d = .11$). This effect increased significantly, however, for judgments of workers' potential for development ($d = .45$) and reversed for judgments of workers' stability ($d = -.67$). In the latter case, older workers were viewed significantly more positively. For the dependent measures of job qualifications and interpersonal skills, the bias against older adults was similar in magnitude to the overall bias ($ds = .10$ and $.11$, respectively). Another meta-analysis (Finkelstein, Burke, and Raju 1995) found similar effects, but also showed that younger people rated older workers more harshly than they rated their younger counterparts in the areas of potential for development, qualification for a physically demanding job, and overall job qualification. For older raters, only the last variable could be examined, but no evidence for age-of-target bias emerged. We address this in-group–out-group bias later in the chapter. Moreover, consistent with our discussion of context, these authors also found that when job-relevant differentiating information was provided, older and younger workers were rated more similarly than when no specific information was available.

When interpreting these findings, it is important to keep in mind that in the literature on age-based job discrimination, the older worker is typically described as between ages 55 and 65 (and the younger worker between ages 24 and 35)—just barely or not quite into the old age group by the standards we discussed earlier for defining "old age." In all likelihood, judgments of even older workers would produce an even greater discrepancy between the older and the younger worker. Unfortunately, and probably because of the available set of studies, neither meta-analysis examined this possibility. We suspect, however, that current economic forces will undoubtedly lead to new research on this topic. That is, given the recent decision not to penalize social security recipients for any level of employment and given the current economic need to attract workers of all ages, understanding how these older individuals are treated in the workforce is even more critical. Such social changes often provide an impetus for research. Another issue is the number of aging female baby boomers in the workforce. Whether patterns of job discrimination will prove to differ between aging women and aging men remains to be seen. The number of women in the workforce, however, suggests the answer to this question will soon be known. At a more general level, perceived sex differences in the aging process have begun to be explored.

Gender and Aging

Our stereotypes about women and men are distinct, so it is not surprising that our views about older women and men are also markedly different. Women, for example, are viewed as warm, emotional, and aware of others' feelings, whereas men are viewed as confident, assertive, and persistent (Deaux and Lewis 1984; Eagly 1987). Perceivers believe these characteristics extend to older women and men as well (Kite 1996). Because gender stereotypes have been so well documented, it is surprising that many researchers, both historically and now, generally ignore target gender when examining attitudes and beliefs about aging. This is especially problematic when one considers that respondents in these studies are probably not making truly gender-neutral ratings. We know, for example, that people generally tend to assume that male is "normal" or "natural" and hence assume maleness in the absence of specific information about gender (see Matlin 2000 for a review). As has been demonstrated in other research, it is unlikely that respondents can or will evaluate group members without also considering the gender of the person being rated (Black and Stevenson 1984; Haddock, Zanna, and Esses 1993). In all likelihood, then, people assume that a person described as simply "older" or "elderly" is male. Yet this tendency may also depend on the contextual information provided. Kite (1996), for example, found that when the gender of the target was unspecified, people assumed an older worker was male and an older homemaker was female. If the information is not specified, raters probably will draw their own conclusions.

Perceived gender differences in aging have not been completely ignored. Beginning with Kogan and Shelton (1962), research has pointed to important differences in how women and men are viewed. Much of this work has addressed the double standard of aging (Sontag 1979)—the belief that women enter the next age category at a younger point than do men. Women are thought to reach middle and old age (Drevenstedt 1976; Kogan 1979; Seccombe and Ishii Kuntz 1991) and the prime of life (Zepelin, Sills, and Heath 1986) earlier than men do. Women are also likely to be stereotyped negatively at a younger age than are men (Hummert, Gartska, and Shaner 1997). Supporting the idea that this double standard exists, particularly for physical appearance, research shows that perceivers are more likely to use facial expressions to categorize older women than older men (Hummert et al. 1994). Similarly, Deutsch, Zalenski, and Clark (1986) found that older men were seen as more attractive than older women, but there were no differences in attractiveness ratings of middle-aged or young women and men.

Overall, however, support for the double standard has been inconsistent, with some studies finding no evidence that men and women are perceived to age at different rates (Drevenstedt 1976; Locke-Connor and Walsh 1980). Kite, Deaux, and Miele (1991) suggested that the presence or absence of such a double standard may depend on the specific age of the target. That is, once a certain age is reached, women may no longer be devalued relative to men (O'Connell and Rotter 1979). Yet whether the sexes are viewed differently as they age may depend on what you ask, with a double standard being more likely for physical appearance ratings, as Hummert et al's (1994) work suggests, or on gender-associated attributes. Women's and men's competence, in contrast, may be viewed similarly regardless of their age (Erber, Szuchman, and Rothberg 1990b). Supporting this proposition, a study of targets 60 years old and older (Canetto, Kaminski, and Felicio 1995) found a gender-based double standard for evaluations of typical aging but not for optimal aging. People apparently believed women could age as successfully as men—under the right circumstances.

The social roles that targets are perceived to occupy matter here too. Research by Walsh, Connor and their colleagues, for example, found that target gender had relatively little effect on evaluations when the quality of a person's work was also known. Older men's and women's essays were evaluated by their quality, not by the author's characteristics (Walsh and Connor 1979), and workers were judged employable based on their interview performance rather than their age or gender (Connor et al. 1978). It is noteworthy, however, that when a gender bias has been demonstrated, it is generally the women who are devalued. An interesting exception to this pattern emerged in a study of attitudes toward the old-old; in this case, men were stereotyped more negatively than the women were (Hummert, Gartska, and Shaner 1997).

Much remains to be learned about our views of older women and men, and researchers should, at a minimum, consistently identify the gender of targets used in their experiments. We also want to point out that very few studies have considered how a target's race or ethnicity affects evaluations of older adults. This oversight surely deserves rectifying. Consider, for example, the complex ways perceptions are influenced by the interaction of gender and race. Judgments of women and men described as black or Asian differ markedly from judgments of white women and men (Niemann et al. 1994). Similarly, gender-associated beliefs about black and white men are similar, but black women are seen as more similar to black men than to white women on male-associated traits (Deaux and Kite 1985). Social class figures in as well. Landrine (1985) found that black women and lower-class women were seen as feminine, but less so than white women and middle-class women. In the literature on aging, a number of studies have examined cultural differences in attitudes toward the elderly (see chapter 10, this volume, for a review). Yet within cultures, little attention has been paid to how the target's ethnicity and social class influence age-related attitudes. An exception, Adams and Hummert (cited in Hummert 1999) recently found that African Americans and whites have similar stereotypes about older adults; more such research is needed to document whether these similarities are the exception or the rule. The differences found in the gender literature testify to the importance of this issue; certainly it is a topic that gerontologists should explore.

Do Perceivers Believe Memory Is the First Thing to Go?

Age discrimination in the workplace rests on the assumption that older workers no longer "make the grade." After all, no employer wants to lose effective workers. This assumption reflects one of the most consistently held beliefs about older adults: that they are less competent than their younger counterparts (Kite and Johnson 1988). There is likely a kernel of truth to this stereotype; at least in terms of some cognitive abilities, age-related decrements have been found (Park et al. 1996; Salthouse 1996). But just as observers would be wrong to conclude that all older adults have poor memories, gerontologists would err in concluding that all stereotype research shows an age bias on that dimension. Instead, research findings show that perceivers have considerable savvy when evaluating older adults' cognitive abilities.

How people view intelligence and competence across the life span is indeed complex. On the one hand, when comparing 30, 50, and 70 year olds, perceivers believe the youngest are most able to deal with novelty and are most likely to show an interest in gaining new knowledge. When the dimensions are verbal competence or the ability to deal with everyday life, however, middle-aged and older targets carry the day (Berg and Sternberg 1992). Similar results emerged when raters guessed how younger and older people would perform on the Wechsler Adult Intelligence Scale (WAIS; see Hendrick et al. 1988; Wechsler 1955). Interestingly, estimates that computational ability and logical ability (as measured by the WAIS) would not decline with age run counter to normative data showing that there are actual age-related declines on those dimensions.

This is not to suggest that an age-related bias does not exist; young people (but not older people) viewed the same type of memory failure (e.g., forgetting the name of a long-time friend) as more serious when the memory lapse was experienced by a 70 year old rather than a 30 year old (Erber 1989). Moreover, attributions about the causes for memory failure differ by target age. For older targets, memory failure is explained by internal, stable causes, such as memory difficulty, whereas for younger targets, the same memory lapse is explained by internal, unstable causes, such as lack of attention (Erber, Szuchman, and Rothberg 1990a). These judgments, too, are qualified by age of rater, with older targets being more forgiving in their evaluations of their peers.

In many situations, however, both the young and the old show a willingness to eschew age-related explanations for memory failure. In these instances, information other than age can be more influential. Erber, Szuchman, and Etheart (1993) found that young people do believe older adults are more forgetful than those who are younger; at the same time, their belief that older people are more responsible led them to judge older neighbors as a "better bet" for getting needed favors done. Moreover, regardless of target age, perceivers saw failures suggesting serious, long-term memory problems (e.g., forgetting familiar information) as more likely due to internal, stable causes than less serious incidents of forgetting (e.g., short-term memory failure or forgetting less familiar information; Erber, Szuchman, and Rothberg 1990a). Similarly, judgments of a person's suitability for a job at a museum gift shop were influenced by evidence of his or her memory capacity but not by age (Erber et al. 1996).

Older adults' competence has been assessed in a variety of ways, each pointing to a complex web of beliefs. When seeking information about the cause of an accident, people want to know whether young drivers have been drinking or speeding; in contrast, they wonder whether older drivers are physically or mentally impaired (Carver and de la Garza 1984). Yet perceptions of a witness's credibility show a bias in favor of the older adult (Ross et al. 1990). And older adults are viewed as unlikely to complete a computer course, but those known to complete the course successfully are perceived as more capable than their younger peers (Ryan, Szechtman, and Bodkin 1992). This returns us to the now-familiar topic of contextual information: simply put, when it is available, perceivers use it. When people performed better than expected for their age group in family and work situations, for example, they were perceived particularly positively; a worse-than-expected performance produced particularly negative ratings (Krueger, Heckhausen, and Hundertmark 1995). Apparently even when the dimensions include cognitive abilities, people are more than willing to set aside ageist assumptions when the evidence allows.

Are Young People Particularly Ageist?

The question of whether younger adults have especially negative attitudes toward older people has long been of interest to gerontologists. Drawing conclusions from a narrative review of this literature is difficult, however. Some studies do find older people to be more favorable toward old age than are younger people (Anantharaman 1979; Deutsch, Zalenski, and Clark 1986; Erber 1989; Jackson and Sullivan 1988), but others report no age differences (Bailey 1991; Berg and Sternberg 1992; Harris, Page, and Begay 1988). Still other studies find older people to be more negative toward old age (Hellbusch et al. 1994). Hummert (1999) points out that older and younger people are in basic agreement about the stereotypes associated with advancing age, although older people list more subcategories for "elderly persons" than younger people do (Brewer and Lui 1984; Hummert et al. 1994). When evaluations are considered, however, the picture is more mixed.

The literature examining whether the young and old have different attitudes toward aging is extensive, and we are reluctant to draw conclusions about this question for several reasons. First, no clear pattern emerges from a narrative review of this literature. Second, even if a clear direction was indicated, interpreting any age-related differences is complicated because the raters of different ages also differ in educational achievement, socioeconomic status, and ethnicity (Kite and Whitley 1996; Sears 1986). This problem is exacerbated because younger respondents are often college students, and older samples are typically convenience samples. It is extremely rare to have directly comparable populations. Relatedly, when respondents rate someone of a different age, they are also rating someone of a different generation, a factor that may be more important than age (Slotterback 1996). Third, it is likely that age-of-respondent effects are moderated by other factors. Determining what those factors may be is limited by our fourth concern: research addressing this question is rarely driven by theoretical questions that frame the issue and aid in the interpretation of results (see Brewer and Lui 1984; Hummert 1999; Linville 1982; Linville, Fischer, and Yoon 1996, for excellent exceptions). The field would benefit greatly from a meta-analysis comparing younger and older adults' attitudes toward aging, but we are not aware of any such summary. Such a review could offer both an overall assessment of whether respondent age differences exist and, if so, the direction of that bias. In addition, such a review could consider which factors might moderate any such bias. Hopefully, examination of these potential factors would be derived from relevant theory. We suggest next how hypotheses derived from social identity theory can inform the study of this issue.

Social Identity Theory

Any understanding of age differences in age-related attitudes must begin by acknowledging that these perceptions include views about ourselves and about others (see Markus and Herzog 1991 for an excellent discussion of the self-concept and aging). When we make age-based judgments, we are evaluating a person who either is or is not a member of our own age group. This important distinction is central to social identity theory (SIT; Tajfel and Turner 1979), which posits that people want to have a positive self-identity. Because a large part of our self-identity is made up of our group identity, we can achieve this goal only by feeling positively about the groups to which we belong. One way to achieve this positive group identity is to seek positive distinctiveness between our group (the in-group) and other groups (out-groups).

When age is the social category into which they are grouped, people should be motivated to view their own age group positively. According to SIT, however, simply feeling good about your own group is not sufficient. To maintain a positive identity, groups are also motivated to elevate their group above others. Applied to aging, both younger and older respondents should evaluate their own age group more favorably than other potential age groups. That is, older adults should show preferences for older adults (in-group bias), and younger adults and middle-aged adults should prefer members of their own age group and devalue people of other ages (out-group bias). Ageist attitudes could then be viewed as the product of younger age groups' creating and maintaining positive social identities. But the complexity of the literature examining this question belies such a simple explanation: age groups do not uniformly derogate people of other ages. A closer look at the dynamic nature of social identity shows how SIT can address these complexities (see Chapter 6, this volume, for a discussion of SIT and workplace ageism).

SIT does not predict that we dislike all out-groups. Rather, what is important is that we are always motivated to see our own group more positively than other groups. If one belongs to a dominant, positively viewed group, then making a favorable comparison for one's own group is easy. But if one belongs to a subordinate, lower-status group, then maintaining a positive group identity becomes more difficult. It is here where the foundation of attitudes is laid and where prejudice can start. A complex interplay between self-identity and attitudes toward others can occur.

As an example of how self-identity can affect attitudes toward others, consider how people acquire a positive self-image if they are in (or may eventually join) a negatively viewed low-status group. In other words, if you are in a group for which others have negative attitudes, like older adults, how do you maintain a positive self-identity? SIT theory predicts that if people do not obtain the positive distinctiveness from their in-group, then they have several options for maintaining a positive self-image: social mobility, social creativity, and social competition (Harwood,

Giles, and Ryan 1995; Tajfel and Turner 1979). The option that a person uses will affect their attitudes toward others. Using social mobility, a person in a negatively viewed group can leave this social group (literally or figuratively). This strategy allows the negative attitude toward that group to remain—after all, you are not one of "them." If leaving a group is difficult, a low-status group member could use social creativity and focus on other positive traits of the in-group, other subgroups of the in-group, or negative traits of other out-groups. This social creativity could lead to greater differentiation of the group whereby positive attitudes are held toward some subgroups and negative attitudes toward others. Finally, using social competition, a low-status group member could change the societal images of his or her group so that a positive identity could be gained from belonging to this group (Harwood, Giles, and Ryan 1995; Tajfel and Turner 1979). Social competition, if successful, should actually change attitudes toward the group. Given the progressive nature of age, all people—younger, middle-aged, and older adults—will eventually need to work to maintain a positive self-identity if they have or are aware of society's negative views of aging. This task will likely become more relevant the closer one gets to old age.

For younger adults, positive distinctiveness of their age group can be made simply by noting that they are not old. Given an awareness of society's negative views of older adults, this comparison will likely confer a positive distinctiveness. The issues younger adults have with age identity, although important, are not relevant for this chapter. Some research and anecdotal information, for example, suggests that young adolescents do see themselves as older than they actually are (i.e., they have older subjective age identities; Montepare and Lachman 1989). We simply note here that age-linked attitudes cut both ways and that the way younger adults see the aging process now may well set the stage for how they look at both their own and others' aging.

Middle-aged adults are in a slightly different circumstance. As members of a dominant group that overall is seen relatively positively, they would not appear to need strategies to create positive distinctiveness for their age group. Yet middle-aged adults are also aging and so are closer to becoming members of a stereotyped group. This impending group change may increase their need for positive distinctiveness from older adults. In contrast with early adolescents, middle-aged adults hold younger subjective age identities, perhaps providing evidence for social mobility (Montepare and Lachman 1989). Again, social mobility would result in the maintenance of attitudes toward older adults. Middle-aged adults could also use social creativity by avoiding older adults and thus avoid thinking about their own aging, or by focusing on certain negatively viewed subgroups of older adults to ensure a positive self-comparison. Using social creativity in this way would strengthen existing negative stereotypes of older adults. If middle-aged adults instead focused on valuing certain subgroups of older adults (again, using social creativity) or worked to change society's view of aging (social competition), then the relatively low status and negative images of older adults might change.

Clearly, younger and middle-aged adults' negative attitudes toward the aged are explained by SIT. But why might younger and middle-aged adults have positive views of aging? As Harwood, Giles, and Ryan (1995) argue, such positive attitudes are not necessarily inconsistent with a SIT framework. Younger and middle-aged adults do not need to derogate older adults in order to maintain positive group images; they simply need relative positive distinctiveness of their own age group on personally relevant traits. Hence, younger adults might see themselves as having more developmental potential than older adults, but they still might think older adults are happier or more settled in their lives.

Research examining older adults' attitudes toward the elderly is more complicated. In support of SIT, Celejewski and Dion (1998) found that older adults did evaluate other older adults more positively than did younger adults. But contrary to a simple SIT prediction, older adults also evaluated younger adults more positively than they did older adults. The research comparing older and younger adults' evaluations of older adults is particularly complex.

Clearly, older adults' attitude toward aging defies simple explanation. Perhaps age is a rather unique social category in that, if SIT is correct, people may spend a lifetime making their own age group positively distinctive from older adults—only to find that they have become an older adult themselves. The knowledge that they are becoming a part of a group about which society holds many negative views requires action— or at least cognitive adjustment—to stay upbeat. According to SIT, these older adults have three options to maintain a positive identity. They can use social mobility and avoid becoming a member of this group by maintaining a youthful demeanor and appearance and by avoiding any behaviors associated with the elderly. They can use social creativity by focusing on the positive attributes of aging or by joining a specific subgroup of the elderly (e.g., perfect grandparent), or they can use social competition to change the status of older adults. Evidence supports the possible use of all these strategies. Avoiding old age through social mobility can be seen when older adults resist using the very things designed to make their lives easier (e.g., refusing to use hearing aids or a walker). Name changes for social groups can be seen as examples of social creativity (Harwood, Giles, and Ryan 1995). That is, by changing the name of one's social category (e.g., from "the aged" to "senior citizens" to "older adults"), one can try to avoid the stigma attached to the less favorable labels. Similarly, an older adult could use social competition by working to change the societal images of aging. Groups such as the Gray Panthers, Older Women's League (OWL), and American Association for Retired Persons (AARP) strive to do just that. Older adults' attitudes toward other older adults may depend heavily on the strategy that they use to maintain a positive self-identity while aging.

The particular strategy for identity maintenance that an older adult adopts (or the failure to adopt one) may explain why and where researchers find age-of-respondent differences in attitudes toward older adults. Adding to the complexity of age-related attitudes is the dynamic nature of social identity. Age is just one social category that may or may not constitute a part of one's identity. Perhaps age is more or less relevant to identity at different ages. Other identities (e.g., gender, marital status) may be more salient than age, at least at some points in life. Moreover, which identity is salient may change in different situations and even at different ages. People may think more about aging, for example, when their fiftieth birthday arrives and their office is decorated with black crepe paper. Obviously, SIT would best predict age-related attitudes when age is an important component of the respondent's identity. This leads us to another important point: awareness of age stereotypes does appear to affect older adults' behavior. Levy (1996) has found that priming negative aging trait terms (e.g., *senile*) decreased memory performance and increased negative attitudes toward aging. In contrast, priming positive aging trait terms (e.g., *wise*) increased memory performance and increased the positivity of attitudes toward aging. Younger adults' memory and attitudes are not influenced by these primes. Priming can influence older adults' physiological functioning as well. Those primed with positive aging trait terms walked at a faster rate than those primed with negative trait terms (Hausdorff, Levy, and Wei 1999). Such findings testify to the power of negative stereotypes, particularly for those who are members of the derogated group. We now examine how culture influences these stereotypes.

Culture

We assume that ageist attitudes stem from cultural beliefs about older adults. Given this assumption, we need to examine our own culture's (and other cultures') influences on the aging process. How cultural issues influence ageism (see chapter 10, this volume) and age-linked communication patterns across cultures (chapter 7, this volume) are described elsewhere in this book, so we comment only briefly on this issue here.

One intriguing advantage of cross-cultural studies is that they can test theoretical propositions that cannot be tested within a culture. There has long been some question, for example, about whether a society's attitudes toward older adults affect older adults themselves (Levy and Langer 1996). Questions about the impact of negative attitudes toward older adults can be partially answered by comparing cultures that differ in their attitudes toward aging. To address this issue, Levy and Langer (1994) examined three cultural groups whose attitudes toward older adults differed in positivity: Chinese culture (most positive toward aging), deaf American culture, and hearing American culture (least positive). After determining that young adults in these cultures did not differ in performance on memory tasks, they showed that Chinese older adults had higher memory performance than the American older adults. This suggests that peoples' attitudes toward aging might affect their own aging process in a sort of self-fulfilling prophecy. For cultures with negative views of aging, this is a disconcerting prospect.

One problem with cross-cultural aging research is that a comprehensive understanding of culture's influence on attitudes toward aging and older adults is lacking. Studies comparing two different countries' ageist attitudes predominate. These kinds of studies can lead to oversimplifying a culture's attitude toward aging, a point Tobin (1987) makes. For example, North Americans idealize the respect and devotion toward older adults in Japan (Tobin 1987) and envy Swedes' access to social services that facilitate independent aging, without a full understanding of each culture's influence on the aging process. To avoid this oversimplification, researchers must be careful to conduct culturally appropriate research to address the full complexity of aging within a culture. Instead of focusing on an idealized view of Japanese aging, Levy (1999) examined how Japanese older adults maintain a positive self-image in the face of what some argue are even stronger ageist attitudes than those encountered in the United States. She found that Japanese older adults maintain a sharp distinction between their inner self and societal views of aging. They do this by sharply differentiating what might apply to the self and what applies to "other older adults." She also demonstrated that Japanese older adults have more negative views of older adults in general than her Chinese or U.S. participants. Additional research on this and similar questions would add much to our understanding of culture and ageism. Another positive model for cross-cultural aging studies is a study of cognitive aging that begins with a well-known cultural difference: Asians tend to focus more on contextual or situational factors, whereas Westerners tend to focus more on the actor or the object. The authors of this study (Park, Nisbett, and Hedden 1999) theorize about the impact of this cultural cognitive difference on cognitive processes as people age. Future work should continue in this complex vein.

Conclusion

This chapter is about attitudes toward older adults. In many cases, this implies "other" older adults ("not me; not us"). But because "the aged" is a group that we will all likely join, it is, at a minimum, also about attitudes toward a current or future in-group. And because there are visible markers that indicate age and we do not live in a completely age-segregated society, it is also about attitudes toward a group with which most of us have had some interaction throughout our lives. Given that we are aging as we speak (or as we type or read), it is also about attitudes toward the aging process in general and our own aging process in particular. These complexities make studying and understanding ageism a challenge.

Gerontologists have not yet fully addressed the implications of these complexities. Indeed, in this chapter we sometimes switch between these different attitudes without comment. Also, theories that predict when these attitudes will overlap and when they will diverge remain undeveloped. We do not know, for example, whether a fear of aging makes people avoid older adults or how much cultural views of aging produce fear of old age. We need to move in this direction to be able to understand the complexity of our attitudes toward older adults, our attitudes toward others' aging, and our attitudes toward our own aging process. Some research is incorporating this complexity. But current theories do not go far enough in delineating the relationship between our own aging and our attitudes toward aging and older adults.

Significant advances have been made toward describing our stereotypes of older adults and toward understanding the role that context plays in age-based evaluations. As we have said throughout this chapter, questions such as, "Are North Americans ageist?" defy simple answers. By continuing to explore the "yes, buts" and "only ifs," great advancements toward understanding have been achieved. This chapter summarizes some of these achievements, and we hope it points to fruitful avenues for continued exploration.

Note

Preparation of this chapter was supported by National Institute on Aging Grant to Mary Kite and was facilitated by our participation in an NIA-supported research training program directed by Chandra M. Mehrotra at the College of St. Scholastica. Order of authorship is alphabetical; the authors contributed equally to this work.

References

Anantharaman, R. N. (1979). Perception of old age by two generations. *Journal of Psychological Researches, 23*(3), 198–199.

Bailey, W. T. (1991). Knowledge, attitude, and psychosocial development of young and old adults. *Educational Gerontology, 17*(3), 269–274.

Bell, B. D., and Stanfield, G. G. (1973). Chronological age in relation to attitudinal judgments: An experimental analysis. *Journal of Gerontology, 28*(4), 491–496.

Berg, C. A., and Sternberg, R. J. (1992). Adults' conceptions of intelligence across the adult life span. *Psychology and Aging, 7*(2), 221–231.

Black, K. N., and Stevenson, M. R. (1984). The relationship of self-reported sex-role characteristics and attitudes toward homosexuality. *Journal of Homosexuality, 10*(1–2), 83–93.

Brewer, M. B., Dull, V., and Lui, L. (1981). Perceptions of the elderly: Stereotypes as prototypes. *Journal of Personality and Social Psychology, 41*(4), 656–670.

Brewer, M. B., and Lui, L. (1984). Categorization of the elderly by the elderly: Effects of perceiver's category membership. *Personality and Social Psychology Bulletin, 10*(4), 585–595.

Butler, R. N. (1969). Age-ism: Another form of bigotry. *Gerontologist, 9*(4, Pt. 1), 243–246.

Byrd, M., and Breuss, T. (1992). Perceptions of sociological and psychological age norms by young, middle-aged, and elderly New Zealanders. *International Journal of Aging and Human Development, 34*(2), 145–163.

Canetto, S. S., Kaminski, P. L., and Felicio, D. M. (1995). Typical and optimal aging in women and men: Is there a double standard? *International Journal of Aging and Human Development, 40*(3), 187–207.

Caporael, L. R. (1981). The paralanguage of caregiving: Baby talk to the institutionalized aged. *Journal of Personality and Social Psychology, 40*(5), 876–884.

Carver, C. S., and de la Garza, N. H. (1984). Schema-guided information search in stereotyping of the elderly. *Journal of Applied Social Psychology, 14*(1), 69–81.

Celejewski, I., and Dion, K. K. (1998). Self-perception and perception of age groups as a function of the perceiver's category membership. *International Journal of Aging and Human Development, 47*(3), 205–216.

Chumbler, N. R. (1994). Black/white comparisons in negative stereotypes toward older people. *Free Inquiry in Creative Sociology, 22,* 149–155.

Connor, C. L., Walsh, R. P., Litzelman, D. K., and Alvarez, M. G. (1978). Evaluation of job applicants: The effects of age versus success. *Journal of Gerontology, 33*(2), 246–252.

Crockett, W. H., and Hummert, M. L. (1987). Perceptions of aging and the elderly. In K. W. Schaie (Ed.), *Annual review of gerontology and geriatrics* (Vol. 7, pp. 217–241). New York: Springer.

Davis-Berman, J., and Robinson, J. D. (1989). Knowledge on aging and preferences to work with the elderly: The impact of a course on aging. *Gerontology and Geriatrics Education, 10*(1), 23–36.

Deaux, K., and Kite, M. E. (1985). Gender stereotypes: Some thoughts on the cognitive organization of gender-related information. *Academic Psychology Bulletin, 7*(2), 123–144.

Deaux, K., and Lewis, L. L. (1984). Structure of gender stereotypes: Interrelationships among components and gender label. *Journal of Personality and Social Psychology, 46*(5), 991–1004.

Deutsch, F. M., Zalenski, C. M., and Clark, M. E. (1986). Is there a double standard of aging? *Journal of Applied Social Psychology, 16*(9), 771–785.

Drevenstedt, J. (1976). Perceptions of onsets of young adulthood, middle age, and old age. *Journal of Gerontology, 31*(1), 53–57.

Eagly, A. H. (1987). *Sex differences in social behavior: A social-role interpretation.* Hillsdale, NJ: Erlbaum.

Eagly, A. H., and Chaiken, S. (1993). *The psychology of attitudes.* Fort Worth, TX: Harcourt Brace.

Eagly, A. H., and Steffen, V. J. (1984). Gender stereotypes stem from the distribution of women and men into social roles. *Journal of Personality and Social Psychology, 46*(4), 735–754.

Eagly, A. H., Wood, W., and Diekman, A. B. (2000). Social role theory of sex differences and similarities: A current appraisal. In T. Eckes (Ed.), *The developmental social psychology of gender* (pp. 123–174). Mahwah, NJ: Erlbaum.

Erber, J. T. (1989). Young and older adults' appraisal of memory failures in young and older adult target persons. *Journals of Gerontology, 44*(6), 170–P175.

Erber, J. T., and Prager, I. G. (1999). Age and memory: Perceptions of forgetful young and older adults. In T. M. Hess and F. Blanchard-Fields (Eds.), *Social cognition and aging* (pp. 197–217). San Diego, CA: Academic Press.

Erber, J. T., Prager, I. G., Williams, M., and Caiola, M. A. (1996). Age and forgetfulness: Confidence in ability and attribution for memory failures. *Psychology and Aging, 11*(2), 310–315.

Erber, J. T., Szuchman, L. T., and Etheart, M. E. (1993). Age and forgetfulness: Young perceivers' impressions of young and older neighbors. *International Journal of Aging and Human Development, 37*(2), 91–103.

Erber, J. T., Szuchman, L. T., and Rothberg, S. T. (1990a). Age, gender, and individual differences in memory failure appraisal. *Psychology and Aging, 5*(4), 600–603.

Erber, J. T., Szuchman, L. T., and Rothberg, S. T. (1990b). Everyday memory failure: Age differences in appraisal and attribution. *Psychology and Aging, 5*(2), 236–241.

Finkelstein, L. M., Burke, M. J., and Raju, M. S. (1995). Age discrimination in simulated employment contexts: An integrative analysis. *Journal of Applied Psychology, 80*(6), 652–663.

Foos, P. W., and Dickerson, A. E. (1996). People my age remember these things better. *Educational Gerontology, 22*(2), 151–160.

Gekoski, W. L., and Knox, V. J. (1990). Ageism or healthism? Perceptions based on age and health status. *Journal of Aging and Health, 2*(1), 15–27.

Gekoski, W. L., Knox, V. J., Johnson, E. A., and Evans, K. R. (1984). Sex of target and sex of subject effects on the perception of 25, 45, 65, and 85 year olds. *Canadian Journal on Aging, 3*(4), 155–164.

Golde, P., and Kogan, N. (1959). A sentence completion procedure for assessing attitudes toward old people. *Journal of Gerontology, 14*, 355–360.

Gordon, R. A., Arvey, R. D., Hodges, T. L., Sowada, K. M., and King, C. M. (2000, May). *The issue of generalizability in age discrimination research: A meta-analytic investigation.* Paper presented at the Midwestern Psychological Association, Chicago.

Graham, I. D., and Baker, P. M. (1989). Status, age, and gender: Perceptions of old and young people. *Canadian Journal on Aging, 8*(3), 255–267.

Haddock, G., Zanna, M. P., and Esses, V. M. (1993). Assessing the structure of prejudicial attitudes: The case of attitudes toward homosexuals. *Journal of Personality and Social Psychology, 65*(6), 1105–1118.

Harris, M. B., Page, P., and Begay, C. (1988). Attitudes toward aging in a southwestern sample: Effects of ethnicity, age, and sex. *Psychological Reports, 62*(3), 735–746.

Harwood, J., Giles, H., and Ryan, E. B. (1995). Aging, communication, and intergroup theory: Social identity and intergenerational communication. In J. F. Nussbaum and J. Coupland (Eds.), *Handbook of communication and aging research* (pp. 133–159). Mahwah, NJ: Erlbaum.

Hassell, B. L., and Perrewe, P. L. (1995). An examination of beliefs about older workers: Do stereotypes still exist? *Journal of Organizational Behavior, 16*(5), 457–468.

Hausdorff, J. M., Levy, B. R., and Wei, J. Y. (1999). The power of ageism on physical function of older persons: Reversibility of age-related gait changes. *Journal of the American Geriatrics Society, 47*(11), 1346–1349.

Heckhausen, J., Dixon, R. A., and Baltes, P. B. (1989). Gains and losses in development throughout adulthood as perceived by different adult age groups. *Developmental Psychology, 25*(1), 109–121.

Hellbusch, J. S., Corbin, D. E., Thorson, J. A., and Stacy, R. D. (1994). Physicians' attitudes towards aging. *Gerontology and Geriatrics Education, 15*(2), 55–65.

Hendrick, J. J., Knox, V. J., Gekoski, W. L., and Dyne, K. J. (1988). Perceived cognitive ability of young and old targets. *Canadian Journal on Aging, 7*(3), 192–203.

Hori, S. (1994). Beginning of old age in Japan and age norms in adulthood. *Educational Gerontology, 20*(5), 439–451.

Hummert, M. L. (1990). Multiple stereotypes of elderly and young adults: A comparison of structure and evaluations. *Psychology and Aging, 5*(2), 182–193.

Hummert, M. L. (1993). Age and typicality judgments of stereotypes of the elderly: Perceptions of elderly vs. young adults. *International Journal of Aging and Human Development, 37*(3), 217–226.

Hummert, M. L. (1999). A social cognitive perspective on age stereotypes. In T. M. Hess and F. Blanchard-Fields (Eds.), *Social cognition and aging* (pp. 175–196). San Diego, CA: Academic Press.

Hummert, M. L., Garstka, T. A., and Shaner, J. L. (1995). Beliefs about language performance: Adults' perceptions about self and elderly targets. *Journal of Language and Social Psychology, 14*(3), 235–259.

Hummert, M. L., Garstka, T. A., and Shaner, J. L. (1997). Stereotyping of older adults: The role of target facial cues and perceiver characteristics. *Psychology and Aging, 12*(1), 107–114.

Hummert, M. L., Garstka, T. A., Shaner, J. L., and Strahm, S. (1994). Stereotypes of the elderly held by young, middle-aged, and elderly adults. *Journal of Gerontology, 49*(5), 240–P249.

Intrieri, R. C., von Eye, A., and Kelly, J. A. (1995). The Aging Semantic Differential: A confirmatory factor analysis. *Gerontologist, 35*(5), 616–621.

Jackson, L. A., and Sullivan, L. A. (1988). Age stereotype disconfirming information and evaluations of old people. *Journal of Social Psychology, 128*(6), 721–729.

Kidwell, I. J., and Booth, A. (1977). Social distance and intergenerational relations. *Gerontologist, 17*(5), 412–420.

Kite, M. E. (1996). Age, gender, and occupational label: A test of social role theory. *Psychology of Women Quarterly, 20*(3), 361–374.

Kite, M. E., and Cano, M. (1998). *The roles of perceived choice and perceived status in beliefs about the elderly.* Unpublished data.

Kite, M. E., Deaux, K., and Miele, M. (1991). Stereotypes of young and old: Does age outweigh gender? *Psychology and Aging, 6*(1), 19–27.

Kite, M. E., and Johnson, B. T. (1988). Attitudes toward older and younger adults: A meta-analysis. *Psychology and Aging, 3*(3), 233–244.

Kite, M. E., and Whitley, B. E., Jr. (1996). Sex differences in attitudes toward homosexual persons, behaviors, and civil rights: A meta-analysis. *Personality and Social Psychology Bulletin, 22*(4), 336–353.

Klemmack, D. L., Durand, R. M., and Roff, L. L. (1980). Re-examination of the relationship between age and fear of aging. *Psychological Reports, 46*(3, Pt 2), 1320.

Kogan, N. (1979). A study of age categorization. *Journal of Gerontology, 34*, 358–367.

Kogan, N., and Shelton, F. C. (1960). Differential cue value of age and occupation in impression formation. *Psychological Reports, 7*, 203–216.

Kogan, N., and Shelton, F. C. (1962). Images of "old people" and "people in general" in an older sample. *Journal of Genetic Psychology, 100*, 3–21.

Krueger, J., Heckhausen, J., and Hundertmark, J. (1995). Perceiving middle-aged adults: Effects of stereotype-congruent and incongruent information. *Journals of Gerontology: Series B: Psychological Sciences and Social Sciences, 50b*(2), 82–93.

Landrine, H. (1985). Race * class stereotypes of women. *Sex Roles, 13*(1–2), 65–75.

Levin, J., and Levin, W. C. (1981). Willingness to interact with an old person. *Research on Aging, 3*, 211–217.

Levy, B. (1996). Improving memory in old age through implicit self-stereotyping. *Journal of Personality and Social Psychology, 71*(6), 1092–1107.

Levy, B., and Langer, E. (1994). Aging free from negative stereotypes: Successful memory in China among the American deaf. *Journal of Personality and Social Psychology, 66*(6), 989–997.

Levy, B., and Langer, E. (1996). Reversing disability in old age. In P. M. Kato and T. Mann (Eds.), *Handbook of diversity issues in health psychology* (pp. 141–159). New York: Plenum Press.

Levy, B. R. (1999). The inner self of the Japanese elderly: A defense against negative stereotypes of aging. *International Journal of Aging and Human Development, 48*(2), 131–144.

Linville, P. W. (1982). The complexity-extremity effect and age-based stereotyping. *Journal of Personality and Social Psychology, 42*(2), 193–211.

Linville, P. W., Fischer, G. W., and Yoon, C. (1996). Perceived covariation among the features of ingroup and outgroup members: The outgroup covariation effect. *Journal of Personality and Social Psychology, 70*(3), 421–436.

Locke-Connor, C., and Walsh, R. P. (1980). Attitudes toward the older job applicant: Just as competent, but more likely to fail. *Journal of Gerontology, 35*(6), 920–927.

Lutsky, N. (1980). Attitudes toward old age and elderly persons. In C. Eisdorfer (Ed.), *Annual review of gerontology and geriatrics* (Vol. 1, pp. 287–336). New York: Springer.

Markus, H. R., and Herzog, A. R. (1991). The role of the self-concept in aging. In K. W. Schaie and M. P. Lawton (Eds.), *Annual Review of Gerontology and Geriatrics* (Vol. 11, pp. 110–141). New York: Springer.

Matlin, M. W. (2000). *The psychology of women* (4th ed.). Fort Worth, TX: Harcourt Brace Jovanovich.

McTavish, D. G. (1971). Perceptions of old people: A review of research methodologies and findings. *Gerontologist, 11*(4, Pt. 2), 90–101.

Mellott, D. S., and Greenwald, A. G. (2000). *Do older adults show automatic ageism? A comparison with young adults.* Unpublished manuscript.

Montepare, J. M., and Lachman, M. E. (1989). "You're only as old as you feel": Self-perceptions of age, fears of aging, and life satisfaction from adolescence to old age. *Psychology and Aging, 4*(1), 73–78.

Neugarten, B. (1974, September). Age groups in American society and the rise of the young-old. *Annals of the American Academy of Political and Social Science,* 187–198.

Niemann, Y. F., Jennings, L., Rozelle, R. M., and Baxter, J. C. (1994). Use of free responses and cluster analysis to determine stereotypes of eight groups. *Personality and Social Psychology Bulletin, 20*(4), 379–390.

O'Connell, A. N., and Rotter, N. G. (1979). The influence of stimulus age and sex on person perception. *Journal of Gerontology, 34*(2), 220–228.

Palmore, E. (1977). Facts on Aging: A short quiz. *Gerontologist, 17*(4), 315–320.

Palmore, E. B. (1988). *The Facts on Aging quiz: A handbook of uses and results.* New York: Springer.

Park, D. C., Nisbett, R., and Hedden, T. (1999). Aging, culture, and cognition. *Journals of Gerontology: Series B: Psychological Sciences and Social Sciences, 54b*(2), 75–84.

Park, D. C., Smith, A. D., Lautenschlager, G., Earles, J. L., Frieske, D., Zwahr, M., and Gaines, C. L. (1996). Mediators of long-term memory performance across the life span. *Psychology and Aging, 11*(4), 621–637.

Perdue, C. W., and Gurtman, M. B. (1990). Evidence for the automaticity of ageism. *Journal of Experimental Social Psychology, 26*(3), 199–216.

Reno, R. (1979). Attribution for success and failure as a function of perceived age. *Journal of Gerontology, 34*(5), 709–715.

Rosen, B., and Jerdee, T. H. (1976a). The influence of age stereotypes on managerial decisions. *Journal of Applied Psychology, 61*(4), 428–432.

Rosen, B., and Jerdee, T. H. (1976b). The nature of job-related age stereotypes. *Journal of Applied Psychology, 61*(2), 180–183.

Rosencranz, H. A., and McNevin, T. E. (1969). A factor analysis of attitudes toward the aged. *Gerontologist, 9*(1), 55–59.

Ross, D. F., Dunning, D., Toglia, M. P., and Ceci, S. J. (1990). The child in the eyes of the jury: Assessing mock jurors' perceptions of the child witness. *Law and Human Behavior, 14*(1), 5–23.

Rubin, K. H., and Brown, I. D. (1975). A life-span look at person perception and its relationship to communicative interaction. *Journal of Gerontology, 30*(4), 461–468.

Ryan, E. B., and See, S. K. (1993). Age-based beliefs about memory changes for self and others across adulthood. *Journals of Gerontology, 48*(4), 199–P201.

Ryan, E. B., Szechtman, B., and Bodkin, J. (1992). Attitudes toward younger and older adults learning to use computers. *Journals of Gerontology, 47*(2), 96–P101.

Salthouse, T. A. (1996). The processing-speed theory of adult age differences in cognition. *Psychological Review, 103*(3), 403–428.

Sanders, G. F., Montgomery, J. E., Pittman, J. F., and Balkwell, C. (1984). Youth's attitudes toward the elderly. *Journal of Applied Gerontology, 3*(1), 59–70.

Schmidt, D. F., and Boland, S. M. (1986). Structure of perceptions of older adults: Evidence for multiple stereotypes. *Psychology and Aging, 1*(3), 255–260.

Sears, D. O. (1986). College sophomores in the laboratory: Influences of a narrow data base on social psychology's view of human nature. *Journal of Personality and Social Psychology, 51*(3), 515–530.

Seccombe, K., and Ishii Kuntz, M. (1991). Perceptions of problems associated with aging: Comparisons among four older age cohorts. *Gerontologist, 31*(4), 527–533.

Slotterback, C. S. (1996). Projections of aging: Impact of generational differences and the aging process on perceptions of adults. *Psychology and Aging, 11*(3), 552–559.

Sontag, S. (1979). The double standard of aging. In J. Williams (Ed.), *Psychology of women* (pp. 462–278). New York: Academic Press.

Tajfel, H., and Turner, J. C. (1979). An integrative theory of intergroup conflict. In W. C. Austin and S. Worchel (Eds.), *The social psychology of intergroup relations* (pp. 33–53). Monterey, CA: Brooks Cole.

Taylor, G. S., Crino, M. D., and Rubenfeld, S. (1989). Coworker attributes as potential correlates to the perceptions of older workers' job performance: An exploratory study. *Journal of Business and Psychology, 3*(4), 449–458.

Tobin, J. J. (1987). The American idealization of old age in Japan. *Gerontologist, 27*(1), 53–58.

Tuckman, J., and Lorge, I. (1952). The effect of institutionalization on attitudes toward old people. *Journal of Abnormal and Social Psychology, 47,* 337–344.

Tuckman, J., and Lorge, I. (1953). The effect of changed directions on the attitudes about old people and the older worker. *Educational and Psychological Measurement, 13,* 607–613.

Tuckman, J., and Lorge, I. (1958). Attitude toward aging of individuals with experiences with the aged. *Journal of Genetic Psychology, 92,* 199–204.

U.S. Bureau of the Census. (1989). Projections of the population of the United States by age, sex, and race: 1988–2080, *Current population reports: Population estimates and projections.* Series P-25, No. 1018. Washington, D.C.: U.S. Government Printing Office.

Walsh, R. P., and Connor, C. L. (1979). Old men and young women: How objectively are their skills assessed? *Journal of Gerontology, 34*(4), 561–568.

Wechsler, D. (1955). *Manual for the Wechsler Adult Intelligence Scale.*

Zepelin, H., Sills, R. A., and Heath, M. W. (1986). Is age becoming irrelevant? An exploratory study of perceived age norms. *International Journal of Aging and Human Development, 24*(4), 241–256.

6

Ageism in the Workplace: A Communication Perspective

Robert McCann and Howard Giles

With medical and scientific advances pushing life expectancy rates increasingly higher, the resultant "aging world" will undeniably affect all of us. It is not unrealistic, for example, to envision a world twenty years hence where "older individuals" wield considerably more political power, are more active in the workplace and in universities, and have a much greater stake in the world's economic output. New attitudes on health care and older people's roles in education will be forged, and questions will be raised about the fairness of social security and other payments that are taken for granted today. This chapter examines one of these developments: changes in the workplace.

Demographic workforce projections for the new millennium paint a mixed picture for older workers. On the positive side, most economists predict future shortages of skilled younger workers (Steinhauser 1998; Walsh and Lloyd 1984), predictions that bode well for older workers who possess advanced job skills. In fact, a recent study by Hall and Mirvis (1994) suggests that the paucity of skilled people in America's workforce is already a problem for management. In this study, 75 percent of employers interviewed stated that filling jobs for skilled workers was an ongoing problem. Moreover, as the baby boom generation moves into the 50- and 60-year-old age brackets, it is likely that there will be a disproportionate number of younger workers to fill the jobs that these baby boomers vacate. This should serve as yet another positive sign for the older individuals of tomorrow who wish to work during their later years.

Another school of thought on workplace trends paints a bleaker picture. Economists and academics who adhere to this line of thinking point to the imbalance between supply and demand of jobs today and question how these figures can be turned around in a matter of decades. With 1989 survey poll results showing that roughly 5.4 million older people reported being "ready and willing to work but unable to secure a job" (Louis Harris and Associates 1989) and labor force projections forecasting that the percentage of people in the workplace aged 55 and above will rise from 27.1 percent in 1990 to 39.1 percent by 2020 (see Williams and Nussbaum 2001), it is not difficult to understand why these economists predict continued difficulties for older workers.

In this chapter, we discuss the role that the particularly problematic, yet increasingly present, concept of ageism plays in the workplace. In this social context, and while recognizing that this concept has not gone unquestioned (Noels et al. 1999, 2001) and should ideally be construed from a life span perspective (Nussbaum and Baringer 2000; Williams and Giles 1998), we shall expend our energies on the "process of systematic stereotyping of and discrimination against people because they are old" (Butler 1987, p. 22; see also Gatz and Pearson 1998). First, we argue that intergenerational communication plays a central, though as yet understudied, role in workplace ageism. As Williams and Giles (1998, p. 159) stated, "Alongside the other 'isms,' [ageism] receives its impact through and is shaped in turn by communication." That said, we construe ageism as a particularly unique -ism given its facility to trigger cognitions and feelings of premature or impending, yet total, demise. Second, we contend that ageist stereotypes are central to the production of ageist attitudes, discourse, and behaviors that are commonplace in the workplace. In making this argument, we present an array of empirical evidence that challenges widely held perceptions that older workers are less adept than their younger counterparts. Third, the issue of age discrimination in the workplace will be examined, with emphasis placed on the role of discourse and communication in cases heard under the Age Discrimination in Employment Act of 1967. Finally, an agenda for future research will be set while simultaneously highlighting two relevant theories that could guide future research into the role of communication management in workplace ageism.

Intergenerational Communication and Workplace Ageism Research: Their Merging

Although aging issues unfortunately do not command mainstream attention in the discipline of communication (Giles 1999), the multidisciplinary study of intergenerational communication is just beginning to enjoy a rich and varied history (Giles 1998; Nussbaum and Coupland 1995). Over the past fifteen years, it has rapidly evolved to encompass an increasingly broad array of social and relational contexts (e.g., medical, family) as well as a full spectrum of levels of analysis (for overviews, see Kemper and Hummert 1997; Nussbaum et al. 1996; Williams and Nussbaum 2000). It features work on ageist beliefs about older people's language and communication skills (Ryan and Kwong See 1993; Ryan et al. 1992), age stereotypes and language performance (Hummert, Garstka, and Shaner 1995; Hummert et al. 1994), perceptions of older communicators (Mulac and Giles 1996; Ryan and Laurie 1990), intergenerational communication satisfaction and dissatisfaction (Williams and Giles 1996), and how elderly and younger people can under- and overaccommodate to, and miscommunicate with, each other (Coupland et al. 1988; Williams 1996). Such Western-oriented research, which now is taking on cross-cultural proportions around the Pacific Rim (Noels et al. 1998, in press; Williams et al. 1997), can be found in areas as diverse as communication between adult children and their elderly parents (Cicirelli 1993), grandparents and grandchildren (Nussbaum and Bettini 1994), elder patients and younger physicians (Ryan and Butler 1996), and care professionals and institutionalized elderly people (Caporael 1981). Interestingly, much work in this tradition approaches intergenerational communication from an explicitly anti-ageist stance, theoretically, methodologically, and ideologically (see Coupland and Coupland 1990, 1993).

Given the scope and obvious importance of intergenerational communication research, as well as the large numbers of older workers in the workforce, one would expect that workplace intergenerational communication would be a vibrant and extensive area of inquiry. After all, given the many hours of daily time spent in organizational activities, let alone the remainder of one's time participating in others' work settings, this would seem a compelling context in which to study the potential for ageisms to occur. Arguably, given the centrality of a work identity and its social meanings for many people, ageist (and hence life-constraining) comments and actions here can be hurtful, especially for those unprepared to be the recipients of them. This, however, has not been the case; in fact, the area has been virtually ignored by intergenerational communication scholars (who have bypassed the workplace context) and gerontologically sensitive organizational scholars (who have tended to ignore communication). Instead, the latter researchers focus on more traditional areas of inquiry, such as older workers' stereotypes (Shea 1991), health issues (Landy 1996; Hall and Mirvis 1994), training (Carnevale and Stone 1994), work performance (Forteza and Prieto 1994; Park 1994), the cognitive and physical capacities of older workers (Hall and Mirvis 1994), demographic changes in the workplace (Steinhauser 1998), and retirement (Levine 1988).

This chapter takes a step in bridging these two literatures in that it seeks to export research and theory from intergenerational communication (albeit from nonorganizational settings) into areas that are of relevance to workplace ageism research. Our intent is that thought-provoking connections can be forged and an agenda for future research proffered, as illustrated in the last section of this chapter.

Ageist Stereotypes: Societal and Organizational

Examples of ageism in the workplace include ageist discourse (ageist jokes and barbs), expressed ageist attitudes ("People should retire by age 60"), and discriminatory practices based on age (training, hiring, and firing decisions). These manifestations, conscious or unconscious, are guided by stereotypical expectations about how elderly people should behave and communicate in the workplace.

Workplace stereotypes do not occur in isolation, and thus they tend to reflect widespread societal stereotypes of older people. These stereotypes include perceptions of them as being nagging, irritable, decrepit, cranky, weak, feebleminded, verbose, and cognitively deficient (Braithwaite 1986; Branco and Williamson 1982; Neussel 1982); asexual, impotent, useless, and ugly (Palmore, 1990); and miserable and unsatisfied with their lives (Palmore 1988). Negative stereotypes are also considered to be the cognitive precursors to discourses such as hostile humor (Wilson and Molleston 1981) and baby talk and patronizing speech directed at the elderly (Hummert and Ryan 1996; Ryan, Hummert, and Boich 1995). Moreover, they have been shown to contribute to increased social distance and avoidance between people of different generations (Ryan and Cole 1990) and span many contexts, including the medical (Green, Adelman, and Majerovitz 1996; Ryan and Butler 1996), media (Bishop and Krause 1984; Robinson and Skill 1995), and caring (Ashburn and Gordon 1981).

Although earlier work addressed some caveats concerning the nature of the judgmental contexts in which age stereotypes are typically elicited (see Kogan 1979; Schonfield 1982), negative stereotypes of the elderly are fairly consistent among several Western countries, such as the United States (O'Connell and Rotter 1979; Perdue and Gurtman 1990), New Zealand (Koopman-Boyden 1993; Wither and Hodges 1987), and Australia (Braithwaite, Lynd-Stevenson, and Pigram 1993), as well as (and perhaps, surprisingly, even more so) in East Asia (Ikels et al. 1992; Harwood et al. 1996; Koyano 1989; Tien-Hyatt 1987). Nonetheless, studies suggest that some positive images of older people also exist (Harwood et al. 1996; Hummert et al. 1994; Kite and Johnson 1988). Indeed, it has been demonstrated that adults tend to hold multiple stereotypes of elderly individuals, such as the lively "golden-ager," the health conscious "activist," and the "shrew" (Brewer, Dull, and Lui 1981; Hummert 1990; Hummert, Garstka, and Shaner 1995).

Although life span development theory (Erickson 1959; Kolhberg 1973) suggests that aging is an individualized, unique process where universal patterns of growth cannot be expected during any one period of life, widely held perceptions that "the elderly" are cognitively deficient, physically unsuitable for work, unable to cope with change, poor performers at work, and pining for retirement still persist in society at large. Unfortunately, when extrapolated to a workplace context, these generalizations may play a part in stereotypical expectations by management and staff, which may serve as harbingers to ageist communication and discriminatory practices toward older workers. The repercussions of such age-laden discourse and practices can be devastating to both older employees, who may suffer declines in self-esteem and mental health, as well as to corporations, which may be the recipients of declining older worker productivity and age discrimination lawsuits from older workers. In what follows, some specific ageist stereotypes in the workplace will be examined, and suggestions will be made as to how these stereotypes may be manifested through intergenerational workplace communication.

Mental Decline
While it is indisputable that cognitive declines in areas such as memory (Nussbaum, Thompson, and Robinson 1988) and language (Estes 1978) skills are to be expected for many older individuals, it is erroneous and even cruel to tag all, or even most, older workers with labels such as *senile* or *out to pasture;* gerontological research suggests that senility afflicts only about 0.5 percent of those over age 65 (Feezel and Hawkins 1988). There is little change in intellectual function for individuals throughout adulthood except in matters pertaining to speed and reaction time (Newton, Lazarus, and Weinberg 1984), and brain activity in healthy people in their 80s is comparable to that of people in their 20s (Driver 1994). Nevertheless, stereotypical beliefs about the mental decrements of older individuals are ubiquitous and are well documented in the research literature. For example, research has demonstrated that individuals attribute both

memory (Ryan 1992; Ryan and Kwong See 1993) and language skill declines (Hummert, Gartska, and Shaner 1995; Ryan et al. 1992) to increasing age, despite the fact that research shows that a complex set of
factors contributes to variability in these skills. With respect to language
performance, this complexity is highlighted by Ryan and associates
(1992) "model of influences on language performance in later life,"
which shows how language ability may be influenced by a variety of factors
that include, but are not limited to, environmental influences, the task
demands and interpersonal demands of the situation, and emotional factors. The issue of cognitive competence clearly is complex. Still, society at
large continues to view "older people" as talking more slowly (Stewart and
Ryan 1982), using less sophisticated grammar (Emry, 1986), and being
overly verbose (Gold, Arbuckle, and Andres 1994), and 25 percent of
companies cited the "mental demands of work" as a factor affecting decisions to hire or retrain workers over the age of 55 (Mirvis 1993).

Several other studies by communication and organizational researchers have demonstrated that observers hold age biases when rating
the cognitive performance of older adults. In studies by Erber (1989) and
Erber and Rothberg (1991), identical memory and communication performance by young and older targets was perceived differently according
to age. More specifically, raters perceived memory failures to be correlated with "lack of ability" when the target was old but with "lack of effort"
when the target was young. These attitudes are also seen in the workplace.
In a Louis Harris survey, for example, 25 percent of managers reported
giving older applicants a "wide berth" due to the mental demands of work
(see Carnevale and Stone 1994).

Evidence exists, albeit in a nonworkplace setting, that stereotypical beliefs and attitudes about the cognitive competence of older individuals
can lead to inappropriate communication in intergenerational interactions. This miscommunication may include patronizing speech (Ryan et al.
1986), which can take the form of childlike vocabulary, demeaning emotional tone, diminutives (Ryan et al. 1986), or its most extreme form, secondary baby talk (Caporael, 1981). Although it is likely that patronizing
speech may be more characteristic of hospital, family, and caring settings
than the workplace setting, workplace language reflecting perceptions
that older workers are less sharp, slower to grasp new material, indecisive,
slow, having declining reasoning abilities, having poor memory, and making more mistakes than younger workers is still common. Comments directed at older workers—*Do you need more time? Do you need me to repeat that?
That's okay, I'll take care of it*—as well as third-party speech—*He's losing it;*

He's out to pasture; Give him some slack; He's getting on; maybe you [a younger worker] should handle the tricky stuff—are all common examples of ageist, and in some cases, patronizing, speech. This cognitively focused ageist language is frequently cited in age discrimination lawsuits.

Physical Decline

As the body ages, a multitude of physical transformations take place. Some of these, such as the wrinkling of the skin and the graying of the hair, are generally expected to occur for most individuals at certain points in their lives, while other transformations, such as certain pathologies (e.g., lung cancer), may be more of a reflection of an individual's genetics or lifestyle choices (e.g., smoking) than of his or her particular stage in life. When this idea is extrapolated to a workplace context, certain assumptions about the physical abilities of older workers may be understandable, and at times even appropriate, but to generalize these assumptions across contexts and to all older workers is problematic. Nevertheless, widespread societal perceptions of the elderly as unhealthy, characterized by physical decline, and unsuitable for work persist. For example, young respondents rated young individuals as more physically qualified than older people for "demanding" work (Finkelstein, Burke, and Raju 1995), while more than half of those polled in a Louis Harris survey believed that people over age 65 had serious health problems (Rosen and Jerdee 1985). Similarly, 40 percent of firms in a Louis Harris labor force 2000 poll cited the physical demands of work as affecting their hiring and retaining decisions for workers over age 55 (see Mirvis 1993). These perceptions are particularly telling in the light of the fact that a relatively small percentage of jobs today involve manual labor. Finally, stereotypes about the imminent physical decline of older workers are also represented in the language that can be heard in the workplace, some of which is beginning to appear in age discrimination lawsuits. Examples of this ageist language includes phrases such as *marking time, fading fast, on the shelf, one foot in the grave,* and *ready for the scrap heap.*

In contrast to widely held stereotypes that depict older workers as chronically absent and injury prone, the research literature on absenteeism and workplace injuries suggests quite a different story. Several studies point to either negative relationships (Rousseau 1978; Wall and Shatshat 1981) or nonsignificant relationships (Froggatt 1970; Nicholson, Brown, and Chadwick-Jones 1977) between advancing age and absenteeism. In a survey conducted by the National Council on the Aging (1997), employers described their older employees as high on dimensions of reliability, dependability, conscientiousness, loyalty, and stability, and an American Association of Retired People's survey of human resource executives found that 91 percent of executives rated older workers as "very good" or "excellent" in attendance and punctuality (cited in Mirvis 1993). With respect to correlations between occupational injury and advancing age, the research is equivocal. The literature does show that older adults take longer to recover from workplace accidents than younger workers (Shea 1991; Sterns, Barrett, and Alexander 1985), yet it also suggests that younger workers are hurt more often than their older counterparts (Root 1981). Taken together, the statistics point to a trade-off of sorts for employers between accident-prone younger workers and older workers who may have longer recovery times from workplace injury. That said, it is important to consider that accident figures are generally more pertinent to jobs that involve manual labor than to the desk or nonphysical jobs where many older workers are employed. Since only 14 percent of American jobs in 1978 required a high degree of physical strength (Anderson 1978), a percentage that will likely decrease considerably in the future, it is clear that fears of injury and absenteeism among older workers are largely overstated.

Results from recent research into three physically demanding types of work, policing, firefighting, and airline piloting, deemphasize the importance of chronological age and instead highlight the value of individual health and personal experience of the worker. With respect to policing and firefighting, Landy (1996) found that police officers and firefighters aged 50 and above were less likely to die of catastrophic illnesses than were workers of the same age in other stressful occupations. Landy points to particularly high levels of physical activity and fitness among older police officers and firefighters, as well as years of accumulated job experience, as being more significant to survival rates than age in these professions. In other words, compensation more than replaced any physical declines. As for airline pilots, research (Kay et al. 1994) on airline safety found no increases in accident rates among pilots after the age of 40. As is the case with police and firefighters, the above findings are consistent with research on the "healthy worker effect," in which older workers, because of deselection on the basis of health, are found to experience lower morbidity rates than the general older population (Nuyts, Elseviers, and De-Broe 1993, cited in Hansson et al. 1997). In sum, societal perceptions of older workers as unhealthy, characterized by physical decline, and chronically absent from work are more often than not erroneous and in many cases represent polar opposites to what research in these areas suggests.

Inability to Cope with Change

Almost any book on the subject of older workers inevitably contains some reference to the commonly held notion that older workers are unable to cope with change. Sometimes this belief is raised in the context of older people's perceived resistance to new technology—a process that itself could contribute to the social construction of ageing and ageism (see Giles and Condor 1988)—while at other times, it stands alone and simply represents an extension of the broader societal belief that older people are set in their ways. The supposed inability of older individuals to cope with change is reflected in stereotypical beliefs that older people are inflexible, rigid, cautious, resistant to apply new methods, careful, critical, cranky, and unadaptable (Neussel 1982; Shea 1991), as well as in younger people's perceptions of older people as communicatively close-minded, out of touch, and focused on the past (Williams et al. 1997).

With respect to the workplace, although survey results show that employers give older workers high marks on loyalty, performance, and job skills (AARP, 1989), the perception that "you can't teach an old dog new tricks" stubbornly persists among American employers. In perhaps no other area is this perception more striking than in the area of training, where study after study points to strongly held societal beliefs that older people are unwilling to change, not worth training because they will not be around long, learn too slowly, do poorly in the classroom, and are computer illiterate. In a study of 400 employers, Hall and Mirvis (1994) found that while older workers were rated better than the average employee on dimensions of performance, attitude, and turnover, these same older workers were rated worse in flexibility, health care costs, and suitability for training. Unfortunately, these negative stereotypes often lead to reluctance to train older workers, a trend that is well documented in the research literature (Rosow and Zager 1980; Simon 1996).

Although some studies support societal perceptions that older workers train more slowly than their younger counterparts (Sieman 1976; Sterns and McDaniel 1994) and have inferior abilities when compared to younger people on tasks that require complex skill acquisition (Kubeck et al. 1996; Park 1994), an equally compelling body of research shows that older workers make excellent learners. In a study that documented adult students at the University of Kansas, over 75 percent of the faculty who taught these students reported that older students learned just as quickly as their younger counterparts (AARP 1989), and in another study, older workers were found to be able to keep up with technological changes and learn new skills at a rate that was on par with younger workers (Mowery and Kamlet 1993). Moreover, several corporations have met with success in the area of training older workers. For example, General Electric, the Russell Corporation, Motorola, Days Inn, 3M, and the Travelers Group have all introduced innovative training programs for their older workers and reported great success in doing so (Carnevale and Stone 1994). These studies indicate that the research literature on the subject of elderly training is divided at best and should not be used as justification for withholding training from older workers, who represent a valuable asset to any organization. Without proper training and access to opportunity, the value of older workers cannot be maximized.

Performance and Productivity

In line with the decremental theory of aging (Botwinick 1978; Shock 1962), which suggests that worker performance naturally declines as a natural function of age, stereotypes about older workers as being unable to perform and produce at levels that are deemed acceptable for the workplace are common. Specifically, research suggests that older workers are perceived by management as being lower in job performance (Britton and Thomas 1973; Cole 1979; Roe 1965), slower in work (Panek et al. 1978), lacking in creativity, and less able to cope with job stress (Rosen and Jerdee 1977). In a recent survey, the 773 chief executive officers asked about worker productivity responded that "peak productivity" occurred, on average, at age 43 (Munk 1999).

Despite these commonly held negative perceptions, a large number of empirical studies and research reviews (Forteza and Prieto 1994; Park 1994; Warr 1994) indicate that a nonexistent or slightly positive statistical significance exists between job performance and the age of a worker. In this vein, research has shown that the output of older workers is equal to that of younger workers (Commonwealth Fund 1993), that older workers are better in terms of accuracy and steadiness of work output and output level (Eisenberg 1980), and that they outperform their younger counterparts in the area of sales (Holley, Field, and Holley 1978). Expectancy theory (Vroom 1964) suggests that motivation and effort may be more important factors than age in gauging worker performance, a claim that has been partially supported in the research literature (Arvey and Neel 1974; Doering, Rhodes, and Schuster 1983). Taken together, these studies suggest that older workers may actually be more productive than their younger counterparts, or at least be on par with them.

Although the communication literature is largely silent on intergenerational issues in the workplace, many studies have been conducted on how individuals rate the successes, achievements, and overall performance of older individuals. For example, a study by Ryan, Szechtman, and Bodkin (1992) found that young participants rated their own age group as more likely to succeed in completing a computer course than older individuals. Interestingly, the young raters gave those in their own age group higher ratings on future success measures despite rating older individuals higher on the measure of computer competence. In another study, young professionals were asked to listen to audiotapes of simulated job interviews. Before the tapes were played, the participants were told that the young and older job candidates possessed very similar work experience and identical job performance ratings. Despite the researcher's efforts to create a high degree of similarity among candidates, the young listeners negatively evaluated older workers as "deadwood" and positively evaluated younger workers as "adequate performers" (cited in Webb 1993). Unfortunately, ratings and evaluations such as these are also seen in the workplace, as is evidenced in another study (cited in Webb 1993) in which workplace evaluation forms were analyzed. Here, it was found that management in a large American bank and a hospital rated older workers consistently lower than younger workers despite no significant differences in work achievements between the two groups.

Lawrence's (1988) theory of age norms may help to shed some light on why negative stereotypes about the elderly can be so dominant in the light of evidence to the contrary. According to this scholar, society has deeply rooted normative expectations regarding the levels of success that should be obtained by certain ages. For example, by one's late 50s, societal expectations are that a person should be in a position of seniority and authority at work; to fall short of this "benchmark" represents a failure on the part of the individual. Lawrence exports this theory to managerial evaluations, arguing that when supervisors evaluate older employees against younger employees who may be viewed as "fast trackers," the supervisor's evaluations will likely be influenced by societal norms that dictate where in the organization each worker should be at his or her respective age. In terms of the theory, the supervisor would therefore downgrade the older worker and upgrade the younger "fast tracker" in performance evaluations.

Just as the social structure around us continuously transforms itself, so do the older workers who operate within it. To judge older workers by erroneous and narrowly focused productivity myths, many of which were likely developed during the middle of the twentieth century when manual labor was predominant in America, is grossly unfair. Moreover, such judgments overlook the valuable wisdom and experience that workers gain through years on the job—wisdom and experience that may more than compensate for potential cognitive or physical declines.

Retirement

The concept of retirement is a relatively new one. Before the twentieth century, Americans rarely lived past age 65, with property owners typically outliving those who did not own land. Moreover, those unfortunate enough to lack adequate economic resources traditionally had to do heavy work or toil the land well into their later years, and they were often victims of injury and early physical demise. With the Industrial Revolution and the rise of government bureaucracy and the civil service in the early 1920s, as well as America's first retirement system in 1921 and the Social Security Act of 1935, this situation soon became a thing of the past. The Social Security Act, in particular, had a profound effect on how Americans viewed retirement because it essentially institutionalized the concept of retirement by dictating that all individuals over the age of 65 who had worked for a certain number of years were eligible for benefits. The age of 65 thus became the official age of retirement for American citizens, and societal views on workplace longevity were forever altered. In more recent years, a new concept of retirement has emerged, known as early retirement. This has pushed typical retirement ages of workers downward to the late 50s and early 60s, resulting not only in a drop in the median retirement age but also a boom in early retirement incentive programs.

Partly as a result of these trends, one of the more pervasive beliefs that operates in today's workplace is that older workers should retire sometime in their mid- to late 50s or early 60s. At this point in one's life, so goes the belief, one should reap the reward of years of hard work and enjoy one's "golden years." Although this view of early retirement appears to be somewhat innocuous and even well intentioned, to those who wish to continue working, it may be seen as dripping with ageism. In fact, the "golden years view" of early retirement may actually reflect underlying attitudes that the future of the corporation lies with the young; that older workers are too rigid, slow, or sick to contribute to the organization; that the needs of the young are more important than those of the old; and that the young have more to give to the organization than do older people. Although each of these assumptions is disturbing on its own, they are not without theory to support them. Disengagement theory (Cumming and Henry, 1961) states that aging individuals loosen ties through lessened social interaction and withdraw from society (e.g., retire) in order to ensure society's optimal functioning. According to this position, ultimately, it is society's need to have people with new skills, rather than the wishes of the older person, that dictates when disengagement occurs. Retirement, whether by an early retirement package or a spoken or unspoken understanding that a worker should leave his or her job at age 65, then becomes less about choice and more about societal pressure and norms.

Popular expressions such as *waiting for the gold watch, take the package and run, golden handshake,* and 30 *and out* reflect widely held societal views that older workers spend much of their time in eager anticipation of their retirement day. Although this is likely true for many older individuals, mounting evidence suggests that a large percentage of older workers would prefer to stay in the workplace. For example, in a recent poll, 58 percent of respondents said that they plan to continue working full or part time after reaching retirement age (*Los Angeles Times,* 2000), and another survey revealed that 76 percent of retirees would like to be working, with 86 percent opposed to mandatory retirement at a fixed age (see Rosen and Jerdee 1985). A 1992 Louis Harris survey reported that 5.4 million older Americans, or one in seven American aged 55 and over, who were not working were willing to work but could not find a suitable job (Louis Harris and Associates 1992). With 12.2 percent of people aged 65 and over living in poverty (U.S. Bureau of the Census 1990), 40 percent of people aged 51 to 61 expecting to have no retirement income except social security (Eaton 1993), and less than 30 percent of older adults receiving private pension income (Rix 1990), many older Americans clearly want, and need, to work. Unfortunately, societal norms often dictate otherwise. Ever since the enactment of the Social Security Act, "age 65" has became a marker of sorts for when older adults are officially "sent out to pasture." Work is suddenly no longer expected from those who have spent a lifetime devoted to their careers, leaving the recently retired feeling isolated and confused. Powerful age norms that dictate that age 65 (or earlier) is the time for rest and relaxation have the potential to clash with the wishes and needs of older individuals.

One commonly held attitude that underlies societal beliefs about early retirement is the view that the future of the organization lies with the young and that older workers should thus "make way for the young." Younger workers, goes the reasoning, have families to support, children's educations to pay for, and great "potential" for future success, while older workers have their pensions, their social security, and their "past." Unfortunately, this view, aside from being degrading toward older workers, also overlooks the tremendous variability of older individuals, especially today, when people are going to school longer, having families later, and living longer. These assumptions do not account for the 50-year-old recent college graduate, the 40 year old just starting a family, or the 45 year old beginning a new career.

Aside from overlooking the variability in older individuals, these views also place the needs of the young over those of the older by assuming that the former have more to give to an organization. In examining this assumption, it is useful to consider research conducted on employee turnover, a so-called organizational giving variable. Interestingly enough, the statistics on worker turnover are perhaps as definitive as any that have been looked at so far, though the results are in direct contrast to the assumption that young people have more to give to an organization. In fact, although younger workers may have the potential to give more years to organizations, research is conclusive in showing that they stay far fewer years in their organizations than do older workers. A meta-analysis of several major studies on voluntary turnover found a clear inverse relationship between age and turnover (Porter and Steers 1973). Still, finding work remains a serious problem for older Americans. Older workers typically suffer extended periods of joblessness after being laid off, and when they do find work, it is often at salary levels far lower than what they have earned in the past. And this is for the "lucky" ones, as can be seen by a U.S. Bureau of the Census (1990) survey that found that 25 percent of workers aged 50 to 59 never found another job after being laid off.

In conclusion, societal assumptions that older individuals should retire and "reap the rewards from a lifetime of hard work" and "enjoy one's golden years" may actually be far less innocuous than they appear at first sight, and indeed may serve as fodder for stereotypical attitudes, ageist communication, and discriminatory practices.

Age Discrimination and the Legal Arena

Negative stereotypes about older workers, as well as about elderly people in general, may act as precursors to ageist discourse or discriminatory practices toward them. Although theoretical-driven findings in the area of age discrimination have only recently begun to emerge (see Finkelstein, Burke, and Raju 1995), strong links remain between communication and age discrimination. In order to forge these links, and using the United States on this occasion as the case study, the Age Discrimination Act of 1967 (ADEA) will be introduced, followed by the amendments that extended the ADEA. Next, the two primary means of establishing age discrimination, disparate treatment theory and disparate impact theory, will be considered. Finally, the role that ageist communication has played in age discrimination lawsuits over the past few decades will be examined.

The Age Discrimination Act of 1967

The magnitude of the age discrimination problem is underscored by recent statistics revealing that an average of 16,000 age discrimination cases per year were filed with the Equal Employment Opportunity Commission (EEOC) between 1995 and 1998, a figure that amounts to roughly 20 percent of all cases filed with the EEOC (EEOC official Web site, 1999). Age discrimination follows race, sex, and disability claims as the type of claim filed most often with the EEOC. Moreover, between 1988 and 1995, the average awards for those claiming age discrimination amounted to $219,000, as compared to $147,799 for race discrimination, $106,728 for sex discrimination, and $100,345 for disability cases (Jury Verdict Research 1999). It is important to note that these figures do not include out-of-court settlements and thus exclude recent settlements by such high-profile corporations as Westinghouse Electric ($14 million), Lennox Industries ($6.2 million), Northrop Gruman ($14 million), Continental Airlines ($9 million), and First Union Corporation ($58.5 million).

The 1967 ADEA, signed into law by President Lyndon Johnson on December 15, 1967, was designed to protect individuals older than age 40 from employment discrimination based on age, as well as to promote opportunities for older workers who were capable of meeting job requirements. The ADEA was amended in 1974 to include coverage of government employees and again in 1978 to abolish mandatory retirement for federal employees. Under the ADEA, it is unlawful for an employer to discriminate against a person because of his or her age with respect to any terms, conditions, or privileges of employment—including, but not limited to, promotion, firing, hiring, layoff, compensation, job assignments, training, and benefits. The ADEA does not apply to elected officials or independent contractors and excludes those who work in companies with fewer than twenty employees.

In addition to the core tenets of the ADEA, a few other important provisions of the ADEA are worthy of mention. First, the ADEA deems it unlawful to include age preferences or specifications in job advertisements. Want ads with language such as "applicants under 40" are thus unlawful under the ADEA. Second, the ADEA was amended, or complemented, in 1990 to include the Older Workers Benefit Protection Act, which prohibits employers from denying benefits to older workers. Under this provision, a legal framework for class action and private suits is provided to older workers. Third, the ADEA stipulates that all requests for age information during an application procedure must be for lawful purposes only. Therefore, although an employer may ask an applicant his or her age during an interview, such requests would be scrutinized carefully if they made their way to the courts. Fourth, and finally, the ADEA holds that it is unlawful for apprenticeship programs to discriminate on the basis of age.

There are three important exceptions to the ADEA, and all have featured prominently in court cases over the years. The first, and most notable exception, is the *bona fide occupational qualification (BFOQ)*, which holds that differentiation based on age is allowed "where age is a bona fide occupational qualification reasonably necessary to the normal operation of the particular business, or where differentiation is based on reasonable factors other than age" (ADEA, 29 U.S.C. 623 (f)). Using the BFOQ as a basis for their defense, companies frequently attempt to demonstrate in the courts that older employees are incapable of doing their job in a way that is "reasonably necessary to the normal operation of their particular business." From this example alone, the complexities of age discrimination lawsuits thus become immediately evident. For example, the courts are left to ponder questions such as whether the hiring of a 25-year-old engineer over an equally qualified 40-year-old engineer reflects the younger applicant's BFOQ or simply a desire for cheaper labor or more years of service. Not surprisingly, the BFOQ exception is also frequently cited in airline and other industries where public safety is an issue.

The second exception to the ADEA, called the *good cause exception,* allows employers to discipline or fire older employees if it can be shown that age was not a determining factor in their disciplinary or termination decision. Under this exception, employers often use performance evaluations as evidence for their termination decisions, though this evidence may well be tainted by stereotypical myths about older workers. The third and final exception, the *seniority system exception,* holds that "differentiation based on age is allowed where the terms of a bona fide seniority system or any bona fide employee benefit plan, such as retirement, pension, or insurance plan, are being observed, and these terms are not a 'subterfuge to evade the purposes' of the act" (ADEA, 29 U.S.C. 623 (f)). In most cases, for a benefit plan or seniority system to be considered as a subterfuge, the system must differentiate its older workers in a disadvantageous manner.

Proving Age Discrimination

There are two distinct ways to establish workplace discrimination: disparate treatment and disparate impact. The vast majority of age discrimination suits have used the disparate treatment theory.

Under disparate treatment theory, the plaintiff must demonstrate that the discrimination was intentional—in other words, show proof (direct, indirect, or both) of a motive to discriminate. In the absence of direct evidence of discrimination, which is common, most courts use a three-stage model of proof. The plaintiff must first establish a prima facie case. In order to do this, the plaintiff must show that he or she is in the protected age group, suffered an adverse reaction, was successfully performing the work according to the legitimate expectations of the employer prior to the adverse action, and was replaced (Bessey and Ananda 1991). Next, the burden falls on the employer to present a nondiscriminatory reason for its actions, and finally, the plaintiff must establish that this reason was simply a pretext for discrimination (Bessey and Ananda 1991). Plaintiffs often point to ageist language in the workplace in their effort to make or support their prima facie case.

With respect to the disparate impact theory, the burden is again on the plaintiff to demonstrate that the employment practices of the employer had a disproportionately negative effect on him or her. Once the plaintiff's evidence has been presented, the defendant must then either demonstrate that the organization required the action or policy for "business reasons" or show that the negative effect was due to non-age-related factors. The disparate impact theory is not used frequently and has been roundly criticized over the years by researchers for the supposed vagueness of its "business necessity" argument. Nevertheless, cases such as *Leftwich v. Harris Stowe State College* (1983) have been won using this method. In this case, Harris State College was accused of reserving certain positions for nontenured faculty, while eliminating senior, tenured faculty positions. In order to support its policy, the college argued that it would be able to save money and promote "innovation and quality" by bringing in nontenured faculty. After hearing the case, the court found against Harris State College, citing that the college's hiring policy was discriminatory in that it was not based on a "business necessity" and instead was an attempt to eliminate older workers who had built up higher salaries than their younger counterparts.

The Role of Language

Our content analysis of age discrimination lawsuits over the past two decades reveals that ageist communication has played a central role in a large percentage of the ADEA cases brought before the courts. For the plaintiff, the defendant's ageist comments typically are perceived as clear evidence of discriminatory animus on the company's behalf, and for the defendant, these same ageist comments or "stray remarks" generally are viewed as proving little except that ageism is prevalent in society at large.

Age-related comments are frequently presented in court to demonstrate evidence of age discrimination, though with varying degrees of success. Comments such as "the old woman," "that old goat," and "too long on the job" have been successfully offered as evidence of the employer's intent to discriminate (Bessey and Ananda 1991), while equally severe language such as "an old, fat, baldheaded man," "a tough old fart" (*Snyder v. AG Trucking*, 1995), and "old ladies with balls" (*Haskell v. Kaman Corporation*, 1984) have not. Many factors must be considered when attempting to prove age discrimination, not the least of which is that the plaintiff must generally prove that it was the decision maker who uttered the remarks (*Stopka v. Alliance of American Insurers*, 1998) and that the ageist remarks were related to the employment decision in question (*McCarthy v. Kemper Life Insurance*, 1991). Nevertheless, in spite of the complexity in establishing proof of age discrimination, ageist language still plays an important role in many age discrimination cases and thus requires further investigation.

"Young Blood" Remarks   One common type of ageist discourse that is frequently introduced as evidence in the courtroom can be referred to as "young blood" remarks. Examples include youth-oriented comments such as, "We need young blood around here," "Let's make room for some M.B.A.s," or "Let's bring in the young guns." Young blood communication has appeared in cases such as *Robb v. Chemetron* (1978), where the company's president detailed his wishes for a "young line of command"; in *Hedrick v. Hercules, Inc.* (1981), where management expressed its wish to "get rid of the good old Joes"; and in *Danzer v. Norden Systems, Inc.* (1998), where a supervisor stated that "we need new bold—new and younger, fresh skills from out of schools." In the first two of these cases, the ageist comments were found as constituting direct evidence of dis-

criminatory motive; in the last one, the court found the comments to be potentially discriminatory and sent the case to jury.

In many other young blood cases, ageist language has not held up on its own as direct evidence or sufficient proof of a prima facie case. For example, in *Scott v. The Goodyear Tire and Rubber Company* (1998), young blood comments made by two executives of the company were found to be insufficient on their own to survive summary judgment. In this case, one Goodyear executive commented that "this company is run by white haired old men waiting to retire—and this must change," while another executive stated that "some people will lose their jobs, but in time, we will replace them with young college graduates at less money." In another widely cited case, that of *Hoffman v. MCA, Inc.* (1998), the court upheld the grant of summary judgment to MCA. In this case, six incidences of ageist language were introduced as evidence in court, with young blood comments represented among them. More specifically, after a business dinner, an MCA supervisor told his sales representative, "I think we're going to have to get fresh legs in Chicago," language that the court found to be overly vague and not discriminatory in nature.

In a final case here, that of *Smith v. Flax* (1980), the plaintiff attempted to make its prima facie case by introducing ageist comments by management into evidence. The plaintiff argued that management's desire to replace older workers with younger employees was reflected in management's comments that "the company's future lay in its young Ph.D.s," and "all employees at some time reach their peak in efficiency." In ruling against the plaintiffs, the court found that "such statements seem only as truisms. In any enterprise, today's juniors will be tomorrow's seniors. Today's seniors can help create a foundation for tomorrow's growth and prosperity, but future realization of the potential of an enterprise lies principally with those who will be in positions of leadership and responsibility in the future" (*Smith v. Flax*, 1980).

"Old" Remarks   Making reference to an individual as old is of itself only occasionally considered as direct evidence of age discrimination. Still, a comment by a supervisor in *Wichman v. Board of Trustees of Southern Illinois University* (1999) that "in a forest you have to cut down the old, big trees so that the little ones underneath can grow" was found as enough to carry the plaintiff's burden of proof regarding age discrimination. More commonly, "old" remarks are used to help establish a prima facie case. For example, in *Danzer v. Norden Systems, Inc.* (1998), the court sent the case to jury, a move considered damaging to the defense because as it found

comments made by the plaintiff's supervisor as potentially discriminatory. In this case, the supervisor commented that his staff was a bunch of *"alte cockers"* ("old fogies" in Yiddish) and then made sure that he translated this into English. Moreover, in another "old fogie" case, this one with "old fogies" being spoken only in English, the court also ruled against the employer (*Abrams v. Lightolier,* 1995). Finally, in *Meschino v. ITT Corporation* (1983), the court ruled that statements that referred to the plaintiff as "old and tired" and "a sleepy kind of guy with no pizzazz" provided sufficient evidence of age bias and subsequent discriminatory practices by the plaintiff's supervisors.

Not all stereotypical remarks about a worker's age are considered discriminatory. In fact, in most cases, ageist remarks cannot stand alone as enough for a prima facie case or direct evidence of discrimination. For example, in *Hoffman v. MCA, Inc.* (1998), in upholding the grant of summary judgment to MCA, the court referred to remarks by an MCA supervisor that his sales representative was "an old fashioned hack salesman" as a reference to his style, and not age. The court also considered the "you're just getting old" comments made by this same supervisor on three occasions as merely truisms about aging. In sum, after collectively and individually examining all of the ageist statements in the *Hoffman v. MCA, Inc.* (1998) case, the court found that the remarks represented only social banter conducted in social settings and amounted to merely conversational jabs that could not be constituted as discriminatory.

Like *Hoffman v. MCA, Inc.* (1998), other "you're getting old" cases have found in favor of the defendant, or employer. These cases include *Walch v. Intecom* (1997), where the manager responded to his employee's complaints about prostate problems with, "That's what happens when you get old"; *Godfrey v. Allen* (1997), where a manager commented to an older employee, "That's what happens when you get old—you get forgetful"; and *Berkowitz v. Allied Stores* (1982), where a supervisor told the plaintiff that he "had been around since the dinosaurs roamed the earth." Moreover, in another case (*Speen v. Crown Clothing Corporation* (1996), lawyers for the plaintiff, William Spleen, argued that a comment made by Spleen's supervisor constituted direct evidence of age discrimination, suggesting that age was a motivating factor in the decision not to hire Spleen. The supervisor's comment, "Why do I need a 71 year old when I can have a 51 year old?" was ultimately found to be insufficient to prove age discrimination in the light of the totality of the circumstances. Finally, in *Robin v. Espo Engineering* (2000), comments by the owner and director of Espo Engineering that the plaintiff was "an old S.O.B." and "getting too old" were also found to be insufficient to constitute discrimination.

Other Media and Complexities

Evidence introduced under the ADEA is not limited to discourse and can include organizational memoranda, organizational surveys, and organizational charts. For example, in *Franci v. Avco Corporation* (1984), the recruiting director of Avco Corp. prepared a memorandum stating that "his department was overloaded with elderly people and that younger people should be brought in" (Denis 1985), and in *Mercer v. K Mart Corporation* (1996), an executive of K Mart sent a confidential internal memorandum to his district managers' informing them to "build a case to terminate low performing store managers" (many of whom were older individuals). Organization charts that list the ages of top management have also been deemed evidence of age-biased decision making (*Bernstein v. Consolidated Foods*, 1984), as have memoranda that list the names of terminated employees alongside the employer's net savings from the termination (*Nalon v. Bank of California*, 1981).

Given widely held perceptions that older workers struggle with new technology (Breakwell and Fife-Schaw 1988), it comes as no surprise that the courts are beginning to hear increasing numbers of "new technology" age discrimination cases. For example, in *Ryther v. KARE* (1997), a supervisor told his 53-year-old sportscaster that he "had bags under his eyes," was "an old fart," "wasn't able to grasp the new computer system," and "couldn't handle the new technology." In this case, the court found for the plaintiff. In another "new technology" case, that of *Horn v. Cushman and Wakefield Western* (1999), the plaintiff was told, "Haven't you ever heard of a FAX before?" when he mentioned to his supervisor that he had sent a document overnight. The court found in favor of Cushman and Wakefield, a large real estate company, in this case.

The "sexism and ageism" suit is also finding its way into the courts, and appears to be the type of case that will proliferate in "aesthetically oriented" industries such as film and television. In *Leopold v. Baccarat Corporation* (1999), however, the problems began in a retail outlet where a supervisor threatened to fire an older female worker because he wanted "a young and sexy saleswoman," while also commenting that another saleswoman had high sales because "she flirts and attracts all male customers." In this case, the court found for the defendant with respect to the age discrimination suit but for the plaintiff with respect to sex discrimination. Finally, in *Sherman v. American Cynamid* (1999), a case that appears to be typical of "sexism and ageism" suits, the plaintiff attempted to argue, without success, that her employer favored older male employees over older female employees.

Epilogue: Theoretical and Empirical Agendas

Given the large numbers of older people in the workforce, the integral role that communication plays in age discrimination lawsuits, and the widespread stereotypical attitudes about older workers, it is imperative that theoretically driven intergenerational communication research begins to make its way into the workplace literature. As scholars embark on this task, there are two well-tested, far-reaching theories that have potential here. The first of these, social identity theory (SIT) (see, for example, Tajfel and Turner 1986), claims that a large part of our identity as individuals is derived from our memberships in salient groups. Tajfel and Turner argue that as people make social comparisons and categorize, they favor their own in-group over out-groups, minimizing in-group differences and creatively accentuating out-group differences during this process (particularly the stereotypic ones). According to SIT, people categorize and favor their in-group in order to enhance their self-esteem.

Social identity theory has been a highly productive theory when applied in broad terms to communication and aging issues (Fox 1999; Fox and Giles 1993; Harwood, Giles, and Ryan 1995). Moreover, several authors (Gardner et al. 2001; Hartley 1996; Kramer 1991) have argued that SIT also has much to offer to organizational understanding. These researchers argue that since individuals in organizations are typically differentiated from each other by their group memberships, whether the groups are formally mandated (project groups, committees), centered on functional roles (secretary, production manger), created by employment status (full time, temporary), or informally created outside the bounds of the organization (age, gender), group-based social identity theory would appear to provide a strong theoretical basis for addressing organizational research issues. In fact, some scholars studying age discrimination have already tested in-group bias elements of social identity theory, finding partial support for an in-group bias hypothesis. In this study, young subjects rated younger workers (the in-group) more favorably than older workers (the out-group) in terms of workers' job qualifications, potential for development, and qualifications for a physically demanding job (Finkelstein, Burke, and Raju 1995).

Although social identity, and arguably relevant other intergroup, theories (social dominance theory and the role of "legitimizing myths" in Sidanius and Pratto 1999) offer many insights into how people may identify and act as group members, communication accommodation theory (CAT; Coupland et al. 1988; Giles, Coupland, and Coupland 1991) examines the ways in which individuals use language in intergroup encounters. Briefly, CAT states that individuals attempt to accommodate or adjust their speech style when communicating with others in order to increase communication efficiency, gain another person's approval, or maintain their own distinctiveness. A fundamental underlying assumption of CAT is that individuals choose certain verbal and nonverbal communicative strategies (e.g., approximation) for personal, situational, and interactional reasons. These strategies may be intergroup or interindividual in their focus. For example, an individual may slow his or her rate of speech to match the speech rate of the other speaker (interindividual) or employ "baby talk" due to existing stereotypes about the other person's group (intergroup). Approximation strategies include convergence, where individuals attempt to match their speech style to that of their interlocutors', and divergence, where individuals seek to accentuate valued communicative differences. For example, a younger speaker may attempt to converge by adjusting his or her rate of speech to that of the older speaker, or diverge by using teen slang that he or she feels the older speaker may not be able to relate to. The name *approximation strategies* is therefore derived from the addressee focus on the productive language and communication of the other interlocutor (see Giles, Coupland, and Coupland 1991). In addition, CAT labels the communicative attempts of the interlocutors as overaccommodating or underaccommodating. Overaccommodation (e.g., patronizing speech) refers to "a miscommunicative process where at least one participant perceives a speaker to go beyond a sociolinguistic style judged to be necessary for attuned talk," while underaccommodation (e.g., excessive talk about one's own life) refers to "some style or quality of talk . . . perceived to be underplayed relative to the needs and/or wishes of at least one interactant" (Coupland et al. 1988).

CAT research has centered primarily on the areas of the sociology of language, communication breakdown, and sociolinguistics, but researchers are also calling for its use in workplace settings (Baker 1991; Bourhis 1991). Recent CAT-oriented studies that have answered this call include research on nonaccommodation and gender in the workplace (Boggs and Giles 1999), job interviews (Willemyns et al. 1997), and supervisor-subordinate interactions (Jones et al. 1999).

Because both SIT and CAT appear to provide a firm foundation for future research in the domain of workplace ageism, it is important to set forth an agenda for future research. Research questions in the occupational and organization spheres might include questions such as: What aspects of social identity theory and communication accommodation theory are most and least suited to answer questions regarding workplace ageism? Looking at social identity theory, when does age become more or less salient (compared with other group and individual identities), and do people categorize in- and out-groups in general terms (older, younger) or in specific terms? What ages subjectively define workers as "older" or "younger"?

Given that elderly people have been found to be less able to suppress stereotypical tendencies than younger adults (von Hippel, Silver, and Lynch 2000), when and how do older workers express prejudicial reactions to and discriminate against *young* workers (Commonwealth of Australia 1999 for blatant exemplars of this; see also Giles and Williams 1994)? Are the latter the very ones who are at the forefront of sustaining prejudice to older workers in due time? In what ways do older workers themselves reiterate ageist stereotypes in their verbalized accounts of their own and peers' behavior? To what extent, when, and why do older workers themselves exchange direct ageist remarks between each other? In regard to these latter two issues, our informal workplace observations over the years lead us to speculate that older workers too can, and sometimes do, participate in the communication climates that sustain ageism. If this is indeed so (under obviously specific conditions), then it is no wonder that certain ambitious younger workers will tend to capitalize on and socially reproduce these patterns for their own purposes.

With respect to social stereotypes, researchers may want to examine how older workers' stereotypes about workers of different ages compare with those of younger and middle-aged workers. What are these stereotypes, and in what types of language are they represented? Moreover, little research has been conducted regarding job stereotypes, begging the question as to whether individuals possess stereotypes about particular jobs or positions, and if so, what types of jobs or positions young, middle-aged, and older workers people feel are appropriate for people of different ages. Following from this, do societal age norms play a part in the types of positions that people may or may not judge to be appropriate?

Researchers may want to focus on whether young, middle-aged, and older adults encounter serious social problems in working (and hence communicating) with individuals of different ages, and if so, what these problems are. Are people of different ages satisfied with their intergenerational workplace conversations, or are they dissatisfied? It seems important, for both theoretical and practical payoffs, to locate where and why workplaces are satisfying as much as it does to focus on contexts that are otherwise (see Williams and Coupland's 1998 critique of the communication and sociolinguistic literatures' biased attention to deficit and problems). Is there underaccommodation or overaccommodation taking place in intergenerational workplace conversations, and if so, in what situations are under- and overaccommodation most and least common? In more general terms, which types of CAT goals and strategies appear to be most frequent in organizational settings, and in what ways are these goals and strategies related to intergenerational interaction? Given that organizations vary among multiple dimensions (size, function, structure), how does ageism in the workplace communicatively manifest itself in different types of organizations and organizational groups? How is it variably managed by recipients (e.g., let it pass versus confrontation), who collude in its performance, and to what effects (e.g., in inhibiting future ageist remarks and actions)? Clearly, a multitude of other factors (e.g., work centrality, gender as it intersects with age; see Paoletti 1998) influence workplace communicative satisfaction or dissatisfaction. What are they, and in what types of situations are they most likely to manifest themselves?

Despite the ever-growing numbers of age discrimination lawsuits, the dynamics of age discrimination are still largely atheoretical and underresearched. Potential research questions in this area may include: What are the differences and similarities of people's perceptions about what constitutes age discrimination, and how do these perceptions compare to the legal definition of age discrimination? How does age discrimination in the workplace communicatively manifest itself, and how does this communication vary across different types of gendered organizations? What is the relationship of stereotypes about older workers, intergenerational workplace communication, and age discrimination?

Many of the issues are also rich for cross-cultural examination. For example, researchers may want to consider questions such as: Does the nature of intergenerational communication climates in the workplace differ across cultures—as reported by young, middle-aged, and older adults in various occupational settings? Does communicative ageism in workplace settings manifest itself differently across cultures? What are the differences and similarities of people's perceptions about what constitutes age discrimination, and how do these perceptions compare to the legal definition (when appropriate) of age discrimination in these countries?

It is beyond question that ageism plays a particularly pernicious role in the workplace. Older workers face widely held societal stereotypes that they are cognitively, socially, and performatively deficient in the workplace. They are also the targets of ageist attitudes, ageist communication, and age discrimination. Nevertheless, older Americans in great numbers continue to work, and as they continue to succeed in their jobs, we become increasingly hopeful for the future. As greater numbers of older Americans continue to break the negative stereotypes toward older individuals that exist in our society, we feel confident that societal perceptions will gradually shift as well. After all, older Americans are not just reminders of our past; they are also our future.

References

Abrams v. Lightolier, Inc. (1995). 50 F.3d 1204 (3rd Cir.).

American Association of Retired Persons (AARP). (1989). *Business and older workers: Current perceptions and new directions for the 1990s.* Washington, D.C.: AARP.

Anderson, Jr., A. (1978). Old is not a four-letter word. *Across the Board, 15,* 20–27.

Arvey, R. D., and Neel, C. W. (1974). Testing expectancy theory predictions using behaviorally based measures of motivational effort for engineers. *Journal of Vocational Behavior, 4,* 229–310.

Ashburn, G., and Gordon, A. (1981). Features of a simplified register in speech to elderly conversationalists. *International Journal of Psycholinguistics, 8,* 7–31.

Baker, M. A. (1991). Reciprocal accommodation: A model for reducing gender bias in managerial communication. *Journal of Business Communication, 28,* 113–130.

Berkowitz v. Allied Stores. (1982). 541 F. Supp. 1209, 1218–19 (E.D., Pa.).

Bernstein v. Consolidated Foods Corp. (1984). 36 Fair Empl. Prac. Cas. 1333, 1339 (N.D., Ill.).

Bessey, B. L., and Ananda, S. M. (1991). Age discrimination in employment: An interdisciplinary review of the ADEA. *Research on Aging, 13,* 413–457.

Bishop, J. M., and Krause, D. R. (1984). Depictions of aging and old age on Saturday morning television. *Gerontologist, 24,* 91–94.

Boggs, K., and Giles, H. (1999). "The canary in the coalmine": The nonaccommodation cycle in the gendered workplace. *International Journal of Applied Linguistics, 9,* 223–245.

Botwinick, J. (1978). *Aging and behavior: A comprehensive integration of research findings*. New York: Springer.

Bourhis, R. Y. (1991). Organizational communication and accommodation: Toward some conceptual and empirical links. In H. Giles, J. Coupland, and N. Coupland (Eds.), *Contexts of accommodation: Developments in applied sociolinguistics* (pp. 27–303). New York: Cambridge University Press.

Braithwaite, V. A. (1986). Old age stereotypes: Reconciling contradictions. *Journal of Gerontology, 41,* 353–360.

Braithwaite, V. A., Lynd-Stevenson, R., and Pigram, D. (1993). An empirical study of ageism: From polemics to scientific utility. *Australian Psychologist, 28,* 9–15.

Branco, K. L., and Williamson, J. B. (1982). Stereotypes and the life cycle. In A. G. Miller (Ed.), *In the eye of the beholder: Contemporary issues in stereotyping* (pp. 364–410). New York: Prager.

Breakwell, G. M., and Fife-Schaw, C. (1988). Ageing and the impact of new technology. *Social Behavior: An International Journal of Applied Social Psychology, 3,* 119–130.

Brewer, M. B., Dull, V., and Lui, L. (1981). Perceptions of the elderly: Stereotypes as prototypes. *Journal of Personality and Social Psychology, 41,* 656–670.

Britton, J. O., and Thomas, K. R. (1973). Age and sex as employment variables: Views of employment service interviewers. *Journal of Employment Counseling, 10,* 180–186.

Butler, R. N. (1987). *"Ageism": The encyclopedia of aging*. New York: Springer.

Bytheway, B. (1995). *Ageism*. Buckingham, UK: Open University Press.

Caporael, L. R. (1981). The paralanguage of caregiving: Baby talk to the institutionalized elderly and their caregivers. *Journal of Personality and Social Psychology, 44,* 746–754.

Carnevale, A. P., and Stone, S. C. (1994). In J. A. Auerbach and J. C. Welsh (Eds.), *Developing the new competitive workforce* (pp. 94–146). Washington, D.C.: National Council on the Aging.

Cicirelli, V. G. (1993). Intergenerational communication in the mother-daughter dyad regarding caregiving decisions. In N. Coupland and J. F. Nussbaum (Eds.), *Discourse and lifespan identity* (pp. 215–236). Newbury Park, CA: Sage.

Cole, S. (1979). Age and scientific performance. *American Journal of Sociology, 84,* 958–977.

Commonwealth of Australia (1999, April). *Age matters: A discussion paper on age discrimination*. Sydney: Human Rights and Equal Opportunity Commission.

Commonwealth Fund (1993). *The untapped resource: Americans over 55 at work*. New York: Commonwealth Fund.

Coupland, N., and Coupland, J. (1990). Language and later life. In H. Giles and W. P. Robinson (Eds.), *Handbook of language and social psychology* (pp. 451–468). New York: Wiley.

Coupland, N., and Coupland, J. (1993). Discourses of ageism and anti-ageism. *Journal of Aging Studies, 7*, 279–301.

Coupland, N., Coupland, J., Giles, H., and Henwood, K. (1988). Accommodating the elderly: Invoking and extending a theory. *Language in Society, 17*, 1–41.

Cumming, E., and Henry, W. E. (1961). *Growing old: The process of disengagement.* New York: Basic Books.

Danzer v. Norden Systems, Inc. (1998). U.S. App. Lexis 16191 (2d Cir.).

Denis, M. K. (1985, Autumn). The roots of age discrimination claims. *Employment Relations Today*, 257–263.

Doering, M., Rhodes, S. R., and Schuster, M. (1983). *The aging worker: Research and recommendations.* Beverly Hills, CA: Sage.

Driver, M. I. (1994). Workforce personality and the new information age workplace. In James A. Auerbach and Joyce C. Welsh (Eds.), *Developing the new competitive workforce* (pp. 185–206). Washington, DC: National Council on the Aging.

Eaton, L. (1993). Cloudy sunset: A grim surprise awaits future retirees: The story behind the numbers. *Barron's, 73*, 8–9.

EEOC Official Web Site. (1999). The U.S. Equal Employment Opportunity Commission. Age Discrimination in Employment Act (ADEA) charges, 1992–1998. http://www.eeoc.gov/stats/adea.html.

Eisenberg, J. (1980). Relationship between age and effects upon work: A study of older workers in the garment industry. *Dissertation Abstracts International, 41* (4A).

Emry, O. B. (1986). Linguistic decrement in normal aging. *Language and Communication, 6*, 47–64.

Erber, J. T. (1989). Young and older adults' appraisal of memory failures in young and older target persons. *Journal of Gerontology: Psychological Sciences, 44*, 170–175.

Erber, J. T., and Rothberg, S. T. (1991). Here's looking at you: The relative effect of age and attractiveness on judgments about memory failure. *Journal of Gerontology, 46*, 116–123.

Erickson, E. H. (1959). Identity and the life-cycle. *Psychological Issues, 1*, 1–171.

Estes, W. K. (1978). *Handbook of learning and cognitive processes: Linguistic functions in cognitive theory.* Hillsdale, NJ: Erlbaum.

Feezel, J., and Hawkins, R. (1988). Myths and stereotypes: Communication breakdowns. In C. W. Carmichael, C. H. Botan, and R. Hawkins (Eds.), *Human com-*

munication and the aging process. (pp. 81–94). Prospect Heights, IL: Waveland Press.

Finkelstein, A. M., Burke, M. J., and Raju, N. S. (1995). Age discrimination in simulated employment contexts: An integrative analysis. *Journal of Applied Psychology, 80,* 652–663.

Forteza, J. A., and Prieto, J. M. (1994). Aging and work behavior. In H. C. Triandis, M. D. Dunnette, and I. M. Hough (Eds.), *Handbook of industrial and organizational psychology* (2nd ed., Vol. 4, pp. 447–483). Palo Alto, CA: Consulting Psychologists Press.

Fox, S. (1999). Communication in families with an aging parent: A review of the literature and agenda for future research. In M. E. Roloff (Ed.), *Communication Yearbook, 22,* 377–429.

Fox, S., and Giles, H. (1993). Accommodating intergenerational contact: A critique and theoretical model. *Journal of Aging Studies, 7,* 423–451.

Franci v. Avco Corp., 538 f. Supp. 250 (D. Conn. 1982).

Froggatt, P. (1970). Short-term absence from industry, I: Literature, definitions, data, and the effect of age and length of service. *British Journal of Industrial Medicine, 27,* 199–210.

Gardner, J., Paulsen, N., Gallois, C., Callan, V., and Monaghan, P. (2001). An intergroup perspective on communication and organizations. In W. P. Robinson and H. Giles (Eds.), *The new handbook of language and social psychology.* (561–584). Chichester: Wiley.

Gatz, M., and Pearson, C. G. (1988). Ageism revised and the provision of psychological services. *American Psychologist, 43,* 184–188.

Giles, H. (Ed.) (1998). Applied research in language and intergenerational communication. *Journal of Applied Communication Research, 26,* 1–154.

Giles, H. (1999). Managing dilemmas in the "silent revolution": A call to arms!. *Journal of Communication, 49,* 170–182.

Giles, H., and Condor, S. (1988). Aging, technology, and society: An introduction and future priorities. *Social Behavior: An International Journal of Applied Social Psychology, 3,* 59–70.

Giles, H., Coupland, N., and Coupland, J. (Eds.). (1991). *Context of accommodation: Development of applied linguistics.* Cambridge: Cambridge University Press.

Giles, H., and Williams, A. (1994). Patronizing the young: Forms and evaluations. *International Journal of Aging and Human Development, 39,* 33–53.

Godfrey v. Ethan Allen. (1997). 113 F.3d 1229 (2d Cir.).

Gold, D. P., Arbuckle, T. Y., and Andres, D. (1984). Verbosity in older adults. In M. L. Hummert, J. M. Wiemann, and J. F. Nussbaum (Eds.), *Interpersonal communication and aging* (pp. 107–129). Thousand Oaks, CA: Sage.

Greene, M. G., Adelman, R. D., and Majerovitz, S. D. (1996). Physician and older patient support in the medical encounter. *Health Communication, 8,* 263–279.

Hall, D. T., and Mirvis, P. H. (1994). The new workplace and older workers. In J. A. Auerbach and J. C. Welsh (Eds.), *Developing the new competitive workforce* (pp. 58–93). Washington, D.C.: National Council on the Aging.

Hansson, R. O., DeKoekkoek, P. D., Neece, W. N., and Patterson, D. W. (1997). Successful aging at work: Annual review, 1992–1996: The older worker and transitions to retirement. *Journal of Vocational Behavior, 51,* 202–223.

Hartley, J. F. (1996). Intergroup relations in organizations. In M. A. West (Ed.), *Handbook of work psychology* (pp. 397–422). New York: Wiley.

Harwood, J., Giles, H., Ota, H., Pierson, H. D., Gallois, C., Ng, S. H., Lim, T. S., and Somera, L. (1996). College students' trait ratings of three age groups around the Pacific Rim. *Journal of Cross-Cultural Gerontology, 11,* 307–317.

Harwood, J., Giles, H., and Ryan, E. B. (1995). Aging, communication, and intergroup theory: Social identity and intergenerational communication. In J. F. Nussbaum and J. Coupland (Eds.), *Handbook of communication and aging research* (pp. 133–160). Hillsdale, NJ: Erlbaum.

Haskell v. Kaman Corporation. (1984). 743 F.2d 113 (2nd Cir.).

Hedrick v. Hercules, Inc. (1981). 658 F.2d 1088, 1092 (5th Cir.).

von Hippel, W., Silver, L. A., and Anderson, A. (2000). Stereotyping against your will: The role of inhibitory ability in stereotyping and prejudice among the elderly. *Personality and Social Psychology Bulletin, 26,* 523–532.

Hoffman v. MCA, Inc. (1998). U.S. App. Lexis 11807 (7th Cir.).

Holley, W. H. Jr., Field, H. S., and Holley, B. B. (1978). Age and reactions to jobs: An empirical study of paraprofessional workers. *Aging and Work, 1,* 33–40.

Horn v. Cushman and Wakefield Western, Inc. (1999). 72 Cal. App. 4th 798 (Cal. Ct. App. 1st Dist.).

Hummert, M. L. (1990). Multiple stereotypes of the elderly and young adults: A comparison of structure and evaluations. *Psychology and Aging, 5,* 182–193.

Hummert, M. L., Garstka, T. A., and Shaner, J. L. (1995). Beliefs about language performance: Adults' perceptions about self and elderly targets. *Journal of Language and Social Psychology, 14,* 235–259.

Hummert, M. L., Garstka, T. A., Shaner, J. L., and Strahm, S. (1994). Stereotypes of the elderly held by young, middle-aged, and elderly adults. *Journal of Gerontology: Psychological Sciences, 49,* 240–249.

Hummert, M. L., and Ryan, E. B. (1996). Toward understanding variations in patronizing talk addressed to older adults: Psycholinguistic features of care and control. *International Journal of Psycholinguistics, 12,* 149–170.

Ikels, C., Keith, J., Dickerson-Putman, J., Draper, P., Fry, C., Glascock, A., and Harpending, H. (1992). Perceptions of the adult life course: A cross-cultural analysis. *Aging in Society, 12,* 49–84.

Jones, E., Gallois, C., Callan, V., and Barker, M. (1999). Strategies of accommodation: Development of a coding system for conversational interaction. *Journal of Language and Social Psychology, 18,* 123–152.

Jury Verdict Research. (1999). Age discrimination claims. Available at: www.amanet.org.

Kay, E. J., Harris, R. M., Voros, R. S., Hillman, D. J., Hyland, D. T., and Deimler, J. D. (1994). *Age 60 study, part III. Consolidated database experiments final report.* Washington, D.C.: Federal Aviation Administration.

Kemper, S., and Hummert, M. L. (1997). New directions in research on aging and message production. In J. O. Greene (Ed.), *Message production: Advances in communication theory* (pp. 127–149). Hillside, NJ: Erlbaum.

Kite, M. E., and Johnson, B. T. (1988). Attitudes toward older and younger adults: A meta-analysis. *Psychology and Aging, 2,* 233–244.

Kogan, N. (1979). Beliefs, attitudes and stereotypes about old people: A new look at some old issues. *Research on Aging, 2,* 11–36.

Kohlberg, L. (1973). Stages and aging in moral development—some speculations. *Gerontologist, 13,* 497–502.

Koopman-Boyden, P. G. (1993). *New Zealand's ageing society.* Wellington: Dalphane Brasell.

Koyano, W. (1989). Japanese attitudes toward the elderly: A review of research findings. *Journal of Cross-Cultural Gerontology, 4,* 335–345.

Kramer, R. M. (1991). Intergroup relations and organizational dilemmas: The role of categorization processes. *Research in Organizational Behavior, 13,* 191–228.

Kubeck, J. E., Delp, N. D., Haslett, T. K., and McDaniel, M. A. (1996). Does job-related training performance decline with age? *Psychology and Aging, 11,* 92–107.

Landy, F. J. (1996). *Mandatory retirement and chronological age in public safety workers.* Testimony before the U.S. Senate Committee on Labor and Human Resources. (March 8, 1996). Washington, D.C.: American Psychological Association.

Lawrence, B. (1988). New wrinkles in the theory of age demography norms and performance ratings. *Academy of Management Journal, 31,* 309–337.

Leftwich v. Harris-Stowe State College. (1983). 540 F. Supp. 37 (D. Mo. 1982), aff'd 702 F.2d 686 (8th Cir. 1983).

Leopold v. Baccarat, Inc. (1999). No. 98-7474, 1999 WL 236509 (2d Cir.).

Levine, M. L. (1988). *Age discrimination and the mandatory retirement controversy.* Baltimore, MD: Johns Hopkins University Press.

Levy, B., and Langer, E. (1994). Aging free from negative stereotypes: Successful memory in China and among the American deaf. *Journal of Personality and Social Psychology, 66,* 989–997.

Los Angeles Times (2000, April 3). pp. A1, A15.

Louis Harris and Associates. (1981). www.irss.unc.edu/irss/dataservices/dataservices.html.

Louis Harris and Associates. (1989). www.irss.unc.edu/irss/dataservices/dataservices.html.

Louis Harris and Associates. (1992). www.irss.unc.edu/irss/dataservices/dataservices.html.

McCarthy v. Kemper Life Insurance Company. (1991). 924 F.2d 683, 686–87 (7th Cir.).

Mercer v. K Mart Corporation. (1996). No. 94-9257, 94-9293 (11th Cir.).

Meschino v. ITT Corp. (1983). 563 F. Supp. 1066, 1071 (S.D.N.Y.).

Mirvis, P. (1993). *Building the competitive workforce: Investing in human capital for corporate success.* New York: Wiley.

Mowery, D. C., and Kamlet, M. S. (1993). New technologies and the aging work force. In S. A. Bass, F. G. Caro, and Y. P. Chen (Eds.), *Achieving a productive aging society* (pp. 81–95). Westport, CT: Auburn House.

Mulac, A., and Giles, H. (1996). "You're only as old as you sound": Chronological, contextual, psychological, and perceptual parameters of elderly age attributions. *Health Communication, 8,* 199–216.

Munk, N. (1999). Finished at forty. *Fortune, 139,* 50–66.

National Council on the Aging. (1997). Cited in S. Steinhauser, Successfully managing an age diverse workforce. *Managing Diversity, 8,* 99.

Naton v. Bank of California. (1981). 649 F.2d 697–698.

Newton, N., Lazarus, L., and Weinberg, J. (1984). Aging: Biosocial perspectives. In D. Offer and M. Sabshin (Eds.), *Normality and the life cycle: A critical integration* (pp. 262–266). New York: Basic Books.

Nicholson, N., Brown, C. A., and Chadwick-Jones, J. K. (1977). Absence from work and personal characteristics. *Journal of Applied Psychology, 62,* 319–327.

Ng, S. H., and Bradac, J. J. (1993). *Power in language: Verbal communication and social influence.* Newbury Park, CA: Sage.

Noels, K., Giles, H., Cai, D., and Turay, L. (1999). Intergenerational communication and health in the United States and the People's Republic of China. *South Pacific Journal of Psychology, 10,* 120–134.

Noels, K., Giles, H., Gallois, C., and Ng, S. H. (2001). Intergenerational communication and health across the Pacific Rim. In M. L. Hummert and J. F. Nussbaum (Eds.), *Communication, aging, and health: Multidisciplinary perspectives.* (249–278). Mahwah, NJ: Erlbaum.

Nuessel, F. (1982). The language of ageism. *Gerontologist, 22,* 273–276.

Nussbaum, J. F., and Baringer, D. K. (2000). Message production across the lifespan: Communication and aging. *Communication Theory, 10,* 200–209.

Nussbaum, J. F., and Bettini, L. M. (1994). Shared stories of the grandparent-grandchild relationship. *International Journal of Aging and Human Development, 39,* 67–80.

Nussbaum, J. F., and Coupland, J. (Eds.). (1995). *Handbook of communication and aging research.* Hillside, NJ: Erlbaum.

Nussbaum, J. F., Hummert, M. L., Williams, A., and Harwood, J. (1996). Communication and older adults. In B. Burleson (Ed.), *Communication Yearbook 19* (pp. 1–48). Thousand Oaks, CA: Sage.

Nussbaum, J. F., Thompson, T., and Robinson, J. D. (1988). *Communication and aging.* New York: Harper.

Nuyts, G. D., Elseviers, M. M., and DeBroe, M. F. (1993). Healthy worker effect in a cross-sectional study of lead workers. *Journal of Occupational Medicine, 35,* 387–391.

O'Connell, A. N., and Rotter, N. G. (1979). The influence of stimulus age and sex on person perception. *Journal of Gerontology, 34,* 220–228.

Palmore, E. D. (1988). *The Facts on Aging quiz.* New York: Springer.

Palmore, E. D. (1990). *Ageism, negative and positive.* New York: Springer.

Panek, P. E., Barrett, G. V., Sterns, H. L., and Alexander, R. A. (1978). Age differences in perceptual style, selective attention, and perceptual-motor reaction time. *Experimental Aging Research, 4,* 377–387.

Paoletti, I. (1998). *Being an older woman: A study in the social production of identity.* Hillside, NJ: Erlbaum.

Park, D. C. (1994). Aging, cognition, and work. *Human Performance, 7,* 181–205.

Perdue, C. W., and Gurtman, M. B. (1990). Evidence for the automaticity of ageisms. *Journal of Experimental Social Psychology, 26,* 199–216.

Porter, L. W., and Steers, R. M. (1973). Organizational, work, and personal factors in employee turnover and absenteeism. *Psychological Bulletin, 80,* 151–176.

Rix, S. (1990). *Older workers: Choices and challenges.* Oxford: Clio Press.

Robb v. Chemetron. (1978). 17 Fair Empl. Prac. Cas. 1535, 1538 (S.D. Tex.).

Robin v. Espo Engineering. (2000). No. 98-3909, U.S. Court of Appeals for the 7th Circuit, 2000 U.S. Lexis 448.

Robinson, J. D., and Skill, T. (1995). Media usage patterns and portrayals of the elderly. In J. F. Nussbaum and J. Coupland (Eds.), *Handbook of communication and aging research* (pp. 359–391). Hillside, NJ: Erlbaum.

Roe, A. (1965). Changes in scientific activities with age. *Science, 150,* 313–318.

Root, N. (1981). Injuries at work are fewer among older employees. *Monthly Labor Review, 104,* 30–34.

Rosen, B., and Jerdee, T. H. (1977). Too old or not too old? *Harvard Business Review, 55,* 97–106.

Rosen, B., and Jerdee, T. (1985). *Older employees: New roles for valued resources.* Homewood, IL: Dow-Jones Irwin.

Rosow, J. M., and Zager, R. (1980). *The future of older workers in America: New options for an extended working life.* Scarsdale, NY: Work in America Institute.

Rousseau, D. M. (1978). Characteristics of departments, positions, and individuals: Contexts for attitudes and behavior. *Administrative Science Quarterly, 23,* 521–539.

Ryan, E. B. (1992). Beliefs about memory changes across the lifespan. *Journal of Gerontology: Psychological Sciences, 47,* 96–101.

Ryan, E. B., and Butler, R. N. (1996). Communication, aging, and health: Toward understanding health provider relationships with older clients. *Health Communication, 8,* 191–197.

Ryan, E. B., and Cole, R. (1990). Perceptions of interpersonal communication with elders: Implications for health professionals. In H. Giles, N. Coupland, and J. Wiemann (Eds.), *Communication health and the elderly: Fulbright international colloquium, 8* (pp. 172–191). Manchester, England: Manchester University Press.

Ryan, E. B., Giles, H., Bartolucci, G., and Henwood, K. (1986). Psycholinguistic and social psychological components of communication by and with the elderly. *Language and Communication, 6,* 1–24.

Ryan, E. B., Hummert, M. L., and Boich, L. (1995). Communication predicaments of aging: Patronizing behavior toward older adults. *Journal of Language and Social Psychology, 13,* 144–166.

Ryan, E. B., and Kwong See, S. (1993). Age-based beliefs about memory change in adulthood. *Journal of Gerontology: Psychological Sciences, 48,* 199–201.

Ryan, E. B., Kwong See, S., Maneer, W. B., and Trovato, D. (1992). Age-based perceptions of language performance among younger and older adults. *Communication Research, 19,* 311–331.

Ryan, E. B., Kwong See, S., Maneer, W. B., and Trovato, D. (1994). Age based perceptions of the conversational skills of younger and older adults. In M. L. Hummert, J. Nussbaum, and J. Weimann (Eds.), *Interpersonal communication and older adulthood: Interdisciplinary theory and research* (pp. 15–39). Newbury Park, CA: Sage.

Ryan, E. B., and Laurie, S. (1990). Evaluations of older and younger adult speakers: The influence of communication effectiveness and noise. *Psychology and Aging, 5,* 514–519.

Ryan, E. B., Szechtman, B., and Bodkin, J. (1992). Attitudes toward younger and older adults learning to use computers. *Journals of Gerontology, 47,* 96–101.

Ryther v. KARE (1997). 108 F.3d 832 (8th Cir.).

Schonfield, D. (1982). Who is stereotyping whom and why? *Gerontologist, 22,* 267–272.

Scott v. The Goodyear Tire and Rubber Company. (1998). Fed. App. 0343P (6th Cir.).

Shea, G. F. (1991). *Managing older employees.* San Francisco: Jossey-Bass.

Sherman v. American Cyanamid Company. (1999). 1999 U.S. App. Lexis 2106 (6th Cir.).

Shock, N. W. (1962). The psychology of aging. *Scientific American, 206,* 100–110.

Sidanius, J., and Pratto, F. (1999). *Social dominance.* Cambridge: Cambridge University Press.

Sieman, J. R. (1976). Programmed material as a training tool for older persons. *Industrial Gerontology, 3,* 183–190.

Simon, R. (1996). Too damn old. *Money, 25,* 118–126.

Smith v. Flax (1980). 618 F.2d 1062 (4th Cir.).

Snyder v. AG Trucking (1995). 1995 Fed. App. 0184P (6th Cir.).

Speen v. Crown Clothing Corporation. (1996). No. 96-1402 (1st Cir.).

Steinhauser, S. (1998). Age bias: Is your corporate culture in need of an overhaul? *HR Magazine, 43,* 86–88.

Sterns, H. L., Barrett, G. V., and Alexander, R. A. (1985). Accidents and the aging individual. In J. E. Birren and K. W. Schaie (Eds.), *Handbook of the psychology of aging* (2nd ed., pp. 703–724). New York: Van Nostrand Reinhold.

Sterns, H. L., and McDaniel, M. A. (1994). Job performance and the older worker. In S. Rix (Ed.), *Older workers: How do they measure up?* Washington, D.C.: American Association of Retired Persons.

Stewart, M. A., and Ryan, E. B. (1982). Attitudes toward older and younger adult speakers: Effects of varying speech rates. *Journal of Language and Social Psychology, 1,* 91–109.

Stopka v. Alliance of American Insurers. (1998). No. 97-1974, WL 146412, *6 (7th Cir.).

Sung, K. T. (1995). Measures and dimensions of filial piety in Korea. *Gerontologist, 35,* 240–247.

Tajfel, H., and Turner, J. C. (1986). The social identity theory of intergroup behavior. In S. Worchel and W. G. Austin (Eds.), *Psychology of intergroup relations* (pp. 7–17). Chicago: Nelson-Hall.

Tien-Hyatt, J. L. (1987). Self-perceptions of aging across cultures: Myth or reality? *International Journal of Aging and Human Development, 24,* 129–148.

U.S. Bureau of the Census. (1990). Persons below poverty level by age, region, race, and Hispanic origin, 1990. Available at: www.census.gov/.

Vroom, V. A. (1964). *Work and motivation.* New York: Wiley.

Wall, J. L., and Shatshat, H. M. (1981). Controversy over the issue of mandatory retirement. *Personnel Administrator, 26,* 25–28.

Walch v. Intecom (1997). WL 452742 (N.D. Tex.).

Walsh, D., and Lloyd, A. D. (1984). Personnel planning's new agenda. *American Demographics, 6,* 34–37.

Warr, P. (1994). Age and employment. In H. C. Triandis, M. D. Dunnette, and L. M. Hough (Eds.), *Handbook of industrial and organizational psychology* (2nd ed., Vol. 4, pp. 485–550). Palo Alto, CA: Consulting Psychologists Press.

Webb, M. (1993, March 29). How old is too old? *New York Magazine, 26*(13), 66–73.

Wichmann v. Board of Trustees of Southern Illinois University (1999). No. 97-2902 (7th Cir.).

Willemyns, M., Gallois, C., Callan, V. J., and Pittam, J. (1997). Accent accommodation in the job interview: Impact of interviewer accent and gender. *Journal of Language and Social Psychology, 8,* 1–22.

Williams, A. (1996). Young people's evaluations of intergenerational versus peer underaccommodation: Sometimes older is better? *Journal of Language and Social Psychology, 15,* 291–311.

Williams, A., and Coupland, N. (1998). Epilogue: The socio-political framing of communication and aging research. *Journal of Applied Communication Research, 26,* 139–154.

Williams, A., and Giles, H. (1998). Communication of ageism. In M. Hecht (Ed.), *Communication prejudice* (pp. 136–160). Thousand Oaks, CA: Sage.

Williams, A., and Nussbaum, J. F. (2001). *Intergenerational communication across the lifespan*. Hillside, NJ: Erlbaum.

Williams, A., Ota, H., Giles, H., Pierson, H. D., Gallois, C., Ng, S. H., Lim, T. S., Ryan, E. B., Somera, L., Maher, J., Cai, D., and Harwood, J. (1997). Young people's beliefs about intergenerational communication: An initial cross-cultural analysis. *Communication Research, 24,* 370–393.

Wilson, D. W., and Molleston, J. L. (1981). Effects of sex and type of humor on humor appreciation. *Journal of Personality Assessment, 45,* 90–96.

Wither, A., and Hodges, I. (1987). *Elderly people in New Zealand: A bibliography of New Zealand research, 1972–1985.* Wellington: Department of Health.

Yum, J. O. (1988). The impact of Confucianism on interpersonal relations and communication patterns in East Asia. *Communication Monographs, 55,* 374–388.

7

Ageist Behavior
Monisha Pasupathi and Corinna E. Löckenhoff

Writing for the majority opinion of the U.S. Supreme Court in *Kimel et al. v. Florida Board of Regents et al.* (1999), Justice Sandra Day O'Connor suggested that older adults do not deserve protection from discrimination in the same way that other groups do: "Older persons . . . have not been subjected to a history of purposeful and unequal treatment. . . . Old age also does not define a discrete and insular minority because all persons, if they live out their normal life, will experience it." In at least one sense, Justice O'Connor is right: Most of us will become elderly. Will we be differentially treated on the basis of our age? If so, is such differential treatment necessarily ageist, or is it necessitated by the other changes occurring with increasing age? This chapter focuses on describing ways in which older adults are treated across a variety of settings. In addition, we elaborate on some of the issues involved in deciding when and whether age-differentiated treatment constitutes ageism and consider future directions for research on ageist and age-differentiated behavior.

Behavior—Ageist and Age Differentiated

We are primarily concerned with research on behavior or actions that potentially affect older adults. We define behavior broadly, from legislation to conversation, and across a variety of settings. The depth of our coverage does vary to reflect that some areas are more fully examined in other portions of this book. We begin by considering some important issues in the definition and examination of ageist behavior.

Much of our review focuses on documenting age-differentiated behavior, which we define as behavior that differs as a function of the age of the target person. Such behavior is not necessarily ageist. We define ageist behavior as a subset of age-differentiated behavior that is either caused by inaccurate negative attitudes and beliefs about aging or older adults or has clear harmful impact on older adults. Distinguishing between age differential and ageist behavior can be difficult, especially in the face of age-related changes that may require age-differentiated treatment. Further, not all research that demonstrates age-differentiated behavior also provides evidence that negative and inaccurate beliefs and attitudes caused the differences in people's behaviors, and not all age-differentiated behavior appears obviously harmful. In fact, as is clear throughout our review, many age-differentiated behaviors have both positive and negative features on the surface.

The Faces of Aging

Because some age-differentiated behavior may reflect appropriate accommodation to real changes in old age, we begin by outlining the impact of typical aging on information processing, language and conversational skills, physical capacities, and social and emotional characteristics. Evaluating whether age-differentiated behavior is actually ageist requires a look at the real characteristics of older adults.

Health and Sensory Functioning

Older adults are typically more variable along almost any dimension considered than adults at earlier ages (Dannefer and Perlmutter 1990). This means that age alone is a poorer cue to functioning in later adulthood than at almost any other age. Further, although it is true that health declines occur in later life, the prevalence of those declines may be overestimated. Consider some statistics. According to national survey data, about 8.5 percent of older adults (those age 65 and older) have significant problems with vision; about 35 percent report difficulties with hearing. Fewer than 2 percent have speech impairments (Adams, Hendershot, and Marano 1999). Thus, although older adults report more hearing impairments than younger adults do, the majority of older adults do not have difficulty with hearing or vision.

Independence and Everyday Living

On average, 64 percent of adults over age 65 report no limitations in major activities (Adams, Hendershot, and Marano 1999), with approximately 2 percent requiring assistance with basic activities of daily living (e.g., eating, dressing, or bathing; Horgas, Wahl, and Baltes 1996). This number does increase with age; about 26 percent of adults over age 85 require such assistance. Once again, however, 26 percent does not constitute a majority of older adults.

Cognition

Cognitive and intellectual changes with age are well documented, although both declines and stability are observed, depending on the specific capacity examined (Baltes, Lindenberger, and Staudinger, 1998; Salthouse, Hambrick, and McGuthry, 1998; Schaie 1994). As is generally true with age, there is considerable intraindividual variability in cognitive changes, and the individual's environment (work, family) influences the likelihood and magnitude of losses (Schaie 1994). Studies of cognitive function often employ artificial laboratory tasks that are designed to reveal basic cognitive processes and often show substantial age-related changes (Baltes et al. 1998), but evidence suggests that the more ecologically valid the task is, the lower is the magnitude of age-related decline (Adams et al. 1990; Baltes et al. 2000; Blanchard-Fields and Chen 1996). Many researchers believe that in everyday life, acquired expertise compensates for declines in the mechanics of cognition. For example, despite showing typical declines in laboratory tasks, older managers may be better at managerial decision making than younger ones (Colonia-Willner 1998; Streufert et al. 1990). Thus, although normal aging is associated with declines in many cognitive abilities, the impact of those declines on everyday functioning is often small or nonexistent.

Language

Age-related changes in language have also been documented. Older adults speak and write using syntactically simpler sentence structures than younger adults, with fewer left-branching clauses (e.g., subordinate clauses that occur to the left of the predicate of the main clause in a sentence; Kemper et al. 1989; Kemper and Kemtes 1999). The effect on communication may be positive in that older adults' speech is clearer and simpler to understand than the speech of younger adults (Kemper et al. 1989). Older adults' ability to understand what others say to them is well preserved in normal aging, unless the speech is presented very rapidly or is complex (Kemper and Kemtes 1999). In general, many aspects of language function are unchanged with age (Bayles, Tomoeda, and Boone 1985; Kemper and Kemtes 1999), and storytelling abilities may actually improve in later life (Kemper et al. 1990; Kemper and Kemtes 1999). Contrary to stereotype, older adults are not necessarily more prone to rambling or irrelevant speech, and such speech may actually be perceived favorably by listeners when it does occur (James et al. 1998).

Social and Emotional Changes

In social and emotional development, gains with adulthood have also been documented. For example, older adults report more frequent positive emotion, less frequent negative emotion, and similar well-being when compared to younger adults (Mroczek and Kolarz 1998; Carstensen, Pasupathi, and Mayr 2000). Older adults report better capacities for emotion regulation (Gross et al. 1997), and adaptive changes in social cognition have also been observed (Berg et al. 1998; Chen and Blanchard-Fields 1997; see also Staudinger and Pasupathi 2000).

Thus far, we have written as though the years between 65 and the end of life are largely similar; they are not. The prevalence of impairment among adults over 85 is greater, with adults over age 85 being twice as likely to exhibit undesirable age-related changes (Smith and Baltes 1999). Further, the likelihood of multiple impairment is higher in very old age, and we have not considered the prevalence of multiple impairments (see, Marsiske et al. 1999). The heterogeneity of the older population, however, remains large across the later years (Smith and Baltes 1999), and our brief tour should suggest that aging is not nearly as negative as the negative stereotypes of aging might suggest.

The Impact of the Findings

Taken together, these findings imply a complex, domain-specific, and multidirectional set of psychological changes in later adulthood. In other words, parallel to studies showing both positive and negative attitudes and beliefs (Brewer and Lui 1989; Heckhausen, Dixon, and Baltes 1989; Hummert 1990; see also chapter 5, this volume), aging appears to have both positive and negative implications for physical and psychological well-being.

Three important points must be emphasized. First, no single age-related impairment affects a majority of older adults. Second, older adults tend to be more different from one another than are younger adults, making age in later life a poor indicator of an individual's competence or functional ability. Third, there are developmental discontinuities in the years from 65 to the end of life; these discontinuities warrant sensitivity to continuing changes within the period we term old age. These three points have implications for considering age-differentiated versus ageist labels for observed behavior in the literature review that follows. In evaluating whether behavior is age differentiated or ageist, important considerations include the assumed and actual attributes of the older adult recipient of differential behavior, including their age. The base rates we have presented imply that in many cases, differential treatment of older adults reflects unfounded and negative assumptions about their competence.

Age-Differentiated Behavior

We now turn to reviewing evidence for age-differentiated behavior across a variety of settings. We consider behavior at the societal or institutional level, including the passage of legislation or the dispersion of media images, and at the level of interpersonal interactions. This broad focus is intended to reveal a wide range of ways in which older adults receive differential treatment. Some areas, however, are richer in research findings than others. We have structured the review within domains (e.g., health, intergenerational interaction) and then draw conclusions about commonalities in age-differentiated behavior across domains.

Health Settings

For older patients, as for younger ones, medical and psychosocial problems are often closely related. Psychological issues such as depression, family problems, or fear of medical procedures influence and are influenced by physical disease. Greene and Adelman (1996) believe that "in every patient's physical complaint, there is a psychosocial component" (p. 85). For elderly patients, diagnosis and treatment decisions with regard to psychological issues are often left to the primary care providers, without further referral to psychologists or psychiatrists. About half of all older patients mention at least one psychosocial problem during a consultation with their physician (Greene and Adelman 1996). Therefore, we address evidence for behavioral ageism with regard to both physical disease and psychosocial issues in one section. To provide a complete picture of age-differentiated and ageist behavior in medical settings, we review research on diagnostic issues and treatment decisions, as well as physician-patient interactions and the specific context of institutional settings.

Diagnostic Issues and Treatment Decisions Age-differentiated behavior in health care settings may manifest itself very early in the medical encounter, when patient and health care professional have to reach agreement about the problems that need to be addressed. It has been suggested that physicians and nurses ascribe certain symptoms of their older patients (such as balance problems and falls, incontinence, constipation, memory loss, or depression) to advanced age instead of viewing them as treatable conditions (Greene et al. 1986; Adelman et al. 1990; Lasser et al. 1998).

Also, the same disorder can manifest itself in different symptoms across the life span, which can lead to misdiagnosis and inappropriate treatment. Up to one-third of the older population may suffer from depression. However, depressive older adults experience more somatic symptoms and anxiety and less subjective sadness than younger patients (Lasser et al. 1998). As a consequence, depression often goes unnoticed in older adults, and misdiagnoses of depression-related cognitive deficits as dementia are frequent (Lamberty and Bieliauskas 1993). Medical problems are also frequently misdiagnosed or not detected at all. Secondary prevention programs such as routine screenings for cancer often ignore older adults (Derby 1991), and many physicians fail to offer adequate preventive counseling to their geriatric patients (Adelman, Green, and Charon 1991).

Even if disorders are correctly diagnosed, treatment biases or lack of information might lead to suboptimal treatment. Gatz and Pearson (1988) suggest that professional psychologists might underestimate older adults' responsiveness to psychotherapy and believe that they are not capable of self-reflection. Because of this misconception, older patients with depression are often treated with drugs instead of psychotherapy, although psychological treatment is equally effective for all age groups (Gatz and Pearson 1988). Also, some physicians fail to take age-related changes in the absorption and effectiveness of medications into account. As a consequence, older adults are more likely to suffer from adverse drug effects and misuse prescription drugs more frequently than any other group of patients (Finlayson 1995).

Another area in which health professionals treat people of different ages differently involves pain management. Pain (both acute and chronic) is common among the elderly (Gagliese and Melzack 1997). However, geriatric pain patients are less likely to receive adequate treatment than younger adults. Gagliese and Melzack (1997) identified three reasons for inadequate management of pain among older people. First, physicians are not properly assessing pain problems among their geriatric patients. Second, there are some risks associated with pharmacotherapy of pain, and older adults are more likely to experience adverse side effects than younger adults. Alternative methods of pain control, such as biofeedback or relaxation techniques, can benefit older people, but physicians often fail to inform their patients about these options. Adequate pain management is also hindered by misconceptions about pain and aging. Some physicians still seem to view pain as a normal consequence of the aging process, not as a treatable condition.

Decisions about the treatment of terminally ill patients require both medical and ethical considerations on the part of health care professionals. Some physicians might put less effort into saving the lives of older patients because they will soon die of old age anyway (Uddo 1986; Bornemann and Ferell 1996). Not chronological age but medical status and patient's quality of life should determine whether treatment is continued or whether food and water are withdrawn in the final stages of a disease (Uddo 1986). Advance directives such as living wills and do-not-resuscitate orders can help health care providers make such decisions when the patient is no longer able to do so. Unfortunately, few physicians inform their patients about the possibility of formulating advance directives. Physicians seem reluctant to discuss end-of-life issues with their older patients, although older adults would like to talk about these topics with their primary health care provider (Resnick, Cowart, and Kubrin 1998).

Physician and Patient Communication Thus far, we have considered primarily differences in the diagnosis of disease and decisions regarding treatments. These differences arise in the course of physician-patient interactions, which serve multiple functions. Putnam (1996) identified three crucial parts of medical interviews: gathering data, establishing a relationship between patient and physician, and educating and treating the patient. In reality, however, goals and roles within the encounter are much less clear-cut, and there is considerable uncertainty and ambiguity for both the patient and the physician (Giles, Williams, and Coupland 1990). Patients usually do not know the exact nature of their problems. They experience certain symptoms but initially have little information about the underlying problem. Some patients have their own explanatory model, derived from folk beliefs about their symptoms, and it might differ considerably from the medical model of the physician (Putnam 1996). Also, patients are often not sure which information about the problem is relevant for the physician to make a clear diagnosis (Haug 1996).

Physicians too can experience considerable uncertainty. As medical science evolves, diagnostic and treatment techniques change, and medical students as well as experienced practitioners are often in doubt as to whether they are in fact providing the right treatment for a certain problem (Gerrity et al. 1992). Further, they are often not sure whether they have gathered all of the necessary information to decide about the right course of action (Haug 1996). Unfortunately, patient-physician interactions often fail to resolve this inherent uncertainty in medical encounters. For example, regardless of age, cancer patients seem to recall very little of the information that physicians gave them about their prognosis and their course of treatment (Siminoff 1989). Similar gaps in comprehension are evident in studies of informed consent (Mann 1994).

Uncertainty and lack of mutual understanding in physician-patient interactions may be greater for older adults, for several reasons. Older adults tend to have more complex medical problems than younger age groups. Many of them suffer from multiple, often chronic, conditions, and they have a higher risk of adverse side effects (Finlayson 1995; Beisecker 1996). Further, the tempting explanation of "old age" may obscure a treatable problem. Older patients certainly represent a subset of the elderly with more serious health problems and perhaps less intact ability to manage their lives. This means that health care professionals may be more susceptible than the general public to ageist attitudes and the assumption that aging and disease go hand in hand (Greene et al. 1986). Uncertainty and ambiguity are even more likely to arise in such situations and could exacerbate the communicative gap between physicians and their older patients, and there is some evidence that this may be the case.

Several studies have found evidence for age-differentiated behavior among physicians. Greene and her colleagues (1986) audiotaped eighty medical interviews during follow-up visits for chronic conditions. Using the Geriatric Interactions Analysis (GIA; Greene et al. 1986) as a coding scheme, they analyzed the interviews with regard to the content and process of the interview and with regard to the behavior of physician and patient. Physician behavior was coded for egalitarian attitude, patience, engagement, and respectfulness. Patients' characteristics were coded for assertiveness, relaxedness, friendliness, and expressiveness. Physicians provided more detailed medical information and were more supportive when interacting with younger patients (under age 45) than with older patients (over age 65). They were also rated as more egalitarian, more patient, more engaged, and more respectful when addressing younger patients. Physicians raised more psychosocial topics in interviews with their younger patients. Finally, they were more responsive to the topics that younger patients raised than to the topics mentioned by older patients. This age-differentiated behavior of physicians could not be explained through age differences in patient behavior because no differences were found in the behavior of younger and older patients. Although older patients' medical problems were judged as more severe than the problems of younger patients, age differences in physician behavior remained significant even if the authors controlled for severity of disease. These findings suggest that physicians communicate more successfully with their younger patients than with their older patients and are more open to the concerns of younger patients.

These differences in interaction have consequences for how patients and physicians later remember an interaction. In a later study Greene and her colleagues (1989) investigated the concordance between patients' and physicians' views of the major topics and goals that were discussed during a medical interview. They analyzed audiotapes of the interview itself and gathered postvisit information from both physicians and patients. There was more agreement about the major topics of the encounter between physicians and their younger patients than between physicians and their older patients.

Rost and Frankel (1993) analyzed the medical visits of one hundred elderly diabetic patients (age 60 or older) and found that most patients were not successful in raising important medical and psychosocial problems. Physicians did not prompt patients to tell them about additional complications, and if patients did mention new problems, physicians often failed to discuss them properly. As a consequence, patients managed to discuss fewer than half of the new problems they wanted to raise during their medical visit. It is not clear whether younger patients would have fared better, but it is clear that older patients' interactions with physicians were less than optimal.

Some of the age differences might be due to the influence of age on the average length of medical encounters. Although Greene and her colleagues (1986) did not find any age differences in the length of the medical interviews they examined, Radecki and colleagues (1988) concluded from a review of several national surveys that physicians spend less time with older patients, especially during follow-up visits. This smaller amount of time may make it more difficult for patients to raise all of the issues that they consider important and certainly reduces the information available to the physician for making diagnostic and treatment decisions.

In contrast to these findings, some studies found age differences in physician behavior that favored older patients. Hooper and colleagues (1982) observed patient-physician interactions and found that physicians were more courteous when interacting with older adults. Such courtesy could be a double-edged sword, preventing physicians from raising sensitive but important topics with patients.

One other age difference in physician-patient encounters has been documented, but its effects are not well understood: Older people are more likely to be accompanied by a third person, usually a relative, during their medical visit (Adelman, Greene, and Charon 1987; Beisecker 1994). The third person in the medical encounter can have different roles, either providing support for the patient and his or her concerns or being antagonistic to the patient's interests (Adelman, Greene, and Charon 1987; Beisecker 1989). Some authors are concerned that the presence of a companion might interfere with communication between patient and physician and contribute to tendencies for passivity among older patients (Beisecker 1994; Greene et al. 1994).

Taken together, there is substantial evidence that physicians treat older patients differently from younger patients. Specifically, this differential treatment involves the potential for misinterpretation of symptoms and inappropriate treatment, is reflected in less open and receptive communication practices, and results in poor concordance between patient and physician about what was accomplished in an interview. Whether such behavior is ageist is more complicated. Consider just the issue of pain management. Some reasons for inadequate treatment of pain in older patients appeared ageist (considering pain normal for older adults), while others appeared legitimate concerns (the higher likelihood of adverse reactions to pain medications in older adults). We return to this issue because the case of physician-patient encounters provides a compelling illustration of complexities in determining whether behavior is ageist.

Nursing Homes

Institutional settings that are specifically designed for older residents, such as nursing homes and assisted living facilities, foster age-differentiated behavior by their very definition. In everyday language, such institutions are often referred to as "old people's homes," a colloquialism that makes the age-differentiated nature of such settings even more obvious. The older people who live in such settings also constitute the subset of the older population who is most vulnerable to the negative consequences of age-differentiated and ageist behavior. Both physical impairment and cognitive decline can lead to the institutionalization of an older person, and the rate of institutionalization increases with age. Among the oldest old (persons over age 85), 22 percent reside in nursing homes (Doty 1992). Over 80 percent of nursing home residents suffer from severe functional limitations, 50 percent show signs of cognitive impairment, and over two-thirds depend on Medicaid and have no private assets (Krauss et al. 1997). These numbers stand in direct contrast to the characteristics of the general elderly population. Such circumstances leave residents with few resources to cope with any additional challenges.

Many nursing homes still fulfill Goffmann's (1961) criteria of total institutions. They have a tight daily schedule, enforce a strict set of rules, and leave little personal freedom for the residents. Residents tend to be deprived of their individuality because tight routines leave little space for specific wishes and needs. According to Goffmann, total institutions are "total" because they completely control the life's of their residents. This is achieved by ritualized processes of initiation (nursing home admission) and degradation (loss of privacy, submission to rules). Thus, residents' identities are first stripped away and then reconstituted within the institutional system; a person becomes a resident, who is defined by his or her age along with specific medical diagnoses. By complying with the rules, residents can gain privileges; noncompliance leads to negative outcomes. Total institutions render their inhabitants quite vulnerable to any negative behaviors on the part of institutional personnel.

Further, the structure of nursing home staff can contribute to problems with treatment of the elderly residents. Usually, the nursing staff is composed of several hierarchical layers. The director of nursing (DON) is the head of this hierarchy. The middle levels include registered nurses (RNs) and practical nurses (LPNs). The lowest and largest level of this hierarchy of care consists of nurses' aides. Nurses' aides have more frequent contacts with residents than other nursing staff, because they provide hands-on care and interact with residents day in and day out (Aroskar, Urv-Wong, and Kane 1990). Nurses' aides' work is physically demanding and emotionally challenging, they deliver physical care and are the closest social contact to the residents. Thus, it is nurses' aides who are confronted with the sadness, anger, fear, or resignation the residents may feel. Additional challenges for the aides result from the hierarchical setup of the care setting. They form the link between the residents and the RNs and LPNs who make the care plans. Nurses' aides are expected to follow tight rules while performing care tasks. Thus, they carry a lot of responsibility without having the authority to change the routines (Aroskar, Urv-Wong, and Kane 1990). Unfortunately, most nursing homes do not have sufficient funds to employ more than the legally required staffing ratio, which usually covers only basic care needs and does not leave sufficient time for social interactions. Thus, nurses' aides often have to refuse one resident's wish for personal attention because another resident requires physical care. In spite of the high demands of their job, nurses' aides are not trained sufficiently. Most receive only the legally required seventy-five hours of theoretical training in addition to some basic instruction on the job (Aroskar, Urv-Wong, and Kane 1990). Thus, nurses' aides are not adequately trained to handle the multiple demands of their job. In addition, most are paid minimum wage. Together with the high stress potential of the job, the low payment leads to an extremely high turnover rate among nursing staff (Kaster, White, and Carruth 1979). Most authors agree that nurses' aide is a highly demanding, low-prestige job that offers little reward for the workers (Goodwin and Trocchio 1987). The problematic working conditions of nursing staff make them more vulnerable to ageist attitudes and a mechanical approach to care that treats residents as cases, and not as individual persons.

Overall, the interactions between residents and nurses' aides are guided by role relationships. Lidz, Fischer, and Arnold (1992) found that health care professionals perceived the maximization of residents' health as their major goal. Within such a medical model of care, the residents are expected to attempt to get better and to comply with recommendations from the nursing staff. Noncompliance with the rules of the institution is perceived as problematic. Often residents with dementia are no longer able to understand the rules of the nursing home; most of the time they do not even know where they are. They also have problems following the recommendations of nursing home staff. Nurses' aides may perceive this as a purposeful noncompliance with the rules of the nursing home and sometimes react by providing less support. The medicalization of care fosters the tendency to value restorative care for patients with acute medical problems over custodial care for residents with progressive diseases like dementia. So not only do residents with progressive disease sometimes violate the explicit rules of the nursing home, they also violate the implicit rules about improving through being cared for or treated and render themselves "unworthy" of attention. Ultimately, even less attention is given to residents who are more vulnerable because of their cognitive or physical impairments (Lidz, Fischer, and Arnold 1992).

When residents do receive attention, that attention has an interesting slant. Nursing staff tend to ignore independent behavior of residents and to foster dependent behavior. This tendency was first described by Baltes as the "dependence-support, independence-ignore script" (Baltes, Burgess, and Stewart 1980; Baltes 1988; Baltes and Wahl 1996). In her research, Baltes used a behavior coding system to code self-care behaviors of nursing home residents (e.g., combing hair, getting dressed) as either dependent (requiring assistance) or independent (performed without help). She found that dependent self-care behaviors were followed by a high amount of social action and congruent responses from the social partners (in most cases nursing staff). In contrast, independent self-care behaviors and independent prosocial behaviors (such as talking to other residents) were ignored most of the time. Thus, dependent behavior was most likely to elicit attention from social partners. Because social contact is rare and desired in nursing homes, such interaction patterns are likely to reinforce dependent behavior among residents. But one criticism of all of this work is that it reflects something about institutions, not about age-differentiated behavior.

To address this concern, Baltes and Reisenzein (1986) compared the situation of institutionalized children with the situation of nursing home residents. They found that children were more likely to be reinforced for independent behaviors, whereas older residents were more likely to receive social attention for dependent behavior. It can be concluded that support for dependent behavior patterns is not a consequence of institutionalization in itself but constitutes a case of age-differentiated treatment within long-term care institutions.

Combined with the dependency-support script, nurses' aides also display tendencies to treat residents like children. This manifests itself not only in comments from nursing staff comparing residents to children (Dolinsky 1984) but also in the frequent use of displaced baby talk in interactions between aides and residents. According to Caporael and Culbertson (1986), baby talk is "a simplified speech register having special lexical items (e.g., 'choo, choo') and constructions . . . , but is identified by its distinctive paralinguistic features. The hallmark of baby talk speech is its high pitch and exaggerated intonation" (p. 99). Baby talk is normally used while talking to infants and young children. However, it is also used with animals, inanimate objects, and older persons. In such cases it is called "displaced baby talk" (Caporael and Culbertson 1986). Baby talk is not without consequences. It affects the self-esteem of nursing home residents. Self-esteem was the lowest in residents who received baby talk frequently and perceived it as negative (O'Connor and Rigby 1996). Further, Ryan, Hamilton, and Kwong See (1994) found that baby talk supported dependent behavior among nursing home residents. Caporael, Lukaszewski, and Culbertson (1983) found that the use of baby talk was associated with caregivers' stereotypes of older persons as dependent. Nursing staff members who perceived older persons as dependent were more likely to use baby talk than others.

Staff attitudes are relevant not only as a predictor for baby talk. They also play an important role in the well-being and the autonomy of nursing home residents in general, probably through their impact on the nature of the care provided. Perhaps for the same reasons we already outlined for physicians, negative attitudes toward the aged are common among health care workers and nursing staff (Penner, Ludenia, and Mead 1984; Heller, Bausell, and Ninos 1984; Sherman, Roberto, and Robinson 1996; DePaola et al. 1992). Several studies have shown that negative or positive attitudes toward the elderly are related to the quality of care provided for nursing home residents. Learman and associates (1990) told nursing staff that some residents had high rehabilitation potential and others only average rehabilitation potential. The residents were randomly assigned to the average- or high-expectancy groups. Learman and associates found that the high-expectancy residents had fewer depressive symptoms and were admitted to hospitals less frequently. Higher expectations about the cognitive, functional, and emotional status of residents are correlated with more positive interactions between residents and staff and better outcomes of care. The findings of Kahana and Kiyak (1981, 1984) suggest that the more positive the attitudes are, the greater is the chance that staff will foster the independence of residents. In turn, negative staff attitudes seem to be correlated to low empathy, a custodial attitude toward treatment, inadequate care, and low perceptions of rehabilitation potential (Hatton 1977; Heller, Bausell, and Ninos 1984; Bagshaw and Adams 1985; Sheridan, White, and Fairchild 1992).

It can be concluded that institutionalized homes for the elderly constitute age-differentiated settings by the very way in which they are defined and organized. Not surprisingly, there is ample evidence for age-differentiated treatment in such settings and some evidence that this treatment is harmful for residents' self-esteem and autonomy. There are also obvious links between negative attitudes toward aging among nursing staff and observed age-differentiated behavior. We can conclude that nursing homes offer many examples of ageist behavior.

Legal Settings

The legal system sometimes treats older adults differently, and sometimes does not. Moreover, this area of research is sparse and ripe for further investigation. Older adults participate in and are affected by the legal system in various ways. These include being victims or perpetrators of crimes and being the recipients of various custodial court decisions, as well as being affected by legislative and judicial acts that concern older adults. We begin with older adults as victims and perpetrators in the criminal justice system and then move on to a brief consideration of legislative and judicial acts.

As victims, older adults may be vulnerable to different types of crime than younger adults are. For example, FBI records in South Carolina suggest that older adults were disproportionately at risk for robbery, intimidation, vandalism, and fraud (McCabe and Gregory 1998), although they may be at lower risks for other types of crime, such as rape and murder (Hirschel and Rubin 1982). When older adults do become victims of crime, their age may affect the way they are perceived and the outcome of a trial. Victims of rape may be differently regarded depending on their age. A study of college students' jury decisions in a rape case manipulated the age of the victim (early 20s or 60s) and examined the verdict, recommendation for sentencing, and degree of victim blaming (Villemur and Hyde 1983). There were no simple effects of the victim's age on these outcomes outside the fact that older victims were judged as more respectable. However, when victims were older, female jurors attributed greater fault to the defendant, and male jurors gave more frequent guilty verdicts when the victim was both elderly and unattractive. These findings can be interpreted as both positive and negative in their implications. They imply that older victims are more likely to see their attackers punished, but also suggest that older adult rape victims are viewed as having less culpability because they are viewed as less attractive generally and thus present fewer "temptations" for a rapist.

Are older offenders treated differently from younger ones by the criminal justice system? This sort of study is difficult to conduct because older adults generally engage in less crime and also are likely to engage in different sorts of crime (e.g., less rape) than younger adults (Wilbanks 1988). The results we do have are mixed. Studies that examine actual cases and sentences tend to show that older adults are treated more harshly in terms of convictions and parole but are sometimes given more lenient sentences (Fishman and Sordo 1984; Wilbanks 1988). Studies examining mock juror decisions on simulated cases tend to show that older criminals are perceived more positively and given more lenient sentences (Silverman et al. 1984; Reynolds and Sanders 1975). Here again, older adults appear to be treated more leniently and more harshly.

Conservatorship or guardianship is intended to protect people who are unable to manage their own affairs. A guardian or conservator may make any number of personal and financial decisions on behalf of the conservatee, depending on the specific ruling of the court. In some cases, conservatorship carries the right to place a conservatee in a locked facility or authorize the use of psychotropic medications.

Conservatorships represent a conflict between preservation of autonomy and protecting a person who may need substantial help. Is that conflict differently resolved for people of different ages? Erring on the side of protection results from negative ageism—the idea that older adults are incompetent and in need of protection—while erring on the side of preserving autonomy results from compassionate ageism—the idea that older adults are especially hurt by overprotection because of their age (Reynolds 1997). In a review of 2,118 conservatorship cases in Los Angeles County, Reynolds concludes that compassionate ageism is more evident than negative ageism. For example, older conservatees were less likely to be placed in locked facilities and less likely to be placed on psychotropic medications. These differences were evident after presenting problems and other demographic characteristics had been statistically controlled. While this treatment appears benevolent, Reynolds cautions that compassionate ageism can result in the failure to protect or treat a person who needs medication or highly protected locked facilities.

A comprehensive review of legislative acts concerning older adults is well beyond our scope. However, as in other areas, legislative acts tend to have both benevolent and harmful implications for older adults. At first glance, recent legislative acts indicate concern with protecting older adults from ageism. These include the 1967 Age Discrimination in Employment Act (ADEA), as well as the amended Older Workers' Benefit Protection Act. The former was designed to protect employees over the age of 40 from differential treatment in all phases of the employment process, including advertising, with small firms being exempt from compliance. The latter act was designed to ensure that early retirement packages and other incentives that require workers to waive their right to sue for age discrimination are offered in a way that does not unduly harm the worker (Pearce and Schultz 1995). The ADEA can be considered among the broadest legislative protections against discrimination (Issacharoff and Harris 1997).

This broad application has received recent challenges. For example, the 1999 Supreme Court ruling described at the chapter opening implies that older adults do not deserve special protections in the workplace, because they do not constitute a group with a history of discrimination. At the least, the ruling strongly argues that age-related discrimination is not like other discrimination (see also Issacharoff and Harris 1997).

Mandatory retirement and increased insurance costs on the basis of age alone, rather than competence or demonstrated health risks, are still legal policies.

In sum, there is evidence that older victims may be seen as less responsible for their victimization and that older perpetrators are treated both more and less harshly by the judicial system, depending on the specific outcome examined. Legislative acts acknowledge age-differentiated treatment, protect against it, and in some cases (e.g., the ADEA) perpetuate it by establishing age limits in the scope of the law's protection. Recent thinking on age discrimination acknowledges that it differs from other group-based discrimination and may require different legislative treatment as well. Still, despite attention to problems for older adults in employment, many forms of age-differential treatment remain permissible under current law; notably, those include the age-based mandatory retirement policies and age-based increases in insurance costs. In an increasingly heterogeneous elderly population, such policies may be unfair and ageist.

The Workplace

Mandatory retirement laws are perhaps the most glaring example of discrimination based on age, particularly because the heterogeneity of older adults means that age is less related to competence in later life than at other times. However, even retirement is an ambiguous prospect with some benevolent features, having been previously sold to older workers as a reward for long and valued service and to younger workers as reducing competition and opening positions (Jefferys 1996).

Hiring and firing practices are certainly age differentiated. For example, the British Broadcasting Corporation, when forced to downsize, targeted early retirements and layoffs at older workers (Plattman and Tinker 1998). In BBC recruiting advertisements during this period, younger adults were targeted. The result was a workforce composition increasingly at odds with England's aging population.

Bendick, Brown, and Wall (1999) examined discrimination in hiring practices directly, using an innovative approach. Pairs of testers were matched in appearance, demeanor, and qualifications (fabricated) but differed in age (32 years old versus 57 years old). Three of the four pairs were male, and all were European Americans. The pairs received additional coaching prior to the study's beginning to ensure that their interview behavior was as similar as possible throughout the study. Pairs of testers then applied for 102 jobs in the Washington, D.C., area. Analyses examined the ways in which employers responded to testers, the offers that were made to older versus younger applicants, and the impact of contextual variables such as the type of job.

The favorability of the response they received during the application process was assessed in both a preinterview stage and at the interview and offer stages, based on statements made by the employer, the timing and length of events (e.g., phone conversations), and the impressions of the applicant. Overall, the younger applicant received a more favorable response at the preinterview stage 31.4 percent of the time; older applicants never received more favorable responses at this stage. At the interview stage, the gap diminished, with younger applicants receiving a more favorable response 10.8 percent of the time, and in 1 percent of cases, older applicants receiving a more favorable response. Interestingly, initial phone contacts between applicants and employers tended to involve more substantive questions when the applicant was older.

In nine cases, both applicants received a job offer, making it possible to compare the offers given to older and younger applicants. In the majority of cases, the offer was the same for both older and younger adults across title, health benefits, salary, full-time versus part-time employment, and advancement opportunities. For job title and advancement opportunities, older and younger applicants were equally likely to be favored. However, in terms of salary, full-time versus part-time status, and health benefits, discrepancies favored younger applicants.

Finally, context mattered in this study. Sales jobs were less discriminating (34 percent of the time) than managerial positions (100 percent of the time). Bendick and colleagues speculate that sales firms, which pay employees partly on commission, can take on an employee perceived as high risk with fewer consequences than other firms can. Further, older applicants were especially disadvantaged by employment agencies that contracted with multiple businesses (84 percent of the time) in comparison to direct employer contact (29 percent of the time).

The exclusion of workers from employment on the basis of age, whether through retirement or hiring discrimination, represents clear evidence for age-differential treatment. Because such practices are likely to be harmful to older adults by restricting their opportunities and because they are likely to be driven by negative attitudes (see Chapter 6, this volume), age-differentiated behavior in the workplace can be viewed as ageist.

Mass Media and Entertainment

Another example of age-differentiated treatment includes portrayals of different age groups on television, in newspapers, and in magazines. The characteristics of mass media images of aging are a result of decisions made by editors, program directors, and advertisers, based on their expectations about audience preferences. Thus, media images reflect general societal opinions. However, mass media coverage can also influence general values and individual behavior through its impact as a socializing force. Langer and associates (1988) suggest that stereotypes of old age start to develop in childhood (see also Isaacs and Bearison 1986) and are shaped by images of aging present in mass media and everyday conversations.

Both the visibility and the valence of television and magazine characters vary by age (Petersen 1973). The visibility of older people in the mass media (compared to their presence in the total population) has been so low that Davis (1984) felt compelled to title his review of the situation, "TV's Boycott of Old Age." Since the 1970s, various studies have found a striking underrepresentation of older adults in both electronic and print media (Davis and Davis 1985; Kubey 1988; Vasil and Wass 1993 for reviews). Aronoff (1974) analyzed 2,741 prime time television characters and found that less than 5 percent were older people (as opposed to a proportion of 10 percent of older adults in the general population in 1974). Harris and Feinberg (1977) observed 312 older characters in three networks across a six-week period. Only 8 percent of the characters were classified as 60 years or older. Gerbner and associates (1980) found that only 2.3 percent of the characters in a sample of prime time television dramas were older than 65 years. This bias remained stable through the decades examined. An analysis of new season characters on major networks from 1966 to 1992 revealed that only 2 percent of the characters were over 65 years old (Greenberg and Colette 1997). Cassata and Irwin (1997) sampled forty-five hours of daytime serial dramas; only 3 percent of the characters could be characterized as senior citizens. Television commercials are biased in a similar way. Francher (1973) found that the characters in a sample of 100 television commercials were almost exclusively young and attractive. In a random sample of 136 television commercials aired in 1981, only 3 percent of the characters were over 60 years old (Hiemstra et al. 1983). More than a decade later, Hajjar (1997) found that only 8 percent of her sample of characters in commercials were 60 years or older. Similar percentages were found in children's television programming. In a sample of 106 cartoon characters, only 7 percent were categorized as "old" (Bishop and Krause 1984).

Evidence of a gross underrepresentation of older adults was also found for various types of print media (see Vasil and Wass 1993 for a review). Wass and associates (1985) noted that less than 1 percent of the space in 263 issues of eleven different Sunday papers was concerned with older adults. This bias remained stable over the two decades 1963 to 1983. With regard to magazine advertisements Ursic, Ursic, and Ursic (1986) found that only 9 percent of more than 5,000 analyzed ads portrayed older adults. Similarly, Bramlett-Solomon and her colleagues (Bramlett-Solomon and Wilson 1989; Bramlett-Solomon and Subramanian 1997) categorized only 1 to 2 percent of advertisement characters in the popular magazines *Life* and *Ebony* as older adults. Only birthday cards (which are by definition related to aging) were found to use aging themes in 30 to 40 percent of the cases (Vasil and Wass 1993).

Women and minority elderly are even more underrepresented. Based on her findings, Petersen (1973) estimated that viewers would have to wait twenty-two minutes to see an older man, but four and a half hours to see an older woman on prime time television. Hiemstra and his colleagues (1983) and Hajjar (1997) found a one-to-two proportion of older female to older male characters in television commercials. In their review of twenty-eight empirical studies investigating mass media portrayals of older adults, Vasil and Wass (1993) found an underrepresentation of women in 65 percent of these studies. Minority elderly are almost invisible on television. Hiemstra and colleagues (1983) and Cassata and Irvin (1997) determined that more than 92 percent of all older soap opera characters were Caucasian. The only evidence for a more realistic proportion of different ethnicities is in Hajjar's analysis of television commercials, although blacks tended to be overrepresented in comparison to other nonwhite ethnicities.

From the evidence, it can be concluded that older characters are clearly underrepresented in electronic and print media. Findings are less clear with regard to the valence of mass media portrayals of older adults. In past decades, most studies found that older characters were described rather unfavorably (see Davis and Davis, 1985, Kubey 1988, and Vasil and Wass 1993 for reviews). Aronoff (1974) found that only 40 percent of older men and 10 percent of older women were depicted in positive ways. Harris and Feinberg (1977) noted that older characters showed less emotional complexity and worse health than younger characters. Only 1 of the 312 analyzed characters was part of a loving couple. Bishop and

Krause (1984) found that older characters on children's comics were described as more negative than younger characters. In Petersen's (1973) analysis of prime time television characters, 30 percent of the older characters were described as socially rejected and unfriendly. However, 93 percent of the older characters were also described as active, and 82 percent were characterized as healthy and independent. Kubey (1988) explained such surprising findings by a tendency toward a "reversed stereotype" (p. 22) of older characters, whose athletic and amorous pursuits are exaggerated and intended to create comical clashes with the existing negative stereotypes. More recently, there has been a positive shift in mass media images of aging that cannot be completely explained through reverse stereotyping. Bell (1992) analyzed the title sequences of five prime time dramas that presented elderly characters and found them to be portrayed as powerful, healthy, wealthy, and sexually attractive. Cassata's and Irwin's (1997) analysis of daytime soap operas had similar findings. The majority of older characters could be described as "fair, sociable, strong, rational, stable, happy, peaceful, independent, assertive, caring, powerful, honest" (p. 226). In Hajjar's analysis of older characters in television commercials, only 8 percent were portrayed unfavorably. These results match findings by Hofstetter and his colleagues (1993), who investigated older adults' perceptions of television images of old age. Only 20 percent of their participants thought that older television characters were portrayed less favorably than younger characters. Old people who had higher exposure to television had an even more positive view of the image of old age conveyed by this medium.

Two conclusions can be drawn. First, there are clear age differences in visibility in the mass media, with older adults grossly underrepresented. Second, mass media reflect the recent emergence of a positive stereotype of aging, with the majority of older characters described as powerful, active, and healthy. Whether such differences reflect ageist assumptions or intentions on the part of mass media directors, editors, and writers is not clear. Further, it is not clear whether such discrepancies are inherently harmful. Nevertheless, there is a striking discrepancy between the increase of television viewing with age (Kubey 1988) and the underrepresentation of older age groups. Marginalization in mass media coverage might support societal neglect of older adults' concerns and undermine older adults' own perceptions of their role in society. As Bell (1992) notes, to the extent that all television viewers look to television for role models and a vision of the real world, underrepresentation of any group is problematic.

Community Settings

In our leisure and everyday lives, outside work, medical, institutional, and legal settings, we also encounter others of varying ages. Here, too, there is evidence for age-differentiated behavior, ranging from subtle to profound. Egregious cases of ageism in everyday settings are easily found. Consider Michael D'Amico, a Manhattan hairstylist who gained notoriety for refusing to cut the hair of women over age 45 ("Age Cutoff" July 5, 1999). D'Amico may sound extreme, and clearly he defines old in ways that many researchers would find questionable (over age 45). Moreover, his story is only an anecdotal piece of evidence that older adults are denied access to services. But D'Amico's hair salon may not be the only place where doors close for older adults. Consider access to housing opportunities. One-hundred twenty individuals advertising rooms for rent were telephoned by an adult male, a young adult female, or an elderly female who posed as prospective renters. Rooms were more likely to be described as unavailable when the elderly person phoned or when another person made calls on her behalf (Page 1997).

The structuring of public spaces may also reflect assumptions about the needs and wants of older adults (Teo 1997). For example, in Singapore, spaces for health-related needs and those intended to meet older adults' social needs are separated. When surveyed about their use of public spaces, older adults report using health-related spaces but not social spaces (Teo 1997). Teo suggests that older adults clearly want to build and maintain their own private geographies and that current approaches to public space are formed by ageist assumptions (for example, the notion that older adults are lonely and in need of intervention to aid them in building a social network). Teo's article addresses a kind of compassionate ageism, like that considered earlier in conservatorships for older versus younger adults.

Ageism can enter into the reactions of the community to proposed spaces designed for elderly adults, and some authors report that communities resist housing directed toward elderly adults, acting to protest or even block the construction of this kind of housing (Lawton and Hoffman 1984; Mangum 1988). However, this resistance may be relative and may have little to do with ageism. Mangum (1988) examined reactions to various types of group housing: housing directed toward the mentally retarded, unwed mothers, welfare recipients, ordinary apartments, and high-priced condominiums, as well as housing for older adults. Interestingly, housing for older adults was less objectionable than all other types of group housing, including high-priced condominiums. Regression analyses were used to predict objections to housing for the elderly from measures of ageism and a measure of general antipathy toward group housing; attitudes toward housing for the elderly were predicted by antipathy toward group housing, not by ageism (Mangum 1988).

Interacting with People We Know In an extension of their work on dependency support to community settings, Baltes and Wahl (1992) studied community-dwelling elderly interacting with others. They coded the older adults' behaviors as sleeping, constructively engaged, destructively engaged, nonengaged, independent self-care, or dependent self-care. The behavior of the older adult's social partner was coded as dependence supporting, independence supporting, engagement supporting, nonengagement supporting, nonresponse, or leaving. Analyses focused on the contingencies surrounding an older person's dependent or independent behaviors. As in nursing home settings, dependent behaviors received support in the form of assistance and attention, but responses to independent behaviors in community settings were more ambivalent. Independent behaviors were supported one-third of the time and responded to with dependency support two-thirds of the time. These findings were elaborated by a consideration of the types of behaviors being employed in dependent-behavior/dependency-support interchanges (Baltes and Wahl 1996). Older adults often received suggestions or requests for activities, and they often responded with compliance. Note that this also illustrates substantial ambiguity. Were requests or suggestions due to the older adult, such as suggesting activities the older adults typically likes, or were they assumptions on the part of the interaction partner? Thus, in community settings, older adults are also reinforced for dependency, and their attempts to be independent receive ambivalent reactions.

This study examined both home care nurses and family members. Family contexts are a particularly interesting place to look at behavior toward older adults, because family members usually know a great deal about one another's capabilities and knowledge across a broad range of situations; in contrast, strangers may rely on obvious information like an individual's age to infer competence. Montepare, Steinberg, and Rosenberg (1992) compared the way that college students spoke to their parents and the way they spoke to grandparents. Speech to grandparents was rated as higher in pitch, more feminine, deferential, and unpleasant than speech to parents. Such speech was not less complex than speech toward parents. These findings were interpreted as reflecting differences in the relationship between a child and his or her parents and that between a child and his or her grandparents. The grandparent-grandchild relationship was viewed as involving greater deference and less intimacy, and the authors believe these differences explain the differences in speech style that they observed.

Other examinations of family interactions and aging have involved mothers and daughters and aging spouses (Carstensen, Gottman, and Levenson 1995; Fingerman 1995, 1996; Levenson, Carstensen, and Gottman 1993). Such studies reveal age changes in communicative interactions, but such changes are difficult to attribute to the age of the target person. For example, aging spouses tend to be more affectionate and less negative during conflict conversations and to have less intense conflicts than younger couples, but this may be a function of age of the spouses or the age of the relationship, or both (Carstensen, Gottman, and Levenson 1995; Levenson, Carstensen, and Gottman 1993). Studies examining elderly mothers and middle-aged daughters with a particular focus on conflict and tension also reveal some age-differentiated behavior. Mothers treat daughters somewhat differently than daughters treat mothers. For example, mothers were more likely than daughters to report feeling excluded or neglected and to experience daughters' concerns about their own health as intrusive (Fingerman 1996). Daughters reported more intrusiveness on the part of mothers than the reverse. Further, mothers may underestimate the degree to which their adult daughters engage in destructive conflict behaviors when the two have conflicts; certainly, daughters report engaging in more destructive behaviors toward their mothers than the reverse (Fingerman 1995). Such behaviors may reflect age or developmental differences (i.e., the fact that the mother is older) and thus constitute age-differentiated treatment. However, the attitudes and harmful impact standards do not easily apply to interchanges between familiar partners.

Communicating with nonfamily acquaintances may be somewhat different. Williams and Giles (1996) asked younger adults to report on recent conversations with older adults, excluding family members. Their participants reported both satisfying and unsatisfying conversations with elderly acquaintances. Unsatisfying conversations involve older adults' ignoring the younger adult's needs, feeling restricted in communication topics, hearing negative emotions, being forced to accommodate to the older adult's interests, feeling defensive, and hearing stereotypes about young adults. Satisfying conversations revolved around being supported, exchanging narratives, mutuality, expressing positive emotions, and feeling as if the older adult accommodated to the young adult's interests and needs. Williams and Giles note that these differences generalized across conversations with strangers and with acquaintances. It is not clear what older adults might say about their intergenerational encounters either; it is noteworthy that older adults may be less motivated by, interested in, and engaged with social interactions involving acquaintances and strangers (Carstensen, Isaacowitz, and Charles 1999).

Interacting with Strangers   One of the most active research areas in age-differentiated behavior has focused on intergenerational communication between previously unacquainted people, and much of this work is reviewed elsewhere in this book (see chapter 6). It is, in fact, a context that should maximize age-differentiated behavior because participants have little else on which they can base their behavior toward one another. Findings in this area suggest that conversations between younger and older adults can be problematic for both sides. Specifically, younger adults may use a version of displaced baby talk, also referred to as *elderspeak*, when talking to older adults (Kemper 1994; Kemper and Harden 1999; Harwood, Giles, and Ryan 1995; Williams 1996; Ryan, Hummert, and Boich 1995; Caporael 1981). Kemper and her colleagues (1995) define elderspeak slightly differently from displaced baby talk, highlighting not only the paralinguistic features (high pitch, slow rate of speaking) but also reductions in syntactic complexity (reduced length of utterances, lower complexity of utterances). Young adults spontaneously use this register in communication tasks with older adult partners (Kemper et al. 1995).

Younger adults who use this mode of speaking may be overaccommodating to the presumed needs of their older social partners (Harwood, Giles, and Ryan 1995; Williams 1996). Older adults, however, may not adequately adapt their communications to the interests and needs of younger adults (Harwood, Giles, and Ryan 1995; Williams 1996). Still, some research suggests that younger adults are more responsive to the age of their partner than older adults, that is, they are more age discriminating. In getting-to-know-you conversations, Coupland and colleagues (1988) paired young and old women with either a same-age peer or a different-age peer. Young women were less disclosing to older women than to same-age peers, while older women tended to behave similarly regardless of their partner's age. Similarly, in giving map directions, older adults do not switch to a simplified way of speaking when addressing age peers; older adults were less age discriminating than younger adults (Kemper et al. 1995). There may be many reasons for this, ranging from the possibility that older adults do not want to patronize their age peers or do not need to adapt their speech style and content to age peers, to the possibility that older adults are unable to adapt speech style or content or are insensitive to the cues that adaptations are required (Kemper and Kemtes 1999).

Tsai and Carstensen (1991) examined how European American and Chinese American young adults interacted with older adults. Because Chinese Americans are purported to hold less ageist attitudes than do European Americans (Chang, Chang, and Shen 1984; Cheung 1989; Lee 1986; Levy and Langer 1994), this study affords a rare chance to examine whether groups that express less ageist beliefs will also behave in less age-differentiated ways. Further, it extends communication research by examining persuasion interactions rather than getting-acquainted or referential communication tasks. Participants between 18 and 21 years of age were paired with other women of the same ethnicity. The partner was either young adult or elderly. Pairs were instructed to reach a consensus about a topic on which they disagreed (as assessed by questionnaires); topics ranged from "mothers' employment outside the home" to "the use of the military to combat drugs." These interactions were videotaped, and raters assessed the respectfulness, politeness, patience, responsiveness, comfort, and directiveness subjects exhibited toward their partners. Both young and old partners elicited the same level of patience, comfort, and responsiveness from subjects. However, older partners elicited greater respect, politeness, and directiveness. Further, they elicited greater opinion change during the interaction, but that change disappeared following the interaction. Subjects also moved their chairs closer to older partners than to younger partners. No differences were found by ethnicity.

Explanations given to older adults are often simpler than those given to younger adult listeners (Rubin and Brown 1975). For example, Rubin and Brown asked younger adults to rate the competence of people of various ages across a variety of cognitive skills. The rated skills included those perceived to decline in later life (e.g., memory) and those believed to increase (e.g., wisdom). Perceptions of competence were generally curvilinear, increasing through middle adulthood and then decreasing. The same subjects then were to explain a game to a hypothetical listener of a particular age. The listener was represented by an age-suggestive ink drawing. Child, adolescent, and elderly listeners elicited simpler speech, as indexed by number of words per utterance. Thus, older adults were treated like children and adolescents rather than adults, consistent with perceptions of their competence.

Explanation or instruction was also examined more recently with differentiated elderly targets (Thimm, Rademacher, and Kruse 1998).

Young adults were to explain a complex technical object to an elderly adult, a younger adult, a positively depicted elderly adult, or a negatively depicted older adult. The instructions were given to a tape recorder, no actual listeners were present. Pretesting revealed that the control old is perceived similarly to the negatively stereotyped older adult in terms of competence with technical objects. Patronizing talk was found in comparisons of the control old and young conditions. Specifically, subjects talking to older targets made more references to age-related deficits, gave more praise, and also produced more requests for feedback. A positively stereotyped elderly target elicited fewer references to age-relevant topics and greater use of English-language words (in a German-speaking sample, this indicates assumptions of greater competence). However, compared to speech toward a young target, even positive stereotypes elicited more intonation variability, greater formality, and longer, slower, and more detailed instructions. Interestingly, women responded with a more generalized approach, using patronizing speech equally for all elderly targets, while men tended to differentiate more among older targets. Some participants explicitly addressed the face-threatening features of elderspeak by acknowledging that they were speaking oddly, and perhaps oversimplistically, but that they wished to ensure a clear understanding of the device to be explained. Thus, an actual listener who gave feedback indicating competence and ease of comprehension might have eliminated age-differentiated behavior. This study also varied the age of the target (who was either 60 or 80), but, interestingly, young adults did not discriminate among elderly targets in a young-old or an old-old age range.

Children also discriminate against older adults behaviorally in collaborative tasks (Isaacs and Bearison 1986). Children at age 4, 6, or 8 were placed in a room with a child-sized table, chairs, and two jigsaw puzzles. The experimenter and an adult confederate were also present. The adult confederate was either an elderly adult (approximately 75 years old) or a younger adult (approximately 35 years old). All confederates were healthy and well dressed, and had professional experience in working with children. The children were asked to work on the puzzle with the confederate. Children sat farther away from, made less eye contact with, spoke fewer words to, initiated less conversation with, and asked for less help from an elderly confederate. These discriminations were largely stable with age, although 4 year olds sought more assistance from and sat closer to older confederates than their older peers did. However, attitudes of the children (assessed previously) did not correlate strongly with observed behaviors.

Elder Abuse

Perhaps the most egregious example of hurtful behavior directed against older adults is elder abuse. By definition, this behavior can only be directed against older adults. Frailty, dependency, and ageism have been viewed as important factors in the etiology of elder abuse (Nadian 1995), and in particular, ageism is viewed as creating a societal environment in which elder abuse can begin and be maintained with greater ease. We were unable to find research explicitly comparing elder abuse with other forms of domestic violence, and only this kind of research can reveal the importance of ageism in elder abuse as compared to other factors. Ageism may influence individuals' responses to suspected elder abuse. Blakeley and Dolon (1998) surveyed more than 300 students about their anticipated behavior toward an older woman who alleged her son was abusing her. Students also completed an ageism inventory. Their responses generally revealed themselves to be kind and helpful (or at least suggested they perceived themselves that way). However, more ageist students reported greater doubts about the reality of the problem (e.g., were more likely to wonder if the woman was senile or seeking attention) and were less likely to respond with action.

Is Age-Differentiated Behavior Ageist?

We have provided substantial evidence for a wide range of age-differentiated behavior across a variety of settings. In some cases, behavior appeared clearly ageist, while in others, the situation was more complex. In summarizing our review, we want to draw attention to at least three issues that must be considered in research on age-differentiated and ageist behavior: the type of behavior, the cause of the behavior, and the appropriateness of the behavior for a specific target.

Type of Behavior

We have reviewed evidence for age-differentiated or ageist treatment of older adults in settings varying from physician-patient encounters to urban planning. In general, three classes of age-differentiated behaviors were observed across these settings.

First are behaviors that distance, ignore, exclude, or underrepresent older adults in comparison to younger adults. Examples of these types of behaviors appear pervasive, occurring in all the settings we examined. These include the way that physicians spend less time with and show less receptivity to older patients, the way that nursing home staff ignore and fail to reinforce independence, the failure to incorporate older adults' concerns in urban planning for older adults, the way that younger adults do not disclose to older adults, and the gross underrepresentation of older adults in mass media.

Second are behaviors that are more positive, beneficial, protective, or compassionate toward older adults than younger adults: legislative protections, positive stereotypes of aging in mass media, more deferential treatment from physicians and other social partners, and more compassionate rulings in conservatorships.

A third class are behaviors that are negative or overtly harmful: negative images of aging in mass media, differential access to treatments, inappropriate use of displaced baby talk or elderspeak, denial of access to jobs and housing despite equal qualifications, and elder abuse.

It may seem that only some age-differentiated behaviors are ageist—in particular, the last category. However, we would contend that all of these types of behaviors may or may not be harmful. Differential access to medical care, differential sentencing, and elder abuse (at the extreme) are clearly harmful to older adults. Behaviors such as simplified language and baby talk can also be harmful because they communicate expectations of lower capabilities. These can result in lower performances (Levy and Langer 1994), as well as lowered self-esteem and poorer care. Positive behaviors, such as more compassionate decision making by conservators, may fail to protect people who need protection. Deference and politeness may also deprive people of intimate connections, which they might prefer. Neglect and underrepresentation may reduce societal interest in the issues of older adults and can create stronger age segregation than is already the case. When older adults are not visible in the media and when they are excluded from housing and job opportunities, there are fewer and fewer places where younger adults encounter them. Even positive images in the mass media may provide unrealistic standards and implicitly suggest that those who are not "successful agers" have somehow failed and are responsible for their own ill health.

That said, some features of age-differentiated behavior can also be helpful. For example, Kemper and Harden (1999) showed that certain features of elderspeak, such as simplified syntactic structures and providing elaborations, resulted in improved comprehension for older adults. Other features, such as slow speech rate, exaggerated intonation, and high-pitched voice, did not improve comprehension and led to reports of greater communication problems. When elderspeak is examined, older adults benefit in terms of comprehension but report communication problems (Kemper et al. 1995).

Cause of Behavior

Is the observed age-differentiated behavior linked to ageist attitudes or assumptions about the incompetence or uselessness of older adults? This is a difficult question to answer, and not all the studies examine relationships between attitudes and assumptions, and actual behavior. Where examined, these studies typically indicate that ageist behavior often, but not always, maps directly onto ageist attitudes (see Mangum 1988). For example, in explanation giving in intergenerational encounters and in nursing home settings, negative attitudes were explicitly related to age-differentiated behavior. Related to attitudinal accounts of age-differentiated behavior is the notion that aging is a stigmatized condition that reminds us of our own mortality and provokes distancing behavior (Goffman 1963; chapter 2, this volume). From this perspective, the wealth of distancing behavior is not surprising, particularly the absence of images of older adults in mass media. When stigmatization or negative attitudes are at the heart of the negative behaviors observed, then it is relatively straightforward to consider the behaviors ageist.

However, other proposed causes of age-differentiated behavior are more ambiguous in terms of ageism. For example, other theories, not explicitly developed to explain age-differentiated behavior, point to discrepant motivations as a cause for age-differentiated behavior. Carstensen, Isaacowitz, and Charles (1999) have proposed that motivations for social contact change across the life span. This may in turn have implications for intergenerational interactions. If, as Carstensen and her colleagues argue persuasively, older adults prefer interactions with familiar partners more than young adults do, then underaccommodation to strangers may be a result. Fingerman (1996) introduced the term *developmental schism* to explain sources of tension between mothers and daughters, arguing that in adulthood, a daughter's need to establish an independent life conflicts with her mother's needs to maintain closeness and contact. The result is greater feelings of exclusion from the mother and intrusion from the daughter. When motivational conflict results in age-differentiated treatment, it seems inappropriate to consider such behavior ageist in the classic sense.

One approach to understanding the age-differentiated interactions between older and younger adults is speech accommodation theory, based on a sociolinguistic framework in which intergenerational interactions are seen as examples of intergroup behavior (Coupland et al. 1988; Giles, Coupland, and Coupland 1991). Coupland and his colleagues assume that both younger and older adults accommodate their communication strategies in order to fit the perceived needs of the other group. Young-to-elderly language strategies tend to be overaccommodative; younger adults tend to change their communication strategies more than necessary when they interact with older adults. This overaccommodation can have different causes, including perceived communication deficits in the older interaction partner. About one-third of older adults are in fact experiencing hearing problems. Speaking clearly and sitting closer to an older adult in order to accommodate this deficit can benefit the communication process. However, overaccommodation occurs if younger adults change their behavior in irrelevant dimensions (e.g., using simpler sentence structure or starting to use elderspeak). Overaccommodation is likely if intergenerational communication is guided by role relationships (such as in nursing homes) and if the older interaction partner is not perceived as an individual but as a member of the group of elderly. In such cases, individual communication competencies are neglected, and language strategies are guided by stereotype-based negative expectations.

According to Coupland, Giles, and their colleagues, elderly-to-young communication strategies tend to be underaccommodative. Older people might actively avoid certain conversation topics that could lead to unfavorable comparisons with the younger partner. They might also engage in self-stereotyping and show communication characteristics (such as speaking slowly, talking about the past) that are regarded as typical for the elderly in response to overaccommodation of the younger interaction partner. Self-handicapping to avoid the pressure of high expectations regarding their communication skills is also frequent.

Ryan and her colleagues (Ryan et al. 1986; Ryan, Hummert, and Boich 1995) developed a model in which they describe a communication predicament of aging that manifests itself from the very first encounter between a younger and an older person. They argue that the younger partner will categorize the older partner as "old" and subsequently tailor his or her communication according to this age stereotype, showing a characteristic pattern of patronizing language and behavior. As a result, the older partner will have less control over the communication process. He or she will lose confidence in his or her communication skills and avoid future social contacts. Also, communication skills will get lost because they are not used anymore. As a consequence, younger interaction partners will find it more difficult to communicate with the older adult and minimize their contacts. Thus, age stereotypes can act as self-fulfilling prophecies and induce a downward spiral of increasingly unsuccessful intergenerational communication. Again, the differences between age-differentiated behavior based on existing communication deficits and ageist behavior (overaccommodation due to negative stereotypes of aging) are blurred. In the vicious circle of the communication predicament, a single instance of patronizing behavior could be interpreted as a cause of subsequent communication deficits in the older person. However, it could also be seen as an accommodative effort that responds to existing communication deficits (which are the result of previous patronizing behavior). Because of these ambiguities, it is necessary to take the individual capabilities of the older person and the specific behavioral context into consideration before a certain behavior can be labeled as ageist.

As a further example, consider the case of age-differentiated treatment of patients by physicians and psychiatrists. Much of the behavior reviewed in the section on health care settings appeared ageist by our definition. But before concluding that physicians and psychiatrists are rampantly ageist, it must be said that older patients as a group differ from younger patients in a number of ways. On average, older adults visit a physician eight times a year compared to five physician visits in the general population (Beisecker 1996). Older adults are more likely to suffer from chronic conditions than younger adults. Thus, often the goal is not to heal a disease but to manage its symptoms and deal with comorbidities on a long-term basis (Adelman, Greene, and Charon 1992). More frequent patient-physician encounters and this longer-term perspective may reduce the number of topics raised on any one occasion. Older patients may also be those who have more functional difficulties and require greater communicative accommodations (Beisecker 1996; McCormick, Inui, and Roter 1996).

Further, older patients may want different things from a physician. They are less likely to have an internal health locus of control, tending instead to ascribe control over their health to their physician or to fate and not to their own actions; they also have less desire to exert control than younger adults do (Smith et al. 1988). Older people were also found to have a lower health-related self-efficacy. They had less desire for information about their medical status and preferred to delegate decision-making processes to their physicians (Beisecker 1988; Woodward and Wallston 1987). Thus, some of the physician's behaviors may reflect differences in what patients of different ages expect, demand, and want.

The issue of what causes age-differentiated behavior is important, and some explanations (e.g., attitudes, overaccommodations) fit our definition of ageist more neatly than others (e.g., motivational discrepancies, appropriate accommodations). Even when behavior appears ageist, as in the case of physicians, it may be more complex than first glances would suggest.

Target Characteristics

We began this chapter with a consideration of characteristics of the older adult population and stressed the heterogeneity of this group. Some older adults do need accommodations in communication, some are less capable for particular types of jobs, and some may indeed fit all the negative stereotypes we associate with aging. In labeling behavior as ageist or simply age differentiated, the appropriateness of a behavior for a specific target is critical. This is particularly the case for discriminatory employment practices and age-differentiated communication. Studies that presented people with actual social partners who were older or that varied characteristics of a hypothetical target are instructive in this regard. First, studies that varied the characteristics of the hypothetical target suggested that people do not always adapt appropriately to positively versus negatively characterized older adults (Thimm, Rademacher, and Kruse 1998). Second, even in the presence of actual social partners, young adults tended to use elderspeak spontaneously in communicating map directions (Kemper et al. 1995).

Gaps in the Evidence: A Research Agenda

As we see it, there are four central issues in future research on ageist behavior. The first is a plea for studying actual social interactions or real rather than hypothetical cases whenever possible. The second concerns the causes of age-differentiated behavior. The third revolves around expanding coverage of domains and behaviors. The fourth concerns crosscultural stability and variability and issues of multiple jeopardy.

Issue 1: Actual Rather Than Hypothetical Behavior

In the absence of real interaction, behavior toward hypothetical targets provides strong evidence of the existence of generalized negative stereotypes of older adults but does not reveal whether such stereotypes are applied to actual people. As in the case of the verdict studies, looking only at hypothetical judgments may reveal only one part of the story. This is especially critical in studies of communication, and the field is certainly moving toward an increasing emphasis on actual interactions. Because real social partners do provide feedback about whether accommodations are necessary or desired, behavior in the presence of real social partners may be considerably less related to ageist attitudes than behavior toward hypothetical targets. That said, the studies we have reviewed that did examine actual interaction typically also found age-differentiated behavior. One important question is what might happen if the older targets in such studies made it clear that the age-differentiated behavior was unwanted or unnecessary. For example, the study of explanations, in which people made explicit reference to their accommodations, suggests that with a real partner, subjects might have shifted back to normal speech given appropriate feedback from the listener (Thimm, Rademacher, and Kruse 1998).

Issue 2: What Causes Age-Differentiated Behavior?

In order to advance theory as well as our understanding of age-differentiated behaviors, issues of causality need to be more consistently addressed empirically. Depending on the theoretical framework at stake, this can be done by assessing the attitude-behavior relationship using both explicit and implicit measures of attitudes, examining accommodative intentions (although accommodations in speech may not be conscious), or using mortality-salience manipulations like those used in terror management experiments, to mention just a few directions. In addition, studies that manipulate characteristics of the target individuals and examine whether behavior changes accordingly can also reveal something about the causes of age-differentiated behavior. The studies we have reviewed that have taken these approaches are noteworthy. First, attitudes often appear to correlate with behavior; that is, negative attitudes about the competence or qualities of older adults accompany age-differentiated treatment. In the cases where this does not happen, the results are revealing. For example, Mangum's (1988) study of endorsement of group housing revealed that resistance to group housing is probably related not to ageism but to attitudes toward group housing in general. Second, despite having differentiated stereotypes of aging, including positive images, people may not adapt their speech to reflect older adults with different capacities, nor do they treat the young-old differently from the old-old.

Issue 3: Expanded Scope of Research

Much of what we know revolves around a handful of important social contexts, including physician-patient interactions, explanations, intergenerational get-to-know-you conversations, media images, and caregiving interactions in nursing homes and community settings. But many other contexts are important and deserve greater attention. Service interactions like those with cashiers, clerks, bank tellers, and postal employees constitute a large portion of our everyday lives but have been largely ignored in the literature. Greater attention to housing access and employment opportunities is also needed, particularly in the light of recent changes allowing retired adults to work part time without penalties in social security income. Many other areas are worthy of attention in the future.

Contrasts between familiar and unfamiliar social partners and between different settings, examining similar behaviors, will also be important for moving this area ahead. The work of Margret Baltes and her colleagues is of note here, because they have revealed similar dependence-supportive scripts in nursing homes and community settings, but different reactions to independent behaviors in those two settings. The results of Montepare, Steinberg, and Rosenberg (1992) are also noteworthy in revealing that grandchildren do not simplify their speech for grandparents in the same ways that college students do for elderly people they do not know (Kemper et al. 1995). The social landscape of older adults is often tilted toward long-term relationships like those with family and long-term friends (Carstensen, Isaacowitz, and Charles 1999). Those social interactions carry with them a wealth of individuating information that can mitigate the impact of stereotypes about aging on someone's behavior, while, in contrast, interactions between strangers may be tilted toward confirming that someone is a "typical old person" (Trope and Thompson 1997).

Issue 4: Multiple Jeopardy, Cross-Cultural Issues

Finally, two open issues are the generality of the findings reviewed above across ethnic and cultural lines. The literature has yet to examine multiple jeopardy—the situation of older adults who are both elderly and belong to another stigmatized or stereotyped group. Consider elderly African Americans. Within their communities and families, older African Americans may have greater respect and status than comparable European Americans (Minkler and Roe 1993). Outside their communities, there are few data. Similarly, cross-cultural comparisons of ageist behavior are rare, although attitude and social cognition research suggests there is good reason to look at behavior across cultures (Levy and Langer 1994). Even more important perhaps, cross-cultural and cross-ethnic work can reveal something about proposed causes of ageist and age-differentiated behavior. For example, terror management accounts imply

that all cultures exhibit ageist behavior because of the mortality awareness that is human and the inevitable associations between aging and
death. In contrast, accommodation and attitude-based accounts suggest
the potential for cross-cultural plasticity, depending on how the groups
"older adults" or "younger adults" are defined and perceived in particular cultures.

Conclusion

We have given a broad tour of age-differentiated and ageist behavior, as
well as raised some issues for consideration in the future. Research on
ageist behavior is largely in its infancy, especially in comparison to research on ageist attitudes. In this vein, there is much work to be done. In
closing, we point out that examinations of ageism may push the envelope
of traditional "-ism" research in interesting ways. We all will become old,
making aging the one stigmatized, discriminated-against group that we
will all join. What are the ramifications of this for ageist attitudes, behavior, and our own aging? Simone de Beauvoir recognized this years ago,
and we end with her words: "If we do not know what we are going to be,
we cannot know what we are. Let us recognize ourselves in this old man
or in that old woman. It must be done if we are to take upon ourselves the
entirety of our human state" (1972, p. 12).

References

Adams, C., Labouvie-Vief, G., Hobart, C. J., and Dorosz, M. (1990). Adult age
group differences in story recall style. *Journal of Gerontology, 45,* P17–27.

Adams, P. F., Herdershot, G. E., and Marano, M. A. (1999). Current estimates
from the National Health Survey 1996. *National Center for Health Statistics Vital
Health Statistics, 10*(200).

Adelman, R. D., Greene, M. G., and Charon, R. (1987). The physician-elderly pa-
tient-companion triad in the medical encounter: The development of a conceptual framework and research agenda. *Gerontologist, 27*(6), 729–734.

Adelman, R. D., Greene, M. G., and Charon, R. (1991). Issues in the physician-
elderly patient interaction. *Aging and Society, 2,* 127–148.

Adelman, R. D., Greene, M. G., and Charon, R. (1992). The content of physician
and elderly patient interaction in the primary medical encounter. *Communication
Research, 19,* 370–380.

Adelman, R. D., Greene, M. G., Charon, R., and Friedman, E. (1990). Issues in the
physician-geriatric patient relationship. In H. Giles, N. Coupland, and J. M. Wie-

mann (Eds.), *Communication, health and the elderly* (pp. 126–134). Glasgow: Manchester University Press.

Age cutoff. When Manhattan stylist Michael D'Amico refused to serve older women in his salon, the hair started flying. (1999 July 5). *People Weekly, 51(25)*, 165.

Age Discrimination in Employment Act. (1967). 29 U.S.C.S. §§ 621 (Congressional Universe, Online Service: Bethesda, MD: Congressional Information Service).

Aronoff, C. (1974). Old age in prime time. *Journal of Communication, 24*, 86–87.

Aroskar, M., Urv-Wong, E. K., and Kane, R. A. (1990). Building an effective caregiving staff: Transforming the nursing services. In R. A. Kane, and A. L. Kaplan (Eds.), *Everyday ethics: Resolving dilemmas in nursing home life* (pp. 3–20). New York: Springer.

Bagshaw, M., and Adams, M. (1985). Nursing home nurses' attitudes, empathy, and ideological orientation. *International Journal of Aging and Human Development, 22(3)*, 235–246.

Baltes, M. M. (1988). The etiology and maintenance of dependency in the elderly: Three phases of operant research. *Behavior Therapy, 19*, 301–319.

Baltes, M. M., Burgess, R., and Stewart, R. (1980). Independence and dependence in self-care behaviors in nursing home residents: An operant-observational study. *International Journal of Behavioral Development, 3*, 489–500.

Baltes, M. M., and Reisenzein, R. (1986). The social world in long-term care institutions: Psychological control toward dependency. In M. M. Baltes and P. B. Baltes (Eds.), *The psychology of control and aging* (pp. 315–343). Hillsdale, NJ: Erlbaum.

Baltes, M. M., and Wahl, H. W. (1992). The dependency-support script in institutions: Generalization to community settings. *Psychology and Aging, 7*, 409–418.

Baltes, M. M., and Wahl, H. W. (1996). Patterns of communication in old age: The dependence support, independence ignore script. *Health Communication, 8(3)*, 217–231.

Baltes, P. B., Lindenberger, U., and Staudinger, U. M. (1998). Life-span theory in developmental psychology. In R. M. Lerner (Ed.), *Handbook of child psychology: Theoretical models of human development* (Vol. 1, pp. 1029–1143). New York: Wiley.

Bayles, K. A., Tomoeda, C. K., and Boone, D. R. (1985). A view of age-related changes in language function. *Developmental Neuropsychology, 1*, 231–264.

Beisecker, A. E. (1988). Aging and the desire for information and input in medical decisions: Patient consumerism in medical encounters. *Gerontologist, 28(3)*, 330–335.

Beisecker, A. E. (1996). Older persons' medical encounters and their outcomes. *Research on Aging, 18(1)*, 9–31.

Bell, J. (1992). In search of a discourse on aging: The elderly on television. *Gerontologist, 32*(3), 305–311.

Bendick, M., Brown, L. E., and Wall, K. (1999). No foot in the door: An experimental study of employment discrimination against older workers. *Journal of Aging and Social Policy, 10,* 5–23.

Berg, C. A., Strough, J., Calderone, K. S., Sansone, C., and Weir, C. (1998). The role of problem definitions in understanding age and context effects on strategies for solving everyday problems. *Psychology and Aging, 13,* 29–44.

Bishop, J. M., and Krause, D. R. (1984). Depictions of aging and old age on Saturday morning television. *Gerontologist, 24*(1), 91–94.

Blakely, B. E., and Dolon, R. (1998). A test of public reactions to alleged elder abuse. *Journal of Elder Abuse and Neglect, 9,* 43–65.

Blanchard-Fields, F., and Chen, Y. (1996). Adaptive cognition and aging. *American Behavioral Scientist, 39,* 231–248.

Bornemann, T., and Ferell, B. R. (1996). Ethical issues in pain management. *Clinics in Geriatric Medicine, 12*(3), 615–628.

Bramlett-Solomon, S., and Subramanian, G. (1999). Nowhere near picture perfect: Images of the elderly in *Life* and *Ebony* magazine ads, 1990–1997. *Journalism and Mass Communication Quarterly, 76*(3), 565–572.

Bramlett-Solomon, S., and Wilson, V. (1989). Images of the elderly in *Life* and *Ebony. Journalism Quarterly, 66,* 185–188.

Brewer, M. B., and Lui, L. N. (1989). The primacy of age and sex in the structure of person categories. *Social Cognition, 7,* 262–274.

Caporael, L. R., and Culbertson, G. H. (1986). Verbal response modes of baby talk and other speech at institutions for the aged. *Language and Communication, 6,* 99–112.

Caporael, L. R., Lukaszewski, M., and Culbertson, G. (1983). Secondary baby talk: Judgements by institutionalized elderly and their caregivers. *Journal of Personality and Social Psychology, 44,* 746–754.

Carstensen, L. L., Gottman, J. M., and Levenson, R. W. (1995). Emotional behavior in long-term marriage. *Psychology and Aging, 10,* 140–149.

Carstensen, L. L., Isaacowitz, D. M., and Charles, S. T. (1999). Taking time seriously: A theory of socioemotional selectivity. *American Psychologist, 54,* 165–181.

Carstensen, L. L., Pasupathi, M., and Mayr, U. (2000). Emotions in everyday life across the adult life span. *Journal of Personality and Social Psychology, 79,* 644–655.

Cassata, M., and Irwin, J. (1997). Young by day: The older person on daytime serial drama. In H. S. Nor Al-Deen (Ed.), *Cross-cultural communication and aging in the United States.* Mahwah, NJ: Erlbaum.

Chen, Y., and Blanchard-Fields, F. (1997). Age differences in stages of attributional processing. *Psychology and Aging, 12,* 694–703.

Chang, B., Chang, A., & Shen, Y. (1984). Attitudes toward aging in the United States and Taiwan. *Journal of Comparative Family Studies, 15,* 109–130.

Cheung, M. (1989). Elderly Chinese living in the United States: Assimilation or adjustment. *Social Work, 34,* 457–461.

Colonia-Willner, R. (1998). Practical intelligence at work: Relationship between aging and cognitive efficiency among managers in a bank environment. *Psychology and Aging, 13,* 45–57.

Coupland, N., Coupland, J., Giles, H., Henwood, K., and Wiemann, J. (1988). Elderly self-disclosure: Interactional and intergroup issues. *Language and Communication, 8,* 109–133.

Dannefer, D., and Perlmutter, M. (1990). Development as a multidimensional process: Individual and social constraints. *Human Development, 33,* 108–137.

Davis, R. H. (1984). TV's boycott of old age. *Aging, 346,* 12–17.

Davis, R. H., and Davis, J. (1985). *TV's image of the elderly: A practical guide for change.* Lexington, MA: Lexington Books.

de Beauvoir, S. (1972). *The coming of aging.* New York: Putnam.

DePaola, S. J., Neimeyer, R. A., Lupfer, M. B., and Fiedler, J. (1992). Death concern and attitudes towards the elderly in nursing home personnel. *Death Studies, 16*(6), 537–555.

Derby, S. E. (1991). Ageism in cancer care of the elderly. *Oncology Nursing Forum, 18,* 921–926.

Dolinsky, E. H. (1984). Infantilization of the elderly. *Journal of Gerontological Nursing, 10,* 12–19.

Doty, P. J. (1992). The oldest old and the use of institutional long-term care from an international perspective. In R. M. Suzman, D. P. Willis, and K. G. Manton (Eds.), *The oldest old* (pp. 251–267). New York: Oxford University Press.

Fingerman, K. L. (1995). Aging mothers' and their adult daughters' perceptions of conflict behaviors. *Psychology and Aging, 10,* 639–649.

Fingerman, K. L. (1996). Sources of tension in the aging mother and adult daughter relationship. *Psychology and Aging, 11,* 591–606.

Finlayson, R. E. (1995). Misuse of prescription drugs. *International Journal of the Addictions, 30*(13–14), 1871–1901.

Fishman, G., and Sordo, I. (1984). Aging and delinquent behavior: The criminal act and the societal response. In S. G. Shoham (Ed.), *Israel studies in criminology* (Vol. 7 pp. 37–53). Northwood, England: Science Reviews, Ltd.

Francher, J. S. (1973). "It's the Pepsi generation. . . ." Accelerated aging and the television commercial. *International Journal of Aging and Human Development, 4*(3), 245–255.

Gagliese, L., and Melzack, R. (1997). Chronic pain in elderly people. *Pain, 70,* 3–14.

Gatz, M., and Pearson, C. (1988). Ageism revised and the provision of psychological services. *American Psychologist, 43,* 184–188.

Gerbner, G., Gross, L., Signorielli, N., and Morgan, M. (1980). Aging with television: Images in television dramas and conceptions of social reality. *Journal of Communication, 30,* 37–47.

Gerrity, M. S., Earp, J. A. L., Devellis, R. F., and Light, D. W. (1992). Uncertainty and professional work: Perceptions of physicians in clinical practise. *American Journal of Sociology, 97*(4), 1022–1051.

Giles, H., Coupland, N., and Coupland, J. (1991). Accommodation theory: Communication, context, and consequence. In H. Giles, J. Coupland, & N. Coupland (Eds.). Contexts of accommodation: Developments in applied sociolinguistics. Studies in emotion and social interaction. (pp. 1–68). New York: Cambridge University Press.

Giles, H., Williams, A., and Coupland, N. (1990). Communication, health and the elderly: Frameworks, agenda and a model. In H. Giles, N. Coupland, and J. M. Wiemann (Eds.), *Communication, health and the elderly* (pp. 126–134). Glasgow: Manchester University Press.

Goffman, E. (1961). *Asylums.* New York: Anchor Books.

Goffman, E. (1963). *Stigma: Notes on the management of spoiled identity.* Englewood Cliffs, NJ: Prentice-Hall.

Goodwin, M., and Trocchio, J. (1987, January–February). Cultivation of positive attitudes in nursing home staff. *Geriatric Nursing,* 32–34.

Greenberg, B. S., and Colette, L. (1997). The changing faces on TV: A demographic analysis of network television's new seasons, 1966–1992. *Journal of Broadcasting and Electronic Media, 41,* 1–13.

Greene, M. G., and Adelman, R. D. (1996). Psychosocial factors in older patients' medical encounters. *Research on Aging, 18*(1), 84–102.

Greene, M. G., Adelman, R. D., Charon, R., and Friedman, E. (1989). Concordance between physicians and their older and younger patients in the primary care medical encounter. *Gerontologist, 29*(6), 808–813.

Greene, M. G., Adelman, R., Charon, R., and Hoffman, S. (1986). Ageism in the medial encounter: An exploratory study of the doctor-elderly relationship. *Language and Communication, 6*(1/2), 113–124.

Greene, M. G., Majerowitz, S. D., Adelman, R. D., and Rizzo, C. (1994). The effects of the presence of a third person on the physician–older patient medical interview. *Journal of the American Geriatrics Society, 42*(4) 413–419.

Gross, J. J., Carstensen, L. L., Pasupathi, M., Tsai, J., Skorpen, C., and Hsu, A. Y. C. (1997). Emotion and aging: Experience, expression, and control. *Psychology and Aging, 12,* 590–599.

Hajjar, W. J. (1997). The image of aging in television commercials: An update for the 1990's. In H. S. Nor Al-Deen (Ed.), *Cross-cultural communication and aging in the United States.* Mahwah, NJ: Erlbaum.

Harris, A. J., and Feinberg, J. F. (1977). Television and aging: Is what you see what you get? *Gerontologist, 17*(5), 464–468.

Harwood, J., Giles, H., and Ryan, E. B. (1995). Aging, communication and intergroup theory: Social identity and intergenerational communication. In J. Nussbaum and J. Coupland (Eds.), *Handbook of communication and aging* (pp. 133–159). Hillsdale, NJ: Erlbaum.

Hatton, J. (1977). Nurses' attitude toward the aged: Relationship to care. *Journal of Gerontological Nursing, 3*(3), 21–26.

Haug, M. R. (1996). Elements in physician/patient interactions in late life. *Research on Aging, 18*(1), 32–51.

Heckhausen, J., Dixon, R., and Baltes, P. B. (1989). Gains and losses in development throughout adulthood as perceived by different adult age groups. *Developmental Psychology, 25,* 109–121.

Heller, B. R., Bausell, R. B., and Ninos, M. (1984). Nurses' perceptions of rehabilitation potential. *Journal of Gerontological Nursing, 10*(7), 22–26.

Hiemstra, R., Goodman, M., Middlemiss, M. A., Vosco, R., and Ziegler, N. (1983). How older adults are portrayed in television advertising: Implications for educators. *Educational Gerontology, 9,* 111–122.

Hirschel, J. D., and Rubin, K. B. (1982). Special problems faced by the elderly victims of crime. *Journal of Sociology and Social Welfare, 9,* 357–374.

Hofstetter, C. R., Schultze, W. A., Mahoney, S. M., and Buss, T. F. (1993). The elderly's perception of TV ageist stereotyping: TV or contextual aging. *Communication Reports, 6*(2), 92–100.

Hooper, E. M., Comstock, L. M., Goodwin, J. M., and Goodwin, J. S. (1982). Patient characteristics that influence physician behavior. *Medical Care, 20,* 630–638.

Horgas, A., Wahl, H. W., and Baltes, M. M. (1996). Dependency in late life. In L. L. Carstensen, B. A. Edelstein, and L. Dornbrand (Eds.), *The practical handbook of clinical gerontology* (pp. 54–75). Thousand Oaks, CA: Sage.

Hummert, M. L. (1990). Multiple stereotypes of elderly and young adults: A comparison of structure and evaluation. *Psychology and Aging, 5,* 182–193.

Isaacs, L. W., and Bearison, D. J. (1986). The development of children's prejudice against the aged. *International Journal of Aging and Human Development, 23,* 175–194.

Issacharoff, S., and Harris, E. W. (1997). Is age discrimination really age discrimination? The ADEA's unnatural solution. *New York University Law Review, 72,* 780–840.

James, L. E., Burke, D. M., Austin, A., and Hulme, E. (1998). Production and perception of "verbosity" in younger and older adults. *Psychology and Aging, 13,* 355–367.

Jefferys, M. (1996). Cultural aspects of ageing: Gender and intergenerational issues. *Social Science and Medicine, 43,* 681–687.

Kahana, E., and Kiyak, H. (1981, July 12–17). *Predicators of attitudes toward the aged by service providers.* Paper presented at the Twelfth International Congress of Gerontology, Hamburg, Germany.

Kahana, E., and Kiyak, H. (1984). Attitudes and behavior of staff in facilities of the aged. *Research on Aging, 6*(3), 395–416.

Kaster, J. M., White, M. A., and Carruth, M. L. (1979). Personnel turn-over: A major problem for nursing homes. *Nursing Homes, 28,* 20–25.

Kemper, S. (1994). "Elderspeak": Speech accommodations to older adults. *Aging and Cognition, 1,* 17–28.

Kemper, S., and Harden, T. (1999). Experimentally disentangling what's beneficial about elderspeak from what's not. *Psychology and Aging, 14,* 656–670.

Kemper, S., and Kemtes, K. (1999). Aging and message production and comprehension. In N. Schwarz, D. Park, B. Knäuper, and S. Sudman (Eds.), *Cognition, aging, and self-reports* (pp. 230–244). Philadelphia: Taylor and Francis.

Kemper, S., Kynette, D., Rash, S., O'Brien, K., and Sprott, R. (1989). Life-span changes to adults' language: Effects of memory and genre. *Applied Psycholinguistics, 10,* 49–66.

Kemper, S., Rash, S., Kynette, D., and Norman, S. (1990). Telling stories: The structure of adults' narratives. *European Journal of Cognitive Psychology, 2,* 205–228.

Kemper, S., Vandeputte, D., Rice, K., Cheung, H., and Gubarchuk, J. (1995). Spontaneous adoption of elderspeak during referential communication tasks. *Journal of Language and Social Psychology, 14,* 40–59.

Kimel et al. v. Florida Board of Regents (1999). No. 98-791, slip op. (S. Ct. January 11, 1999).

Krauss, N. A., Freimann, M. P., Rhoades, J. A., Altmann, B. M., Brown, E., and Potter, D. E. B. (1997). *Medical Expenditure Panel Survey, 2,* 1–3.

Kubey, R. W. (1980). Television and aging: Past, present, and future. *Gerontologist, 20*(1), 16–35.

Lamberty, G. J., and Bieliauskas, L. A. (1993). Distinguishing between depression and dementia in the elderly: A review of neuropsychological findings. *Archives of Clinical Neuropsychology, 8*(2), 149–170.

Langer, E., Perlmutter, L., Chanowitz, B., and Rubin, R. (1988). Two new applications of mindlessness theory: Alcoholism and aging. *Journal of Aging Studies, 2,* 289–299.

Lasser, R., Siegel, E., Dukoff, R., and Sunderland, T. (1998). Diagnosis and treatment of geriatric depression. *CNS Drugs, 9*(1), 17–30.

Lawton, M. P., and Hoffman, C. (1984). Neighborhood reactions to elderly housing. *Journal of Housing for the Elderly, 2,* 41–53.

Learman, L. A., Avorn, J., Everitt, D. E., and Rosenthal, R. (1990). Pygmalion in the nursing home. The effects of caregiver expectations on patient outcomes. *Journal of the American Geriatric Society, 38,* 797–803.

Lee, J. (1986). Asian-American elderly: A neglected minority group. *Ethnicity and Gerontological Social Work, 4,* 103–116.

Levenson, R. W., Carstensen, L. L., and Gottman, J. M. (1993). Long-term marriage: Age, gender, and satisfaction. *Psychology and Aging, 8,* 301–313.

Levy, B., and Langer, E. (1994). Aging free from negative stereotypes: Successful memory in China and among the American deaf. *Journal of Personality and Social Psychology, 66,* 989–997.

Lidz, C. W., Fischer, L., and Arnold, R. M. (1992). *The erosion of autonomy in long-term care.* New York: Oxford University Press.

Mangum, W. P. (1988). Community resistance to planned housing for the elderly: Ageism or general antipathy to group housing? *Gerontologist, 28,* 325–329.

Mann, T. (1994). Informed consent for psychological research: Do subjects comprehend consent forms and understand their legal rights? *Psychological Science, 5*(3), 140–143.

Marsiske, M., Delius, J., Maas, I., Lindenberger, U., Scherer, H., and Tesch-Römer, C. (1999). Sensory systems in old age. In P. B. Baltes and K. U. Mayr (Eds.), *The Berlin Aging Study* (pp. 360–383). Cambridge: Cambridge University Press.

McCabe, K. A., and Gregory, S. S. (1998). Elderly victimization: An examination beyond the FBI's index crimes. *Research on Aging, 20,* 363–372.

McCormick, W. C., Inui, T. S., and Roter, D. L. (1996). Interventions in physician–elderly patient interactions. *Research on Aging, 18,* 103–136.

Minkler, M., and Roe, K. M. (1993). *Grandmothers as caregivers: Raising children of the crack cocaine epidemic.* Thousand Oaks, CA: Sage Publications.

Montepare, J., Steinberg, J., and Rosenberg, B. (1992). Characteristics of vocal communication between young adults and their parents and grandparents. *Communication Research, 19,* 479–492.

Mroczek, D. K., and Kolarz, C. M. (1998). The effect of age on positive and negative affect: A developmental perspective on happiness. *Journal of Personality and Social Psychology, 75,* 1333–1349.

Nadian, M. B. (1995). Elder violence (maltreatment) in domestic settings: Some theory and research. In L. L. Adler and F. L. Denmark (Eds.), *Violence and the prevention of violence* (pp. 177–190). Westport, CT: Praeger.

O'Connor, B. P., and Rigby, H. (1996). Perceptions of baby talk, frequency of receiving baby talk, and self-esteem among community and nursing home residents. *Psychology and Aging, 11*(1), 147–154.

Page, S. (1997). Accommodating the elderly: Words and actions in the community. *Journal of Housing for the Elderly, 12,* 55–61.

Pasupathi, M., Carstensen, L. L., and Tsai, J. L. (1995). Ageism in interpersonal settings. In B. Lott and D. Maluso (Eds.), *The social psychology of interpersonal discrimination* (pp. 160–182). New York: Guilford Press.

Penner, L. A., Ludenia, K., and Mead, G. (1984). Staff attitudes. Image or reality. *Journal of Gerontological Nursing, 10*(3), 110–117.

Petersen, M. (1973). The visibility and image of old people on televisions. *Journalism Quarterly, 50,* 569–573.

Plattman, K., and Tinker, A. (1998). Getting on in the BBC: A case study of older workers. *Ageing and Society, 18,* 513–535.

Putnam, S. M. (1996). Nature of the medical encounter. *Research on Aging, 18,* 70–83.

Radecki, S. E., Kane, R. L., Solomon, D. H., and Mendenhall, R. C. (1988). Do physicians spend less time with older patients? *Journal of the American Geriatrics Society, 36,* 713–718.

Resnick, L., Cowart, M. E., and Kubrin, A. (1998). Perceptions of do-not-resuscitate orders. *Social Work in Health Care, 26,* 1–21.

Reynolds, D. E., and Sanders, M. S. (1975). Effect of defendant attractiveness, age, and injury on severity of sentence given by simulated jurors. *Journal of Social Psychology, 96,* 149–150.

Reynolds, S. L. (1997). Protected or neglected: An examination of negative versus compassionate ageism in public conservatorship. *Research on Aging, 19,* 3–23.

Rost, K. A., and Frankel, R. (1993). The introduction of the older patient's problems in the medical visit. *Journal of Aging and Health, 5,* 387–401.

Rubin, K. H., and Brown, I. (1975). A life-span look at person perception and its relationship to communicative interaction. *Journal of Gerontology, 30,* 461–468.

Ryan, E. B., Giles, H., Bartolucci, G., & Henwood, K. (1986). Psycholinguistic and social psychological components of communication by and with the elderly. *Language and Communication, 6,* 1–24.

Ryan, E. B., Hamilton, J. M., and Kwong See, S. K. (1994). Patronizing the old: How do younger and older adults respond to baby talk in the nursing home? *International Journal of Aging and Human Development, 39,* 21–32.

Ryan, E. B., Hummert, M. L., and Boich, L. H. (1995). Communication predicaments of aging: Patronizing behavior toward older adults. *Journal of Language and Social Psychology, 14,* 144–166.

Salthouse, T. A., Hambrick, D. Z., and McGuthry, K. E. (1998). Shared age-related influences on cognitive and noncognitive variables. *Psychology and Aging, 13,* 486–500.

Schaie, K. W. (1994). The course of adult intellectual development. *American Psychologist, 49,* 304–313.

Sheridan, J. E., White, J., and Fairchild, T. J. (1992). Ineffective staff, ineffective supervision, or ineffective administration? Why some nursing homes fail to provide adequate care. *Gerontologist, 32,* 334–341.

Sherman, M. M., Roberto, K. A., and Robinson, J. (1996). Knowledge and attitudes of hospital personnel towards older adults. *Gerontology and Geriatrics Education, 16,* 25–35.

Silverman, M., Smith, L. G., Nelson, C., and Dembo, R. (1984). The perception of the elderly criminal when compared to adult and juvenile offenders. *Journal of Applied Gerontology, 3,* 97–104.

Siminoff, L. A. (1989). Cancer patient and physician communication: Progress and continuing problems. *Annals of Behavioral Medicine, 11,* 108–112.

Smith, J., and Baltes, P. B. (1999). Trends and profiles of psychological functioning in very old age. In P. B. Baltes and K. U. Mayr (Eds.), *The Berlin Aging Study* (pp. 197–226). Cambridge: Cambridge University Press.

Smith, R. P., Woodward, N. J., Wallston, B. S., Wallston, K. A., Rye, P., and Zylstra, M. (1988). Health care implications of desire and expectancy for control in elderly adults. *Journals of Gerontology, 43,* P1–P7.

Staudinger, U. M., and Pasupathi, M. (2000). Life-span perspectives on self, personality, and social cognition. In F. I. M. Craik and T. A. Salthouse (Eds.), *The handbook of aging and cognition* (pp. 633–688). Mahwah, NJ: Erlbaum.

Streufert, S., Pogash, R., Piasecki, M., and Post, G. M. (1990). Age and management team performance. *Psychology and Aging, 5,* 551–559.

Teo, P. (1997). Space to grow old in: The availability of public spaces for elderly persons in Singapore. *Urban Studies, 34,* 419–439.

Thimm, C., Rademacher, U., and Kruse, L. (1998). Age stereotypes and patronizing messages: Features of age-adapted speech in technical instructions to the elderly. *Journal of Applied Communication Research, 26,* 66–82.

Trope, Y., and Thompson, E. P. (1998). Looking for truth in all the wrong places? Asymmetric search of individuating information about stereotyped group members. *Journal of Personality and Social Psychology, 73,* 229–241.

Tsai, J. L., and Carstensen, L. L. (1991). *Social interaction with the elderly: A comparison of Chinese-American and Caucasian students.* Unpublished honors thesis, Stanford University.

Uddo, B. J. (1986). The withdrawal or refusal of food and hydration as age discrimination: Some possibilities. *Issues in Law and Medicine, 2,* 39–59.

Ursic, A. C., Ursic, M. L., and Ursic, V. L. (1986). A longitudinal study of the use of the elderly in magazine advertising. *Journal of Consumer Research, 13,* 131–133.

Vasil, L., and Wass, H. (1993). Portrayal of the elderly in the media: A literature review and implications for educational gerontologists. *Educational Gerontology, 19,* 71–85.

Villemur, N. K., and Hyde, J. S. (1983). Effects of sex of defense attorney, sex of juror, and age and attractiveness of the victim on mock juror decision making in a rape case. *Sex Roles, 9,* 879–889.

Wass, H., Hawkins, L. V., Kelly, E. B., Magners, C. R., and McMorrow, A. M. (1985). The elderly in the Sunday newspapers: 1963 and 1963. *Educational Gerontology, 11,* 29–39.

Wilbanks, W. (1988). Are elderly felons treated more leniently by the criminal justice system? *International Journal of Aging and Human Development, 26,* 275–288.

Williams, A. (1996). Young people's evaluations of intergenerational versus peer underaccommodation: Sometimes older is better? *Journal of Language and Social Psychology, 15,* 291–311.

Williams, A., and Giles, H. (1996). Intergenerational conversations: Young adults' retrospective accounts. *Human Communication Research, 23,* 220–250.

Woodward, N. J., and Wallston, B. S. (1987). Age and health care beliefs: Self-efficacy as a mediator of low desire for control. *Psychology and Aging, 2,* 3–8.

8

The Paradox of Well-Being, Identity Processes, and Stereotype Threat: Ageism and Its Potential Relationships to the Self in Later Life

Susan Krauss Whitbourne and Joel R. Sneed

How does it feel to grow old in a society that values youth and youthfulness? This central question is the organizing theme of this chapter, in which we examine the impact on sense of self or identity of society's attitudes toward older adults. Whether and why ageism exists will not be questioned or analyzed; we assume that there is sufficient evidence from within all sectors of Western society to present aging individuals with challenges to their identities and will not document these. The focus of the chapter is the question of how it is that the majority of older adults maintain a positive sense of the self despite the fact that they are confronted on a daily basis with fear and devaluation from others within society. At the same time, there is evidence that for at least some older adults, negative attitudes about aging and the aged are internalized in ways that affect their ability to perform well on tasks in the laboratory and in everyday life. Thus, although the majority of older adults maintain high self-esteem and positive feelings of self-worth, there is the potential for some (or perhaps most) to behave in ways that are similar to those of other discriminated against subgroups within Western society. Ironically, such self-fulfilling properties of their behavior may reinforce negative stereotypes about the abilities of older adults to carry out tasks that are vital to their adaptation.

The Nature of Aging Stereotypes: Myth and Reality

Negative attitudes toward aging take several forms (Kite and Johnson 1988). The first is that older adults are lonely and depressed. This stereotype portrays older adults as lacking close friends and family and as having a higher rate of mood disorders than is true of younger adults. Both components of this stereotype clearly are myths (Cooley et al. 1998; Whitbourne, 2001). They conflict with the weight of evidence supporting the view that older adults are high on psychosocial resources, both personal and interpersonal. Related to myths of lack of psychosocial resources are the views of older adults as rigid and unable to cope with the declines associated with aging. Again, data on flexibility in later life (Schaie 1994) and on the adequacy of coping resources (Diehl, Coyle, and Labouvie-Vief 1996) refute this myth. Older adults are not inherently less flexible in terms of attitudes or personality styles than are younger adults. Furthermore, older adults have a wealth of coping resources that allow them to manage stress in personally and interpersonally more effective ways than do young adults.

The second stereotype of aging is that older adults become increasingly similar as they grow old—and the similarity is one that has negative connotations. This stereotype portrays aging as unidimensional and unidirectional, again a view that conflicts with the evidence. A considerable body of research within gerontology has established that older adults are more rather than less different from each other in terms of the extent to which their scores vary on a range of physical, psychological, and sociological measures (Nelson and Dannefer 1992).

The third aging stereotype is that older adults are sick, frail, and dependent, a stereotype unfortunately reinforced by the use of the term *frail elder* promoted in some of the gerontological literature. This stereotype conflicts with the evidence on self-assessed and objectively rated health in older adults (National Center for Health Statistics 1999). The majority of older persons, even those objectively in poor health and limited economic circumstances, rate their health as "good" or "very good."

Fourth, older adults are seen as cognitively and psychologically impaired, a view that fits with the notion of aging as involving inevitable "senility." Here again the evidence presents a conflicting viewpoint. Although clearly there are losses in attention and working memory with increasing age in adulthood, only a minority (7 percent) of older adults develop extreme impairment in the form of dementia (Brookmeyer and Kawas 1998).

Ageism is not only reflected in common myths held by the public at large, but is also reflected in psychological theories about older adulthood. For example, disengagement theory (Cumming and Henry 1961) proposed that older adults voluntarily reduce their contact with society rather than being excluded from participation in their former social roles. This theory conflicted with the views held previously by professional advocates working with elders that older adults are involuntarily forced to give up valued participation in society. The inherent ageism of disengagement theory, which justifies the withdrawal of social institutions from the lives of older adults, led many researchers to question its conclusions, and it has since been refuted (Atchley 1989). However, the theory provides a justification for those who wish to argue that older adults are best left to rest on the shelf.

In addition to its appearance within the social-psychological literature on aging, ageism has made its way to the undergraduate psychology textbooks used in colleges and universities to teach tomorrow's psychologists. In a study of undergraduate psychology textbooks published between 1949 and 1989, Whitbourne and Hulicka (1990) documented the extent to which older adults and the aging process are portrayed in a negative light. For example, the "everything goes downhill" theme was prominent in descriptions within these texts of research on cognition, personality, and physical functioning. Although not all portrayals of aging and the aged were as negative, there was sufficient evidence to justify concern that undergraduates are not being given accurate information about the aging process. More recent analyses of undergraduate texts reveal continued examples of ageist portrayals in areas such as introductory, cognitive, and abnormal psychology (Whitbourne and Cavanaugh, in press). Other gerontologists have provided evidence of ageism in psychological research (Schaie 1988, 1993) and in the provision of treatment to older adults (Gatz and Pearson 1988).

Given that society's attitudes toward aging are more negative toward women than toward men (the "double standard of aging"; Sontag 1979; Wilcox 1997), women are seen as particular targets of ageism. In part, such a view relates to social definitions of attractiveness, which, in turn, can create a challenge for women's body image (Whitbourne and Skultety, in press). Countering the negative views of aging adults are forms of ageism in which older adults are seen in an overly positive but equally stereotyped light (Hummert et al. 1994). Older adults are seen as "cute" or "kindly," and although these views may bring a smile to the face of a younger person, they still involve placing all older adults into the same category and therefore limiting appreciation of their individuality.

The need to counteract ageist myths and stereotypes remains a pressing concern within the field of gerontology. As the generation of baby boomers reaches their mature adult years and heads into the years traditionally thought of as old age, these negative views of aging and the aged could potentially have negative effects on the social treatment and regard of many millions of individuals.

The Paradox of Well-Being and Successful Aging

Having just made the case for the need to revise views of aging and the aged, we now arrive at a startling fact: Despite the existence of ageism and other negative social indicators associated with aging, the majority of older adults maintain a positive sense of subjective well-being. This phenomenon has been referred to as the "paradox of well-being" (Mroczek and Kolarz 1998), a term that seems to be an apt description of this puzzling phenomenon. Support for this phenomenon emerged from analysis of data from over 32,000 Americans studied from 1972 to 1994 obtained in the Midlife in the United States Survey (MIDUS) carried out within the context of the MacArthur Study of Successful Midlife Development. The large majority of individuals in the later adult years within this sample were found to rate themselves as "very" or "pretty" happy. Findings from countries around the world support this positive image of aging as a time of increased feelings of satisfaction (Diener and Suh 1998). In general, the majority of people report having a favorable evaluation of themselves and their lives, and this rosy view does not become dimmed in old age (Diener 1998).

Related to the paradox of well-being is another more long-standing observation within social gerontology, referred to as the phenomenon of "successful aging" or "optimal aging" (Rowe and Kahn 1987). This notion is related to the paradox of well-being, but is a more explicit approach that emphasizes the positive aspects of growing older. The tradition of studying successful aging has existed for many years within the field of social gerontology, but it has been gaining ascendance with a growing emphasis on positive psychology. Another study founded by the MacArthur Foundation designed to investigate this phenomenon identified the three theorized aspects of successful aging as absence of disease or disability, maintaining high cognitive and physical functioning, and being actively engaged with life (Rowe and Kahn 1998). According to this definition of successful aging, the majority of older adults are in fact successful. The paradox of well-being may be explained in part by the fact that most older adults meet the objective criteria for successful aging. The fact that they feel good about themselves follows from their having met these criteria. Perhaps lacking from this definition is a sense of self-actualization or self-expression. Although the criterion of active engagement with life conjures up a sense of an individual's reaching out to others, there is no criterion in the definition of successful aging that relates to full expression of the self, or what Erikson and colleagues refer to as "ego integrity" (Erikson 1963) or "vital involvement" (Erikson, Erikson, and Kivnick 1986).

Despite its limitations, the concept of successful aging adds an important counterpoint to the view of aging as a time of inevitable disease and decline. What remains interesting, however, is the fact that despite so many negative portrayals of aging, which persist even in the face of evidence to the contrary, the majority of older adults are able to achieve positive well-being. We will turn next to theories that attempt to provide explanations for this intriguing phenomenon.

Theorized Processes of Maintaining Well-Being in Later Life

Within personality theories concerning aging and the sense of self, or identity, the older adult is viewed as maintaining both positive self-esteem and enhanced abilities to cope with negative life events. Four mechanisms are theorized to account for this improved ability to manage such problems. The first is a mature set of defense mechanisms or coping abilities. The second is the ability to select emotionally rewarding social partners. The third proposed mechanism involves accommodation of goals by older adults in the face of actual and impending age-related changes. The last, which we focus on most heavily, is the use of processes of interpreting experiences in which information consistent with present (positive) views of the self is preserved.

Use of Mature Defense Mechanisms

There is evidence to suggest that older adults possess an adaptive set of defense mechanisms with which to handle emotional challenges. Vaillant (1993) proposed a hierarchical model of defense mechanisms in which immature defenses such as denial predominate in early life, and more mature mechanisms such as humor and altruism come to the fore in later life. Along similar lines, Haan (1977) suggested that coping and defensive processes develop across the life span. Haan proposed that the use of coping strategies that involve cognitive mediation and mature emotional expression increase with age, whereas defensive processes that lack conscious cognitive mediation and distort reality decrease with age.

Both the Vaillant and Haan models have received considerable empirical support in investigations of defense mechanisms in later adulthood. Across a variety of measures, immature coping and defensive strategies decrease with age, and more mature strategies increase with age (Diehl, Coyle, and Labouvie-Vief 1996; Ihilevich and Gleser 1986; Labouvie-Vief,

Hakim-Larson, and Hobart 1987). Clearly, older adults have the ability to handle negative emotions in a more productive and positive manner than do their younger counterparts. This ability allows them to engage in extensive "damage control" when exposed to potentially negative emotional interchanges in which they are made to feel weak, inferior, or rejected by virtue of their status as older adults.

Socioemotional Selectivity Theory

Related to the notion of enhanced psychosocial maturity in later life is socioemotional selectivity theory, which proposes that older adults have found ways to control successfully the potentially negative outcomes of their life experiences (Carstensen 1992; Carstensen, Isaacowitz, and Charles 1999). Rather than spend time with strangers, who may base their interactions with older adults on social stereotypes instead of personal knowledge, older adults prefer to spend their time with family and close friends, who are more likely to provide positive emotional feedback. Through this mechanism of selection, older adults are able to maintain positive rather than negative emotions.

Socioemotional selectivity theory postulates that the underlying impetus for changes in the choice of desired social partners is the perception of time as limited, not age. When people of any age perceive time to be limited, as opposed to expansive, they tend to weigh the regulation of positive emotional states more heavily than the acquisition of knowledge (novelty). In other words, when time is perceived as expansive, people tend to be more acquisitive in their desire for new information. When people perceive that their time will be limited, they become more present oriented and turn their social goals from acquisition of information to the securing of emotionally significant interactions with significant others. Older people perceive their future time as limited, and therefore engage in a process of reducing the size of their social networks.

Through the process of selection, socioemotional selectivity theory explains the empirical fact that older adults have smaller social networks. In contrast to the disengagement theory, however, socioemotional selectivity theory accounts for the fact in a positive light, presenting older adults as active agents in the construction of their social worlds. Furthermore, older adults do not restrict their social networks because they value emotional experiences any less than do younger adults, a process implied by disengagement theory; in fact, it is for the opposite reason. Thus, older adults are seen within this framework as having the potential to control their emotional experiences by controlling the nature of their social interactions.

Goal Accommodation

A third mechanism that older adults may use to maintain a positive sense of self despite objective evidence of losses and exposure to negative stereotypes is to accommodate or reduce their level of aspiration or goals. According to Brandstädter and Greve (1994), successful aging results from an "accommodative shift" in which adults gradually relinquish the desired aims and objectives of their younger years to ones that are more compatible with their more restricted set of abilities in later life. Such a shift allows them to maintain a positive sense of self because they are no longer faced with their objectively based physical and cognitive limitations (Brandstädter and Greve 1994).

Along similar lines, Heckhausen and Schulz (Heckhausen 1997; Heckhausen and Schulz 1995) postulate that older adults shift from primary control of their environment, in which they try to impose their will onto situations, to secondary control, in which they change their goals so that they can derive a sense of achievement and accomplishment. Downward social comparison, habituation, and negative scaling of aspirations are other related mechanisms theorized to account for the maintenance of positive well-being in the face of objective social losses (Mroczek and Kolarz 1998).

Identity Processes

The final theoretical approach we examine to explain the maintenance of positive views of the self is based on the theory of identity processes (Whitbourne 1986). Identity process theory proposes that people interpret their perceptions of experiences through the Piagetian-like process of identity assimilation: the interpretation of experiences through the template provided by the individual's self-schemas or identity. The theory postulates that the majority of adults attempt to maintain a positive sense of self—as competent, well regarded, and ethical. As in Piaget's theory, however, some situations are not amenable to identity assimilation, and this sense of the self must undergo some change. For example, if an older person with reduced muscle strength cannot lift a heavy box (one that could formerly have been lifted with ease), identity assimilation will be defeated. Instead, the individual must undergo a change in the self, which occurs through identity accommodation. Through this process, the older person with reduced muscle strength must make a shift to viewing the self as having lost some of his or her former competence.

Ideally, however, as in Piaget's theory, there is a balance or dynamic equilibrium between identity assimilation and identity accommodation.

When an individual is faced with experiences that challenge his or her self-definition, identity assimilation should gradually give way to identity accommodation. However, identity accommodation should not become so predominant that the individual's identity is based entirely on the ups and downs of life experiences. Instead, the individual should be able to make changes in identity as necessary but maintain a coherent and integrated sense of self.

The integration of aging into identity process theory is represented by the multiple threshold model, a proposal that personal recognition of the physical and cognitive aspects of aging occurs in a stepwise process across the years of adulthood (Whitbourne and Collins 1998). According to this model, individuals pass through a set of thresholds of feeling old at different times for different systems of the body (what is popularly called a "senior moment"). Each new age-related change brings with it the potential for another threshold to be crossed. The area or areas that are of greatest significance to an adult's identity are likely to observed with great care or vigilance. Some thresholds are crossed without creating a challenge for identity because they are in areas that are not of particular importance to that individual. At the point of crossing a threshold, the individual is stimulated to recognize the reality of the aging process in that particular area of functioning. At that point, the individual moves from identity assimilation to identity accommodation in an attempt to adjust to the crossing of the threshold and reach a new state of balance.

Implied in the identity process model is the notion that the most important challenges to occur from a psychological standpoint in later adulthood pertain to the sense of self. However, unlike theories that propose shifts in ego defenses, coping styles, and goals as reactions to aging, identity process theory proposes that individuals can shape the aging process to fit their own sense of identity. In keeping with the notions of contextualism and reciprocity as life span developmental processes (Lerner 1995), identity process theory also assumes that identity influences the actions people take with regard to their own aging. They can maintain an active "use it or lose it approach" to the aging process that allows them to slow or ward off the negative effects of aging, such as taking advantage of aerobic exercise. On the other hand, people can fall into the many traps that are present within contemporary culture to accelerate the aging process, such as for fair-skinned people to acquire a suntan or people with cardiovascular disease to eat food with high fat content.

According to the identity process model, older individuals maintain a positive sense of well-being despite objective losses and exposure to ageism through the mechanism of identity assimilation. A series of studies conducted within our laboratory has led us to hypothesize the existence of an identity assimilation effect (IAE), which is the positive relationship between age and self-esteem that is accounted for by a positive relationship between age and the use of identity assimilation. Through the IAE, older adults are able to preserve their sense of identity by using identity assimilation to minimize or alter the nature of the experiences to which they are exposed by virtue of their moving into the status of older adult. The "successful" ager does not pretend that aging is not occurring. Instead, aging is adapted to at the level of behavior. Older adults maintain their overall positive sense of identity while at the same time making the behavioral microaccommodations that allow them to preserve their health and functioning at optimal levels. Older adults vary in their ability to take these measures to protect and express the self in later life. After examining the research supporting the IAE, we turn to the challenge presented by aging to the sense of self that stimulates the use of identity processes. Finally, we explore the notion of identity styles as alternate ways of managing the threats to identity created by negative stereotypes of aging.

The Identity Assimilation Effect: How Individuals May Ward Off the Effects of Ageism

Our position is that older adults are able to combat the potentially negative attitudes toward aging and the aged that are observed in Western society through a variety of mechanisms, but the one of most relevance is identity assimilation. The IAE is a product of the older individual's desire to preserve a positive sense of self in the face of increasingly threatening images of aging as a negative state of existence. The IAE works for most individuals, but as we shall also see not for all.

Previous Research on the IAE

The IAE has been observed in a series of studies examining the relationship between identity processes and self-esteem in middle and later adulthood. The first evidence of such an effect was noted in an investigation of the relationship between the identity processes of assimilation, accommodation, and balance, and perceptions of physical and cognitive functioning in older adults (Whitbourne and Collins 1998). Using a questionnaire designed to tap the use of the identity processes in response to age-related physical and cognitive changes, a strong relationship was observed between the use of identity assimilation and the maintenance of self-esteem in older adults. Specifically, identity assimilation was (1) used by adults between the ages of 40 and 65 to maintain self-esteem in the areas of appearance and cognition, (2) positively related to self-esteem in the area of appearance for adults 65 and older, and (3) positively related to self-esteem in the area of basic functioning for the sample as a whole. According to Whitbourne and Collins (1998), people using identity assimilation may make behavioral changes to cope with the aging process, but without ruminating about them.

In a subsequent investigation (Sneed and Whitbourne 2001), we examined the relationship between self-esteem and identity processes using a fifty-five-item version of the Identity and Experiences Scale–General, a Likert-type self-report measure developed to assess an individual's use of identity assimilation (IAS), identity accommodation (IAC), and identity balance (IBL) in the domain of personality. Items for this measure were originally derived from an interview study in which ninety-four adults shared their thoughts and feelings regarding family, work, values, and aging (Whitbourne 1986). Statements such as, "Have many doubts and questions about myself," tap the IAC dimension; "Don't spend much effort reflecting on 'who' I am," tap the IAS dimension; and "Try to keep a steady course in life but am open to new ideas," tap the IBL dimension. We administered this measure along with Rosenberg's (1965) Self-Esteem Scale to a community sample of older adults ranging in age from 40 to 95 years (M = 63.31, SD = 13.31). As expected, both identity balance and identity assimilation were positively correlated with self-esteem, whereas identity accommodation was negatively correlated with self-esteem. Supporting the concept of the IAE, we also found positive correlations between identity assimilation and age.

The relationships observed in our research between the identity processes and self-esteem are buttressed by the independent observation that self-concept clarity is negatively associated with self-report measures of negative affect and neuroticism (anxiety and depression) and positively correlated with self-esteem (Campbell 1990; Campbell et al. 1996). In other words, identity accommodation should negatively relate to self-esteem because it is an identity process associated with a loosely organized identity structure, whereas identity balance and self-esteem should positively correlate because these processes are associated with self-concept clarity. Identity assimilation is conceptualized as being primarily a defensive strategy; it protects the individual from realizing a shortcoming in the self. As a result of this self-protective strategy, identity assimilation is positively related to an increased sense of self-worth.

Using a refined thirty-three-item version of the IES (Sneed and Whitbourne 2000), we examined the relationship between the identity processes and self-esteem, need for cognition, and self-consciousness in a community sample of 173 adults (108 females and 65 males) ranging in age from 42 to 85 years (M = 60.80; SD = 12.58). Bivariate correlations and multiple regression analysis yielded partial support for the predicted relationships among the variables in the study. As expected, identity balance was positively correlated with internal state awareness and self-esteem, suggesting that individuals using identity balance are self-accepting and tend to be aware of their internal moods and feelings. Identity accommodation was positively associated with self-reflection, social anxiety, and self consciousness, which was also anticipated. Because of their loosely integrated identities, people high on identity accommodation were predicted to be concerned with their self-presentation and consequently to be socially anxious. This prediction was upheld. Identity assimilation was negatively correlated with self-reflection, indicating that individuals using this process tend not to examine their internal states in an attempt to avoid discovering shortcomings in the self. In this study, we also found partial support for the IAE hypothesis. Although identity assimilation did not positively correlate with self-esteem, a positive association was observed between identity assimilation and age. Furthermore, we predicted that identity accommodation would vary inversely with age and self-esteem, and this prediction was upheld. These findings suggest that older individuals are more likely than younger persons to decrease their use of identity-accommodative processes and increase their use of identity assimilation–like processes in order to maintain a positive view of the self.

Subsequent research (Skultety 2000) suggests that the IAE is more likely to occur in women. The double jeopardy of ageism and sexism places a greater strain on identity processes, and to avoid self-esteem losses, women turn, perhaps defensively, to identity assimilation as their buffer (Whitbourne, Sneed, and Skultety 2001).

Research Related to the IAE

The IAE hypothesis directly contrasts with Brandstädter and Greve's (1994) model of accommodative shifting in later adulthood. According to these researchers, successful aging occurs when goals and aspirations are adjusted in accordance with one's age-related abilities. Although at first glance these models share much in common (both are based loosely on Piagetian-like constructs), a closer inspection shows that they diverge considerably. Most important, in Brandstädter and Greve's model, people are motivated to achieve consistency between what they want to do and what they are able to do; that is, we see this as primarily a goal-directed model. In our view, people seek to maintain consistent and positive views of themselves, and the identity process styles refer to the means through which they accomplish this goal. This model places identity squarely at center of experience (Whitbourne and Connolly 1999). Successful adaptation to the aging process refers not to what is external (e.g., goals) but to what is most internal: one's self.

According to the IAE, the modus operandi of the normally functioning individual is to maintain, perhaps at the expense of accuracy, a positive self-view or "positive ego-enhancing bias" (Whitbourne 1996, p. 280). Along related lines, Baumeister (1996, 1997) proposes that individuals prefer to see themselves as stable and predictable. They distort the way they interpret their own actions and experiences to make this positive view seem plausible. As in identity process theory, normal adults are theorized to prefer to view themselves as being personally competent and as having desirable personality traits (Newman, Duff, and Baumeister 1997).

Greenberg, Pyszczynski, and Solomon (1986) have summarized a variety of experimental findings from social psychology that highlight the individual's need to protect self-esteem, which we argue is maintained in later adulthood through the use of identity assimilation: (1) Individuals tend to take credit for their successes and deny responsibility for their failures; (2) they will inhibit performance or undermine their own chances for success (i.e., self-handicap) if they are able to conjure up external attributions to explain their failure; (3) when self-esteem in a particular domain is threatened, people compensate by overly valuing their skills in an unrelated domain; (4) when individuals fail at a task that is important to them, they overestimate how many others will also fail; conversely, when they succeed, they underestimate how many others will succeed; (5) people prefer to compare themselves to others who perform worse than they do on dimensions that are important to them (e.g., downward social comparisons); and (6) when research participants are outperformed by confederates on tasks that are personally relevant (identity salient), they subsequently downplay or minimize the importance of that domain to their self-concept.

The identity processing perspective conceives of self-esteem as tantamount to evaluating the self as loving in relations with others, competent in abilities, and morally good, a position consistent with the view that self-esteem serves as a buffer against anxiety. According to this view, identity challenges cause anxiety (i.e., threaten the unity of the self; Lecky

1945) because they challenge this set of beliefs. Similarly, terror management theory (Greenberg et al. 1992) holds that the awareness of one's mortality causes paralyzing anxiety and that one's cultural worldview imbues the world with meaning to prevent this realization. Self-esteem serves as a guide in determining how well an individual is meeting the prescribed standards of the culture and functions as an anxiety buffer against mortality salience. These authors have shown that high self-esteem is associated with experiencing less anxiety following exposure to threatening stimuli. Conversely, decreases in self-esteem are related to increases in anxiety following exposure to threatening stimuli.

The IAE hypothesis is also consistent with the accumulated body of research evidence challenging the view that accurate perception of the self and the social world is necessary for psychological health. Taylor and Brown (1988) persuasively argued that people have unrealistically positive self-views, exaggerated perceptions of control, and unrealistic optimism. In addition to the many self-esteem-protective mechanisms, evidence that people have unrealistically positive self-views comes from the fact that most people believe they are better than the average person, which Taylor and Brown note is a logical contradiction. People also have exaggerated perceptions of control. For example, they believe they have control over chance situations such as rolling dice and believe they have more control over the outcome if they throw the dice themselves than if someone else does it for them. Indeed, the only group of people that does not display this illusion of control are those who are depressed. Taylor and Brown also document the unrealistic optimism of nondepressed individuals. Over a variety of experimental tasks, most people's predictions about the future closely correspond to what they would like to see happen. Furthermore, most people believe that the likelihood of experiencing positive outcomes in the future is greater than that of their peers, and the likelihood of experiencing negative events is less than that of their peers. These authors make the important point, which is underscored here, that high self-esteem, a sense of self-efficacy or perceived personal control, and a positive outlook on life are all associated with psychological health, whereas low self-esteem, lack of perceived control, and a pessimistic outlook on life are associated with depression and anxiety.

There appears to be a developmental progression in the use of defense mechanisms over the life span from less sophisticated and mature defenses such as projection to more mature and complex defenses such intellectualization. However, what seems to be overlooked by most researchers, which is particularly relevant to the IAE hypothesis, is that it is consistently observed that the defense mechanism of denial (also called "reversal") tends to increase with age. In a sex- and age-stratified random sample of adults from low, medium, and high socioeconomic backgrounds, Diehl, Coyle, and Labouvie-Vief (1996) observed that older adults had significantly higher reversal scores than all other age ranges. This finding is of particular importance because it may indicate that the negative stereotypes associated with aging may be combated using denial, which is consistent with the IAE hypothesis. Moreover, their findings cut across a wide range of income and education levels, increasing the generalizability of our hypothesis, which has been tested in more limited populations. It is particularly interesting to note that mean scores on reversal level off in the over-70 age group in this study. This indicates that it is during the critical late middle age and retirement age period that the effects of ageism may be strongest and defenses such as denial necessary to counter its deleterious effects. In all, an impressive body of research support exists from a variety of disciplines within psychology suggesting that assimilative processes such as denial are increasingly used in later adulthood to maintain self-esteem.

Identity Styles: On the Road to Individual Differences in Reactions to Ageism

There is reason to maintain that not all older individuals are able to withstand the challenges to identity presented by negative views of aging in Western society. In this section, we present a model of identity styles that describes alternative combinations of the identity processes of assimilation, accommodation, and balance (Whitbourne et al. 2001). We then relate the variations among the identity styles to the challenges presented by ageism.

Characteristics of the Identity Styles

How one characteristically handles identity challenges can be thought of as one's identity style, an individual's characteristic way of processing information about the self that theoretically predicts adaptation to the physical, psychological, and social role changes inherent in the aging process (Berzonsky 1990; Whitbourne 1987). Identity styles are similar in scope and function to cognitive styles, which are conceptualized as bridges between an individual's cognitions and personality (Sternberg and Grigorenko 1997).

Identity Assimilators   Identity assimilators possess fragile identities. At all costs, they attempt to fit identity-discrepant experiences into their existing identities because to recognize discrepancies is painful. A notion similar to extreme identity assimilation is Robins and John's (1997) metaphor of the Egoist, an individual who seeks self-enhancement and distorts information regarding the self because experiences that reflect poorly on the self produce negative affect. The inflated self-esteem of identity assimilators may serve as a defense against a weak and fragile ego that is defensively compensating for feelings of worthlessness and self-doubt (Kernberg 1975).

To maintain a positive identity, the identity assimilator characteristically uses defensive processes that cause potentially negative information about the self to be warded off or prevented from entering or invading identity. These individuals may blame others for their shortcomings, seek out only information that is consistent with identity, or defensively assert, sometimes in the face of contradictory evidence, that they are loving, competent, and good. It is interesting to note that these individuals may pride themselves on their flexibility and adaptability in keeping up with the standards and values of the day. Furthermore, they refuse to engage in self-reflection both because they do not value the process and because they unconsciously fear the outcome.

Identity Accommodators   Identity accommodators have unstable and incoherent identities and therefore are easily shaped by new experiences and ideas. They are compelled to seek information about themselves to assuage their feelings of self-doubt and low self-esteem. At the same time, however, they continually recognize their own limitations and lack of integration. They also tend to be highly responsive to external influences; that is, they tend to look to the outside rather than the inside for inner guidance.

Robins and John's (1997) metaphor of the Politician is conceptually similar to this characterization of the identity accommodator. The Politician lacks a core sense of self or identity and can be seen solely as a product of the social context. According to Robins and John, the self-concept of such individuals can be thought of as a public performance. Politicians are primarily concerned with the impression they make on people and change their self-presentation to gain approval. When these individuals fail to gain approval, they experience negative affect and anxiety.

Given the theoretical relationship among identity accommodation, self-doubting, and low self-esteem, it would be predicted that identity accommodation correlates with depression and depressogenic tendencies. Indeed, depression and self-esteem are inversely correlated (Tennen and Herzberger 1987), and it is believed the mechanisms underlying low self-esteem and depression are the same (Watson and Clark 1984).

Identity Balanced   A dynamic balance between the opposing processes of identity assimilation and accommodation is considered the optimal approach to aging. Identity-balanced individuals are flexible enough to change in response to identity-salient discrepancies but not so flexible and unstructured that every new experience causes them to question fundamental assumptions about their self-definition. Identity-balanced individuals are theoretically in the best position to age successfully because they can flexibly adapt to and integrate age-related changes into their identities while simultaneously not losing their sense of self as consistent over time. People who are identity balanced regard the changes they have experienced as favorable (even if challenging), take a flexible approach to new experiences, and are able to engage in honest self-evaluation.

The notion of identity balance is conceptually similar to the Scientist metaphor of Robins and John (1997). Scientists are concerned with acquiring accurate self-knowledge. Thus, they construct theories about the self that are based on observation and can be tested. Because they are relatively objective in their approach to information about the self, they are neither devastated by nor unwilling to recognize changes that may potentially detract from the view they have of themselves as loving, competent, and good.

Theory predicts that identity-balanced individuals are free of debilitating psychopathology because they have a strong sense of personal control and self-efficacy. Indeed, individuals relatively free of psychopathology have a greater sense of personal control than do clinical populations (Shapiro, Schwartz, and Astin 1996). Because actual or perceived personal control is associated with decreased mortality (Alexander et al. 1989; Rodin and Langer 1977) and weak self-efficacy beliefs predict perceived declines in physical functioning (Seeman et al. 1999), it is believed that identity-balanced individuals adapt most successfully to the aging process. However, this may not result in the most positive account of later adulthood.

The possible liability associated with the balanced approach is as follows. The majority of age-related changes are in fact out of the individual's control, as is, of course, the individual's inevitable progress toward death with advancing age in adulthood. Individuals who pride themselves on personal control and self-efficacy may be adversely affected when important events that are uncontrollable affect them (Diehl 1999; Shapiro, Schwartz, and Astin 1996). Given the relationship between anxiety and the inability to perceive control over stressful experiences, periodic bouts of anxiety may be associated with identity balance as individuals face the prospect of loss of control over their mortality.

Reactions to Ageism

How do individuals who predominantly use one identity-processing style over another react to the age-related negative stereotypes present in our society? On the one hand, older adults seem to be able to withstand the difficulties of aging by using identity assimilation to preserve a positive view of the self. Assimilators characteristically exude optimism, perceive themselves as healthy, and take pride in their life's accomplishments. Nevertheless, the use of such a defensive process may lead to social isolation, exhaustion from constantly defending against reality, and failure to engage in age-related compensatory activities (Whitbourne 1987). Identity assimilators may excessively use downward social comparisons (changing the comparison standard in order to remain in a favorable light), which may alienate them from important social contacts like family and friends. This is particularly significant given the importance of close friends and family in later life to the maintenance of well-being and life satisfaction, as predicted by socioemotional selectivity theory.

On the other hand, older adults may suffer negative consequences by buying into social stereotypes about aging that lead them to overaccommodate to age-related changes. They assume that their life will follow a downward trajectory regardless of what actions they take, and as a result, they encounter even more negative changes in physical and cognitive functioning than would otherwise be the case.

In the other words, identity accommodators are expected to overreact and overgeneralize the consequences of age-related changes. For accommodators, stereotyped notions of old age provide a concrete set of external self-referents, and they adopt these stereotypes because they lack the internal identity structure that enables negotiating these challenges. For example, adults approaching their later years may react to the negative stereotype that older adults are cognitively impaired by becoming forgetful. What this buys the individual is the comfort of belonging to a group of similar others, but at the cost of losing healthy cognitive functioning. Individuals who accommodate may respond to medical diagnoses by "adopting" the disease, which protects them against identity instability and, paradoxically, against the existential worry associated with aging. In a sense, accommodators escape from the freedom to choose to live healthily and happily.

Balanced individuals should adjust to age-related setbacks with the most positive outlook. When they cannot adjust to age-related physical, psychological, and social role changes, they readily take advantage of therapeutic interventions, both psychological and physical, by becoming actively involved in social activities and exercise programs. As a result, these individuals will be more able to adjust realistically to age-related changes instead of denying that they are aging (extreme assimilation) or accepting prematurely that they are "over the hill" (overaccommodation).

Potential Consequences of Ageism: Stereotype Threat and Identity

Ageism, defined as a prejudiced attitude toward aging and older adults that is characterized by myths and stereotypes that depict aging as a process of decay (Whitbourne and Hulicka 1990), is not simply an abstract concept of academic interest; the psychological effects or consequences of ageism are very real. As we have seen, although the IAE protects older individuals from having negative stereotypes invade their sense of identities, there are some older individuals at particular risk: those who use identity accommodation. Fortunately, identity accommodators are in the minority. However, all older individuals, whether or not they are aware of this, are vulnerable to the effects of ageism on more subtle aspects of their ability to perform the tasks of daily life.

Older adults share beliefs (both negative and positive stereotypes) about aging that are similar to those of younger and middle-aged individuals, although these stereotypes are more complex. Hummert and her colleagues (1994) demonstrated using a trait generation task that the stereotypic self-representations possessed by older adults are similar to those held by young and middle-aged adults. They believe, for example, that older persons are severely impaired (e.g., senile, feeble, and slow-thinking), despondent (e.g., depressed, sad, and hopeless), shrewd or curmudgeonly (e.g., complaining and bitter), and socially inept or isolated (poor, timid, and quiet). Although the stereotypes that older adults hold were more complex and differentiated, these beliefs generally represented subsets of the broader categories endorsed by younger adults. As a result, it appears that the content of the negative stereotypic representations of older adults remains stable over the life course, but as one moves from out-group to in-group member, these beliefs become more complex.

The Priming of Poorer Performance by Ageist Stereotypes: Evidence from the Laboratory

Although research on beliefs and stereotypes is inherently of interest to this discussion, of most significance are the findings of studies illustrating the self-fulfilling nature of ageist representations of older adults. One remarkable study demonstrated the surprising finding that the priming of negative stereotypes can influence the walking speed of college-aged individuals. Bargh, Chen, and Barrows (1996) primed negative stereotypes of older adults using a scrambled-sentence priming task. In this task, five words were presented in scrambled order, one of which is a negative stereotype prime, and participants were asked to write down a grammatically correct sentence using only four of the five words. Walking speed was measured at a time when participants believed they were not involved in an experimental task: walking to the next part of the experiment. As predicted, undergraduates primed with stereotypes of older adults walked more slowly down the hall than those in a neutral priming condition. Of particular interest is the fact that no primes related to walking speed were included in the task.

A similar phenomenon was demonstrated on a sample of older adult men and women, using ageist stereotypes as primes (Hausdorff, Levy, and Wei 1999). The walking speeds of forty-seven community-dwelling older adult men and women (aged 63 to 80 years) were investigated after subliminal activation of both negative and positive stereotypes. Participants played computer games for approximately thirty minutes, during which they were given subliminal cues about aging. As was predicted, participants who received positive stereotype priming significantly increased their walking speed and percentage of swing time (percentage of time with one foot in the air and one foot on the ground). Walking speed and swing time of participants who received negative stereotypes priming did not change, however. The observed improvements in gait under positive priming were independent of age, gender, health status, or psychosocial status, strongly suggesting, as Bargh and his colleagues had previously shown, that negative stereotypes of aging can alter what might otherwise be thought of as strictly a physiological function.

Bringing this methodology into the cognitive domain, Levy (1996) examined the effects of implicit self-stereotyping on memory using a computer priming method that subliminally presented words associated with wise (positive) or senile (negative) images of older adulthood. Using this procedure, Levy was able to demonstrate that positive primes increased memory performance and self-efficacy beliefs, and negative stereotype primes had a detrimental impact on memory performance and self-efficacy beliefs. These findings challenge the wealth of data showing negative effects of aging on memory in later adulthood. They strongly suggest that the memory deficits that are observed in later adulthood stem not from biological decline but rather from implicit negative self-stereotypes that have been acquired from the environment over the life span without awareness.

These self-fulfilling prophecies that negative stereotypes about aging can produce appear to be specific to Western society, where predominantly negative stereotypes of aging abound (Kite and Johnson 1988). Levy and Langer (1994) observed that mainland Chinese older adults outperform American older adults on immediate, learned, delayed, and probed recall tasks. In fact, the older Chinese adults performed similarly to the younger Chinese adult participants. In contrast to Americans, who learn from an early age to fear and dislike old age, the Chinese learn from an early age to revere, respect, and honor older adults. Therefore, from an early age, the Chinese form positive beliefs regarding the role and function of older adults in society. These positive beliefs may help buffer the inevitable biological changes that take place in later adulthood.

Negative Stereotype Threat and Ageism

Steele's (1997) notion of disidentification following negative stereotype threat offers a compelling account of why and how older adults might take in negative stereotypes and what the possible consequences may be. Steele's analysis may help to explain why the ageism priming paradigm produces such powerful results.

According to Steele, African Americans and women underperform scholastically (women in math and physical sciences and African Americans in general) because, paradoxically, these domains are the most central to their sense of self-definition or identities. Stereotype threat is the fear of becoming like the stereotype in this valued aspect of functioning. In response to stereotype threat, members of these groups disidentify or reconceptualize their identities in order to remove the domain as a basis for self-evaluation. Consequently, they no longer care about the domain in question, and their performance suffers proportionately.

Previous attempts to explain negative stereotypes took the form that exposure to negative stereotypes leads to the internalization of these attitudes and consequently to self-hatred and own-group rejection. Based on this view, however, the self-esteem of stigmatized group members should be less than the self-esteem of nonstigmatized group members. This, however, is not true. Self-esteem is as high in stigmatized groups as it is in nonstigmatized groups (Crocker and Major 1989). Viewed from the perspective of negative stereotype threat and domain disidentification, the self-esteem of stigmatized group members remains high because they have removed the self-relevant domain as a basis for self-evaluation.

Steele and his colleagues have conducted several studies examining the academic performance of African Americans and math performance in women to test the basic postulates of his model and its predictions. In one study, Spencer, Steele, and Dione (1999) manipulated negative stereotype threat to determine its effect on the math test performance of women self-identified as high-level math students and for whom mathematics was an important part of their self-definition. In the first condition, participants were told that the mathematics test would demonstrate gender differences. Presumably this information activated the negative stereotype that women are less capable than men in mathematics. In the second condition, participants were told that the test would not show gender differences. As expected, in the gender-difference condition, women performed more poorly than did men; by contrast, in the no-gender-difference condition, women performed as well as men. Interestingly, these differences were not observed in a similar experiment in which students self-identified as English literature students were tested on the advanced literature section of the Graduate Record Exam (in which women are not threatened by negative stereotypes). In both conditions, women performed as well as men.

In another study, Steele and Aronson (1995) investigated the effect of negative stereotype threat on the standardized test performance of African Americans. In one condition, black and white participants were randomly assigned to either an ability-diagnostic condition or an ability-nondiagnostic condition. Black students underperformed in the ability-diagnostic condition but equaled their white counterparts in the ability-nondiagnostic condition. The researchers produced the same results simply by having participants in an ability-nondiagnostic condition record their race on a demographics questionnaire just prior to taking the examination.

In spite of the obvious parallels, researchers have yet to extend the notions of negative stereotype threat, domain identification, and disidentification to the study of aging. It is possible, as Steele (1997) notes, that older adults too suffer from a "threat in the air" (p. 614). Given the multitude of negative stereotypes that exist about older adults, it seems that disidentification following negative stereotypes threat offers a possible mechanism by which older adults suffer from the negative attitudes Americans hold toward them. We can assume that older people wish to see themselves as unchanged in their ability to engage in competent and positively valued behavior. Given this reality, it is possible that to avoid being reduced to a negative stereotype, older individuals disidentify with the domains of certain physical and cognitive abilities in order to remove these as a basis for self-evaluation. They too, in a sense, underperform. If a woman who is strongly identified with mathematics or an African American who is strongly identified with academics disidentifies, there are other domains in which they can excel. In contrast, if an older adult disidentifies from life satisfaction as a basis for self-evaluation, the alternatives appear rather grim. Although disidentification is meant to serve an adaptive function of maintaining positive self-regard, the consequences are damaging and maladaptive.

Conclusion

This analysis of ageism and its possible relationship to identity and well-being has taken us through a variety of literatures in exploring such phenomena as the paradox of well-being and the existence of successful aging in a world where, by all other reasonable accounts, most older people should in fact be depressed rather than happy. Having invoked the notion of the identity assimilation effect as a primary mechanism through which this process occurs, we have nevertheless identified the possibility of variations in the outcomes of evaluating the self by older individuals exposed to the specter of aging as a downward trajectory. Some individuals do not engage in the IAE: those who use identity accommodation and those balanced individuals who are at least temporarily looking at their own changes in a negative light. Moreover, due to the combined effects of ageism and sexism, women may find identity assimilation to be a necessary strategy to use to maintain their self-esteem in the face of age-related changes that otherwise may be threatening or anxiety provoking.

The possibility that stereotype threats do in fact invade the performance of even the staunchest identity assimilator is perhaps the most intriguing implication to emerge from this analysis. The few studies on priming through ageist stereotypes suggest that if you look below the surface of this identity assimilator, you will find the hidden fears of becoming old that inhibit performance or cause the reactions of those suffering from stereotype threat. Although the next logical question is one of reducing these harmful effects on the performance and well-being of older adults, gerontologists need to find more evidence to support the existence of these mechanisms. We hope that this chapter will provide just such an impetus.

References

Alexander, C. N., Langer, E. J., Newman, R. I., Chandler, H. M., and Davies, J. L. (1989). Transcendental meditation, mindfulness, and longevity. *Journal of Personality and Social Psychology, 57,* 950–964.

Atchley, R. C. (1989). A continuity theory of normal aging. *Journal of Personality and Social Psychology, 29,* 183–190.

Bargh, J. A., Chen, M., and Burrows, L. (1996). Automaticity of social behavior: Direct effects of trait construct and stereotype activation on action. *Journal of Personality and Social Psychology, 71,* 230–244.

Baumeister, R. F. (1996). Self-regulation and ego threat: Motivated cognition, self deception, and destructive goal setting. In P. M. Gollwitzer and J. A. Bargh (Eds.), *The psychology of action: Linking cognition and motivation to behavior* (pp. 27–47). New York: Guilford Press.

Baumeister, R. F. (1997). Identity, self-concept, and self-esteem: The self lost and found. In R. Hogan, J. A. Johnson, and S. R. Briggs (Eds.), *Handbook of personality psychology* (pp. 681–710). San Diego, CA: Academic Press.

Berzonsky, M. D. (1990). Self-construction over the life-span: A process perspective on identity formation. In G. J. Neimeyer and R. A. Neimeyer (Eds.), *Advances in personal construct theory* (Vol. 1, pp. 155–186). Greenwich, CT: JAI Press.

Brandtstaedter, J., and Greve, W. (1994). The aging self: Stabilizing and protective processes. *Developmental Review, 14,* 52–80.

Brookmeyer, R., and Kawas, C. (1998). Projections of Alzheimer's disease in the United States and the public health impact of delaying disease onset. *American Journal of Public Health, 88,* 1337–1342.

Campbell, J. D. (1990). Self-esteem and clarity of the self-concept. *Journal of Personality and Social Psychology, 59,* 538–549.

Campbell, J. D., Trapnell, P. D., Heine, S. J., Katz, I. M., Lavallee, L. F., and Lehman, D. R. (1996). Self-concept clarity: Measurement, personality correlates, and cultural boundaries. *Journal of Personality and Social Psychology, 70,* 141–156.

Carstensen, L. L. (1992). Social and emotional patterns in adulthood: Support for socioemotional selectivity theory. *Psychology and Aging, 7,* 331–338.

Carstensen, L. L., Isaacowitz, D. M., and Charles, S. T. (1999). Taking time seriously: A theory of socioemotional selectivity. *American Psychologist, 54,* 165–181.

Cooley, S., Deitch, I. M., Harper, M. S., Hinrichsen, G., Lopez, M. A., and Molinari, V. A. (1998). What practitioners should know about working with older adults. *Professional Psychology: Research and Practice, 29,* 413–427.

Crocker, J., and Major, B. (1989). Social stigma and self-esteem: The self-protective properties of stigma. *Psychological Review, 96,* 608–630.

Cumming, E., and Henry, W. E. (1961). *Growing old: The process of disengagement.* New York: Basic Books.

Diehl, M. (1999). Self-development in adulthood and aging: The role of critical life events. In C. D. Ryff and V. W. Marshall (Eds.), *The self and society in aging processes* (pp. 150–183). New York: Springer.

Diehl, M., Coyle, N., and Labouvie-Vief, G. (1996). Age and sex differences in coping and defense across the life span. *Psychology and Aging, 11,* 127–139.

Diener, E. (1998). Subjective well-being: Three decades of progress. *Psychological Bulletin, 125,* 276–302.

Diener, E., and Suh, E. (1998). Age and subjective well-being: An international analysis, *Annual Review of Gerontology and Geriatrics, 17,* 304–324.

Erikson, E. H. (1963). *Childhood and society* (2nd ed.). New York: Norton.

Erikson, E. H., Erikson, J. M., and Kivnick, H. Q. (1986). *Vital involvement in old age.* New York: Norton.

Gatz, M., and Pearson, C. G. (1988). Ageism revised and the provision of psychological services. *American Psychologist, 43,* 184–188.

Greenberg, J., Pyszczynski, T., and Solomon, S. (1986). The causes and consequences of a need for self-esteem: A terror management theory. In R. F. Baumeister (Ed.), *Public self and private self* (pp. 189–207). New York: Springer-Verlag.

Greenberg, J., Solomon, S., Pyszczynski, T., Rosenblatt, A., Burling, J., Lyon, D., Simon, L., and Pinel, E. (1992). Why do people need self-esteem? Converging evidence that self-esteem serves as an anxiety-buffering function. *Journal of Personality and Social Psychology, 63,* 913–922.

Haan, N. (1977). *Coping and defending: Processes of self-environment organization.* New York: Academic Press.

Hausdorff, J. M., Levy, B. R., and Wei, J. Y. (1999). The power of ageism on physical function of older persons: Reversibility of age-related gait changes. *Journal of the American Geriatrics Society, 47,* 1346–1349.

Heckhausen, J. (1997). Developmental regulation across adulthood: Primary and secondary control of age-related challenges. *Developmental Psychology, 33,* 176–187.

Heckhausen, J., and Schulz, R. (1995). A life-span theory of control. *Psychological Review, 102,* 284–304.

Hummert, M. L., Garstka, T. A., Shaner, J. L., and Strahm, S. (1994). Stereotypes of the elderly held by young, middle-aged, and elderly adults. *Journals of Gerontology, 49,* P240–P249.

Ihilevich, D., and Gleser, G. C. (1986). *Defense mechanisms: Their classification, correlates, and measurement with the Defense Mechanisms Inventory.* Owosso, MI: DMI Associates.

Kernberg, O. F. (1975). *Borderline conditions and pathological narcissism.* New York: Jason Aronson.

Kite, M. E., and Johnson, B. T. (1988). Attitudes toward older and younger adults: A meta-analysis. *Psychology and Aging, 3,* 233–244.

Labouvie-Vief, G., Hakim-Larson, J., and Hobart, C. J. (1987). Age, ego level, and the life-span development of coping and defense processes. *Psychology and Aging, 2,* 286–293.

Lecky, P. (1945). *Self-consistency: A theory of personality.* New York: Island Press.

Lerner, R. M. (1995). Developing individuals within changing contexts: Implications of developmental contextualism for human development, research, policy, and programs. In T. J. Kindermann and J. Valsiner (Eds.), *Development of person-context relations* (pp. 13–37). Hillsdale NJ: Erlbaum.

Levy, B. (1996). Improving memory in old age through implicit self-stereotyping. *Journal of Personality and Social Psychology, 71,* 1092–1107.

Levy, B., and Langer, E. (1994). Aging free from negative stereotypes: Successful memory in China and among the American deaf. *Journal of Personality and Social Psychology, 66,* 989–997.

Mroczek, D. K., and Kolarz, C. M. (1998). The effect of age on positive and negative affect: A developmental perspective on happiness. *Journal of Personality and Social Psychology, 75,* 1333–1349.

National Center for Health Statistics. (1999). *Health: United States, 1999.* Hyattsville, MD: National Center for Health Statistics.

Nelson, E. A., and Dannefer, D. (1992). Aged heterogeneity: Fact or fiction? The fate of diversity in gerontological research. *Gerontologist, 32,* 17–23.

Newman, L. S., Duff, K. J., and Baumeister, R. F. (1997). A new look at defensive projection: Thought suppression, accessibility, and biased person perception. *Journal of Personality and Social Psychology, 72,* 980–1001.

Robins, R. W., and John, O. P. (1997). The quest for self insight: Theory and research on accuracy and bias in self-perception. In R. Hogan, J. Johnson, and S. Briggs (Eds.), *Handbook of personality psychology* (pp. 649–679). New York: Academic Press.

Rodin, J., and Langer, E. (1977). Long-term effects of a control-relevant intervention with the institutionalized aged. *Journal of Personality and Social Psychology, 35,* 897–902.

Rosenberg, M. (1965). *Society and the adolescent self-image.* Princeton, NJ: Princeton University Press.

Rowe, J. W., and Kahn, R. L. (1987). Human aging: Usual and successful. *Science, 237,* 143–149.

Rowe, J. W., and Kahn, R. L. (1998). *Successful aging.* New York: Pantheon Books.

Schaie, K. W. (1988). Ageism in psychological research. *American Psychologist, 43,* 179–183.

Schaie, K. W. (1993). Ageist language in psychological research. *American Psychologist, 48,* 49–51.

Schaie, K. W. (1994). The course of adult intellectual development. *American Psychologist, 49,* 304–313.

Seeman, T. E., Unger, J. B., McAvay, G., and Mendes de Leon, C. F. (1999). Self-efficacy beliefs and perceived declines in functional ability: MacArthur studies of successful aging. *Journals of Gerontology: Psychological Sciences, 54,* P214–P222.

Shapiro, D. H., Schwartz, C. E., and Astin, J. A. (1996). Controlling ourselves, controlling our world: Psychology's role in understanding positive and negative consequences of seeking and gaining control. *American Psychologist, 51,* 1213–1230.

Skultety, K. M. (2000). Gender differences in identity processes and self-esteem in middle and later adulthood. Unpublished Master's thesis, University of Massachusetts Amherst.

Sneed, J., and Whitbourne, S. K. (2000). *Identity processing styles: Ways of adjusting to change in later adulthood.* Manuscript submitted for publication.

Sneed, J. R., and Whitbourne, S. K. (2001). Identity processing styles and the need for self-esteem in middle-aged and older adults. *International Journal of Aging and Human Development, 52,* 323–333.

Sontag, S. (1979). The double standard of aging. In J. Williams (Ed.), *Psychology of women* (pp. 462–478). San Diego CA: Academic Press.

Spencer, S. J., Steele, C. M., and Diane, M. (1999). Stereotype threat and women's math performance. *Journal of Experimental Social Psychology, 35,* 4–28.

Steele, C. M. (1997). A threat in the air: How stereotypes shape intellectual identity and performance. *American Psychologist, 52,* 613–629.

Steele, C. M., and Aronson, J. (1995). Stereotype threat and the intellectual test performance of African Americans. *Journal of Personality and Social Psychology, 69,* 797–811.

Sternberg, R. J., and Grigorenko, E. L. (1997). Are cognitive styles still in style? *American Psychologist, 52,* 700–712.

Taylor, S. E., and Brown, J. D. (1988). Illusion and well-being: A social psychological perspective on mental health. *Psychological Bulletin, 103,* 193–210.

Tennen, H., and Herzberger, S. (1987). Depression, self-esteem, and the absence of self-protective attributional biases. *Journal of Personality and Social Psychology, 52,* 72–80.

Vaillant, G. E. (1993). *The wisdom of the ego.* Cambridge, MA: Harvard University Press.

Watson, D., and Clark, L. A. (1984). Negative affectivity: The disposition to experience negative emotional states. *Psychological Bulletin, 96,* 465–490.

Whitbourne, S. K. (1986). *The me I know: A study of adult identity.* New York: Springer-Verlag.

Whitbourne, S. K. (1987). Personality development in adulthood and old age: Relationships among identity style, health, and well-being. In K. W. Schaie (Ed.), *Annual review of gerontology and geriatrics* (pp. 189–216). New York: Springer.

Whitbourne, S. K. (1996). *The aging individual: Physical and psychological perspectives.* New York: Springer.

Whitbourne, S. K. (2001). *Adult development and aging: Biopsychosocial perspectives.* New York: Wiley.

Whitbourne, S. K., and Cavanaugh, J. C. (Eds.) (0000). *The aging dimension in undergraduate psychology courses: A practical guide for teaching.* Washington, DC: American Psychological Association.

Whitbourne, S. K., and Collins, K. C. (1998). Identity and physical changes in later adulthood: Theoretical and clinical implications. *Psychotherapy, 35,* 519–530.

Whitbourne, S. K., and Connolly, L. A. (1999). The developing self in midlife. In J. D. Reid and S. L. Willis (Eds.), *Life in the middle: Psychological and social development in middle age* (pp. 25–45). San Diego: Academic Press.

Whitbourne, S. K., and Hulicka, I. M. (1990). Ageism in undergraduate psychology texts. *American Psychologist, 45,* 1127–1136.

Whitbourne, S. K., and Skultety, K. M. (in press). Body image development: Adulthood and aging. In T. F. Cash and T. F. Pruzinsky (Ed.) *Body images: A handbook of theory, research, and clinical practice.* New York: Guilford.

Whitbourne, S. K., Sneed, J. R., and Skultety, K. M. (in press). Identity processes in adulthood: Theoretical and methodological challenges. *Identity: An International Journal of Theory and Research.*

Wilcox, S. (1997). Age and gender in relation to body attitudes: Is there a double standard of aging? *Psychology of Women Quarterly, 21,* 549–565.

III

Reducing Ageism and Future Directions

9

Acting Your Age
Sarit A. Golub, Allan Filipowicz, and
Ellen J. Langer

Stereotypes regarding the negative consequences of old age are widely
known and almost unconditionally accepted, at least in the West. Older
people are seen as forgetful, slow, weak, timid, and set in their ways
(Langer 1982; Levy and Langer 1994). Research suggests that children
develop negative stereotypes about old age starting at about 6 years of
age, around the same time that they develop negative stereotypes concerning race and gender (Isaacs and Bearison 1986). In their meta-
analysis of studies measuring Americans' attitudes toward aging, Kite and
Johnson (1988) found that expressions of negative stereotypes in aging
were greatest when subjects were asked to evaluate the physical attractiveness or mental competence of the elderly. Research has demonstrated
that many negative stereotypes about aging are experienced as unconscious or automatic processes (Perdue and Gurtman 1990; Rudman et al.
1999).

In addition to their impact on the way older adults are viewed or
treated, age-related stereotypes are often internalized by the elderly and
may affect their ability and willingness to engage with younger people. An
application of mindfulness theory (Langer 1989) to the issue of age-
related stereotypes may prove beneficial in understanding the ante-
cedent of such stereotypes and suggesting strategies to combat their
negative consequences.

One can process information, or carry out any other activity for that
matter, in one of two ways: mindfully or mindlessly. Mindful engagement
involves actively drawing novel distinctions, questioning new information
and its implications, and considering new information from multiple
perspectives. Mindless engagement means relying on distinctions that
have already been drawn and accepting preestablished categories as im-
mutable. The construct of mindfulness/mindlessness may be critically
important to the topic of stereotypes about the elderly at three stages:

when stereotypes are constructed and learned, primarily by the non-elderly; when stereotypes are enacted and confirmed, primarily by the elderly; and when there is an attempt to counteract the effect of the stereotypes.

In this chapter, we begin by examining four lessons from mindfulness research that may be helpful in reframing stereotypes about the elderly and counteracting their negative effects. Second, we turn to the question of how stereotype information is learned and encoded, focusing on premature cognitive commitments, framing effects, and actor-observer biases. Finally, we look at the ways in which stereotypes about the elderly are maintained by the environments in which older adults are often placed, focusing primarily on the pitfalls of self-induced dependence. Increasing awareness of processes that lead to stereotype generation, encoding, and confirmation may increase individuals' openness to mindful reconsiderations of both the elderly and the aging process.

Beyond Stereotypes: Toward a Mindful Understanding of Aging

For young children, the admonition to "act your age" is accompanied by expectations of industry, gravity, and the acceptance of responsibility. For the elderly, however, the idea of acting one's age takes on a more burdensome connotation. Ironically, older people are often expected to act more like children, relinquishing a degree of agency, responsibility, and control over their own lives. At its most extreme, the expectation that adults over a certain age will (or should) begin to "act like old people" can become oppressive, suggesting that behavior is and must be determined by a chronology over which the individual has no control. In this section, we argue for a mindful reconsideration of many of our assumptions about aging and suggest ways in which the experiences of the elderly should be reconsidered in the light of their strengths and unique perspectives on our world.

Fish cannot ride bicycles; therefore, by criteria established by bicycle riders, fish seem less competent. The difference between the (anthropomorphic) fish in this joke and the elderly lies mainly in how both the elderly and nonelderly view the relationship between an individual and his or her environment. It seems obvious to us that considering their inability to ride a bicycle as a deficit in fish is ridiculous. The utility of a bicycle should be judged by its ability to be used by a fish; the utility of a fish should not be judged by its ability to use an apparatus that was designed for organisms with two arms, two legs, and well-defined bottoms. Ironically, we often forget this hierarchy of utility when evaluating the competence of the elderly. If an older person has difficulty getting out of a car, for example, we may attribute this difficulty to the weakening of leg muscles and the loss of a sense of balance. Instead, we might consider the inadequacies of a car seat that does not swivel to allow the passenger to emerge straight up as opposed to sideways. While a focus on the inadequacies of automobiles may seem radical, consider how ridiculous it would seem to conclude that a 25 year old's difficulty riding a tricycle is due to an enlargement of the limbs and a loss of flexibility. Tricycles were not made with 25 year olds in mind; car seats were not made with 75 year olds in mind. However, that does not mean that the 75 year old is deficient when it comes to emerging from cars any more than it means that 25 year olds are incompetent at tricycle racing. We might extend this analogy to a large percentage of environments that are considered mainstream—for example, most buildings are made with steps instead of ramps; most kitchen cabinets are made for people over 5 feet 6 inches; most scissors (at least the expensive ones) are made for right-handed people. Every day, older adults are forced to negotiate an environment that was designed neither by them nor for them. A focus on external attributions for perceived deficits, or adapting the bicycle to the fish and not the other way around, might decrease negative perceptions of the elderly and might encourage creative environmental solutions that benefit people of all ages.

Similarly, the elderly's mental capacities are often evaluated as if their desires, intentions, and interests were equivalent to those of younger people. To return to the fish joke, it may also seem readily apparent to us that fish do not care much about bikes. However, such an analogy is rarely used to explain (or understand) the behavior of the elderly. When a child's parents cannot tell different cartoon characters apart or are unable to identify a top-forties hit from its opening bars, the children do not conclude that their parents have lost either their ability to recognize faces or their memory for music. Rather, they conclude (correctly) that their parents do not care about Pokemon or Brittany Spears. It is possible that older adults appear more forgetful simply because they do not care about the same things that younger people care about, including performance on memory tests. An individual who is told a piece of information and does not care about remembering it may not process that information so as to encode it in memory. If the person is later asked a question about the information and cannot answer it, has the information been forgotten? Perhaps the elderly are not more forgetful; they are simply selective encoders. It is often observed, anecdotally, that older people have intact memories of events that occurred in their childhoods but quickly eroding memories for events of the recent past. Perhaps longer-term memories are more meaningful to the elderly; this type of information was worthy of encoding in the past and is worthy of retrieval in the present. When the performance of an older person falls short on some measure, we invariably see this as a failure of the individual rather than question the relevance of the measure. And yet we never doubt the competence of the fish. What keeps nonelderly people from shifting their attention to the inadequate measure?

It is difficult to see past one's own level of development. Ask a child what it would be like to be 30 years old, and he or she will show remarkably little insight. Ask an adult what it would be like to be 80 years old, and whether we care to admit it or not, the same thing happens. The behavior of older people is often judged as if they are ascribing to the same set of values and reference points as those who perceive them. For example, older adults are often considered childlish, and some researchers have suggested that in old age, one naturally regresses to childhood status. However, there is a significant difference between the resumption of behaviors that one exhibited in the past and the enactment of these behaviors for the first time. For example, if both 7-year-old Jimmy and 97-year-old James tell a dinner guest that her stories are boring, they may be using the same words, but they are hardly exhibiting the same behavior. A mindful analysis would suggest that Jimmy is *un*inhibited, meaning that he has not yet learned the socially appropriate response to dinner conversation. In contrast, James is *dis*inhibited; he is well aware of the norms of social behavior but has chosen to ignore them. The observed similarity in the two behaviors is clearly a false equation of levels.

Not being able to see past one's own level of development, coupled with a tendency to understand behaviors in ways that are most relevant to the observer, can lead to a whole range of incorrect but stereotypically coherent attributions about elderly behavior. We suggest trying to consider other reasons for which the elderly exhibit stereotypic (and "negative") behaviors. For example, forgetfulness might be seen as the ability to focus intensely on the present, and driving slowly might reflect an accumulated wisdom of the risks involved. Those with doubts might want to observe the driving habits of someone who has just narrowly avoided a particularly messy accident.

Aging means change, but change does not mean decay. Let us mindfully reconsider the relationship between development and aging and apply this perspective to an understanding of the unique abilities of older adults. While the term *development* can be applied to changes over the entire life cycle of a person, the term is commonly taken to refer only to qualitative change in cognitive structuring and skills during the first two decades of life. The influence of this attitude is persistent. Young persons are described as "developing," whereas persons changing in their later years are typically described as "aging." It is like day and night, where *day* might formally refer to the entire twenty-four-hour span but is informally used to refer to the brighter side of day. So, too, *aging* has come to refer to the darker side of development. In this case, however, the nominal distinction has great consequence. To make changes in later life, one must fight against all sorts of consensually held preconceptions before they are recognized as growth. This struggle for legitimate recognition would be less strenuous if development were cast in other frames. Right now, our stereotypes about the negative aspects of aging prevail.

For example, an 80-year-old man is frustrated by the fact that he can no longer play tennis the way he could when he was 50. But perhaps the problem is not that he can no longer play the same way, but that he is still trying to do so. Venus Williams, who is 6 feet 3 inches and has one of the largest grip sizes in women's tennis, and Amanda Coetzer, who is 5 feet 2 inches and has one of the smallest, cannot possibly play with comparable strategies, nor would it occur to them to do so. However, Coetzer is well aware that her small stature allows her to be quick on the court, and Williams understands that her height gives her stroke tremendous power. Because his social environment and mindless encoding of stereotypes has taught the 80-year-old tennis player that his game is aging, not developing, it may never occur to him to adapt his game based on the identification of new skills. Because differences between young and old people are taken not as differences but as decrements, we are not likely to find ways that older people might metaphorically change their game. If we do begin to notice such potential adaptations, we might still make the mistake of seeing these changes as compensatory, instead of looking for ways in which they might be advantageous to individuals of all ages.

One way to encourage this mind-set among both young and older individuals might be to encourage the generation of social comparisons in a wide spectrum of domains. Chronology aside, age is relative and may vary depending on the domain in question. Mary may feel old when playing bridge with her neighbors but young when playing Monopoly with her grandchildren, and even younger when playing French horn in the community orchestra. Certain contexts place labels on older people that then become difficult to escape. The more that older and younger adults are able to see themselves and each other in a variety of social contexts, taking on a diversity of social roles, the more each will be viewed mindfully.

The relationship between age-related changes and physical and mental decline is not a universal truth. We (Levy and Langer 1994) recruited young and elderly members of two communities that hold their aged members in high esteem: the mainland Chinese and American Deaf. The hypothesis was that if negative views contribute to memory loss in old age, and Deaf and Chinese people hold more positive views of aging than American hearing people, the Deaf and Chinese individuals should show less memory loss with aging. This hypothesis was confirmed; elders in both the mainland Chinese and American Deaf cultures outperformed the American hearing elders on four memory tasks. If memory loss in old age were determined only by a biological mechanism of decay, the old of these two cultures would not be expected to demonstrate better memory skills than the old American participant. The results indicate that age-related changes do not inevitably mean decline. Research on memory loss in general bears out this conclusion. Although some researchers have argued that such a decline is inevitable and have documented consistent trends (Baddeley 1986; Johansson, Zarit, and Berg 1992; Light and Burke 1988), others believe that some aspects of the deterioration of memory may be environmentally determined, shaped by expectations and social contexts (Holland and Rabbit 1992; Langer et al. 1979; Sinnett and Holen 1999).

Changing the environment can promote mindfulness. While we have argued that certain environments can perpetuate stereotypes and stereotyped behavior, there is also research that suggests that altering environments for the elderly may allow individuals to break free from stereotypical attitudes and behavior. As we showed (Langer and Rodin 1979; Rodin and Langer 1977), giving elderly patients in a nursing home autonomy to make decisions and responsibility over a plant resulted in significant differences on measures of alertness, happiness, active participation, and a general sense of well-being three weeks later. Eighteen months later, these differences had expanded not just to measures of physical and psychological health but also mortality rates (four of the forty-seven participants in the experimental group versus thirteen of the forty-four in the control group). In a somewhat similar study, Schultz (1976) found that increasing control by providing institutionalized elderly adults with the opportunity to decide when they would be visited also resulted in improvement on psychological and physical health measures.

These results were replicated in a later study (Alexander et al. 1989), where both active distinction making and transcendental meditation (predicted to enhance mindfulness after meditation practice) were used to promote mindfulness. Both mindfulness-producing groups showed marked enhancement in intellectual functioning and physical health. They also exhibited an increase in perceived control, felt significantly younger, and were rated by nurses as improved on mental health. Further, both groups appeared to live longer during the three-year follow-up period: none of the subjects in the transcendental meditation group and 12.5 percent in the active distinction-making mindfulness group died, as opposed to 28.8 percent of those in the comparison groups and 37.5 percent of the remaining elderly adults ($N = 478$) in the institutions studied during the follow-up period. These findings suggest that creating environments in which the elderly are challenged to counteract stereotypes rather than expected to express them may diminish their negative effects.

Relatedly, it is possible that encouraging mindful approaches to the world may reduce prejudice and stereotyping by increasing discrimination not *against* persons but *between* them. Mindfulness through active distinction making about a given individual prevents one characteristic from dominating or defining them. As such, global characteristics such as "Tom and Joan are old" might become more differentiated, and may be perceived as specific attributes of an individual rather than a class of persons: "Tom has gray hair and whistles; Joan wears red nail polish and walks with a cane." For example, the correlation between apparent age and chronological age is likely to be exaggerated as a result of illusory correlation. Consider the fact that while older people are more likely to have gray hair than younger persons, we can all think of exceptions. However, the strangers we see every day are typically taken as confirmation of this hypothesis; young people with gray hair are assumed to be chronically older than they are, and old people with darker hair are assumed to be younger. So the correlation may not be nearly as high as we presume (Rodin and Langer 1980). The same would be true for characteristics and abilities. By noticing increasing distinctions about individuals in the world around us, we may improve our ability to discriminate among them and our understanding of the futility of arbitrary categorizations.

Langer, Bashner, and Chanowitz (1985) tested a mindful intervention designed to increase active distinction drawing among sixth graders in terms of its impact on attitudes toward disabled others. The mindfulness manipulation in this study consisted of four exercises spread over four days. In the first exercise, children were shown slides of individuals with and without disabilities in specific jobs and asked to write down four reasons that the person depicted in the slide might be good at his or her profession and four reasons that he or she might be bad at it. Children in the low-mindfulness condition were asked to list only one reason. In the second exercise, children were asked either to list as many ways as they could to solve a specific problem faced by a disabled person (high-mindfulness group) or whether the problem could be solved (low-mindfulness group). In the third exercise, children were shown a slide and given a brief description of an event (e.g., a girl spilling coffee) and asked to come up with several different explanations for the event (high-mindfulness group) or one explanation. For the high-mindfulness group, the number of explanations required was increased throughout the training. Finally, the last exercise consisted of asking several aspects (high-mindfulness) or one aspect (low-mindfulness) of one role (e.g., four ways to enjoy a trip, five alternatives for a possible job).

Children in the high-mindfulness condition were more likely to recognize function-specific competencies of the disabled than were the remaining groups. For example, they were more likely to choose a blind partner for a game of Pin the Tail on the Donkey and a partner in a wheelchair for a wheelchair race. They were also less likely to avoid the disabled person overall. The high-mindfulness group who had been exposed to pictures of disabled people expressed the most interest in attending a picnic with those people. The extension of these results to the elderly is easily seen.

Mindfulness on the part of elderly holders of an age-related stereotype could also be beneficial. Remember that mindfulness allows one to notice more ways in which he or she is different from others. In this way, an older person could realize ways in which he or she is like other older people, but more important, ways in which he or she is different, negating the applicability of stereotypes.

We are not suggesting that older adults do not face real difficulties associated with aging or that certain phenomena that have been observed as part of the development of the mind and body toward the end of the life cycle do not exist. However, both the elderly and the not yet elderly might be better off by questioning the applicability of age-sensitive measures of competence, realizing that one cannot see past one's own level of development, accepting that aging means change but not necessarily decay, and promoting autonomy, active distinction making, and sensitivity to context in ourselves and those around us.

Mindful Acceptance of Age-Related Stereotypes

Let us now address the issue from a slightly different angle and examine how premature cognitive commitments, or the mindless acceptance of information, can lead people to form, and then to fall victim to, stereotypes about aging. Research suggests that information is more likely to be processed mindfully if it is learned within a context that satisfies one of the following conditions: it is personally relevant, it requires cognitive effort, or it contradicts previous experience or beliefs. (Langer 1989, 1997; Chanowitz and Langer 1981). While most of us are aware of the fact that we are getting older with the passage of each birthday, many of us ignore the possibility that we will someday "grow old." Therefore, although information about the elderly will be important in the future, few young people have the perspective to appreciate this information in their youth. When individuals are presented with information that is apparently irrelevant to them, there is no reason for them to examine it critically, since cognitive efforts would seem to be better spent dealing with relevant matters. In abstaining from a critical examination of the information, the individual may prematurely commit himself or herself to the unconditional "truth" of the information, and this rigid representation of the information is then encoded for future reference. This type of mindless encoding has been termed a *premature cognitive commitment* (Chanowitz and Langer 1981). Premature cognitive commitments are defined as beliefs that are accepted unconditionally, without benefit of consideration or awareness of alternative interpretations of the information. Once a person processes information unconditionally and forms a premature cognitive commitment, his or her understanding of the information becomes fixed, making it unlikely that the person would be willing to reconsider the information, even when such reconsideration would be beneficial. In fact, once a person makes a premature cognitive commitment, this type of cognition may affect not only one's mind-set but one's behavior as well.

Chanowitz and Langer (1981) used a two-by-two design to test the hypothesis that information must be viewed as relevant or must be processed with cognitive effort in order to be encoded mindfully. Subjects were given information about a (fictional) perceptual deficit called chromosintosis. Chromosintosis was described as similar to dyslexia or color-blindness, in that one can be affected by the deficit without being aware of it and that an appeal to one's own senses would not make the disease apparent. Relevance was manipulated by telling subjects that this deficit was either rare (only 10 percent of the population is affected by it) or widespread (over 80 percent of the population is affected by it). It was expected that this type of prevalence data would make the information about the disorder either irrelevant to subjects in the "rare" condition (because if it affects only 10 percent of the population, chances are they did not have it) or relevant to subjects in the "widespread" condition (because if 80 percent of people like them have it, chances are they do too).

The degree of cognitive effort was manipulated by instructing subjects in each relevance condition to think about ways they might cope with the disorder if they had it. The remaining half was not giving the coping instructions. All subjects were then given a perceptual test in which they were led to discover that they had the disorder. It was hypothesized that only the group that originally thought that it was unlikely that they would have the disorder, and was not instructed to generate strategies for coping with it (irrelevant—no cognitive effort condition), would display subsequent deficits, in accordance with the information they had been given about the disorder. These deficits would be a reflection of the mindless, and therefore unquestioning, way in which they had originally processed the information. A subsequent performance test that required the use of abilities that the subjects in fact possessed, but ones they had been told that individuals who have the disorder do not, revealed strong support for the hypothesis. Relative to the other three groups who had mindfully processed information, either because it was perceived as relevant or because they were asked to engage cognitively with it, the irrelevant–no cognitive effort condition showed severe decrements in performance. A subsequent study showed similar results, but this time using a perceptual skill rather than a deficit. Mindful encoding of information, either through making it relevant or expending cognitive effort, would reduce stereotype formation.

A third way in which stereotype formation might be avoided would be to gain personal (and disconfirming) experience with the stereotype target. Hale (1998) conducted a study in which she surveyed fifty young (18 to 25 years of age) and fifty older (64 to 79 years of age) adults about their degree of contact with the elderly and their belief in aging stereotypes. She found no significant differences in stereotype scores between young and old participants; however, both young and older participants who experienced high levels of contact with the elderly evinced lower stereotype scores. Of course, mere contact is not enough to counter stereotyping. The contact must be engaged in mindfully (Amir 1969; Pettigrew 1997).

We would expect young people to encode stereotypes about old age as premature cognitive commitments to the extent that stereotype information is not processed mindfully. This will happen because the information is not perceived as personally relevant, processing the information does not require cognitive effort, and counterexamples are not readily available. Once a person makes a premature cognitive commitment, however, this type of cognition may affect not only one's mind-set but one's behavior as well. For example, consider the younger person for whom his or her own old age has no psychological reality who is told that senility accompanies old age and is characterized by forgetfulness. If the information is initially accepted unconditionally, what happens later if this initially irrelevant information becomes relevant?

As occurred in the chromosintosis study, mindlessly encoded stereotypes about aging might act as a self-induced prime, causing individuals to act in ways that are consistent with these premature cognitive commitments when they perceive themselves to be aging. Bargh, Chen, and Burrows (1996) showed that stereotypes about the elderly can affect the behavior of college students. Undergraduates were primed with stereotypes about the elderly by solving scrambled sentences that included words such as *forgetful, Florida,* and *bingo.* Following the prime, students were timed as they walked to the elevator. Compared to students who had been primed with unrelated stimuli, students who had been primed with old age walked significantly slower. Imagine the strength of this effect on someone who is no longer 20. Consider a situation in which an older man spends the day working with his granddaughter in the garden and wakes up the next morning with a sore back. Because he knows that older people are likely to have aches and pains, he attributes his sore back to his advanced age. This association, "My back hurts; I must be old," can act as a self-generated prime, causing the grandfather to walk more slowly than the sore back would dictate, which in turn confirms additional age-related stereotypes. Because of the grandfather's premature cognitive commitments, it never occurs to him to discover that his granddaughter awoke with an equally sore back, which she attributed to four hours of weeding.

Similarly, it is possible that when a younger person who has initially mindlessly processed stereotypes about aging becomes elderly and finds himself or herself forgetting things, he or she may attribute this forgetfulness to senility, and begin to behave as if senile. Prematurely committing oneself to an unconditional relationship between a cue in the environment (forgetting) and the behavioral response that it calls for (acting senile) will then direct a person's behavior in a fixed way directed by the original information. It would not occur to the person that there are possibly more efficient ways of defining and responding to that cue. Once the link between the cue and the behavior has been accepted, suggestions of the contingent nature of that relationship may not be effective. The premature cognitive commitment may make subsequent suggestions by others appear to be rationalizations or well-meant but untrue palliatives, since they are after the fact.

Premature cognitive commitments are not the same as self-fulfilling prophecies. They are beliefs that are accepted unconditionally, usually because the information seems irrelevant to the person hearing it. Later, when conditions change and the information becomes relevant to the person, he or she acts as if it were true, creating a self-fulfilling prophecy.

We (Langer et al. 1988) assessed the relationship between premature cognitive commitments one made about aging and the success of one's own aging. Elderly subjects who had lived with a grandparent before they were 2 years old were compared with those who had lived with a grandparent after they were age 13 (the age of the parents was held constant). For the former group, the grandparents were likely to be and act younger than for the latter group. Thus, the former group should have more "youthful" premature cognitive commitments about old age than the latter group; therefore, the younger group should act out a "younger" version of old age. Indeed, this was found to be true. The elderly subjects were independently evaluated by raters unaware of our hypothesis; those whose earliest premature cognitive commitments were youthful were considered more alert. There was also a tendency for them to be more active and more independent. The results suggest that many of us inadvertently may have been taught to grow old inadequately.

The Downward Spiral of Stereotype Confirmation

Information about the elderly tends to be accepted uncritically, mainly because it seems irrelevant to us at the time of encoding. Later, when that information becomes salient, we use it as if it were true to guide our behavior. Having blindly accepted that old people walk more slowly, we end up walking more slowly as soon as cues in the environment make our more advanced age salient. We then take the reduced walking speed as further proof of both our age and the truth of the stereotype. We now examine the second cycle that promotes stereotype confirmation: self-induced dependence. Self-induced dependence, driven by stereotypic labels, unnecessary helping, or doubts about one's competence, leads to decrements in performance, which leads to more dependence.

It has long been known that it is often not the exercise of control that is important but rather the belief (veridical or not) that if one wanted to, one could exercise control in a given situation. If a person is used to exercising control and either environmental constraints or physical limitations deny this opportunity, in the majority of cases that person will soon perceive the loss. The familiar concept of learned helplessness describes a situation in which once individuals experience a situation in which they are unable to control their environment, they often continue to act in this manner even when such perceptions are incorrect (Seligman 1975; Seligman and Maier 1976). The concept of self-induced dependence refers to the process through which an individual erroneously infers his or her own incompetence from situational factors. Research has shown that individuals can erroneously infer similar types or levels of incompetence from seemly innocuous interpersonal cues, such as being assigned a label the connotes inferiority, engaging in a previously performed task that is now performed by another, or simply permitting personal assistance. These interpretations have been hypothesized to result in self-induced dependence if the factors are salient to the person involved (Langer and Imber 1979).

The label *elderly* or *old,* according to the broadly accepted stereotype, connotes incompetent. What happens when you call someone elderly? Langer and Benevanto (1978) had individuals engage in and be successful at a given task (solving math puzzles) and then asked them to perform a second task while assigned to either the superior role of "boss" or the inferior role of "assistant." Individuals then repeated a task that was similar to the first. In spite of their earlier success on the first task, individuals given the inferior role of assistant showed a decrement in performance relative to those who were assigned the role of boss.

Several points of this study need to be emphasized. First, individuals in the inferior condition did not simply try less hard. There were no differences in performance between the assistants or bosses during the second task, when the subjects were asked to assume these two roles. Second, receiving a label of inferiority (assistant) reduced performance on a subsequent task in spite of prior success on that task. Third, this decrement in performance held even when the label of inferiority was explicitly assigned at random.

Stereotypic labels can lead to both increments and decrements in performance, even when presented subliminally or outside of conscious

awareness. Levy (1996) found that activating positive or negative stereotypes associated with old age can differentially affect performance on
tasks that are thought to decline with age: memory performance and
memory self-efficacy. An intervention designed to subliminally activate
negative stereotypes about aging worsened memory performance and
self-efficacy, whereas the opposite effect was found when positive stereotypes were subliminally activated. It is possible that environments that
subtly reinforce age-related stereotypes through environments or interactions designed to "help" the elderly may actually be exacerbating deficits.

Langer and Benvento (1978) hypothesized that self-induced dependence can come not only from receiving an inferior label but also from engaging in a consensually defined demeaning task, no longer engaging in
a previously performed task that is now engaged in by another, or allowing someone else to do something for one. A study conducted by Avorn
and Langer (1982) tested the hypothesis that "overhelping" can lead individuals to infer their own helplessness and incompetence, causing
them to do poorly at a task that they had previously been able to accomplish. Nursing home residents were given ten-piece jigsaw puzzles, spe-
cially designed to require basic skills such as hand-eye coordination,
manual dexterity, and the use of strategy. Seventy-two residents consented
to participate in the study, and each was given a pretest trial of puzzle as-
sembly performance. Then residents were randomized into three groups:
(1) the *encouraged-only* condition, in which an experimenter sat with the
subject and offered encouragement while he or she solved the puzzle; (2)
the *helped* condition, which was similar to the encouraged condition, but
the experimenter also actively assisted in finding correct pieces, suggesting where they should be placed, and at times even solving the puzzle
"with" the subject; and (3) *no contact*, in which subjects has no puzzle sessions other than the pretest and posttest trials.

Subjects in the helped condition completed fewer pieces on the
posttest before giving up than subjects in either of the other two groups,
and despite the practice sessions, they performed less well on the posttest
than they had on the pretest. Subjects in the other two conditions performed better on the posttest. In addition, subjects in the helped condition were significantly less confident that they would be able to complete
similar puzzles in the future and ranked the task as significantly more difficult than those in the encouraged-only condition. From these findings,
the authors concluded that a helping intervention reduced the subjects'
ability to perform the task themselves.

Situations where one's competence can be called into question makes one particularly vulnerable to self-induced dependence and stereotype-confirming cycles. When one first approaches a task, one is necessarily attentive to its particulars. As the task is repeated, practiced, and mastered, the components of the task may coalesce to form a cohesive unit. People who know how to drive cars with manual transmission often describe getting "the feel" of the clutch, but may have difficulty describing exactly what steps their legs, feet, and arms take to shift into first when stopped on an incline. Repeated practice with a task, to the point in which it can be performed almost mindlessly, may produce an ironic loss of knowledge. Following complete mastery, an individual may often be in the position of knowing that he or she can perform a given task without being able to articulate fully the steps required to accomplish it. When future circumstances lead people to question their competence at the same task, they may misinterpret their inability to articulate the components of the task as proof of incompetence. This hypothesis was tested explicitly in set of studies by Langer and Imber (1979). Subjects were introduced to a task and assigned to one of three conditions: no practice, moderate practice, or overpractice. Then subjects were asked to perform a different task in which they were given one of two label assignments: assistant or boss. Finally, subjects were asked to return to the original task, and perform it again. Subjects who were labeled assistants performed poorly in both the overlearned condition and in the no-practice condition, while moderate-practice groups did not seem to be affected by the assistant label. When external factors (i.e., the assistant label) led subjects to question their competence, only the moderate-practice group was able to summon the evidence that they could perform the task (call up the steps necessary to perform it). While younger people might not be likely to question their competence at tasks they have mastered, older adults may be more vulnerable to stereotypes that label them as incompetent. Overexposure to these types of labels, especially in the context of other tasks in which it is assumed they are in need of assistance, may cause the elderly to question their own competence and may even affect their performance.

At its most extreme, aging stereotypes may be internalized to the extent that they interfere with the value that the elderly place on their own lives. A recent study primed old and young adult subjects with negative or positive stereotypes of old age. Subjects were asked to make a medical decision in a hypothetical situation involving the acceptance or rejection of life-prolonging treatment. Positively primed older subjects were more likely to accept the treatment; negatively primed older subjects were more likely to reject it (Levy, Ashman, and Dror 2000).

Conclusion: A New Meaning of Acting Your Age

We have argued that stereotypes about aging are processed mindlessly by individuals in their youth and that this mindless encoding may lead to erroneous perceptions about the elderly and even the enactment of learned stereotypes as one ages. Further, mindlessly encoded stereotypes can lead to treatment of elderly in ways that perpetuate these stereotypes and to the creation of social environments that accentuate their prevalence. Such stereotypes are manifest in the environments in which older people are often placed at two levels: in terms of the institutional structure of the environments themselves and in terms of the one-on-one interactions fostered by such environments. Thus, stereotypical perceptions of helplessness, weakness, and forgetfulness in old age, held by the elderly and those around them, who cannot see beyond their own level of development, can be as disabling as actual physical and mental deficits, or even more so.

A mindful reconsideration of both the vicious cycle of stereotype encoding, confirmation, and expression and of the underpinnings of aging stereotypes themselves provides a more hopeful view. By questioning aging stereotypes, we free ourselves from their mindless repetition and fulfillment. By reexamining the bases for judgments about the elderly, we improve our ability to look beyond our own level of development. By increasing awareness of the role of environmental standards and cues, we improve our ability to foster environments that promote personal growth. A mindful understanding of "acting your age" necessarily acknowledges that such actions are different for different individuals and in different contexts. Increased mindfulness on the part of individuals of all ages will encourage a focus on positive change and development throughout the life span. Moreover, it should lead us to an increased awareness of instances in which a reexamination of what are currently perceived as decrements may actually reveal more evolved behavior and perspective.

References

Alexander, C., Langer, E., Newman, R., Chandler, H., and Davies, J. (1989). Aging, mindfulness and meditation. *Journal of Personality and Social Psychology, 57,* 950–964.

Amir, Y. (1969). Contact hypothesis in ethnic relations. *Psychological Bulletin, 71,* 319–342.

Avorn, J., and Langer, E. (1982). Induced disability in nursing home patients: A controlled trial. *Journal of American Geriatric Society, 30*(6), 397–400.

Baddeley, A. (1986). *Working memory.* New York: Oxford University Press.

Bargh, J. A., Chen, M., and Burrows, L. (1996). Automaticity of social behavior: Direct effects of trait construct and stereotype activation on action. *Journal of Personality and Social Psychology, 71*(2), 230–244.

Chanowitz, B., and Langer, E. (1981). Premature cognitive commitment. *Journal of Personality and Social Psychology, 41,* 1051–1063.

Hale, N. M. (1998). Effects of age and interpersonal contact on stereotyping of the elderly. *Current Psychology: Developmental, Learning, Personality, Social, 17*(1), 28–47.

Holland, C., and Rabbit, P. (1992). Effects of age-related reductions in processing resources on text recall. *Journal of Gerontology: Psychological Sciences, 47,* 129–137.

Isaacs, L., and Bearison, D. (1986). The development of children's prejudice against the aged. *International Journal of Aging and Human Development, 23,* 175–194.

Johansson, B., Zarit, S., and Berg, S. (1992). Changes in cognitive functioning of the oldest old. *Journal of Gerontology: Psychological Sciences, 47,* 75–80.

Kite, M. E., and Johnson, B. T. (1988). Attitudes toward older and younger adults: A meta-analysis. *Psychology and Aging, 3*(3), 233–244.

Langer, E. (1982). Old age: An artifact? In S. Kiesler and J. McGaugh (Eds.), *Aging: Biology and behavior.* New York: Academic Press.

Langer, E. (1989). *Mindfulness.* Reading, MA: Addison-Wesley.

Langer, E. (1997). *The power of mindful learning.* Reading, MA: Addison-Wesley.

Langer, E., Bashner, R., and Chanowitz, B. (1985). Decreasing prejudice by increasing discrimination. *Journal of Personality and Social Psychology, 49,* 113–120.

Langer, E., and Benevento, A. (1978). Self-induced dependence. *Journal of Personality and Social Psychology, 36,* 886–893.

Langer, E. J., and Imber, L. (1979). When practice makes perfect: Debilitating effects of overlearning. *Journal of Personality and Social Psychology, 37,* 2014–2025.

Langer, E., Perlmuter, L., Chanowitz, B., and Rubin R. (1988). Two new applications of mindlessness theory: Alcoholism and aging. *Journal of Aging Studies, 2*(3), 289–299.

Langer, E., and Rodin, J. (1979). The effects of enhanced personal responsibility for the aged: A field experiment in an institutional setting. *Journal of Personality and Social Psychology, 34,* 191–198.

Langer, E., Rodin, J., Beck, P., Weinman, C., and Spitzer, L. (1979). Environmental determinants of memory improvement in late adulthood. *Journal of Personality and Social Psychology, 37,* 2003–2013.

Levy, B. (1996). Improving memory in old age through implicit self-stereotyping. *Journal of Personality and Social Psychology, 71*(6), 1092–1107.

Levy, B., Ashman, O., and Dror, I. (2000). To be or not to be: The effects of aging stereotypes on the will to live. *Omega—Journal of Death and Dying, 40*(3), 409–420.

Levy, B., and Langer, E. (1994). Memory advantage for deaf and Chinese elders: Aging free from negative premature cognitive commitments. *Journal of Personality and Social Psychology, 66*(6), 989–997.

Light, L., and Burke, D. (1988). Patterns of language and memory in old age. In L. Light and D. Burke (Eds.), *Language, memory, and aging* (pp. 241–271). Cambridge: Cambridge University Press.

Perdue, C. W., and Gurtman, M. B. (1990). Evidence for the automaticity of ageism. *Journal of Experimental Social Psychology, 26*(3), 199–216.

Pettigrew, T. F. (1997). Generalized intergroup contact effects on prejudice. *Personality and Social Psychology Bulletin, 23,* 173–185.

Rodin, J., and Langer, E. (1977). Long-term effects of a control-relevant intervention among the institutionalized aged. *Journal of Personality and Social Psychology, 35,* 897–902.

Rodin, J., and Langer, E. (1980). Aging labels: The decline of control and the fall of self-esteem. *Journal of Social Issues, 36,* 12–29.

Rudman, L. A., Greenwald, A. G., Mellott, D. S., and Schwartz, J. L. K. (1999). Measuring the automatic components of prejudice: Flexibility and generality of the Implicit Association Test. *Social Cognition, 17*(4), 437–465.

Schulz, R. (1976). Effects of control and predictability on the psychological well-being of the institutionalized aged. *Journal of Personality and Social Psychology, 33,* 563–573.

Seligman, M. E. P. (1975). *Helplessness.* San Francisco: Freeman.

Seligman, M. E. P., and Maier, S. F. (1976). Learned helplessness: Theory and evidence. *Journal of Experimental Psychology: General, 103,* 3–46.

Sinnett, E. R., and Holen, M. C. (1999). Assessment of memory functioning among an aging sample. *Psychological Reports, 84*(1), 339–350.

10

Will Families Support Their Elders? Answers From Across Cultures

Sik Hung Ng

When life was short, people carried on working to support themselves (and others) until they dropped. When only a handful of the population could survive beyond working age, they posed no unbearable burden to the rest of society. But times have changed. The postwar baby boomers can expect to live well beyond the retirement age (usually but not always at 65), and their children and grandchildren will live even longer. The older sector of the population (those over age 65) has increased in both absolute numbers and as a proportion of the general population, and the trend will accelerate for the next twenty years and beyond. In short, the age wave is already upon a large part of today's world, giving new urgency to the age-old question: Who will support the old?

In principle, there are four possible answers to the question: the state, the seniors themselves, a third party, or, sadly, no one. The first three, of course, are not mutually exclusive but can be combined in varying proportions. Let us take a look at history. In ancient Rome and Greece, seniors themselves were the answer (Parkin 1998). A rugged individualism underlined this type of self-support, best captured in the words of Cicero in 44 B.C.: "Old age will only be respected if it fights for itself, maintains its own rights, avoids dependence on anyone, and asserts control over its own to the last breath" (Parkin 1998, p. 38). Despite the rugged individualism and contrary to the stereotype of elder neglect in western countries, family support, encouraged by Christianity, has long been in place alongside self-support (Hashimoto and Kendig 1992).

In ancient China, where interdependent familial relations between the young and the old prevailed over individualism and the quest for personal independence, seniors were supported by a third party comprising primarily younger family members. In all three places cited, the state moralized about family obligations without entering into a formal support system as a provider. The latter development came about only after the turn of the twentieth century.

The social welfare era as we know it is relatively new by historical standards, and it is already coming to a close in the United States (since Reagan), the United Kingdom (since Margaret Thatcher), New Zealand (since Douglas) and China (since market reforms in the 1980s), to name but a few. In New Zealand, for example, a married couple's superannuation entitlement declined from 89 percent of the national average wage in 1986 to 67 percent in 1997. The retrenchment of state support is partly a response to the ageist perception, rightly or wrongly, of the increasing number of longer-living pensioners as an economically unsustainable and ideologically undesirable burden on the state. This retrenchment will inevitably cause a shift in income-maintenance and health care responsibilities from the state back to seniors themselves or a third party, such as family members. The pendulum of change is on its way back to ancient times.

But if the state finds it economically unaffordable to support seniors and ideologically uncomfortable even if it were able to, would the situation be any easier for seniors and third parties? Clearly the question has multiple facets. Some of the crucial facets have to do with the wealth of the nation, ideology, workforce participation, and demography. More than that, the senior rights movement in the United States has clearly demonstrated that political processes, issues of intergenerational equity, and societal ageism are also intimately involved (Powell, Williamson, and Branco 1996). Ageism in the workplace has meant that older workers who stay on past the traditional retirement age are being looked at suspiciously as having passed their prime or as selfishly hanging on to their jobs at the expense of younger (and more deserving?) workers. The cumulative effect due to insecurity of work income in old age and reduced pension is that seniors may find it harder and harder to remain self-sufficient or independent. Without belittling the resourcefulness of seniors to take care of themselves, there is a need to explore support from third parties. In this chapter, because of the traditional importance of family support, I focus on families as a source of support and review cross-cultural studies that have made use of the traditional Chinese concept of filial piety.

Family Support

Largely as a result of industrialization and urbanization, most families living in urban areas today are monogenerational except when parents have dependent children living with them. Fragmentation of the dual or multi-generational family structure calls into question the viability of the family to function as a central element in the informal support system for elderly family members.

A further complication is the increasing number of reconstituted or blended families made up of individuals from two or more previous marriages. From the point of view of the children, their "parents" now comprise a biological parent and a stepparent who live with them, but also a biological parent who does not. Are they supposed to support all three in their old age? Research in this new and important area yields complex results indicating a fluid situation affected not only by kinship and genetic ties but also legal considerations and the quality of interpersonal relationships (Coleman and Ganong 1997; Ganong and Coleman 1998; Ganong et al. 1998).

Concurrent with those family changes, age peers have become the focal point of social life outside the family and have largely displaced older family members as the principal reference group (Chudacoff 1989). The resultant generational gap raises serious questions about the willingness of younger family members to support family elders.

A big difference between family support and support from the formal system is the nature of social-emotional relations that mediate the provision and uptake of support. Family support is provided out of a sense of obligation that goes back to childhood attachment bonds, whereas support from the formal system is more of a job or a vocation, whether it is performed by professionals (e.g., doctors, nurses, police officers), semi-professionals (e.g., home carers) or bureaucrats (e.g., pension officers). Family transactions occur in a particular social-emotional relationship that is highly personal and relatively long-lasting. On the downside, the personal nature of family relationship may make exit from the relationship difficult, and as a result, it creates strain on younger family members who have to provide long-term support year in and year out. Financially, such long-term support may bankrupt the young; support in other areas of need such as disabilities, nursing care, or mental deficits can be just as crippling if it too is long term without a break. The strain gets worse, and exit from it more difficult, if the younger family members are providing the support under emotional blackmail. It takes courage out of years of endurance and suffering to call on support from the formal system. For family elders depending on the particular family relationships, there is the possibility of unmet expectations and, just as bad if not worse, feigned support aimed at inheritance or asset stripping and even outright abuse.

Despite those shortcomings and risks, family support remains irreplaceable amid the ebb and flow of institutionalized care, deinstitutionalization, and community care, whether it is in the United States (Litwak 1985), China (Mok and Xiong 1998), Hong Kong (Chow 2001), or New Zealand (Prime Ministerial Task Force on Positive Ageing 1997). Within the family, younger family members (adult children and their spouses) remain an important group of caregivers, second only after the elder's spouse but ahead of friends and neighbors. Hashimoto and Kendig (1992, p. 3) sum up the overall situation this way: "As people move through their lives in a changing world, it is principally through families that they receive and provide support to those who came before them, and those who follow after them. The importance of family support has been recognized further given that the Welfare State has not solved the health and welfare problems in the industrial countries."

Thus, it behooves researchers to understand support for elders by younger family members, its strengths and weaknesses, or the lack of it as the case may be. Crucially, researchers need to develop conceptual models for differentiating various aspects of support. The family, as an element of the third party, can provide particular aspects of support but not others, whereas other third-party elements, such as neighbors, friends, and community care, may play various complementary roles (Litwak 1985).

In a major work on family function and change, Kagitcibasi (1989) distinguished between material and emotional support ("interdependencies"). In principle, families may be high on both types of interdependencies (pattern X), low on both (pattern Z), or high on one and low on the other. Pattern Z is often taken to be the destiny of Western technological societies. This stereotype about family change is in fact a myth. "The main shift in the world" is not from X to Z, but from X to a pattern that retains emotional support as the main form of family interdependence.

In a discussion of family support in India, Gore (1992) made a similar distinction between material and emotional support, but also reminded us that a fully supportive family would also provide its elders with "meaningful familial roles" (p. 269). If elders can take part in caring for and bringing up their grandchildren, in housework, in contributing to the household income, and contributing in other ways, and be recognized and valued for such roles, they would feel as if they were an integral part of the family instead of being bored or emotionally estranged. Sadly, such familial roles may be the first to disappear when the family support system begins to break down as a result of residential separation and changing ideas about child rearing. Further "atrophy" in family support, according to Gore's (1992) hypothesis, would lead to a decline in emotional and in material support, in that order. This hypothetical order, admittedly speculative, is interesting in that it reverses the order in Kagitcibasi (1989).

If Gore's hypothetical order of family atrophy is valid, in which material support remains the last bastion of family support even after the breakdown of familial roles and emotional support, there would be some basis of success for the social policy of shifting material support from the state to the family. This may well be true in countries such as India. Indeed, a survey reported by Esterman and Andrews (1992) showed that in Fiji, the Republic of Korea, Malaysia, and the Philippines, the family remained the major source of income for as many as 40 to 70 percent of elders. Kagitcibasi's (1989) observation, on the other hand, would question the practicality of a social policy that tries to ask the family to provide for family elders' material well-being. Instead, social policy should be based on what is available: the willingness of family members to engage in emotional support for their elders, and on this basis try to mobilize families to enhance elders' quality of life and intergenerational linking. The dilemma is that the emotional function may suffer under the pressure of a social policy change that now attempts to revive the family as a viable social unit to provide material support for elders at a time when younger family members, having grown accustomed to cradle-to-grave state provisions, may not accept material support for elders as one of their filial obligations. This brings us to research on younger people's acceptance of filial obligations toward elderly family members.

Filial Piety

From a social policy perspective, it would be important to know how strongly family members believe they should fulfill particular filial obligations that have implications for government spending. These obligations are mostly material in nature, especially those relating to income maintenance and health care, that is, to assist financially and look after family elders (Binstock 1991; Gunn 1986; Hudson 1997). But emotional bonds and respect (or the lack thereof) often have an impact on these decisions and are important to the psychosocial well-being of elders, so it is important to widen the scope of research on filial obligations to cover emotional bonds and respect.

A wider perspective for thinking about filial obligations is the Confucian ethic of familial relations that covers mutual obligations between spouses, between generations (parents and children), and among members within the same generations (siblings). It is a highly elaborated code of human ethics that would, like the biblical and other religious teachings on familial obligations, provide a useful framework for thinking about the topic. In the Confucian ethic of familial obligations, primary significance has traditionally been accorded to the parent-child component, which comprises parental obligations toward their children and, reciprocally, children's obligations toward their parents. The latter, commonly known as filial piety, is regarded developmentally as the first, or the root, of all virtues (Hwang 1999; Yue 1995). It incorporates material obligations such as finance and caregiving, but more than that, it calls for (and also proscribes) a range of attitudinal and social-interactional obligations. Importantly, it extols the cultivation of a genuine reverence for elders and a concern for family honor as the motivating force behind all filial obligations. It is this attitude of reverence, more so than the fulfillment of material obligations, that distinguishes human filial piety from the humanitarian caring of one's pets. The following excerpt taken from the Analects, the most reliable source of Confucius's teachings, makes plain the point: "Tzu-yu asked about filial piety. Confucius said, 'Filial piety nowadays means to be able to support one's parents. But we support even dogs and horses. If there is no feeling of reverence, wherein lies the difference?'" (translated by Chan 1963, p. 23).

As Kim (2000) has pointed out, when interpreting an ancient text or teaching such as Confucian filial piety for social scientific research, one should go beyond mechanical translation to tease out the meaning of the text in psychological terms and scrutinize its contemporary relevance. In psychological terms, the prime value of the filial piety concept is that it captures the motivational force, emotions, and intergenerational reciprocity that underlie the support of one's own aging parents or grandparents. Nonfilial motivations and considerations, such as charity, pecuniary rewards, and vocational commitments, are less relevant to the family, although they are likely to be more applicable than filial piety to formal and community care.

Recent research has identified several attitudinal and social-interactional elements of Confucian filial piety in addition to finance and caregiving. The most common of these are respect for older family members, pleasing and making them happy, maintaining contact with them, and listening patiently to (or obeying) them (e.g., Gallois et al. 1999; Ng, Loong, Liu, and Weatherall 2000). Other filial elements relating to ancestral worship and continuation of the family line, though important in traditional societies, are generally regarded as less applicable to contemporary times and are seldom included in research (see Ho 1996; Sung 1995).

Relevant studies have shown that the six material, attitudinal, and social-interactional obligations were moderately intercorrelated (Gallois 1998; Gallois et al. 1996), suggesting that filial piety, thus measured, is a unitary concept. However, this does not necessarily imply that support for all six obligations is uniformly high or uniformly low. Instead, it is likely that some obligations are more or less strongly supported than others. Variation across obligations provides important descriptive information on how individuals hierarchically order filial obligations; equally, it facilitates the testing and developing of theoretical ideas about filial obligations for comparisons between and within cultures.

Hierarchy of Filial Obligations

In a study by Ng et al. (2000), about 100 European and 100 Chinese families in New Zealand were sampled. From each family, between one and two middle-aged parents and between one and two children completed a questionnaire containing the six filial obligations (to be answered on a five-point scale). Overall, both ethnic groups said they would support rather than not support the six obligations. However, because of the possible effect of social desirability, one can never be sure of the actual level of support. Hence, it would be more meaningful to interpret the results in terms of their relative ranks than in terms of absolute ratings. Across both ethnic groups, the same hierarchy of obligations emerged, with obedience and financial support at the bottom, care and to please in the middle, and respect and social contact at the top (see figure 10.1). In broad terms, this hierarchy is similar to that found in Beijing (Yue and Ng 1999) and several other cities around Pacific Rim countries (Gallois et al. 1999).

As obedience has been shown in studies of human values to be one of the least favored values (Chinese Cultural Connection 1987; Ng et al. 1982), any obligation that is as low as obedience, in this case financial support, can be interpreted as out of favor with people. Social-emotional support, by contrast, enjoys much greater support, particularly in the case of respect and social contact. Thus, there is self-report evidence in support of Kagitcibasi's (1989) thesis that families have opted out of material support for elders while retaining social-emotional support. The separation between material and social-emotional support, as we shall see, is stronger in Western than in Eastern cultures.

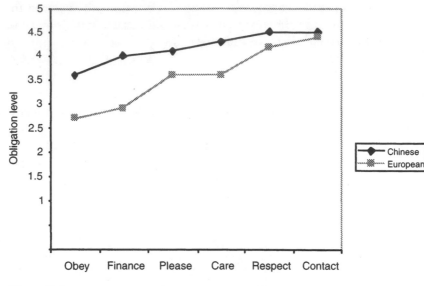

Figure 10.1
Obligations toward older parents by Chinese and Europeans.

So far only the order of filial obligations within the hierarchy has been discussed, leaving out the steepness of the hierarchy or the degree of separation among the various obligations. Ng et al. (2000) reported an interesting difference in hierarchical steepness between Chinese and European New Zealanders (see figure 10.1). Chinese had a relatively flat hierarchy, suggesting that the six elements of filial piety were still relatively intact for them. The cross-cultural difference in the steepness of the hierarchy, after ruling out statistically the possibility of acquiescence on the part of Chinese respondents, was due to Europeans' giving a significantly lower endorsement of all obligations except for social contact. In particular, Europeans were much less enthused than Chinese about financial support, obedience, and caregiving. In the light of this more finely grained finding, Kagitcibasi's (1989) thesis needs to be revised to allow for a greater degree in the retention of material obligations. It is noteworthy that even with the development of social welfare provisions in the People's Republic of China, family members are still required by law to support their family elders who are financially unable to provide for themselves (Constitution of the People's Republic of China 1982, Chapter 2, Article 49). This reflects the deeply rooted sense of financial obligation toward elders among Chinese, and possibly also among overseas

Chinese. In England (whose legal system has been closely followed in New Zealand), neither financial nor caregiving responsibilities are enjoined by law (Twigg and Grand 1998).

Correlates of Filial Obligations

Ethnic and cultural, demographic, and psychological variables are three major categories of correlate of filial piety. *Ethnicity* correlates with filial obligations in the direction of a stronger sense of family obligations for Chinese than for European New Zealanders (Ng et al. 2000). This ethnic difference is especially marked with regard to financial support, caregiving, and obedience. A study in the United States comparing Chinese, Japanese, and Korean Americans found that insofar as services and emotional support for elders are concerned, Koreans are the most pious of the three (Masako 1997). These two studies are concerned with comparisons of ethnic groups living in the same country, within either New Zealand or the United States.

Cross-country comparisons from a major Pacific Rim project revealed a pattern similar to that found in the work by Ng and associates (2000). In this Pacific Rim survey, college students from eight nations or regions were asked, among other questions, to indicate how much they would agree or disagree that young adults should fulfil the six family obligations (Gallois 1998). The results showed a systematic East-West difference between Hong Kong, Japan, the Philippines, and South Korea on the one hand, and Australia, Canada, New Zealand, and the United States on the other. Compared to Western respondents, East Asian respondents more strongly endorsed financial support, caregiving, respect, and to please, the same as that found between Chinese and Europeans in New Zealand. For social contact, Western students were more supportive than East Asian students (whereas Chinese and Europeans in New Zealand did not differ significantly on this). Obedience was not asked in the survey, but instead, "listen patiently to elders" was. On this last item, the comparison favored the West.

Several *demographic* variables have been looked at for possible correlations with filial obligations. In the study by Ng and associates (2000), generational gaps between respondent and elders and the age of respondents were found to have a strong bearing on filial obligations. The bigger the generational gap was, the weaker were the obligations. That is, middle-aged respondents' felt obligations were weaker toward their aging grandparents (bigger generational gap) than toward their aging parents (smaller generational gap); and similarly for younger respondents. Second, the older the respondents, the stronger were their felt obligations. In other words, middle-aged parents were more pious than their children. Third, contrary to gender stereotypes, females were not stronger (or weaker) than males in felt obligations. The age and gender findings contradict an American study that found an inverse age effect (felt obligations were stronger among young adult than middle-aged respondents) and a main effect of gender in favor of females (Stein et al. 1998). The differences between the two studies may be a reflection of true differences between the two countries, but this possibility remains to be tested because the two studies also differ significantly in their methodologies. For example, whereas the family was used as the unit of sampling in Ng and associates' study (2000), unrelated individuals were sampled in Stein and associates' study (1998).

Various *psychological* correlates of filial piety have been identified in research. Many of these have been reviewed by Ho (1996) and integrated under the theoretical constructs of *authoritarian moralism* and *cognitive conservatism*. In a recent study, Zhang and Bond (1998) compared the powers of universal personality traits (derived from the West) and indigenous Chinese ones in predicting filial piety among Chinese college students. Among the five factors of the universal Five Factor Inventory, Neuroticism and Openness significantly predicted filial piety. Beyond that, the indigenous personality traits of Harmony and Renqing (relational orientation) significantly improved the prediction of filial piety.

Another recent study revealed an interesting relationship between filial obligations and group-based social identity. Liu, Ng, Weatherall, and Loong (2000) obtained two separate measures of identity for their New Zealand Chinese respondents—one relating to their identification with Chinese and another relating to their identification with New Zealand, their adopted country. Chinese identity, not surprisingly, was positively correlated with filial obligations. For New Zealand identity, a similarly positive correlation with filial obligation also emerged. When a strong New Zealand identity was combined with a strong Chinese identity, adherence to filial piety was stronger still. It was only when respondents had neither a strong Chinese nor New Zealand identity would they disavow filial piety.

The identity results suggest that a strong sense of identity is more important than its particular content for the development of filial piety. In the context of Chinese immigrants, this means that both the retention of a Chinese identity and the acquisition of a New Zealand identity are compatible with filial piety. There are two Chinese sayings that capture these two identities well: "fallen leaves return to their roots" and "grow your roots where you stand." Through the former, immigrants achieve a strong sense of identity by reuniting with and reaffirming their cultural heritage; through the latter they achieve a similarly meaningful sense of identity by putting down their roots where they currently live. Either way, immigrants have a psychological home to belong to and from which they can feel secure enough to respect elders, maintain social contact with them, look after them, and so on.

Conclusion

There is evidence from the research that filial obligations now mean first and foremost respect for and maintaining social contact with older family members. The other four obligations, including health care and financial assistance, are of moderate importance only, although they are still relatively high in Asian cultures, especially among Koreans. One of the implications is that the all-too-popular myths about the East and the West—that elders in Eastern cultures are well looked after by their families, whereas those in the West are abandoned by their families—are grossly exaggerated. Another implication is that social policy that aims at encouraging families to take on material obligations does not have enough motivational support from younger family members. In Asian cultures, the policy may capitalize on the relatively high level of avowed support for material obligations; even then, the depth of *genuine* motivation to provide material support remains uncertain as the results of the New Zealand Chinese have shown (support for financial obligation is only as high as the willingness to obey elders, which can be interpreted as being low). Worse, such a policy runs the risk of straining family relations. As Szinovacz and Ekerdt (1996, p. 391) have put it, "When aging parents are not economically beholden to the wealth of their children and can maintain independent households, intergenerational relationships can be founded on sentiment and affection that are uncomplicated by financial obligation and the strain it engenders. Voluntary emotional bonds, rather than material duty, can tie older people with their adults children and grandchildren."

If a community or country can develop in the direction that Szinovacz and Ekerdt (1996) propose, the burden of filial piety would be lighter and its practice more focused on what younger family members are already most willing to do: respect and maintain social contact with family elders.

These attitudinal, social-interactional, and communicative supports (Coupland, Coupland, and Giles 1991; Ng 1998; Nussbaum et al. 1996) are just as valuable as material supports for elders to age well (Rowe and Kahn 1998). Equally, those supports and the satisfying experience of providing them would promote intergenerational solidarity and healthy mutual respect. What better way there is to reduce ageism against the old by the young, or the young by the old?

The concept of filial piety, stripped of its feudal and patriarchic overtones, can offer a useful way of looking at family support for elders. The concept is broad and for this reason can free up research beyond the narrow focus of material support. It grounds the motivational force of filial obligations in the bonding among members of a social group who partake in everyday life for years and share a common identity.

Our knowledge about the development of filial piety is extremely limited. The various correlates of it, reviewed above, suggest that cultural-political processes, socialization processes, and identification processes are involved. Given this, advances in research can best come through multidisciplinary research across nations and across subcultures within nations. As aging is rapidly becoming an issue of global concern, this calls for international cooperation in research and in the dissemination of knowledge.

References

Binstock, R. H. (1991). Aging, politics, and public policy. In B. B. Hess and E. W. Markson (Eds.), *Growing old in America* (4th ed., pp. 325–340). New Brunswick, NJ: Transaction Publishers.

Chan, W.-T. (1963). *A source book in Chinese philosophy.* Princeton, NJ: Princeton University Press.

Chinese Cultural Connection. (1987). Chinese values and the search for culture-free dimensions of culture. *Journal of Cross-Cultural Psychology, 18,* 143–164.

Chow, W. S. (2001). The practice of filial piety among the Chinese in Hong Kong. In I. Chi, N. L. Chappell, and J. Lubben (Eds.), *Elderly Chinese in Pacific Rim countries: Social support and interaction* (pp. 125–136). Hong Kong: Hong Kong University Press.

Chudacoff, H. P. (1989). *How old are you?* New Jersey: Princeton.

Coleman, M., and Ganong, L. (1997). Beliefs about women's intergenerational family obligations to provide support before and after divorce and remarriage. *Journal of Marriage and the Family, 59,* 165–176.

Coupland, N., Coupland, J., and Giles, H. (1991). *Language, society and the elderly.* Oxford: Blackwell.

Esterman, A., and Andrews, G. R. (1992). Southeast Asia and the Pacific: A comparison of older people in four countries. In H. L. Kendig, A. Hashimoto, and L. C. Coppard (Eds.), *Family support for the elderly: The international experience* (pp. 271–289). Oxford: Oxford University Press.

Gallois, C. (1998). Intergenerational communication and respect of older people around the Pacific Rim. In S. H. Ng, A. Weatherall, J. H. Liu, and C. S. F. Loong (Eds.), *Ages ahead: Promoting intergenerational relationships* (pp. 112–128). Wellington: Victoria University Press.

Gallois, C., Giles, H., Ota, H., Pierson, H. D., Ng, S. H., Lim, T. S., Maher, J., Somera, L., Ryan, E. B., and Harwood, J. (1999). Intergenerational communication across the Pacific Rim: The impact of filial piety. In J.-C. Lasry, J. Adair, and K. Dion (Eds.), *Latest contributions to cross-cultural psychology* (pp. 192–211). Lisse, Netherlands: Swets and Zeitlinger B. V.

Ganong, L., and Coleman, M. (1998). Attitudes regarding filial responsibilities to help elderly divorced parents and stepparents. *Journal of Aging Studies, 12,* 271–290.

Ganong, L., Coleman, M., McDaniel, A. K., and Killian, T. (1998). Attitudes regarding obligations to assist an older parent or stepparent following late remarriage. *Journal of Marriage and the Family, 60,* 595–610.

Gore, M. S. (1992). Family support to elderly people: The Indian situation. In H. L. Kendig, A. Hashimoto, and L. C. Coppard (Eds.), *Family support for the elderly: The international experience* (pp. 260–270). Oxford: Oxford University Press.

Gunn, P. A. (1986). Legislating filial piety: The Australian experience. *Ageing and Society, 6,* 135–167.

Hashimoto, A., and Kendig, H. L. (1992). Aging in international perspective. In H. L. Kendig, A. Hashimoto, and L. C. Coppard (Eds.), *Family support for the elderly: The international experience* (pp. 3–14). Oxford: Oxford University Press.

Ho, D. Y.-F. (1996). Filial piety and its psychological consequences. In M. H. Bond (Ed.), *The handbook of Chinese psychology* (pp. 155–165). Hong Kong: Oxford University Press.

Hudson, R. B. (1997). The history and place of age-based public policy. In R. B. Hudson (Ed.), *The future of age-based public policy* (pp. 1–22). Baltimore, MD: John Hopkins University Press.

Hwang, K.-K. (1999). Filial piety and loyalty: Two types of social identification in Confucianism. *Asian Journal of Social Psychology, 2,* 163–183.

Kagitcibasi, C. (1989). Family and socialization in cross-cultural perspective: A model for change. *Nebraska Symposium on Motivation, 37,* 135–200.

Kim, U. (2000). Indigenous, cultural, and cross-cultural psychology: A theoretical, conceptual, and epistemological analysis. *Asian Journal of Social Psychology, 3,* 265–287.

Litwak, E. (1985). *Helping the elderly: Complementary roles of informal networks and formal system.* New York: Guilford Press.

Liu, J. H., Ng, S. H., Weatherall, A., and Loong, C. S. F. (2000). Filial piety, acculturation, and inter-generational communication among New Zealand Chinese. *Basic and Applied Social Psychology, 22,* 213–223.

Masako, I. K. (1997). Intergenerational relationships among Chinese, Japanese, and Korean Americans. *Family Relations, 46,* 23–32.

Mok, B. H., and Xiong, Y. (1998). Community care for urban elderly in an aging society: A theoretical exploration of the linkage between the family, the community and the government. *Hong Kong Journal of Gerontology, 12,* 8–16.

Ng, S. H. (1998). Social psychology in an ageing world: Ageism and intergenerational relations. *Asian Journal of Social Psychology, 1,* 99–116.

Ng, S. H., Akhtar Hossain, A. B. M., Ball, P., Bond, M. H., Hayashi, K., Lim, S. P., O'Driscoll, M. P., Sinha, D., and Yang, K. S. (1982). Human values in nine countries. In R. Rath, H. S. Asthana, D. Sinha, and J. B. P. Sinha (Eds.), *Diversity and unity in cross-cultural psychology* (pp. 196–205). Lisse: Swets and Zeitlinger B. V.

Ng, S. H., Liu, J. H., Weatherall, A., and Loong, C. S. F. (1998). Intergenerational relationships in the Chinese community. In S. H. Ng, A. Weatherall, J. H. Liu, and C. S. F. Loong (Eds.), *Ages ahead: Promoting intergenerational relationships* (pp. 85–104). Wellington: Victoria University Press.

Ng, S. H., Loong, C. S. F., Liu, J. H., and Weatherall, A. (2000). Will the young support the old? An individual- and family-level study of filial obligations in two New Zealand cultures. *Asian Journal of Social Psychology, 3,* 163–182.

Nussbaum, J. F., Hummert, M. L., Williams, A., and Harwood, J. (1996). Communication and older elders. In B. R. Burleson (Ed.), *Communication yearbook* (Vol. 19, pp. 1–47). Thousand Oaks, CA: Sage.

Parkin, T. G. (1998). Ageing in antiquity: Status and participation. In P. Johnson and P. Thane (Eds.), *Old age from antiquity to post-modernity* (pp. 19–42). London: Routledge.

Powell, L. A., Williamson, J. B., and Branco, K. J. (Eds.) (1996). *The senior rights movement: Framing the policy debate in America.* New York: Twayne.

Prime Ministerial Task Force on Positive Ageing. (1997). *Facing the future.* Wellington: Department of Prime Minister.

Rowe, J. W., and Khan, R. L. (1998). *Successful aging.* New York: Pantheon Books.

Stein, C. H., Wemmerus, V. A., Ward, M., Gaines, M. E., and Jewell, T. C. (1998). "Because they're my parents": An intergenerational study of felt obligations and parental caregiving. *Journal of Marriage and the Family, 60,* 611–622.

Sung, K.-T. (1995). Measures and dimensions of filial piety in Korea. *Gerontologist, 35*, 240–247.

Szinovacz, M., and Ekerdt, D. J. (1996). Families and retirement. In R. Blieszner and V. II. Bedford (Eds.), *Aging and the family: Theory and research* (pp. 375–400). Westport, CT: Praeger.

Twigg, J., and Grand, A. (1998). Contrasting legal conceptions of family obligation and financial reciprocity in the support of older people: France and England. *Ageing and Society, 18*, 131–146.

Yue, Q. P. (1995). Filial piety and modernization. In J. Qiao and N. G. Pan (Eds.), *Chinese concepts and behavior* (pp. 123–136). Tianjin, China: Tianjin People's Press.

Yue, X., and Ng, S. H. (1999). Filial obligations and expectations in China: Current views from young and old people in Beijing. *Asian Journal of Social Psychology, 2*, 215–226.

Zhang, J., and Bond, M. H. (1998). Personality and filial piety among college students in two Chinese societies: The added value of indigenous constructs. *Journal of Cross Cultural Psychology, 29*, 402–417.

11

Reducing Ageism
Valerie Braithwaite

Ageism, used to describe "systematic stereotyping of and discrimination against people because they are old" (Butler 1969), is an umbrella concept that manifests itself in the beliefs, attitudes, expectations, attributions, and behaviors expressed by a community toward older people. The problem that ageism poses for a society increases in seriousness with the depth of its institutional creep. At the microlevel, ageist predispositions shared by a community are likely to be organized into a coherent set of cognitions and practices that are verbalized and reinforced in social contexts. If such views are widely held and systematically applied, they adversely affect the elderly population through limiting their opportunities and restricting their freedom. In the absence of resistance, ageism inevitably frames the ways in which policymakers think and shapes policy design, in effect, serving to legitimize past domination. Ultimately, ageism, if unchecked, makes it more difficult for everyone to think outside the square to reverse patterns of institutionalized passivity or dependency that have come to be regarded as part of normal aging. This describes the cultural context in which Butler coined the term *ageism* more than thirty years ago.

The facets of ageism that remain the greatest threat to the well-being of elderly people are those that are hardest to deal with: negative stereotyping, prejudice, stigmatizing behaviors, and our own fears about the aging process. Stereotypes pose a threat because they are often widely held and take on a social truth that goes unquestioned (Haslam et al. 1998). Prejudice is harmful because it is charged with negative emotion that undermines reason and destroys cooperative social relationships (Allport 1954; Harding et al. 1968). Stigmatizing behaviors are among the most potent weapons for driving people out of their communities, destroying their sense of self in the process (Crocker 1995; Goffman 1963). Finally, inability to resolve fear of aging limits the capacity to focus on others and their needs. With limited capacity to take in information and empathize with older people, cooperative problem solving and enlightened policy formulation are seriously compromised. While these different facets of ageism are challenged more than they were thirty years ago, they continue to have a presence in our communities. They reinforce each other in creating a distinct and readily recognizable social group of "older person" in our society.

Ageism, like racism and sexism, is a form of domination of one group by another that threatens social harmony. Unlike racism and sexism, the domination achieved through ageism involves rescinding the opportunities and freedom afforded in adulthood. For all these reasons, ageism is an appropriate topic for political debate and for political intervention when domination is perceived to have reached a point where shared societal values, in particular basic human rights, are violated.

The past three decades have been characterized by the active pursuit of interventions to counter ageism. Butler (1989) has identified central interventions in the war against ageism in the United States, among them (1) the sharing of knowledge to demonstrate that the elderly could be productive; (2) assurance that intergenerational conflict was not warranted over the distribution of limited resources, associated particularly with health care and income transfers; and (3) the enhancement of opportunities for older persons to take control of their lives and maintain a healthy and dignified old age. While embracing the progress that has been made in reducing ageism, Butler warned of its reemergence: "Ageism is a primitive disease, and unfortunately, our fears about ageing are so deep that ageism will probably never totally disappear" (p. 146).

Not too distant from any "-ism" are fear and the perception of threat to security. Consequently, racism, sexism, and ageism are never eliminated or resolved in a society, just managed and contained. But as Butler points out, management of ageism takes on a special dimension. The phenomenon of aging is part of the expected journey of life for all of us and brings us closer to our own mortality. Whether this realization makes us recoil in horror or zealously work to make old age better depends on one's point of view. According to Guttman (1988), medical establishments are peopled by both gerophiles who want to protect and help and gerophobes who would rather deny that old age can give rise to difficulties.

This chapter reviews ways in which the most damaging facets of ageism—stereotypes, prejudice, stigma, and fear of the aging process—can be reduced through policies and intervention programs. It considers how the different facets of ageism are interrelated and warns against addressing one facet without considering the implications for other facets. Theories of stereotyping, prejudice, stigma, and fearful aging point to different sources for the emergence of an ageist stance. In particular, fears about not having dignity in old age may have a pronounced impact on how we respond to policies that are designed to break down barriers between age-defined social groups. This problem is discussed within the context of caregiving, where problems of stigma, shame, and closeness to the negative aspects of the aging process can undermine the best-laid policy initiatives for successful aging. Finally, society's readiness and willingness to engage with the process of degeneration and loss is proposed as the new challenge that must be met if ageism in all its guises is to be kept at bay.

Reducing Negative Stereotypes of Old Age

In the tradition of Lippmann (1922), stereotypes can be defined as "societally shared beliefs about the characteristics (such as personality traits, expected behaviors, or personal values) that are perceived to be true of social groups and their members" (Stangor 1995, p. 628). Stereotypes, positive or negative, are thought to provide us with a short-cut for perceptual processing (Fiske and Neuberg 1990). They allow us to avoid the time-consuming and cognitively demanding task of sifting through information about an individual to make a judgment about that person's interests, capacities, or needs. Instead, we rely on a heuristic that tells us that people who belong to a certain group are more likely to have interests, needs, and capacities of a particular kind. The perspective of the cognitive miser provides one theoretical lens for understanding stereotyping at work.

A second theoretical perspective has focused on the social dimension of stereotyping. According to Tajfel (1981), stereotypes serve a number of social functions, all of which revolve around the notion of providing individuals with a social identity. At the microlevel, stereotypes provide us with a well-differentiated social world, regulating our behavior and enabling us to maintain a relatively positive self-view through a process of defining ourselves as part of an in-group that is distinctive, in important and valued ways, from competing out-groups. At the macrolevel, Tajfel saw stereotypes serving not only the function of defining and differentiating status groups within society, but also of explaining the relationships among these various groups. Stereotypes are a convenient tool for bestowing status on groups and can be used to make out-groups the scapegoats for society's problems. Most significant, stereotypes provide one means by which challenges to institutional legitimacy and cries of institutional injustice can be quelled. Members of society can be reassured that the problems lie outside, not within, the dominant group, and arguments for the need for social change can be discredited. In these ways, the security provided by society's institutions can be affirmed and maintained.

From either a cognitive miser or social identity perspective, policy initiatives that seek to counter stereotypes of older people need to highlight the variability in the characteristics, interests, and capacities of this age group. Resistance to persuasion may come from a number of sources. Most notably, individuals may dislike the complexity of the message, preferring the order, predictability, and efficiency that comes with knowing that someone belongs to a particular social group that can be broadly characterized in certain ways.

This type of resistance is sidestepped by initiatives that promote positive stereotypes of older age groups. Research has shown that individuals hold multiple stereotypes of older people (Brewer, Dull, and Lui 1981) that are both positive and negative (Braithwaite 1986a; Braithwaite, Gibson, and Holman 1986; Golde and Kogan 1959; Lachman and McArthur 1986; Luszcz and Fitzgerald 1986; Schmidt and Boland 1986). The portrayal of positive elderly role models through advertisements, literature, film, and news stories on television, in the papers, and on radio provide alternative images to traditional negative stereotypes. Broadening the base and nature of stereotypes about a social group so that stereotype diversity and complexity becomes the norm is one step forward in the terms Butler (1989) outlined.

Positive stereotyping to counter negative stereotyping should be recognized as only a partial answer, however. Although we know that each individual can hold a number of stereotypes, we also know that priming is crucial in determining whether a positive or negative stereotype is triggered in a particular situation. The hard problems for combating ageism arise when individuals are visibly losing their capacities to perform tasks that they had been able to perform in the past. It is unlikely to be beneficial for a perceiver to have positive stereotypes in one's repertoire of responses if the perception of failing capacities triggers a negative stereotype instead. Stereotypes are highly sensitive to context (Hummert et al. 1998), and we often have little control over the context or priming event (Bargh, Chen, and Burrows 1996).

On the other hand recent research has provided some evidence that we are not always at the mercy of our primed cognitions. Individuals are able to suppress negative stereotypes (von Hippel, Silver, and Lynch 2000). Willingness to make the effort to suppress stereotypes is likely to be bolstered by providing increased exposure to the diversity of social roles performed by the elderly population. Observing elderly people carrying out a variety of social roles has been shown to override the more restrictive stereotypes of the past (Kite 1996). As long as opportunity to contest new stereotypes is welcomed, the restrictive implications of stereotyping for individual freedom hopefully can be limited.

Reducing Prejudice toward the Elderly

A concept that is closely related to stereotypes theoretically and empirically is prejudice. Negative stereotypes of old people are likely to fuel prejudice toward the elderly and vice versa. Prejudice is used to describe "the holding of derogatory attitudes or beliefs, the expression of negative affect, or the display of hostile or discriminatory behavior toward members of a group on account of their membership in that group" (Zebrowitz 1995, p. 450). As with stereotyping, respect for individual differences disappears when prejudice comes into play. Prejudice differs from stereotypes, however, in its emphasis on affect or emotion. Stereotypes about a group have a quality of social truth and may be held as statements of fact by large segments of the population with little emotional overtone. At best, stereotypes represent ignorance, not hostility. Prejudice, on the other hand, is emotionally charged. The sources of prejudice are multiple (Allport 1954; Duckitt 1992) and the relative importance of the sources poorly understood (Agnew, Thompson, and Gaines 2000). Socialization experiences that take into account cultural history and social norms provide one source for understanding prejudice. A second approach has been psychodynamic, conceiving of prejudice as a manifestation of internal conflict and the displacement of hostility onto less powerful groups (Adorno et al. 1950). A third approach has recognized the importance of specific experiences and the interpretation of those experiences in relation to the negatively evaluated group.

Common to all these perspectives is the relevance of threat, of feeling deprived, frustrated, or hurt in some way by the presence of the other group. Prejudice is thought to be fueled by competition for limited resources and reduced by cooperative ventures where interdependency furthers the agendas of both groups (Zebrowitz 1995). Attempts to improve intergenerational relations through intergenerational cooperation have been documented in the literature. Butler (1989) has described Generations United in the United States as a program that has built a coalition across age groups that is working together to improve life prospects for children and elders alike. As governments throughout the world look to social capital as a means of strengthening care provisions, cooperative ventures across age groups are emerging. The Homeshare program, first trialed in the United States, has spread to Britain and Australia. The programs enable older people to remain in their homes and allow younger people to have rent-free accommodation in exchange for some housework and meal preparation.

Providing opportunities for different age groups to help each other is likely to meet with opposition in some quarters, particularly if the prejudice of one group toward the other is deep. Social identity theorists would argue that cooperation is dependent on the parties developing a shared social identity. Contact and communication are not enough. In this respect, openness to establishing a positive relationship to others is an important quality. Agnew, Thompson, and Gaines (2000) have shown that attitudes of openness and flexibility are important determinants of who is most likely to express prejudice toward the elderly and who is not.

Consistent with this line of argument are the findings of Galinsky and Moskowitz (2000). In their study, perspective taking, the strategy of imagining how we would feel and act if we were in the same situation as the other, increased self-other overlap when undergraduates evaluated an older target. Moreover, when the undergraduates expressed their views about the older person, they were more positive in their evaluations, and their tendency to stereotype was reduced.

Galinsky and Moskowitz (2000) have argued strongly for the superiority of perspective taking over suppression as an approach for controlling stereotyping and prejudicial behavior. They liken suppression to an avoidance response, which does nothing to cure the problem. In contrast, perspective taking is a preventive strategy that appears to forge links between young and old, at least for the duration of that particular encounter. From a practical point of view, perspective taking poses a new challenge in the quest to reduce ageism. Those who are old, middle aged, and young must find time to spend with each other, an issue to which we return later in this chapter.

According to Harding and associates (1968), prejudice is an attitude that departs from three ideal norms: the norm of rationality, the norm of justice, and the norm of human-heartedness.[1] Departure from rationality refers to persistence in relying on stereotypes even when they have been exposed, a lack of interest in uncovering new evidence, and resistance to recognizing individual differences. Departure from justice describes unequal treatment and is closely allied to discrimination, where opportunities are denied to individuals for reasons that are irrelevant to the requirements of the situation. Departure from the norm of human-heartedness is the most unusual of the three ideal norms, not because it does not exist in the community (Braithwaite and Blamey 1998) but because commonly it is not part of our scientific vocabulary. The norm of human-heartedness may be the most important norm to activate in countering ageism. It "enjoins the acceptance of other individuals in terms of their common humanity, no matter how different they may be from oneself. The acceptance is a direct personal response, in either feeling or action, and includes the area of 'private' as well as 'public' relationships" (Harding et al. 1968, p. 5). The norm of human-heartedness is society's expression of endorsement for the kind of intervention advocated by Galinsky and Moskowitz (2000) in their work on perspective taking.

Reducing Stigma in Relation to the Elderly

Stigma has been defined as any peculiar marking of the body thought to be a sign of somewhat general degeneration (English and English 1958). The definition helps focus our understanding of stigmatizing where individuals are rejected from the social group because they have an attribute that compromises their humanity in the eyes of others (Jones et al. 1984). Crocker (1995, p. 633) uses Goffman's (1963) terms to capture the essence of the concept: "the stigmatized have a 'spoiled identity.'" *Stigmatizing* and *stereotyping* are used interchangeably in the gerontological literature, but from the perspective of ageism reduction, there is merit in at least attempting to tease them apart.

All three concepts of stereotyping, behaving prejudicially, and stigmatizing involve labeling the whole person. In the case of stereotyping, the core issue is inaccurate labeling because group homogeneity is assumed and individuality is not taken into account. In short, imperfect knowledge renders the individual invisible. In the case of behaving prejudicially, the core issue is unfair labeling because truths, half-truths, and untruths are stitched together in a loose, but often indefensible, psychologic to underscore dislike for a group and domination of that group. In the case of prejudice, unsubstantiated ideology justifies derogatory treatment that renders the individual invisible. In both cases, an onlooker might question the legitimacy of the perceiver's judgment on the basis of information adequacy or distortion.

Stigmatization is different. The problem is not with the information that the perceiver takes in but rather with the perceiver's response to that information. The core issue in stigmatizing is that an individual has an attribute that is visible, in most cases uncontroversially so, and the perceiver finds the attribute so unacceptable that he or she wants the bearer out of sight. The offending attribute may be a facial blemish. Options for restoring social harmony are limited: The bearer can stay out of sight or have the blemish removed, or the perceiver can become desensitized to the blemish. When there is no evidence that the stigma poses a threat to a society, the process of desensitization would appear to be the respectful option. Desensitization should be relatively simple, providing the perceiver accepts the principle that stigmatizing another person is inappropriate. In practice, stigmas are often bolstered by prejudices and stereotypes that lend them an air of legitimacy. In such cases, convincing a group to break with stigmatizing practices may be a challenge.

The stigma of fading physical attractiveness, for instance, continues to flourish and appears to be almost the prime feeder of the beauty industry. Interestingly, the stigma is thought to affect women more strongly than men (Snyder and Miene 1994). There is little doubt that cosmetic companies and cosmetic surgeons trade on stigmatizing practices: Wrinkles and sags are visible, they are unacceptable in a world that hankers after status, and they are consequently removed from view by cosmetic companies and cosmetic surgeons for a handsome fee. High status for women demands success in battling wrinkles and sagging skin, a stigmatizing tradition that was exposed to much acclaim by Wolf in *The Beauty Myth* (1991). In spite of our assault on ageism and the support of feminism in debunking beauty truisms, wrinkles and sags remain almost universally targets to erase, not embrace.

Many personal characteristics that elicit a stigmatizing response cannot be removed or changed easily. Immobility, frailty, forgetfulness, and widowhood are among the physical, psychological, and social characteristics that are known to elicit stigmatizing responses. While these characteristics have rightly been uncoupled from aging because they are not inextricably tied to aging, they nevertheless are more likely to occur as we grow older. Consequently, any discussion of reducing ageism must give some consideration to the stigma of loss.

We stigmatize other human beings through displays of displeasure or disapproval, the creation of social distance, and avoidance. Stigmatized individuals respond by feeling rejected by their social group—not for what they have done but because of whom they are. Unless the stigmatized individual has the capacity to remove the stigma, rejection is global and enduring and can be damaging to identity.

Institutionalized stigmatizing, that is, removing people from mainstream society because of increased age or an age-related loss, has become less common over the past three decades, but examples are still familiar to most of us. Elderly people with dependency needs routinely were moved out to aged-care homes and hospitals. Workers as they approach 65 still face compulsory retirement in some countries, including Australia. In these cases, the stigmatizing conditions of being removed from mainstream institutions have been offset by a concerted effort to reinterpret these events as points of transition rather than as breaks with normal life. The stigma of "being put out to pasture" has been replaced by notions of new opportunities and, in some cases, "greener pastures."

These changes have been executed and accepted in a relatively short period of time. At the University of Queensland from 1966 to 1976, Elsie Harwood and George Naylor directed a research program called Operation Retirement. They recognized the importance of involving older citizens in mainstream institutions postretirement (Harwood 1974; Naylor and Harwood 1970). On a regular basis, a group assembled to learn German and to play the recorder at the university. Programs of this kind are hardly innovative these days. Senior citizens attending universities, offering special tuition for children with learning disabilities, or operating advice services for new business owners are among the many stories that continue to make the news. We may wonder, however, why they are not more commonplace and still newsworthy after thirty years. Longino, McClelland, and Peterson (1980) have described how elderly communities develop their own subcultures that are integrated, pro-elderly, and self-affirming. They also note, however, that these communities are retreatist and do not foster a politically active aging consciousness. Possibly, older citizens shy away from commitments with mainstream society. Possibly, older citizens are wary of offering their services unless they know that they will be welcomed and valued.

It may be that the social damage of stigmatizing lies not so much in implementing transitions but in the message of disrespect that can be communicated through downgrading the status of individuals and cutting them off from society (Blaney 1994). This point is an important one for interventions. Transitions may be an inevitable part of the aging process, but as a society, we have choice and responsibilities for how they are managed. They can be managed with respect, consultation, and inclusion or, alternatively, with disrespect, domination, and deceit.

To the extent that we are social beings, our self-worth depends on the worth ascribed to us by others. Arendt (1967) has described the devastating effects of Hitler's policies of segregation in relation to the Jewish population in Germany during the Third Reich. Stigmatizing actions that separate us from others destroy the essence of our social being and induce a passivity that robs us of ourselves. Thus, aged-care policies that rob individuals of their identity need to be identified and resisted at all times.

It would be a mistake to consider such policies a thing of the past or to underestimate the difficulty of identifying and reversing them. Transitions are constantly the concern of policymakers, and stigmatizing behavior creeps in when arrangements for transitions are handled disrespectfully. Here are two Australian examples of policy that perpetuates stigmatizing behavior.

The first example relates to nursing home regulation. For a short period in Australia's history, nursing home regulation was resident focused, more so than anywhere else in the world (J. Braithwaite 1993; J. Braithwaite et al. 1993). Government nursing home inspectors were obligated to talk to residents and their families about the care that they were receiving. The regulatory procedure was hailed a great success (J. Braithwaite et al. 1993) until the government decided to go down an audit trail and downgrade the role of residents and their families to that of "the complaints mechanism." This change raises an interesting question. Who among us would think it appropriate for someone to inspect our own home without explaining to us why they were coming and without showing an interest in what we thought about it all?

Admissions procedures to nursing homes in Australia provide a second example of how policy can inadvertently foster stigmatization. Nursing home beds are subsidized by the government, but in order to qualify for the subsidy, the bed has to be occupied. Thus, when an offer is made to someone on the waiting list, the individual, or more often families, are pressured into accepting immediately unless they have the money to hold a bed for future use. Most families cannot afford to pay to hold a bed. In these circumstances, how would we respond to being told by our families that we would be moving out in the next day or two and would need to get our things together to move into a nursing home room that we would be most likely sharing with a stranger? If this happened to us tomorrow, what would we do? If Arendt is right, we would do nothing. We would be herded off with others like us, we would be decultured, and before long, we would lose our sense of self.

Examples of implementing separation with strategies of disrespect, domination, and deceit are not uncommon, and they are not necessarily strategies that are explained by stereotypes or prejudice. Sometimes they have more to do with the way stigma is handled by those with power and an unquestioning sense of their superior knowledge and understanding. When we look at nursing home placements and workplace terminations, disrespect, domination, and deceit often are responses to social awkwardness and a well-meaning desire to minimize the anguish and pain of the situation for everyone. As a society, we struggle with failure and loss. It is hard to acknowledge that we or a loved one cannot take care of ourselves, or that we put others at risk because we can no longer do things as well as we could. The stigma of poor performance remains at the heart of our capitalist economies and our social structures. Inevitably, the identities of those so affected are threatened, highlighting the need to pursue policies that encourage the adoption of new and valued social identities when the time for residential or work transitions arrives.

Sometimes, however, the new identities challenge some basic values of society, and there is nothing to be done other than to face the value conflict head on. Nowhere is this more evident than in dealing with degeneration of a cognitive or social kind. An interesting example of stigma associated with mental deterioration came to attention recently with the publication of Bayley's (2000) book about the last year of the life of his wife, the renowned novelist Iris Murdoch. In this book, Bayley shares his experiences as he cares for his wife in the final stages of Alzheimer's disease. At the time of the book's release, reports of outrage attracted the attention of the world's news media.[2] The story was one of shock that a husband would expose the details of his wife's degenerating condition and in so doing tarnish the memory of someone who was revered for her fine intellect and literary talents. The well-intentioned desire to remember Murdoch at her peak reveals one of our yet unchartered stigmas, that of mental deterioration. The question that needs answering when we consider a talented person who is losing her mental capacities is, Where does disrespect lie? Is disrespect to be owned by a husband who struggled to come to terms with his wife's deterioration, or by a society that cannot truly value a life lived with stigma?

For members of a stigmatized group, anticipating the reactions of others is somewhat unpredictable. The literature documents not only reactions of distaste and displeasure, but also a second reaction that seeks to counter the negativity of the first through offering sympathy and concern (Langer et al. 1976; Scheier et al. 1978; Katz 1981). In some cases, sympathy and concern can backfire because it is expressed in an exaggerated and unnatural manner (Crocker 1995). This observation provides some interesting conflicts for ageism reduction. The perspective taking advocated earlier may lead the nonstigmatized to share the humiliation of the stigmatized to the point where they overcompensate. Research relating to communication patterns reveals that an overaccommodating style by the young toward the elderly can be seen as patronizing (Hummert et al. 1998; Williams and Giles 1998), and elderly people have their own way of dismissing the unwanted attention (Williams and Giles 1998).

Stigmatizing is a problem that requires coordinated action at both the individual and the societal levels. Considerable progress has yet to be made in uncoupling loss from the negative emotions of repulsion and shame. Resolving this societal problem shows signs of being a major challenge. The first step, however, may be more manageable.

Langer and associates (1976) have raised questions about the extent to which stigmas follow from feelings of dislike or disgust, as has always been assumed. Instead, they have put an argument for interpreting reactions to stigma in terms of discomfort arising out of novelty (Langer et al. 1976). They investigated this idea in the context of physical disability. They noted that novel stimuli give rise to the desire to stare. Staring is part of normal exploratory behavior, but it is also deemed socially unacceptable. Consequently, the individual who encounters something unfamiliar in a social context where staring is prohibited will be in a state of conflict. Conflict generates discomfort, which leads to avoidance.

Langer and associates (1976) tested this hypothesis by giving subjects in one experimental group time to familiarize themselves with a physically disabled confederate whom they could observe through a one-way mirror. In a subsequent interaction with the person, the research team observed seating arrangements and found that compared to a control group, those who had time to familiarize themselves with the disability sat closer to the confederate and were less likely to seat themselves at an angle so that the confederate was out of view. Most interestingly, this effect was not mediated by self-reports of liking for the confederate. These findings suggest that stigma as novelty should be the first port of call when planning interventions to deal with stigmatizing behaviors.

If this is so, the stigma associated with old age should be reduced through giving more public exposure to those aspects of aging that leave us feeling conflict ridden, confused, inept, or ill at ease. Of central importance in the context of aging is the stigma of loss. In an achievement- and success-oriented society, the norms and scripts for dealing with failure and loss with the appropriate amounts of respect, concern, and acceptance are strikingly absent. Awkwardness and overcompensation are the more common scripts that we encounter.

Overcoming these boundaries may require stepping outside real life into the world of make-believe and the institutions of the arts. Comedy has always been an important forum for broaching taboo subjects and finding ways to talk about that which is unspeakable. Film, drama, television, and literature can ease us into coming to terms with stigma. Documentaries and public affairs programs can then ride on the coattails of an arts-initiated desensitization process and provide the information and shared experience required to break down barriers that separate older persons psychologically, socially, and physically from society.

Reducing the Fear of Aging

Fear of aging is conceptualized here as holding a negative attitude to one's own aging process, making an appraisal that the final life stage will be the least pleasant because it is dominated by loss. As Berezin puts it (1972), "The older one becomes, the more losses he [or she] sustains" (p. 34). Physical and physiological changes are likely to adversely affect one's health, friends and other loved ones die, and financial resources diminish. Berezin points out that "what is significant about the changes that do occur, both internally and externally, is not the fact of their occurrence but rather how they are met and mastered" (p. 34).

Fear of aging can be conceptualized like any other threat to our well-being. We can allow the fear to grow and dominate our view of aging, we can deny its existence, or we can try to come to terms with it, lessening its power over us in the process. In the last case, fear of acquiring attributes that will limit quality of life is likely to become a motivator for adaptation (Markus and Nurius 1986; Cross and Markus 1991; Hooker and Kaus 1992; Ogilvie 1987). The literature on stress suggests that successful adaptation can be accomplished in two ways.

First, the early stress and coping research identified the value of interpreting outside events as challenges rather than threats or losses, and of seeking and finding solutions to the problems at hand (Folkman et al. 1986; Lazarus and Folkman 1984). Pursuing an active problem-solving approach to aging at all stages of life is likely to prove beneficial. Individuals can learn more about the aging process, adopt a healthier lifestyle to lower the risk of poor health, plan for retirement, and make provisions for care, should that be required. Providing individuals with the belief that they can take steps to improve the quality of life in their old age is likely to help reduce fear of the aging process significantly and strengthen the resolve of individuals to be a "golden ager."

The essence of this approach is control. The second approach, represented by the work of Antonovsky (1972, 1979, 1987), reminds us that some things are beyond control. One of Antonovsky's major contributions to our understanding of adaptation is to shift our frame beyond personal control to management. Antonovsky conceptualizes demands, that is, life events and hassles, not as abnormal experiences but as part of the normal state of living. In other words, Antonovsky starts from the premise that the normal state of living for everyone is more chaotic than orderly and that adaptation is a continuous creative process that involves us in learning, critical thinking, and effort. For Antonovsky, the never-ending threats from the inner and outer environments create tension that we relieve through using our resistance resources: freedom to enter new social roles, modify existing norms, feel connected to others, and have a strong sense of meaning in life and a belief that life can be managed. Without resistance resources, the tension produced by threats and demands eventually leads to breakdown. Part of the account Antonovsky offers is that successfully negotiating one's way through the life course has more to do with an ability to transcend difficulties through giving them meaning than through shaping them directly to suit our liking. Antonovsky uses the term *sense of coherence* to describe the capacity to make sense out of what happens to us, to incorporate our experiences, good and bad, into a meaningful whole, and to comprehend our situation to the point of managing it. Antonovsky's sense of coherence, when applied to the context of elderly people, raises issues similar to those discussed by Erikson in his work on the search for ego integrity in later life and the avoidance of despair (Erikson, Erikson, and Kivnick 1986). The difference is that Antonovsky's account of successful adaptation is an ongoing process on offer to all age groups.

The solutions to problems of stereotyping, prejudice, stigma, and fear of ageing offered in this chapter all head in the same direction: facilitating more open communication, perspective taking, more information exchange, less censoring of taboo topics, more problem solving, and developing the capacity to transcend a need to control events that are not to our liking. These are all desirable outcomes, but how can these goals be achieved in our society, particularly in relation to ageism?

The Interrelationships among Stereotypes, Prejudice, Stigma, and Fear of Aging

A widely held assumption in the gerontological literature is that the components of ageism are loosely interconnected and together lead to discriminatory actions whereby older people are denied the opportunities, benefits, and quality of life offered to other age groups. Questions regarding overlap among the different facets of ageism were raised by Langer and associates (1976), who challenged the assumption that nonverbal expressions of avoidance were more credible indicators of prejudice than verbal measures in which respondents denied having negative feelings. They suggested that people might be telling the truth and that behaviors that were being interpreted as derogation may have really been expressions of discomfort and conflict.

Ageist Ideology versus Discrimination

In 1988–1989, research on the components of ageism was conducted using a sample of 195 students at the Australian National University. The purpose of the study was to find out if endorsement of commonly held stereotypes, negative attitudes to elderly people, fear of one's own aging, and discriminatory behavior were interrelated.[3] If the components of ageism are not tied together at least loosely, initiatives to reduce one problem cannot be expected to have a spin-off effect that will solve other problems. If the various facets operate somewhat independently, many different approaches will be required to make an impact on ageism. Finally, if some components are inversely related, attempts to bring about change on one front may undermine progress elsewhere.

Part I of the ageism study (Braithwaite, Lynd-Stevenson, and Pigram 1993; Pigram 1987) involved constructing scales to measure four facets of ageist ideology along with a measure of awareness of ageism in the society. The Attitudes to Elderly People scale measured comfort with elderly people, feelings of closeness and friendship, through to avoidance and lack of interest in them. The Attitudes to One's Own Aging scale measured fear of loss and concerns about one's capacity to manage through to enthusiasm about the opportunities of old age. The Negative Stereotype Endorsement scale measured the extent to which respondents believed elderly people are slow, forgetful, and distractable as opposed to focused, able, and energetic. The Positive Stereotype Endorsement scale measured the extent to which respondents believed elderly people are friendly, accepting, and sympathetic as opposed to intolerant, biased and unsociable. The Awareness of Ageism scale measured the extent to which individuals believed that elderly people were given respect, consideration, appreciation, and opportunity by members of society through to the extent to which they were targets of discrimination.

Scores on the ageism scales were intercorrelated to find out the extent to which they cohered to form an ageist ideology. Having a negative attitude

Table 11.1
Pearson Product Moment Intercorrelations among Scales Measuring Facets of Ageism

Scales[a]	1	2	3	4
1 Negativity to elderly				
2 Negativity to ageing	.37***			
3 Incapable-capable stereotype	.28***	.36***		
4 Unsociable-sociable stereotype	.29***	.10	.28***	
5 Awareness of ageism	−.18**	−.02	−.08	.01

[a]For all these scales a low score indicates high levels of negativity about older people, and awareness that ageism exists in society.

to elderly people was significantly correlated with feeling negative about one's own aging. Butler (1987) has argued that fear of aging is a key driver of ageism in our society. Those with negative attitudes to the elderly and the aging process were also more likely to endorse the stereotype of elderly people as incapable and ineffective. Systematic denial of the positive stereotype did not come from those with a fear of aging but rather from those who held a negative attitude to the elderly as a group. This finding suggests that the presentation of positive stereotypes is probably of limited use in moving the more prejudiced away from their ageist position.

The results in table 11.1 support the notion that the components of ageism are interrelated. Endorsement of negative stereotyping, negative attitudes to elderly people, and fear of one's own aging work together to promote an ageist ideology. While awareness of ageism in society was high in this sample (78 percent expressed at least some support for this view), awareness was poorly related to holding an ageist ideology oneself. Thus, exposure of ageist practices through the media or advocacy groups may do little to change the ageist ideology of individuals.

Part II of the ageism study examined age discrimination. Prior to completing the ageism questionnaire, participants took part in an experiment to assess ageist practices. Using a two-by-two between-subjects experimental design, each student was given a transcript of an employment interview, purportedly conducted with a woman who had applied for the position of tutor in psychology. Half the students were told that the tutor was 27 years old, the other half that she was 59. Transcripts varied also in terms of the applicant's interest in being primarily a teacher or researcher. Those who participated in the study were required to make two judgments. First, they were asked how much they would like the person as a tutor (rated on a five-point scale from "not at all" to "very much"), and second, they were asked how likely it was that the candidate would actually get the job on a four-point rating scale from "less than a 25 percent chance" to "more than a 75 percent chance."

Having found evidence of ageist ideology and awareness of ageism in society, we were not surprised to find age discrimination when it came to tutor preference and expectations of success. The 27 year old was given higher ratings on how much the students would like her as a tutor and on likelihood of success in getting the job. What surprised us was that when we looked at the ninety-one students who had evaluated the 59 year old as a tutor, we were unable to find any relationship between any of the ageism scales and either liking or expected success. We had hypothesized that those with ageist attitudes would be among those who gave the lowest ratings to the older applicant on both personal liking and likelihood of success (see Braithwaite, Lynd-Stevenson, and Pigram 1993 for further details).

These findings show ageism and age discrimination as being unconnected. The reasons at this stage are unclear. Some may rightly question whether a 59 year old is old. The problem may be one of mistakenly measuring "old-ageism" as opposed to "middle-ageism," although for 18-year-old students who made up most of this sample, the distinction between a 59 year old and a 69 year old is relatively subtle. Alternatively, it may be that the behaviorally damaging component of ageism in this experimental context is covert. Dovidio and Gaertner's (1986) research suggests that the worst side of ageism, like sexism and racism, has "gone underground" and cannot be measured through conscious beliefs. Or it may be, as Langer and associates have proposed, that discrimination is fueled by something more benign, such as novelty.

In the ageism study, the test for discrimination was an employment context. The novelty-familiarity explanation fits the findings to a point. Most tutors were doing postgraduate studies so that students would be most familiar with tutors in their late 20s. In keeping with the familiarity hypothesis, students preferred the younger applicant and also thought that the younger applicant was more likely to be offered the job by the university. The younger applicant matched the prototype of university tutor better than the older applicant.

But the familiarity argument did not explain the second preference the students expressed. The applicant with a commitment to teaching rather than research was the preferred choice of students even though they were not convinced that her chances of success were higher. A broader but not dissimilar concept that has been put forward to explain discrimination is social attractiveness (Puckett et al. 1983). We choose people whom we perceive as enhancing our quality of life. Fitting in, being easy to get on with, and bringing knowledge or status to the workplace are factors that drive personal preferences. This is not to dismiss novelty. Novelty, as described by Langer and associates (1976), may simply be one factor that reduces social attractiveness.

This argument suggests that older job applicants should be as successful as younger applicants, providing they are armed with social attractiveness. It needs to be acknowledged at this point, however, that social attractiveness is a far more complex phenomenon in the outside world than it is in the laboratory. Social attractiveness is likely to be lower in cases where older job applicants have been denied access to new technologies, they are not familiar with new ways of doing work, and superannuation and employment policies make appointment costly and difficult. At the level of individual preferences, social attractiveness may well be the important factor. But social attractiveness may be shaped not by an individual's efforts, achievements, and abilities but by a society that regulates, both intentionally and unintentionally, access to opportunities.

When societies recognize deficiencies in the social system that deny opportunities on a systematic basis to a group, multiple remedial steps can be taken. Among these are affirmative action and antidiscrimination legislation. Both types of legislation are important in signaling the intent of a society to combat discrimination, but their effectiveness is bound by human ingenuity. In the normal course of events, selection processes are devised to suppress the pull of social attractiveness and put appointment by merit in its place. Legislation is devised to rule out age (or race or sex) as a reason for nonappointment. There is, however, no safeguard against a committee's developing a shared and unspoken view that an applicant does not suit the job as well as others. It is not so much that the applicant lacks the desirable qualities; rather, others have more of these qualities. In this context, ageism as lower social attractiveness goes undetected and unchecked.

The ageism study illustrates how advances in combating an ageist ideology may require deeper change in how one thinks about aging than is provided through increasing community exposure to positive stereotypes. It also warns that a less ageist ideology, even when inscribed in law, may have a limited impact on discriminatory actions. While we remain uncertain about the nature of the relationship between ageist ideology and discriminatory action, we can be relatively confident that the relationship is not simple.

Caregiving, Stress, and Stigma

The ageism study illustrated independence between ageist ideology and discriminatory practices; work with caregivers has revealed how policies designed to be inclusive of older people are undermined by the stigma of degeneration.

The initial focus of our caregiving work was understanding the burden of care, defined as the extent to which caregiving frustrated the satisfaction of basic human needs for order, belonging, and self-esteem (Braithwaite 1990, 1992, 1996). The theoretical framework for this work was provided by the crisis-of-decline model. The essential propositions of the model that were supported by data were as follows: Caregiving burden is related to (1) care receiver degeneration, which bears a heavy stigma, (2) caregiver unpreparedness in the form of not having cultural knowledge about this type of care, (3) relationship damage as caregiver and care receiver unsuccessfully battle decline in one partner, (4) enmeshment as the caregiving role becomes all-consuming, and (5) coercion, since no alternative is on offer for most caregiving dyads.

Caregiving in circumstances where degeneration is occurring can be interpreted as a story of stigma and isolation. In Western societies, caregiving eventually tends to become the responsibility of one person. As this person takes on more and more, the caregiving dyad retreats, becoming increasingly isolated from society. It is interesting to note how caregivers receive many more offers of support than they ever accept or feel comfortable accepting (Braithwaite 1986b, 1987). Caregivers and care receivers conspire to preserve their privacy, not wanting to involve too many others in their affairs. At the same time, all indications are that they do not retreat into blissful solitude. The overwhelming proportion of caregivers say they would not wish the caregiving role on their children (Braithwaite 1990).

Stigma affects the caregiver in two ways: through being the person responsible for the care receiver, particularly when the care receiver engages in socially inappropriate behavior, and through a shared identity with the care receiver, often built over many years as a beloved parent or spouse. Either way, the caregiver becomes engulfed in a state of shame. Shame is felt on behalf of the care receiver who can no longer attract the status of earlier times and causes embarrassment and shock to others. Shame also creeps in as caregivers fail in their bid to restore their care receiver to good health. Shame of either kind leads to the same outcome: withdrawal and avoidance of others (Ahmed et al. 2001).

The role that stigma plays in isolating caregiver and care receiver becomes evident in respite care usage. Caregivers are strong advocates of respite care, but their usage patterns belie their agitation for more and better services (George 1988; Gibson et al. 1996; Lawton, Brody, and Saperstein 1989; Montgomery and Borgatta 1989; Oktay and Volland 1990). In investigating the impediments to using respite, great reluctance emerged among those who had an intimate and loving relationship with the person they were caring for (Braithwaite, 1998). They used respite in emergencies, but always hoped that they would not need it again. These findings were interpreted as a sign of the dependency, trust, and intimacy in caregiver–care receiver relationships that could not be equaled by those outside. Added to this may be elements of distrust in a society that is not always tolerant or respectful of vulnerability.

In 1997, the Commonwealth Department of Health and Family Services sponsored the Caregiver Recreational Respite Program, a trial program geared toward increasing the use of respite care among caregivers and giving them an opportunity to reengage with the community (Braithwaite, Pollitt, and Roach 2000). The program recruited thirty-nine caregivers who took part in a leisure activity of their choice through attending weekly sessions over a seven-week period. The program was an enormous success for those who attended, but the recruitment process was painfully slow. We anticipated that we would be flooded with applications, but this was far from the case.

The program was designed to offer support at a number of levels. Respite was organized through professional agencies, taxis were organized to take caregivers to and from the sessions, materials were provided through the research program, and we had good contacts with doctors and caregiving networks in the district. We were open to arranging programs of any kind, responding to public demand. Two specific responses from caregivers surprised us. First, most caregivers preferred to make their own respite arrangements through their informal network rather than use professional services of their choice that we would pay for. It also surprised us that most caregivers were recruited through informal networks with a go-between who encouraged the participant to come forward and become involved. In the course of the evaluation study, we were interested in understanding the reluctance to come forward, who benefited most, and why.

Some caregivers had difficulty accepting the role of caregiver. Such acceptance meant recognizing deterioration in someone they cared for that could not be dismissed as "normal." The stigma of disability prompted the protection offered by denial. Regardless of acceptance of terminology, caregiving that was demanding brought with it enmeshment. Of most concern was the harm induced by two types of enmeshment: relationship enmeshment, whereby caregivers tried in vain to find a sense of their own worth in the eyes of the care receiver, and role enmeshment, whereby caregivers and care receivers excluded others from participating in the caregiving process. Interestingly, those who benefited most from taking part in the program were caregivers with a strong commitment to caregiving who were facing loss through a degenerating relationship with the care receiver.

These findings demonstrate that policies offering respite support make sense from the point of view of relieving the caregivers' stress, but their likely effectiveness is complicated by other factors. Respite provides escape from a situation that is laden with stigma. Whether caregivers feel they can or should take advantage of respite depends on their relationship with the care receiver (Braithwaite 1998). On the positive side, it seems highly likely that respite can disrupt the buildup of tension and fatigue (Braithwaite, 1986b, 1987), but it cannot address the basic source of the problem: stigmatization, shame, and isolation. More broadly, stigma and shame appear to be major impediments to caregivers' feeling willing and able to take advantage of formal and informal services. Ironically, these services are often supported by governments in a bid to be inclusive of caregivers and care receivers and responsive to their needs.

A Ten-Point Plan for Ageism Reduction

This chapter suggests ten action plans for ageism reduction:

1. Heightening sensitivity to the stereotyping of older people.

2. Creating greater exposure to diversity in the personal characteristics of older people.

3. Having greater commitment to recognizing and responding to diversity in dealings with older people.

4. Making deliberate use of perspective taking to see the older person as an individual.

5. Seeking out opportunities for intergenerational cooperation.

6. Taking advantage of opportunities to promote the social attractiveness of older people.

7. Strengthening institutional practices that promote the norm of human-heartedness.

8. Desensitizing ourselves to the stigma of degeneration and dependency.

9. Reviewing policies and practices for evidence of stigmatizing through disrespect, particularly the disrespect communicated through treating older people as an invisible group.

10. Mandating inclusiveness of older people in policy planning and implementation.

In order to implement these ten steps, we need to consider whether the institutions are in place to deliver on them. This question is beyond the scope of this chapter, but I wonder if the institutions of family, work, and governance provide the time and space for reflective dialogue over issues relating to ageism. Common to all the steps is the assumption that nestled within our institutions are places for cooperation, reflective dialogue, shame acknowledgment, and collective problem solving. Such space is often held hostage to competitive struggles for dominance, efficiency, and ritualized outputs that result in the generation of much activity without coming to terms with the problems at hand. Stepping back to take a broader view of our institutional structures for dealing with all types of "-isms" may be a necessary first step for making progress on addressing ageism. The second step should be the definition or creation of spaces where young, middle-aged, and elderly people from all walks of life can get to know each other enough to build mutual respect, develop cooperative relationships, and reignite the norm of human-heartedness.

Notes

1. *Ideal norms* are defined by Williams (1960) as standards of conduct that everyone feels an obligation to follow, even if they are not always followed.

2. Later reviews of the book were positive, reflecting the often observed pattern of stigmatizing reactions being followed by more sympathetic ones.

3. Previous work in this population had identified negative stereotypes relating to competence and positive stereotypes relating to sociability (Braithwaite 1987). In this study, 70 percent of participants endorsed the negative stereotype of low capability, and 63 percent endorsed the positive stereotype of high sociability.

This study did not set out to measure prejudice in the form of threat or hate or stigmatizing in the form of disgust. The focus was on negative attitudes associated with lack of interest in and affection for elderly people and conscious discomfort with elderly people. In this work, these attitudes were highly correlated and formed one scale.

References

Adorno, T. W., Frenkel-Brunswik, E., Levinson, D. J., and Sanford, R. N. (1950). *The authoritarian personality.* New York: Harper.

Agnew, C. R., Thompson, V. D., and Gaines, S. O. (2000). Incorporating proximal and distal influences on prejudice: Testing a general model across outgroups. *Personality and Social Psychology Bulletin, 26,* 403–418.

Ahmed, E., Harris, N., Braithwaite, J., and Braithwaite, V. (2001). *Shame management through reintegration.* Cambridge: Cambridge University Press.

Allport, G. (1954). *The nature of prejudice.* Reading, MA: Addison-Wesley.

Antonovsky, A. (1972). Breakdown: A needed fourth step in the conceptual armamentarium of modern medicine. *Social Science and Medicine, 6,* 537–544.

Antonovsky, A. (1979). *Health, stress and coping.* San Francisco: Jossey-Bass.

Antonovsky, A. (1987). *Unraveling the mystery of health: How people manage stress and stay well.* San Francisco: Jossey-Bass.

Arendt, H. (1967). *The origins of totalitarianism.* London: Allen and Unwin.

Bargh, J. A., Chen, M., and Burrows, L. (1996). Automaticity of social behavior: Direct effects of trait construct and stereotype activation on action. *Journal of Personality of Social Psychology, 71,* 230–244.

Bayley, J. (2000). *Iris and her friends: A memoir of memory and desire.* New York: Norton.

Berezin, M. (1972). Psychodynamic considerations of aging and the aged: An overview. *American Journal of Psychiatry, 128,* 1483–1491.

Blaney, B. C. (1994). Adulthood or oldness: In search of a vision. In V. J. Bradley, J. W. Ashbaugh, and B. C. Blaney (Eds.), *Creating individual supports for people with disabilities: A mandate for change at many levels* (pp. 141–151). Baltimore: P. H. Brookes Publishing Company.

Braithwaite, J. (1993). The nursing home industry. In M. Tonry and A. Reiss, Jr. (Eds.), *Beyond the law: Crime in complex organizations.* Chicago: University of Chicago Press.

Braithwaite, J., Makkai, T., Braithwaite, V., and Gibson, D. (1993). *Raising the standard: Resident centred nursing home regulation in Australia.* Canberra: Department of Health, Housing and Community Services.

Braithwaite, V. A. (1986a). Old age stereotypes: Reconciling contradictions. *Journal of Gerontology, 41,* 353–360.

Braithwaite, V. (1986b). The burden of home care: How is it shared? *Community Health Studies, 10,* 3 (supplement), 7.s–11.s.

Braithwaite, V. A. (1987). Coming to terms with burden in home care. *Australian Journal on Ageing, 6,* 20–23.

Braithwaite, V. (1990). *Bound to care.* Sydney: Allen and Unwin.

Braithwaite, V. (1992). Caregiving burden: Making the concept scientifically useful and policy relevant. *Research on Aging, 14,* 3–27.

Braithwaite, V. (1996). Understanding stress in informal caregiving: Is burden a problem for the individual or for society? *Research on Aging, 18,* 139–174.

Braithwaite, V. (1998). Institutional respite care: Breaking chores or breaking social bonds? *Gerontologist, 38,* 610–617.

Braithwaite, V., and Blamey, R. (1998). Consensus, stability and meaning in abstract social values. *Australian Journal of Political Science, 33,* 373–390.

Braithwaite, V. A., Gibson, D. M., and Holman, J. (1986). Age stereotyping—Are we oversimplifying the phenomenon? *International Journal of Ageing and Human Development, 22,* 315–325.

Braithwaite, V., Lynd-Stevenson, R., and Pigram, D. (1993). An empirical study of ageism: From polemics to scientific utility. *Australian Psychologist, 28,* 9–15.

Braithwaite, V., Pollitt, P., and Roach, G. (2000). *A cameo of re-creation: The caregiver recreational respite program.* Canberra: Department of Health and Family Services.

Brewer, M., B., Dull, V., and Lui, L. (1981). Perceptions of the elderly: Stereotypes as prototypes. *Journal of Personality and Social Psychology, 41,* 656–670.

Butler, R. N. (1969). Age-ism: Another form of bigotry. *Gerontologist, 9,* 243–246.

Butler, R. N. (1987). Ageism. In G. L. Maddox (Ed.), *The encyclopedia of aging* (pp. 22–23). New York: Springer.

Butler, R. N. (1989). Dispelling ageism: The cross-cutting intervention. In M. W. Riley and J. W. Riley, Jr. (Eds.), The quality of aging: Strategies for intervention (May) special issue, *Annals of the American Academy of Political and Social Science, 503,* pp. 138–147.

Crocker, J. (1995). Stigma. In A. S. R. Manstead and M. Hewstone (Eds.), *The Blackwell encyclopedia of social psychology* (pp. 633–635). Oxford: Blackwell.

Cross, S., and Markus, H. (1991). Possible selves across the lifespan. *Human Development, 34,* 230–255.

Dovidio, J. F., and Gaertner, S. L. (Eds.) (1986). *Prejudice, discrimination, and racism.* Orlando, FL: Academic Press.

Duckitt, J. (1992). Psychology and prejudice: A historical analysis and integrative framework. *American Psychologist, 47,* 1182–1193.

English, H. B., and English, A. C. (1958). *A comprehensive dictionary of psychological and psychoanalytical terms.* London: Longmans.

Erikson, E. H., Erikson, J. M., and Kivnick, H. Q. (1986). *Vital involvement in old age.* New York: Norton.

Fiske, S. T., and Neuberg, S. L. (1990). A continuum of impression formation, from category-based to individuating processes: Influences of information and motivation on attention and interpretation. In M. P. Zanna (Ed.), *Advances in experimental social psychology* (Vol. 23, pp. 1–74). New York: Academic Press.

Folkman, S., Lazarus, R. S., Gruen, R. J., and DeLongis, A. (1986). Appraisal, coping, health status, and psychological symptoms. *Journal of Personality and Social Psychology, 50,* 571–579.

Galinsky, A. D., and Moskowitz, G. B. (2000). Perspective taking: Decreasing stereotype expression, stereotype accessibility, and in-group favoritism. *Journal of Personality and Social Psychology, 78,* 708–724.

George, L. K. (1988). *Why won't caregivers use community services? Unexpected findings from a respite care demonstration evaluation.* Paper presented at the 41st Annual Meeting of the Gerontological Society of America, San Francisco.

Gibson, D., Butkus, E., Jenkins, A., Mathur, S., and Liu, Z. (1996). *The respite care needs of Australians: Respite Review supporting paper 1.* Canberra: Australian Institute of Health and Welfare.

Goffman, E. (1963). *Stigma: Notes on the management of spoiled identity.* Englewood Cliffs, NJ: Prentice Hall.

Golde, P., and Kogan, N. A. (1959). A sentence completion procedure for assessing attitudes toward old people. *Journal of Gerontology, 14,* 355–363.

Guttman, D. L. (1988). The two faces of gerontology. *Center on Aging, 4*(1), 1–2.

Haslam, S. A., Turner, J. C., Oakes, P. J., McGarty, C., and Reynolds, K. J. (1998). The group as a basis for emergent stereotype consensus. In W. Stroebe and M. Hewstone (Eds.), *European review of social psychology, 8* (pp. 203–239). Chichester: Wiley.

Harding, J., Proshansky, H., Kutner, B., and Chein, I. (1968). Prejudice and ethnic relations. In G. Lindzey and E. Aronson (Eds.), *The handbook of social psychology* (2nd ed., Vol. 5, pp. 1–76). Reading, MA: Addison-Wesley.

Harwood, E. (1974, June). Reactivation: The Bethesda Programme. *Growing Older,* 8–9.

Hooker, K., and Kaus, C. R. (1992). Possible selves and health behaviours in later life. *Journal of Aging and Health, 4,* 390–411.

Hummert, M. L., Shaner, J. L., Garstka, T. A., and Henry, C. (1998). Communication with older adults: The influence of age stereotypes, context, and communicator age. *Human Communication Research, 25,* 124–151.

Jones, E. E., Farina, A., Hastorf, A. H., Markus, H., Miller, D. T., and Scott, R. A. (1984). *Social stigma: The psychology of marked relationships.* New York: Freeman.

Katz, I. (1981). *Stigma: A social-psychological perspective.* Hillsdale, NJ: Erlbaum.

Kite, M. E. (1996). Age, gender, and occupational label: A test of social role theory. *Psychology of Women Quarterly, 20,* 361–374.

Lachman, M. E., and McArthur, L. Z. (1986). Adulthood age differences in causal attributions for cognitive, physical, and social performance. *Psychology and Aging, 1,* 127–132.

Langer, E. J., Fiske, S., Taylor, S. E., and Chanowitz, B. (1976). Stigma, staring and discomfort: A novel-stimulus hypothesis. *Journal of Experimental Social Psychology, 12,* 451–463.

Lawton, M., Brody, E., and Saperstein, A. (1989). A controlled study of respite service for caregivers of Alzheimer's patients. *Gerontologist, 29,* 8–16.

Lazarus, R. S., and Folkman, S. (1984). *Stress, appraisal, and coping.* New York: Springer.

Lippmann, W. (1922). *Public opinion.* New York: Hartcourt and Brace.

Longino, C. F., Jr., McClelland, K. A., and Peterson, W. A. (1980). The aged subculture hypothesis: Social integration, gerontophilia and self-conception. *Journal of Gerontology, 35,* 758–767.

Luszcz, M., and Fitzgerald, K. M. (1986). Understanding cohort differences in cross-generational, self, and peer perceptions. *Journal of Gerontology, 41,* 234–240.

Markus, H., and Nurius, P. (1986). Possible selves. *American Psychologist, 9,* 954–969.

Montgomery, R. J., and Borgatta, E. F. (1989). Effects of alternative support strategies. *Gerontologist, 29,* 457–464.

Naylor, G. F. K., and Harwood, E. (1970). Mental exercise for grandmother. *Education News, 12* (11), 15–18.

Ogilvie, D. M. (1987). The undesired self: A neglected variable in personality research. *Journal of Personality and Social Psychology, 52,* 379–385.

Oktay, J., and Volland, P. J. (1990). Post-hospital support program for the frail elderly and their caregivers: A quasi-experimental evaluation. *American Journal of Public Health, 80,* 39–45.

Pigram, D. (1987). *A clarification of the constructs of ageism and age stereotypes in non-experimental and experimental paradigms.* Unpublished honours thesis, Australian National University, Canberra.

Puckett, J. M., Petty, R. E., Cacioppo, J. T., and Fischer, D. L. (1983). The relative impact of age and attractiveness stereotypes on persuasion. *Journal of Gerontology, 38,* 340–343.

Scheier, M. F., Carver, C. S., Schulz, R., Glass, D. C., and Katz, I. (1978). Sympathy, self-consciousness, and reactions to the stigmatized. *Journal of Applied Social Psychology, 8,* 270–282.

Schmidt, D. F., and Boland, S. M. (1986). Structure of perceptions of older adults: Evidence for multiple stereotypes. *Psychology and Aging, 1,* 255–260.

Snyder, M., and Miene, P. K. (1994). Stereotyping of the elderly: A functional approach. *British Journal of Social Psychology, 33,* 63–82.

Stangor, C. S. (1995). Stereotyping. In A. S. R. Manstead and M. Hewstone (Eds.), *The Blackwell encyclopedia of social psychology* (pp. 628–633). Oxford: Blackwell.

Tajfel, H. (1981). *Human groups and social categories: Studies in social psychology.* Cambridge: Cambridge University Press.

von Hippel, W., Silver, L. A., and Lynch, M. E. (2000). Stereotyping against your will: The role of inhibitory ability in stereotyping and prejudice among the elderly. *Personality and Social Psychology Bulletin, 26,* 523–532.

Williams, R. M., Jr. (1960). *American society: A sociological interpretation* (2nd ed.). New York: Knopf.

Williams, A., and Giles, H. (1998). Communication of ageism. In M. L. Hecht (Ed.), *Communicating prejudice* (pp. 136–160). Thousand Oaks, CA: Sage.

Wolf, N. (1991). *The beauty myth.* London: Vintage.

Zebrowitz, L. A. (1995). Prejudice. In A. S. R. Manstead and M. Hewstone (Eds.), *The Blackwell encyclopedia of social psychology* (pp. 450–455). Oxford: Blackwell.

12

Thirty Years of Ageism Research
Jody A. Wilkinson and Kenneth F. Ferraro

Robert N. Butler, former director of the National Institute on Aging, coined the term *ageism* (1969). He identified age discrimination when the District of Columbia proposed a public housing project designed for poor seniors in Chevy Chase, Maryland. Local residents met the project with vigorous disapproval on grounds such as tax losses, costs, zoning, and property values. Butler argued, however, that the financial concern was only part of the anger and irritation that residents expressed. Rather, the disapproval was a result of ageism, which he described as "the subjective experience implied in the popular notion of the generation gap . . . a deep seated uneasiness on the part of the young and middle-aged—a personal revulsion to and distaste for growing old, disease, disability, and fear of powerlessness, 'uselessness,' and death" (1969, p. 243).

Butler (1980) further defined the term *ageism* so that it would be useful for social scientists. Ageism comprises three distinguishable yet interconnected aspects: (1) prejudicial attitudes toward older persons, old age, and the aging process, which includes attitudes held by older adults themselves; (2) discriminatory practices against older people; and (3) institutional practices and policies that perpetuate stereotypes about older adults, reduce their opportunity for life satisfaction, and undermine their personal dignity. Attitudes and beliefs, discriminatory behaviors, and institutional policies and practices are related and mutually reinforcing. Butler argues that each aspect has to some degree contributed to the transformation of aging from a natural process into a social problem in which older adults experience detrimental consequences.

This chapter reviews ageism research over the past thirty years in order to summarize major findings and identify areas of research that merit systematic investigation. It focuses on the definition of ageism, its use within the social sciences, and parallels between ageism directed toward older adults and younger persons; reviews ageism research in four main areas of inquiry; and explores the consequences of ageism research for gerontology.

Parallels between Ageism Directed toward Older Adults and Younger Persons

Maggie Kuhn (1987) substantially helped to popularize the term *ageism* through her experience in 1970 with mandatory retirement at the age of 65 from the United Presbyterian church. She felt anxious and depressed about the prospects of leaving a job she loved, for an isolated retirement where she was expected to care for a disabled mother and a brother with emotional problems. Kuhn, along with five of her friends facing similar situations, started an intergenerational organization committed to social justice and peace known as the Gray Panthers. Their slogan was "Age and Youth in Action."

While it is often thought that older adults are more similar than different, the exact opposite is the case. It is also thought that older people have little in common with young people, yet important similarities between younger and older people exist (Kuhn and Bader 1991): many younger and older people are poor or financially dependent; many younger and older people are physically or emotionally dependent and need extensive care; younger and older people are seen as high-risk drivers; and women are often the primary socializing influences in their lives.

The Definition of Ageism

The definition of *ageism* that has become most widely accepted is prejudice and discrimination against older people based on the belief that aging makes people less attractive, intelligent, sexual, and productive (Atchley 1997; Macionis 1998). Prejudice refers to attitudes, while discrimination focuses on behavior. Institutional discrimination refers to a bias in actions inherent in the operation of any of society's institutions, including schools, hospitals, the police, and the workplace. While ageism is generally thought to be negative, it can also be positive, which would reflect prejudice or discrimination in favor of older people. A common example of positive ageism would be Medicare, an insurance program designed primarily for older adults that is not accessible to most young or middle-aged persons.

Areas of Inquiry within Ageism Research

In 1969, Butler surmised that ageism would become the great issue of the next twenty to thirty years. Studies of mass media content found that racism dealt with most of the space devoted to discrimination issues in the 1960s. By 1975, approximately half of the space dealt with racism, while the other half focused on sexism. In 1977, the focus began to shift toward ageism, and in the 1980s ageism occupied about two-thirds of the space (Naisbitt 1982).

One of the largest factors that has precipitated this interest in ageism is the "aging of America" and concern over the resources necessary to support this segment of the population, both now and in the future. Proposals for issues such as the federal debt, social security, health care, and housing are continually debated among legislators and in the media. In addition, there is concern over the "disproportionate" share of political power this age group possesses due to their increasing numbers (Binstock 1992). One can readily see how central the issue of ageism has become in America and other modern societies. As Butler predicted, research on ageism has expanded greatly within the past thirty years and has been studied across disciplines.

Culture

Many aspects of our culture support ageism. Yet as individuals and as a society, we have become so conditioned by the prejudice and discrimination against age that we often fail to recognize its existence. Ageism permeates our culture through a variety of ways, such as language, physical appearance, mass media, and values.

Language   One of the most pervasive ways that ageism exists and persists in our society is through language. Word use has proven to be a good indicator of the perceptions a society holds toward its older people (Butler 1975). Covey (1988) semantically traced terms used to represent old people, aging, and the effects of aging and found a definite pattern in the evolution of the terminology. This pattern focused on the decline in the status of older people and the debilitative effects of aging. Beliefs and ideologies of aging are manifest in intergenerational discourse and social interaction (Coupland, Coupland, and Giles 1991).

Within the field of gerontology, two of the major refereed journals, *Journals of Gerontology* and *Gerontologist,* have adopted an editorial policy regarding the use of terms such as *elderly* or *aged.* They permit neither word to be used as a noun; however, each may be used as an adjective. For example, it is suitable to refer to "elderly people" or "the elderly population," but not as "the elderly." The Gerontological Society of America (GSA) recommends using any of the following terms: *older people, older adults, older persons,* or *elders.* (Parallel to ethnic and racial groupings, we prefer to speak of African Americans or black adults but not blacks or Hispanics.) The point is to emphasize the humanity of the individuals: older people.

There is evidence that our language influences the prejudices that we hold (Berelson and Steiner 1964). Sixty care receivers and thirty-nine care providers were asked to judge vocal nonverbal messages on audiotape of caregivers interacting with their coworkers and elderly nursing home residents (Caporael, Lukaszewski, and Culbertson 1983). Results showed that elderly people who were functioning at lower levels responded positively to baby talk messages. Caregivers with low expectations of the care recipients were more likely to predict that baby talk would be preferable by the care receiver and more effective in their interactions. On the other hand, caregivers with low expectations predicted that adult speech would not be effective in dealing with elderly residents. The authors concluded that the caregivers' use of speech was related to their expectation of elderly people, while the positive interpretation of baby talk by the elderly person was related to their functional status.

Further research examined whether the relationship between the nurturing quality of the baby talk tone of voice would compensate for the lack of respect associated with this type of speech toward elderly people (Ryan, Hamilton, and Kwong See 1994). Respondents expressed that this type of speech style conveyed less respect to the elderly recipient. In addition, baby talk was associated with lower competence of the provider. Baby talk addressed to cognitively alert residents was not perceived as having a nurturing quality.

Not all stereotypes of older adults are negative; some are positive. Hummert (1994a) proposed a model that would identify which factors influence an individual to select a negative stereotype over a positive stereotype of older persons and which stereotype leads to patronizing speech. Whether the perceiver enacts a positive or negative stereotype depends on characteristics such as their age, cognitive complexity, and contact with older adults. The type of stereotype selected by the older adult target depends on his or her physique, personal appearance, and physiognomic cues to age. The resulting type of speech need not be dependent on the stereotypes chosen; rather, the situation and the communication behavior also influence the verbal communication.

Physical Appearance   People are often judged by their physical looks and appearance. This is no different for older adults, but may be even more relevant when examining ageism. For older adults, there are more cues that alert us to their age and lead us to our perceptions and prejudices about age and the aging body. Research has shown, for example, that social perceptions are affected by age-related changes in facial structure (Berry and McArthur 1986; McArthur 1982).

Young adults associate physiognomic (facial) cues with stereotypes of elderly people. Hummert's (1994b) research subjects were undergraduate students who sorted photographs of elderly adults based on the perceived age of the individual. Positive stereotypes were associated with photographs of elderly adults aged 55 to 64, while negative stereotypes were associated with photographs of elderly people sorted in the old-old age group, 75 and over. Physiognomic cues for photographs of older people aged 65 to 74 were equally considered to be associated with positive and negative stereotypes. The age stereotype association pattern was particularly strong for women compared to men in which physiognomic cues of women in advanced age were negative.

Feminists have strongly voiced their concerns about the effects of ageism on the body and gender relations. Cosmetic surgery, skin treatments, and hair coloring are reflections of our society's focus on youth; this produces pressure for women to look young and resist the natural process of aging (Gerike 1990; Melamed 1983). Most of these procedures to "look young" reinforce the notion that beauty is in the domain of youth. Although men's consumption of these products has increased, the dual forces of ageism and sexism still emphasize youthful appearances for women.

Mass Media, Advertising, and Consumerism   In the past, newspapers and magazines generally either ignored older adults or recognized them in relation to a negative stereotype (Palmore 1999). Since the mid-1970s, newspapers have become more sensitive in developing their coverage toward older adults not only as consumers but as stories of human interest (Vesperi 1994). Four formats have been used in accomplishing this: an "age page" that targets older readers; special sections devoted to aging; the "aging beat," which uses age-related stories as news; and coverage that integrates social, political, and medical information about aging that relates to a general readership.

Television is considered a leading pastime of middle-aged and older adults (Kelly 1993; Moss and Lawton 1982; Pfeiffer and Davis 1971). Yet television supports and perpetuates ageism. Less than 3 percent of adult characters on prime time television have been judged to be over the age of 65 (Robinson and Skill 1995). Of those, only 8.8 percent were found to be in major roles. In addition to the ageist bias in older adult characters, older women are far less likely to appear on television (Davis and Davis 1985). Moreover, the portrayal of older people in the news is often focused on a serious problem or having suffered some disaster that prompted either a commentary or a human interest story (Atchley 1997).

Cohort differences in the media portrayal of older adults and change in these portrayals have also been examined. Between 1974 and 1981, Ferraro (1992b) found that younger respondents in 1981 thought that the media portrayed older adults more positively than in reality. In addition, younger respondents felt that the media did not do an adequate job of documenting the continuing needs of older people. On the other hand, older adults felt that the media presented a more negative picture of the elderly population given their current status at the time.

Older adults' perceived quality of coverage by the news media was examined using older adults from Dallas, Texas (Chafetz et al. 1998). Respondents consisted of 868 independent-living seniors who attended one of twenty-eight programs within Dallas County. Two-thirds of the respondents stated that they were interested in news media stories about older people, yet 86 percent described the news media as either being not interested or somewhat interested in news stories about older adults. This finding would suggest that the media are not meeting the needs of the older population in terms of information stories. In terms of the media's accuracy in their reporting of older adults, 80 percent of the respondents believed the media are moderately accurate, despite their lack of interest in stories about older adults.

Twenty-eight studies were used to examine the quantity or quality of the representation of older people in the mass media, including electronic media and print media, summarized from a review of the literature between 1974 and 1988 (Vasil and Wass 1993). The authors concluded that regardless of the type of media in question, the portrayal of older people is widely misrepresented. This misrepresentation occurred in two forms. First, the true size of the elderly population was not represented accurately in the media. Of the twenty-two studies that measured the quantity of portrayals, twenty concluded that older adults were underrepresented according to their proportion in the U.S. population. "The message conveyed by this underrepresentation is that the elderly are unimportant and noncontributing members of society and less worthy of media attention than are other age groups" (p. 80). Second, negative images of older people are supported and strengthened by both the electronic and print media. The quality of the media representation was found to be poor and inadequate. In addition, elderly characters were typically marginalized, rarely appeared in major roles or positions, were rarely developed fully as characters, and were frequently described in stereotypical terms.

Television commercials also reflect an underrepresentation bias of older persons. Roy and Harwood (1997) performed a content analysis regarding the portrayal of older adults in television commercials for one week in October 1994. Commercials were recorded from 5:30 P.M. to 9:30 P.M. on the three major networks. Older adults were underrepresented in television commercials based on their proportion in the U.S. population but were generally portrayed in a positive light.

Positive portrayals, however, do not eliminate ageist messages. A positive and humorous portrayal of an active, healthy, dynamic older adult may resonate with viewers even though the message expresses that this is not the case in reality. If this were a realistic case, such a portrayal might actually reinforce the stereotype that it violates. Indeed, approximately half of the commercial characters were coded as "comical" in this study (Roy and Harwood 1997).

Advertisers may include an older person in a commercial simply because they do not want to alienate older adult consumers. It is thought that the small number of positive portrayals may prevent offending older adults. This is an important marketing consideration when one considers that older adults are the most affluent group in marketing history and will continue to be so in the next twenty years (Light 1990).

It has been argued that the mass media influence people's identities, shape self-identification and body perception, and affect the ways in which self and others look at each other (Laws 1995). The media are both alluring and consequential to millions of people because "we respond to the representation of an older person as much as, if not more than, we respond to old people. We are forced to respond to images on billboards, in newspapers, and on television" (p. 116). In short, the mass media provide a powerful site to define or redefine the meaning of aging.

Values   Values are culturally defined standards of desirability, goodness, and beauty that serve as broad guidelines for social living (Macionis 1998). Williams's (1960) landmark study of American values identified major value orientations. Forty years later, three of these values still provide indirect support for ageist stereotypes within our culture:

Active mastery versus passive acceptance. Older adults are often viewed as more passive and accepting.

Rationalism versus traditionalism. Older people are often referred to as being too traditional and focusing on the past rather than the future.

Concern with horizontal versus vertical relationships. As people age, there is often a shift in relational focus from horizontal to vertical. This is not surprising when one considers that older adults' social networks are reduced horizontally through retirement and death but grow vertically through marriage and births.

Most modern societies support these value orientations, which predispose people to consider older adults as less central to the social fabric.

Productivity, especially at work, is highly valued in most modern societies. Although most older adults are actively engaged in a wide variety of productive activities (Ekerdt 1986; Herzog and Morgan 1992), retirement and age segregation often lead people to believe that older adults are not as active and productive as younger people. The nature of productivity may change across the adult life course from involvement at work to involvement in family and civic roles. In short, older adults are productive, but the types of activities in which they engage may not be as highly valued in modern societies.

Public Image

Negative images held toward a group of people can result in negative behaviors enacted against members of that group. For years, gerontologists have fought against the inaccurate images of older adults and their lives (Brubaker and Powers 1976). Many gerontologists recognize that inaccurate images of older adults can lead to negative or harmful consequences for older adults. In addition, the image of older people held by the public is an important factor in gaining support for social programs established for the benefit of the older adult population. A lack of political support for elder entitlement programs or apathy in volunteer efforts to aid older people may result in the public underestimation of the scope and severity of the problems older adults face. Conversely, if the public overestimates the scope and severity of the problems faced by older adults, then a potentially excessive political solution may result, or the image reifies the negative stereotype.

Substantial change in the image of older persons has occurred in recent decades, as the image of older adults has slowly become more positive (Bultena and Powers 1978; Chafetz et al. 1998; Kimmel 1988). At the same time, it has been suggested that the positive image of older adults has the potential to become problematic due to the oversimplification of the status of the older population. A critical shift in the public image of older adults has moved from one of compassion toward the "disadvantaged elderly" to scapegoating of the "well-off elderly" during the late 1970s and early 1980s (Binstock 1983). While it is true that the economic status of the older population has improved over the past two decades, insensitivity regarding the diversity of the older population is problematic and has implications for shaping social interaction and public policy.

The United States categorizes older people according to their chronological age, which is typically defined as 65 years or older. While one would expect that older adults' personal identification would be based on this age marker, research has shown that some embrace the identification, while others abhor it (Foner 1974; Riley 1987; Rose 1968). Social psychologists have long been concerned about how people view themselves in relation to others, and it has dominated the development of symbolic interactionism (Stryker 1980). Hedley (1986) revealed that people tend to give more favorable evaluations when they are asked about themselves or their problems compared to when they are asked about "other people" or "people in your position."

Ferraro (1992a) examined self- and older-people referents in evaluating life problems. Using data from two cross-sectional surveys, cohort differences were tested for the years 1974 and 1981 for adults aged 18 and over. Eight life problems were examined: not having enough money to live on, poor health, loneliness, poor housing, fear of crime, not enough education, not enough job opportunities, and not enough medical care. First, results revealed that regardless of age, respondents felt that typical older adults have more severe problems than they do themselves. Second, the perceived severity of life problems increased over time, but this was mainly due to personal evaluations of younger people. Third, younger respondents, compared to older respondents, were more likely to evaluate "older people" as having serious life problems. This difference also increased over time. Lastly, older respondents decreased their evaluation of the severity of life problems among other older people. Ferraro concluded that social change occurred for both younger and older cohorts; younger people tend to view older people as being needier or more disadvantaged than the older people are themselves, resulting in what may be termed "compassionate ageism" (Ferraro 1992b).

Although needy and beneficent views of older adults have been common (Schuck 1979), resentment toward the older population also developed in the late 1980s and early 1990s. This was probably due to the growing entitlements and political power of older people (Longman 1987). The image of elders as "greedy geezers" was used to stereotype older people in a "generational equity" debate.

Attitudes and stereotypes are particularly important when considering intergenerational politics because "it is the social image of the aging as much as any other social attribute that has fortified the elderly's political status" (Rosenbaum and Button 1993, p. 481). Using a 1990–1991 random sample of the Florida public, Rosenbaum and Button posited that the state of Florida was a precursor of political and economic transformations based on the demographic aging of the United States. Generational tensions were clear in Florida. Results revealed that a substantial portion of the younger respondents agreed to a variety of statements that older adults in their county were an economic burden, were an economically selfish voting bloc, or had a generationally divisive influence. Moreover, the higher the proportion of older adults in the county, the more critical were the views about the civic impact of older people. As a result, it was suggested that intergenerational political conflict may grow as the population ages, and "the most important source of this conflict may be the community level and the 'image' of the aging that is developing among younger community residents" (p. 481).

Work

To reduce age discrimination in employment, the federal government enacted the Age Discrimination in Employment Act (ADEA) in 1967. This act was later amended in 1974, 1978, and 1986. The ADEA now prohibits mandatory retirement for most federal, state, and private employees based on age. A few exceptions exist, based on certain occupations where the employer can prove that age is an occupational qualification, such as for airplane pilots. The Federal Aviation Administration (FAA) currently prohibits employment of persons over the age of 60 from flying commercial jet airplanes. In addition, mandatory retirement based on age is still allowed for elected public officials and their staff and highly paid executives with minimum annual retirement benefits of $44,000 (Palmore 1999).

Although the ADEA legislation has allowed many older workers to continue employment, there are still some areas of age discrimination that are not covered under this legislation or not sufficiently clear. For example, discrimination of commercial airplane pilots by age is the most litigated violation against the ADEA (Bessey and Ananda 1991). A second type of discrimination, more subtle in character, occurs when qualified older adults are not hired for positions. Job displacements for middle-aged or older workers make it difficult to find employment.

Beyond these two forms of age discrimination, Borgatta (1991) outlines other manifestations of ageism in employment. First, a rational basis may exist for observed patterns of employment that favor younger workers over older workers due to physical attributes, which change as people age, and ingrained work habits, attitudes, and expectations that older workers have learned over the years. These factors could result in additional time and costs in training older workers. Second, age discrimination has typically been applied to older adults with regard to employment, yet discrimination also exists for younger persons. This, however, has not been the focus of age discrimination legislation, which has focused solely on older workers. Third, seniority systems reward employees based on their length of tenure rather than their loyalty or proven productivity. Seniority deals with issues such as higher pay for length of time on the job and job security.

Declining earnings by older workers have been examined in relation to age discrimination (Mueller, Mutran, and Boyle 1989). Data from the National Longitudinal Survey of the Labor Market Experience of Mature Men 1966 and 1976 were used. Only men between the ages of 45 and 66 in 1966 who reported earnings in both 1966 and 1976 were included in the study. The analysis was performed based on the distinction of the core and periphery market sector because individual characteristics such as age are differentially evaluated and rewarded (Tigges 1988). The authors concluded that the 1967 ADEA did not eliminate age discrimination in wages within the core market sector; rather, the effect was stronger in 1976. Controlling for variables such as worker background, education, training, experience, job characteristics, and labor market conditions did not eliminate age differences in wages.

Americans' beliefs about older adults at work were examined using data collected prior to and after the 1978 ADEA amendment (Ferraro 1989). Two models were proposed to understand the relationship between age and public support for older workers. The civil liberty model argues that certain age groups are more likely to favor the civil liberties of others. A group benefit orientation asserts that those members of a particular group who would benefit from the policy would support the perceived outcome of the ADEA policy. Results from the cohort analysis showed that general support was found for the civil liberty model. More recent cohorts were found to support the work privileges and opportunities of older people. Moreover, from 1974 to 1981, support generally grew for older workers' privileges.

Ferraro (1990) later extended the research surrounding the 1978 ADEA amendment to examine its relationship to intergenerational relations. Two primary questions were studied using a cohort analysis of data collected from 1974 and 1981. First, how do people of different ages feel about the opportunities and privileges provided to older adults? Second, is there generational conflict? Again, more recent cohorts were more likely to support the work rights of older workers. With regard to intergenerational relations, "results suggest substantial change in American society in the direction of greater tolerance of and support for the rights of older people" (p. S227).

Health Care

Ageism among Medical Care Professionals   Research has consistently shown that the attitudes of health care professionals regarding older adults tend to be the same as or even worse than society in general (Quinn 1987). Medical ageism is developed in medical school, and this is where Butler (1994) first became aware of prejudice based on age. Terminology learned in many medical schools advances ageism and prejudicial attitudes, which can potentially affect behavior. The term *crock* is sometimes applied to people who have no apparent organic basis for their disease. It is commonly applied to patients thought to be hypochondriacs, especially women and older people. Other terms commonly used are *gomer* (get out of my emergency room) and *gork* (God only really knows [what the basis of the person's symptoms really are]).

Some argue that medical schools continue to underscore this ageist attitude in students through several avenues (Butler 1994). One of the first ways is through the encounter of a cadaver, which is typically an older person. This encounter forces the students to confront death and their own anxieties about death. Soon after, students are exhausted from the long hours of studying and subjected to hostility by trying to learn all of the necessary material. By the third or fourth year of medical school, students are ripe for cynicism, and then their internship follows. During the internship period, students are working in excess of eighty hours per week, and caring for one more "gork" does not instill empathetic emotions within the student. Butler asserts that many physicians do not invest the same amount of time treating older patients as they do younger patients. Some doctors question why they should even care for older patients, especially since some of their problems appear irreversible, unexciting, or untreatable. As a result of this socialization process, it is not surprising that few medical schools graduate students in the field of geriatrics.

Butler's last reference to ageism within the medical profession concerns hospitals themselves. In the past two decades, with financial concerns about the hospitals' bottom line, there has been great concern about the treatment of older people. It can be expensive to care for and treat this population, and Medicare reimbursements may not always cover the cost of treatment; therefore, there is concern that hospitals will view elderly patients as quite unattractive.

Medical student attitudes toward older adults spanning nine years were observed using the Aging Semantic Differential (ASD) instrument, which measures valences and content of stereotypic attitudes toward older adults (Cammer Paris et al. 1997). Results showed that the 1986 and 1994 medical students entered with neutral attitudes toward older people while the 1991 students entered with significantly poorer attitudes. Overall, there was no improvement in attitudes toward older adults between 1986 and 1994 despite a heightened awareness of the health care needs of older adults and the medical community's increased efforts to stimulate interest in the field of geriatric medicine. The authors concluded that medical schools need to be more proactive in developing curricula to improve the attitudes held by medical students toward older people. Two areas of the education process were identified as high priority: eliminate the commonly used negative stereotypes and references aimed at older adults and stimulate interest in students within the field of geriatrics.

Ageism among Other Service Professionals Ageism extends beyond medicine to other health and mental health professionals dedicated to human services. For instance, comprehensive training in geropsychology is rarely offered in clinical psychology programs (Santos and VandenBos 1982). Other issues of concern focus on Alzheimer's disease and dementia (Kimmel 1988). The emphasis placed on dementia should not detract from other mental health needs or imply that dementia occurs in all older adults. More attention needs to be focused on financial support to care for individuals with these disorders.

Ageism was examined within an outpatient social work practice at Massachusetts General Hospital with oncology patients aged 18 and over (Rohan et al. 1994). Of the 502 adult oncology patients who received initial outpatient social work treatment between June 1990 and May 1991, results showed that the number of psychosocial problems that social workers addressed did not differ by age; however, differences were observed in the types of psychosocial problems addressed. First, adults aged 65 and over were assisted with regard to transportation, while adults under age 65 were helped with problems relating to their adjustment to their illness. In addition, social workers addressed housing problems, insurance and medical coverage, and financial problems with younger adults more often than with older adults. Second, social workers engaged in significantly more individual treatment with younger patients than with older patients. Third, the social worker received referrals from family members for the older adult group, while younger adults were identified as needing services by the social workers themselves. Finally, older adults were significantly underrepresented within each measure of social work treatment, including overall time spent, individual treatment time, fewer patient-social worker contacts, and shorter treatment duration compared to adults under 65. The authors concluded that an age bias exists among social workers treating adult oncology patients.

It is clear that there is a clinical bias in most helping occupations because the neediest elders are the ones served in daily practice. Still, Golden and Sonneborn (1998) argue that the ethics of working with older adults must be considered because "little attention has been given to the development of the clinicians' knowledge of his or her own values and how these might affect work with the client" (p. 82). Previous work addressing ethical issues in working with older adults has focused on the ethics surrounding a client's particular situation, but the clinician's personal biases may also affect and influence decisions surrounding the client's care and treatment.

Biases are not determinedly "bad" or "wrong"; all humans have them. It is important, however, to understand the origins of those biases so that one's actions can be better understood and modified appropriately. Personal biases can result in countertransference, which refers to the link between the professional's personal feelings and his or her interventions and "helping behaviors" (Genevay and Katz 1990). The clinician may "overhelp" or "underhelp" the client based on his or her own feelings rather than based on the client's situation if countertransference is left unchecked. Genevay and Katz identified frequently reported countertransference issues in working with older people such as denial, fear of growing older and being helpless, fear of dying, anger, need for control, and professional omnipotence. Beyond countertransference, an individual's personal code of conduct can affect the nature and quantity of care.

For example, if independence is valued, then treatment is based on doing things with a client rather than for a client.

Consequences of Ageism Research for Gerontology

The field of gerontology has contributed much to the study of ageism over the past thirty years. A steady stream of research on ageism has helped to uncover not only the blatant forms of age discrimination but also the more subtle ways in which ageism manifests itself in the social fabric. From greeting cards to medical school, from advertisements to the workplace, it is clear that ageism is prevalent. A myriad of social, cultural, biological, and psychological forces converge to shape ageism, and it will take a concerted effort on many fronts to peel back the layers of ageism that are woven into society.

Figure 12.1 conceptualizes the confluence of these many forces. It is a heuristic tool that summarizes what may be seen as the dialectical confluence of ageism. There is a dialectic between the individual and society; the individual is shaped by social structures and social processes, yet the individual also helps define the structure and process in what is referred to as human agency. Individuals often internalize ageist ideas, but they may choose to resist or attack those same ideas. Interpersonal relations provide

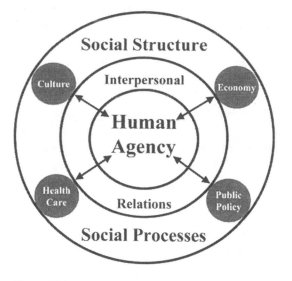

Figure 12.1
The dialectical confluence of ageism.

the immediate context for shaping human agency, but the influence of societal structures and processes helps shape both the individual and his or her interpersonal relations. In this way, ageism exists at both an individual level, as designated by human agency, and a social structural level.

Within the social structure, ageism occurs within our culture, economic and health care systems, public policy agendas, and social relationships. Change occurs through social processes, which can originate at either level. For example, previous public policy that required mandatory retirement influenced an individual's ability to work at older ages. Or, grass-roots organizations such as the Gray Panthers have become a strong lobby in advancing an age-neutral society.

One of the most exciting aspects of ageism research within gerontology is the diversity of disciplines focusing on ageism and the variety of approaches in examining ageism within the United States. Ageism is being studied within several disciplines, such as sociology, psychology, linguistics, consumer sciences, economics, communications, history, and medicine. This research has addressed different ageist issues, such as self and identity, stereotypes, language, attitudes and behaviors, personal and group interactions, consumer behavior, and institutional discrimination. It will take continuing research on these elements of the dialectical confluence of ageism in order to induce meaningful social changes.

The topic of ageism has also fostered some interdisciplinary research, but we believe more interdisciplinary collaboration is key. It is through the intersection of disciplines that a deeper knowledge of the dialectical confluence of ageism is understood. Researchers are encouraged to advance ageism research in the following ways. First, a large body of research exists that addresses various institutional forms of ageism. While this research provides insight into the effects of ageism on the individual, it does not probe deeply enough into the psychosocial effects of ageism on the individual. Second, more ageism research is needed in the area of interpersonal relations and social networks for its consequences on both the individual and the group. Finally, ageism research is often examined in terms of the effect of structural changes on the individual, yet individual efforts and group processes also influence the social structure. These processes have rarely garnered systematic examination.

Gerontologists have a responsibility to advance knowledge surrounding ageism, and within the past twenty to thirty years, they have done just that. Yet as researchers, we must be cautious about reporting our research findings. Schaie (1988) warned of ageism in psychological research, but this can be applied to other disciplines as well. He argued that "inappropriate interpretations of age-related data may become accepted as the scientific basis for policy positions that lead to discrimination against and disadvantages for our older citizens" (p. 179). As gerontologists, it should be one of our duties to disseminate research findings on ageism so that persons of all ages can optimize their well-being.

Note

This research was supported in part by grants from the National Institute on Aging to Kenneth Ferraro (AG11705, AG13739).

References

Atchley, R. C. (1997). *Social forces and aging (8th Edition)*. Belmont, CA: Wadsworth.

Berelson, B., and Steiner, G. A. (1964). *Human behavior.* New York: Harcourt, Brace.

Berry, D. S., and McArthur, L. Z. (1986). Perceiving character in faces: The impact of age-related craniofacial changes on social perception. *Psychological Bulletin, 100,* 3–18.

Bessey, B. L., and Ananda, S. M. (1991). Age discrimination in employment: An interdisciplinary review of the ADEA. *Research on Aging, 13,* 413–457.

Binstock, R. H. (1983). The aged as scapegoat. *Gerontologist, 23,* 136–143.

Binstock, R. H. (1992). The oldest old and intergenerational equity. In R. Suzman, D. Willis, and K. Manton (Eds.), *The oldest old.* New York: Oxford University Press.

Borgatta, E. F. (1991). Age discrimination issues. *Research on Aging, 13,* 476–484.

Brubaker, T. H., and Powers, E. A. (1976). The stereotype of old: A review and alternative approach. *Journal of Gerontology, 31,* 441–447.

Bultena, G. L., and Powers, E. A. (1978). Denial of aging: Age identification and reference group orientations. *Journal of Gerontology, 33,* 748–754.

Butler, R. N. (1969). Age-ism: Another form of bigotry. *Gerontologist, 9,* 243–246.

Butler, R. N. (1975). *Why survive? Being old in America.* New York: Harper and Row.

Butler, R. N. (1980). Ageism: A foreword. *Journal of Social Issues, 36,* 8–11.

Butler, R. N. (1994). Dispelling ageism: The cross-cutting intervention. In D. Schenk and W. A. Achenbaum (Eds.), *Changing perceptions of aging and the aged.* New York: Springer.

Cammer Paris, B. E., Gold, G., Taylor, B., Fields, S. D., Mulvihill, M. N., Capello, C., and deBeer, K. (1997). First year medical student attitudes toward the elderly:

A comparison of years 1986, 1991 and 1994. *Gerontology and Geriatrics Education, 18,* 13–22.

Caporael, L. R., Lukaszewski, M. P., and Culbertson, G. H. (1983). Secondary baby talk: Judgments by institutionalized elderly and their caregivers. *Journal of Personality and Social Psychology, 44,* 746–754.

Chafetz, P. K., Holmes, H., Lande, K., Childress, E., and Glazer, H. R. (1998). Older adults and the news media: Utilization, opinions, and preferred reference terms. *Gerontologist, 38,* 481–489.

Coupland, N., Coupland, J., and Giles, H. (1991). *Language, society and the elderly: Discourse, identity, and ageing.* Cambridge, MA: Basil Blackwell.

Covey, H. C. (1988). Historical terminology used to represent older people. *Gerontologist, 28,* 291–297.

Davis, R. H., and Davis, J. A. (1985). *TV's image of the elderly.* Lexington, MA: D. C. Heath.

Ekerdt, D. J. (1986). The busy ethic: Moral continuity between work and retirement. *Gerontologist, 26,* 239–244.

Ferraro, K. F. (1989). The ADEA amendment and public support for older workers. *Research on Aging, 11,* 53–81.

Ferraro, K. F. (1990). Group benefit orientation toward older adults at work? A comparison of cohort analytic methods. *Journal of Gerontology: Social Sciences, 45,* S220–227.

Ferraro, K. F. (1992a). Self and older-people referents in evaluating life problems. *Journal of Gerontology: Social Sciences, 47,* S105–114.

Ferraro, K. F. (1992b). Cohort change in images of older adults, 1974–1981. *Gerontologist, 32,* 296–304.

Foner, A. (1974). Age stratification and age conflict in political life. *American Sociological Review, 39,* 187–196.

Genevay, B., and Katz, R. S. (1990). *Countertransference and older clients.* Beverly Hills, CA: Sage.

Gerike, A. E. (1990). On gray hair and oppressed brains. *Journal of Women and Aging, 2,* 35–46.

Golden, R. L., and Sonneborn, S. (1998). Ethics in clinical practice with older adults: Recognizing biases and respecting boundaries. *Generations, 22,* 82–86.

Hedley, R. A. (1986). Everybody but me: Self-other referents in social research. *Sociological Inquiry, 56,* 245–258.

Herzog, A. R., and Morgan, J. N. (1992). Age and gender differences in the value of productive activities. *Research on Aging, 14,* 169–198.

Hummert, M. L. (1994a). Stereotypes of the elderly and patronizing speech. In M. L. Hummert, J. M. Wiemann, and J. F. Nussbaum (Eds.), *Interpersonal communication in older adulthood.* Thousand Oaks, CA: Sage.

Hummert, M. L. (1994b). Physiognomic cues to age and the activation of stereotypes of the elderly in interaction. *International Journal of Aging and Human Development, 39,* 5–19.

Kelly, J. R. (1993). *Activity and aging.* Newbury Park, CA: Sage.

Kimmel, D. C. (1988). Ageism, psychology, and public policy. *American Psychologist, 43,* 175–178.

Kuhn, M. E. (1987). Politics and aging: The Gray Panthers. In L. Carstensen and B. Edelstein (Eds.), *Handbook of clinical gerontology.* New York: Pergamon Press.

Kuhn, M. E., and Bader, J. E. (1991). Old and young are alike in many ways. *Gerontologist, 31,* 273–274.

Laws, G. (1995). Understanding ageism: Lessons from feminism and postmodernism. *Gerontologist, 35,* 112–118.

Light, L. (1990). The changing advertising world. *Journal of Advertising Research, 30,* 30–35.

Longman, P. (1987). *Born to pay.* Boston: Houghton Mifflin.

Macionis, J. J. (1998). *Sociology (4th Edition).* Upper Saddle River, NJ: Prentice Hall.

McArthur, L. Z. (1982). Judging a book by its cover: A cognitive analysis of the relationship between physical appearance and stereotyping. In A. Hastorf and A. Isen (Eds.), *Cognitive social psychology.* New York: Elsevier North-Holland.

Melamed, E. (1983). *Mirror, mirror: The terror of not being young.* New York: Simon & Schuster.

Moss, M. S., and Lawton, M. P. (1982). Time budgets of older people: A window of four lifestyles. *Journal of Gerontology, 37,* 115–123.

Mueller, C. W., Mutran, E., and Boyle, E. H. (1989). Age discrimination in earnings in a dual-economy market. *Research on Aging, 11,* 492–507.

Naisbitt, J. (1982). *Megatrends.* New York: Warner Books.

Palmore, E. B. (1999). *Ageism: Negative and positive.* New York: Springer.

Pfeiffer, E., and Davis, G. C. (1971). The use of leisure time in middle life. *Gerontologist, 11,* 187–195.

Quinn, J. (1987). Attitudes of professionals toward the aged. In G. Maddox (Ed.), *The encyclopedia of aging.* New York: Springer.

Riley, M. W. (1987). On the significance of age in sociology. *American Sociological Review, 52,* 1–14.

Robinson, J. D., and Skill, T. (1995). The invisible generation: Portrayals of the elderly on prime-time television. *Communication Reports, 8,* 111–119.

Rohan, E. A., Berkman, B., Walker, S., and Holmes, W. (1994). The geriatric oncology patient: Ageism in social work practice. *Journal of Gerontological Social Work, 23,* 201–221.

Rose, A. (1968). The subculture of the aging: A topic for sociological research. In B. Neugarten (Ed.), *Middle age and aging.* Chicago: University of Chicago Press.

Rosenbaum, W. A., and Button, J. W. (1993). The unquiet future of intergenerational politics. *Gerontologist, 33,* 481–490.

Roy, A., and Harwood, J. (1997). Underrepresented, positively portrayed: Older adults in television commercials. *Journal of Applied Communication Research, 25,* 39–56.

Ryan, E. B., Hamilton, J. M., and Kwong See, S. (1994). Patronizing the old: How do younger and older adults respond to baby talk in the nursing home? *International Journal of Aging and Human Development, 39,* 21–32.

Santos, J. F., and VandenBos, G. R. (1982). *Psychology and the older adult: Challenges for training in the 1980s.* Washington, D.C.: American Psychological Association.

Schaie, K. W. (1988). Ageism in psychological research. *American Psychologist, 43,* 179–183.

Schuck, P. H. (1979). The graying of civil rights law: The Age Discrimination Act of 1975. *Yale Law Journal, 89,* 27–93.

Stryker, S. (1980). *Symbolic interactionism.* Menlo Park, CA: Benjamin/Cummings.

Tigges, L. M. (1988). Age, earnings, and change within the dual economy. *Social Forces, 66,* 676–698.

Vasil, L., and Wass, H. (1993). Portrayal of the elderly in the media: A literature review and implications for educational gerontologists. *Educational Gerontology, 19,* 71–85.

Vesperi, M. (1994). Perspectives on aging in print journalism. In D. Schenk and W. A. Achenbaum (Eds.), *Changing perceptions of aging and the Aged.* New York: Springer.

Williams, R. M. (1960). *American society* (2d ed.). New York: Knopf.

Index

Conservatorship, 215–216
Consumerism, research on ageism
and, 343–345
Cooperation, intergenerational, 315–
316
Coping
with change, older workers and, 171–
172
strategies, for maintaining well-
being, 251–252
Criminal justice system, differential
treatment of elderly, 215
Cross-cultural issues
in age-differential behavior, 235–236
in aging research, 152
hierarchy of obligations, 301–303
Culture
ageist attitudes and, 151–153
children's age attitudes and, 91–92
research on ageism and, 341
valuing, of elderly, 42–43

D'Amico, Michael, 222
Danzer v. Norden Systems, Inc., 180, 181–
182
Death
aging and, 28–30
awareness of, 30–32, 43
denial, 32, 259–260
fear of, 34–35, 39, 42
transcendence, 32–33, 34
De Beauvoir, Simone, 38
Decremental theory of aging, 172
Defense mechanisms
aging and, 259–260
distal, 39–40
mature, 251–252
to terror, elderly characteristics and,
40–41
Demographic variables, filial piety
and, 303–304
Denial, 32, 259–260
The Denial of Death (Becker), 32
Dependence, self-induced, 288–292
Depression, elderly, 206
Derogation
of elderly, negative stereotype, 137

of elderly, self-esteem and, 39
terminology, 38
Devaluation, 133
Development
age-related change and, 280–281
through adulthood, 11
Developmental schism, 230
Diagnostic issues, age-differentiated
behavior in, 205–207
Disabled persons, stereotypes of, 9
Discrimination. *See* Age discrimination
Disengagement theory, 174–175, 248–
249
Disparate impact theory, 179
Disparate treatment theory, 179
Distal defenses, 36–37
Distal terror management defenses, in
response to elderly, 39–40
Distancing strategies, 37–39
Domination, 312
"Double standard of aging," 249

Education, in reducing ageism, 44
EEOC (Equal Employment Opportunity Commission), 177
Ego integrity, 250–251
Egoist, 261
Elder abuse, 228
Elderly
ageist attitudes of, 150–151
antiquated worldview of, 28–29
categorization levels of, 6–7
employees, 11–12
exemplars of, 5–6
group attitudes of, 66–67
healthy/fit, mortality salience reduction and, 40–41
identity maintenance, 151
impact of implicit age stereotypes on,
57–63
name changes for, 151
population demographics, 129
prejudice toward, reducing, 315–317
prototype of, 5–6
proximal defenses against, 37–39
stereotype-consistent information,
18–19